THE PSYCHOLOGY
OF LEARNING AND MOTIVATION

Advances in Research and Theory

VOLUME 47

Categories in Use

A Volume In **THE PSYCHOLOGY OF LEARNING AND MOTIVATION**

Advances in Research and Theory

EDITED BY ARTHUR B. MARKMAN

    DEPARTMENT OF PSYCHOLOGY
    UNIVERSITY OF TEXAS, AUSTIN
    AUSTIN, TEXAS

    BRIAN H. ROSS

    BECKMAN INSTITUTE AND
    DEPARTMENT OF PSYCHOLOGY
    UNIVERSITY OF ILLINOIS AT URBANA-CHAMPAIGN
    URBANA, ILLINOIS

Volume 47

ELSEVIER

AMSTERDAM • BOSTON • HEIDELBERG • LONDON
NEW YORK • OXFORD • PARIS • SAN DIEGO
SAN FRANCISCO • SINGAPORE • SYDNEY • TOKYO
Academic Press is an imprint of Elsevier

Academic Press is an imprint of Elsevier
525 B Street, Suite 1900, San Diego, California 92101-4495, USA
84 Theobald's Road, London WC1X 8RR, UK

This book is printed on acid-free paper.

Copyright © 2007, Elsevier Inc. All Rights Reserved.

No part of this publication may be reproduced or transmitted in any form or by any means, electronic or mechanical, including photocopy, recording, or any information storage and retrieval system, without permission in writing from the Publisher.

The appearance of the code at the bottom of the first page of a chapter in this book indicates the Publisher's consent that copies of the chapter may be made for personal or internal use of specific clients. This consent is given on the condition, however, that the copier pay the stated per copy fee through the Copyright Clearance Center, Inc. (www.copyright.com), for copying beyond that permitted by Sections 107 or 108 of the U.S. Copyright Law. This consent does not extend to other kinds of copying, such as copying for general distribution, for advertising or promotional purposes, for creating new collective works, or for resale. Copy fees for pre-2007 chapters are as shown on the title pages. If no fee code appears on the title page, the copy fee is the same as for current chapters.
0079-7421/2007 $35.00

Permissions may be sought directly from Elsevier's Science & Technology Rights Department in Oxford, UK: phone: (+44) 1865 843830, fax: (+44) 1865 853333, E-mail: permissions@elsevier.com. You may also complete your request on-line via the Elsevier homepage (http://elsevier.com), by selecting "Support & Contact" then "Copyright and Permission" and then "Obtaining Permissions."

For information on all Elsevier Academic Press publications
visit our Web site at www.books.elsevier.com

ISBN-13: 978-0-12-543347-1
ISBN-10: 0-12-543347-6

PRINTED IN THE UNITED STATES OF AMERICA
07 08 09 9 8 7 6 5 4 3 2 1

Working together to grow
libraries in developing countries

www.elsevier.com | www.bookaid.org | www.sabre.org

ELSEVIER   BOOK AID International   Sabre Foundation

CONTENTS

Contributors ix
Preface xi

RELATIONS AND CATEGORIES
Viviana A. Zelizer and Charles Tilly

    I. Introduction 1
   II. Local Money 3
  III. Legal Tenders 7
  IV. The Euro 10
   V. Remittances 13
  VI. Trust Networks 17
 VII. Nationalism and Citizenship 24
VIII. Conclusions 26
      References 28

LEARNING LINGUISTIC PATTERNS
Adele E. Goldberg

  I. Constructions 33
 II. Can Constructions Be Learned on the Basis of the Input? 35
III. Children Can Learn to Map Novel Phrasal Patterns onto
     Novel Meanings 37
IV. How Constructions Can Be Learned: A Facilitory Factor 40
 V. Parallel Facilitory Effect in Nonlinguistic Categorization 44

VI. Why Argument Structure Generalizations Are Learned: What Is the Advantage?	45
VII. Motivating the Particular Form–Function Pairings That Exist in Languages	54
VIII. Conclusions	56
References	57

UNDERSTANDING THE ART OF DESIGN: TOOLS FOR THE NEXT EDISONIAN INNOVATORS

Kristin L. Wood and Julie S. Linsey

I. Motivation and Overview	65
II. A Product Development and Concept Generation Process	69
III. The Scaffolding of Concept Generation: Category Representations	79
IV. Basic Concept Generation Methods: Transforming Representation to Physical Layouts	96
V. Discussion and "Golden Nuggets"	115
References	117

CATEGORIZING THE SOCIAL WORLD: AFFECT, MOTIVATION, AND SELF-REGULATION

Galen V. Bodenhausen, Andrew R. Todd, and Andrew P. Becker

I. Introduction	123
II. A Schematic Model of Social Categorization	124
III. Motivational Influences	128
IV. Affective Influences	137
V. Identification-Based Affect, Motivation, and Inference	144
VI. Conclusions	146
References	148

RECONSIDERING THE ROLE OF STRUCTURE IN VISION

Elan Barenholtz and Michael J. Tarr

I. Introduction	157
II. Defining Structure	160
III. Why Be Structural?	166
IV. Conclusions	177
References	178

CONVERSATION AS A SITE OF CATEGORY LEARNING AND CATEGORY USE

Dale J. Barr and Edmundo Kronmüller

I.	The Importance of Setting in Categorization Research	181
II.	Categorization Processes in Conversation	182
III.	The Multimodal Nature of Conversation: Confidence Cues in Category Learning	185
IV.	The Historical Nature of Conversation: Establishing and Using Conversational Precedents	189
V.	The Collaborative Nature of Conversation: Socially Emergent Categories and Conceptual Alignment	201
VI.	Challenges and Prospects	207
	References	209

USING CLASSIFICATION TO UNDERSTAND THE MOTIVATION-LEARNING INTERFACE

W. Todd Maddox, Arthur B. Markman, and Grant C. Baldwin

I.	Introduction	213
II.	A Framework for Examining the Motivation-Classification Learning Interface	215
III.	Applying the Regulatory Fit Framework to Classification	218
IV.	Regulatory Fit Effects on Rule-Based Classification Learning	224
V.	Regulatory Fit Effects on Information-Integration Classification Learning	233
VI.	Summary of Classification Learning Results	235
VII.	Regulatory Fit Effects on Decision Criterion Learning	235
VIII.	Summary and Future Directions	238
IX.	Closing Remarks	245
	References	245

Index	251
Contents of Recent Volumes	263

CONTRIBUTORS

Numbers in parentheses indicate the pages on which the authors' contributions begin.

Grant C. Baldwin (213), Department of Psychology, University of Texas, Austin, Texas 78712

Elan Barenholtz (157), Department of Cognitive and Linguistic Sciences, Brown University, Providence, Rhode Island 02912

Dale J. Barr (181), Department of Psychology, University of California, Riverside, California 92521

Andrew P. Becker (123), Department of Psychology, Northwestern University, Evanston, Illinois 60208

Galen V. Bodenhausen (123), Department of Psychology, Northwestern University, Evanston, Illinois 60208

Adele E. Goldberg (33), Department of Psychology, Princeton University, New Jersey 08544

Edmundo Kronmüller (181), Department of Psychology, University of California, Riverside, California 92521

Julie S. Linsey (65), Department of Mechanical Engineering, The University of Texas, Austin, Texas 78712

W. Todd Maddox (213), Department of Psychology, University of Texas, Austin, Texas 78712

Arthur B. Markman (213), Department of Psychology, University of Texas, Austin, Texas 78712

Michael J. Tarr (157), Department of Cognitive and Linguistic Sciences, Brown University, Providence, Rhode Island 02912

Charles Tilly (1), Department of Sociology, Columbia University, New York, New York 10027

Andrew R. Todd (123), Department of Psychology, Northwestern University, Evanston, Illinois 60208

Kristin L. Wood (65), Department of Mechanical Engineering, The University of Texas, Austin, Texas 78712

Viviana A. Zelizer (1), Department of Sociology, Princeton University, Princeton, New Jersey 08544

PREFACE

Categories are essential for intelligent thought and action. They support a wide variety of cognitive activities, such as inference, problem solving, explanation, and communication. Despite the widespread use and importance of categories, the voluminous examination of categories in the adult literature in cognitive psychology has been very restricted with an almost exclusive focus on how people learn categories consisting of unstructured lists of features in the course of classifying new instances. This focus has led to relative ignorance on many important questions about how categories might be learned and used. George Bernard Shaw is quoted as saying, "Youth is wasted on the young." Perhaps categorization research is wasted on the categorization researchers.

As an antidote to this restricted view, one might approach categorization from a goal-oriented perspective. Categories are useful because items in different categories require different action or inferences or must be referred to in different ways. That is, categories are mental representations that support a person's cognitive goals. From this perspective, category learning consists of acquiring the groupings that are useful for those goals the person is learning to accomplish. In addition, because not all future goals can be anticipated, a critical part of category learning is to develop flexible representations that can be applied across a wide range of situations that are likely to be encountered.

About ten years ago, we independently embarked on research programs exploring how the uses of categories influence what is learned about them. The aim of this research was to look at a broad range of categorization behavior, and we explored tasks like predictive inference, decision making, problem solving, and referential communication. We summarized much of this work in a 2003 paper in *Psychological Bulletin* (Markman & Ross, 2003).

Still, though, we both felt something was missing. Categorization researchers spend their time studying categories. Perhaps (to butcher a phrase by John Lennon this time), categories are what happens while you are busy making other plans. To address this possibility, we hatched the idea for this volume. We chose a set of authors who (for the most part) do not study categorization and asked them to discuss their work by explicitly thinking about its implications for categorization. Indeed, to ensure that most of these papers would look quite different from the typical categorization researcher's take on categorization, many of the people we asked to write chapters are not even psychologists.

We think that there are two ways to read each of the chapters in this volume. At one level, each of them is a fascinating study of a topic within a particular discipline. Zelizer and Tilley talk about social relationships and money. Goldberg discusses the role of concepts in linguistic structures. Wood and Linsey describe the influence of representations on the development of innovations in mechanical engineering. At a deeper level, though, all of these chapters present views of the way that categories are used in domains that lie outside of psychology.

We also have chapters from psychologists. Bodenhausen, Todd, and Becker discuss the role of categories in our social world. Barenholtz and Tarr present the influence of categories and representation on visual object recognition. Barr and Kronmüller discuss the influence of categories on referential communication. Finally, Maddox, Markman, and Baldwin discuss motivational influences that affect people's ability to acquire and use categories. Of these, only the last of them is written by individuals who might describe their research program as being about categories, but they all have important implications for the nature of categorization.

The goal of this volume is to consider category learning and use across a wide variety of domains, in cognitive psychology, other areas of psychology, and other fields of expertise. We need to look beyond the boundaries of typical studies of categorization to understand how categories are used when people do not necessarily realize that they are using categories. We hope that a broad examination of categories, with a focus on the way they are used, will be of interest to many researchers in fields in which categories are so important. In our view, these chapters raise more questions about people's categories than they answer, but they do provide directions to look for new answers.

Arthur B. Markman and Brian H. Ross

REFERENCE

Markman, A. B., & Ross, B. H. (2003). Category use and category learning. *Psychological Bulletin, 129*(4), 592–613.

RELATIONS AND CATEGORIES

Viviana A. Zelizer and Charles Tilly

I. Introduction

During the late 1990s, a team of French social researchers led by Jean-Michel Servet investigated what was then a rapidly spreading form of organization in France: the Systèmes d'Échange Local (SEL). They conducted close studies of these proliferating local money groups in a number of urban and rural communities. Annie, a member of a local money circle in the Pyrenees, told them how "In the regular system, I have cash, I pay, I am free; in the SEL, I am not free, I forge a relation." Similarly, Y a 60-year-old retiree from the SEL of la Garrigue reported: "The exchange [within the SEL] inevitably leads to something else, while when I give someone a 100 franc note, I hand him the 100 franc note and it's over. There we discuss what's going on, politics, the economy, the SEL" (Servet, 1999, p. 144).

Annie and Y clearly see a sharp difference between economic transactions occurring inside and outside the SEL. That boundary between insiders and outsiders matters. It matters both because people on either side of the boundary have different relations to each other and because when members of the SEL cross the boundary to interact with outsiders they change their own behavior. The boundary, as members describe it, separates a local world of authentic interpersonal solidarity from another world tainted by commercialism.

Parallel monetary systems have existed since the invention of money millennia ago. The distinction between "real" money—legal tender backed by governments—and alternative currencies took on serious consequences when states began establishing monopolies of monetary production during the nineteenth century (Helleiner, 1999). But an ideologically tinged worldwide movement to create alternative local currencies of superior moral value only took root during the 1980s and began sprouting around the globe during the 1990s.

Yet the movement grew fast. In his comprehensive survey of SEL-like local currencies, Jérôme Blanc estimates 250,000 members of such organizations across the world in the year 2000 (Blanc, 2000, p. 243). As of 2001, a semiofficial international website lists over 1500 groups (Lets-Linkup, 2005). In one place after another on all the inhabited continents, people are drawing boundaries and creating consequential insider–outsider categories by establishing local monetary systems.

Local money provides just one example of a much more general process. In a wide variety of situations, people engaged in everyday social interaction establish boundaries between insiders and outsiders that sustain crucial social activities. Those boundaries then create consequential connected categories—not only insiders and outsiders but also us and them, worthy and unworthy, intimate and impersonal, congenial and threatening. To be sure, general cognitive processes affect perception and use of those categories. But the categories themselves emerge from social interaction, and their contents depend on social interaction (Tilly, 2005b; Zelizer, 2005).

This chapter pursues that insight, first within the zone of money and then outside. We return to local monies for a closer look, then move on to parallels with legal tender, including a perplexing new currency, the euro. Immigrant remittances provide a doorway into related phenomena, in this case still mainly monetary, but now involving long-distance and long-term creation of categories through complex social interaction.

From immigrant remittances we turn to other forms of category creation in which money occupies a less central place: interpersonal networks of trust and relations between nationalism and citizenship. Each case illuminates a different aspect of a general argument:

- Social interaction generates, informs, and then responds to a significant set of connected categories.
- Those categories depend on interaction among three elements: (1) socially maintained boundaries, (2) relations within the boundaries, and (3) relations across the boundaries.
- They regularly involve mental accounting systems, of which short-term quid pro quo exchanges constitute only one special type.
- People complement mental accounting systems with earmarking practices; they establish subdivisions within ostensibly homogeneous money and other media by signaling commitment of media segments to distinct relations and transactions.

- Relational work—the effort of establishing, terminating, negotiating, and transforming interpersonal relations—goes on continuously, shaping boundaries, accounting systems, and categories.

By the end we hope to have established not that all categories result from interpersonal interactions, much less that all categories are somehow essentially social, but that coherent social processes regularly generate, deploy, and alter an important set of human categories.

II. Local Money

From the French "grain de sel" and the Australian "green dollars" to the Italian "Misthòs," the German Talent, the Mexican Tlaloc, the Argentine "créditos," the Japanese "ecomoney," or the "Seeds" of Mendocino, California, local currencies mark geographically circumscribed economies (see Helleiner, 1999, 2000; Powell, 2002; Rizzo, 1999; Schroeder, 2002; Servet, 1999; Yen Rivals, 2001). These currencies belong to well-organized, localized, and voluntary groups that go by names such as SEL, local exchange and trading systems (LETS), Banca del Tempo (Bdt), Sistema di Reciprocità Indiretta (SRI), Club del Trueque, Tauschring, and HOURS.

In all this bewildering variety of monetary groups, people are building categories that insulate internal operations of their system from the kinds of economic activities that go on outside. They do so via a series of elements: they mark a boundary distinguishing life inside and outside, assign contrasting meanings to those worlds, use a distinctive idiom for their internal exchanges, set up tailor-made accounting systems, adopt media to represent those accounting systems, and establish a limited set of transactions among members. All this amounts to the construction of connected categories separating insiders from outsiders. Relational work with local money creates new categories.

Of course, the process varies in different kinds of local money groups. Discussions of local money often mention, and sometimes confuse, four rather different phenomena: pegged currencies, time exchanges, commodity-based systems, and barter. Pegged currencies, as in the SEL or LETS, establish a distinct local medium whose value corresponds to that of legal tender. Time exchanges, such as New York's pioneering Ithaca HOURS, take their value from hours of effort contributed by their members. Commodity-based systems involve coupons, vouchers, and credits that are ultimately redeemable only in certain earmarked goods or services. Barter includes direct exchange of goods and services for each other without intervention of a currency. Although combinations of all four systems appear here and there, the overwhelming majority of deliberately organized local monetary systems fall in the range of the first two, from pegged currencies to time exchanges.

For illustration, we focus here on the world's most widespread system: LETS. LETS members transfer goods and services using a locally circumscribed medium, ordinarily pegged to a national currency. At least two major variants of LETS exist. Some create tokens to represent their currency, while others rely on telephone-linked or computer-based central accounts without physical tokens. Participants generally pay an entrance fee and subscribe to a service listing available goods and services provided by members of a group. Buyers and sellers contact each other and negotiate a price; their transaction is then recorded by the local LETS office.

Although some enthusiasts for these local arrangements imagine they are doing away with money entirely, in fact they are creating new forms of money devoted to distinctive groups. As Servet and his collaborators note, the SEL are in search of a "good money" (*bonne monnaie*) (Servet, 1999, p. 12).

How do members of these groups distinguish themselves and their relations from others outside? As we saw with Annie and Y, participants draw emphatic boundaries between themselves and a diffuse commercial world. The groups' self-descriptions commonly emphasize this distinction between an inside world of sociable solidarity and an outside world of self-interested commercialism.

Language further marks that divide: LETS enthusiasts discourage participants from using traditional economic terminology, such as "price," "money," or "sales," referring instead to "estimated amounts," "units," "favours," or "exchanges" (Blanc, 2000, p. 261; Servet, 1999, pp. 28–30; Taris, 2005). Indeed, the effort of Manchester LETS organizers to integrate their exchanges extensively into the national economy outraged other British LETS organizers. Critics of the Manchester plan, Keith Hart (1999, 283) reports, preferred "sealing off a more wholesome kind of circuit from the contamination of capitalism."

LETS participants regularly draw additional, very different boundaries between themselves and their intimates. Nonmember lovers, close friends, and family members belong to a separate set of relations from their LETS partners. Denis Bayon, an investigator at the University of Lyon, comments:

> One may, of course, fall in love in a SEL (as elsewhere) or make friends; but then the romantic or friendly relationship breaks out of the SEL domain; a couple, friends, certainly don't count the services they provide for each other, which from now on belong to their private life and could have been, in other circumstances, exchanges mediated by the SEL. (Bayon, 1999, p. 61 fn.1)

The distinction also operates in the other direction. When friends become LETS partners, they redefine their relationships. In her interviews with local money participants in Ontario and New York state, Mary-Beth Raddon found respondents struggling to readjust their personal relations to the new LETS media for their ongoing transactions. She reports, for instance, one mother's uneasy transition from free babysitting for friends to a local money system. As Erin explained:

> You know, I would watch my friend's child and she would watch mine, and we sort of kept track of the hours so that we were even, but once we were both members of LETS we'd always pay each other in green [dollars]. But there was a change that happened once a currency got attached to it that made it feel a bit different, sort of more formalized and less a currency of friendship. (Raddon, 2003, p. 79)

Establishing boundaries between themselves and the various "them" outside the group, however, is only part of the category-building social process. LETS participants further solidify their internal connections by marking their own economic activities and relations as distinctive. They do so most notably by creating specialized media and accounting systems, as well as by control of membership, transactions, and commodities.

Participants often reinforce their community by incorporating locally meaningful symbols into their monetary tokens. LETS networks that do not rely on physically distinct media use symbolically charged names, usually with transparent local meaning. In Britain, for instance, Greenwich uses "anchors," Canterbury "tales," and Totnes "acorns" (Helleiner, 2000, pp. 46–47). In France, the Pyrénées SEL uses "grains," "cailloux" serve the Lyon Croix-Rousse SEL, while the "fil" circulates in the textile region of Sailly-sur la-Lys, Pas de Calais (Blanc, 2000, p. 265).

How do LETS regulate their membership? Although almost anyone can sign up, once inside the group new members enter into a particular set of relations, and must agree to abide by certain standards that distinguish insiders from outsiders. For instance, item 18 in the Lyon-Croix-Rousse SEL's "Charte d'adhésion" states: "Exclusion of a participant whose behavior contradicts the good functioning of the SEL constitutes a right of the general assembly" (Servet, 1999, p. 30). LETS groups fortify their distinctive economic world by regulating transactions across boundaries. LETS currency, for instance, is not convertible into legal tender. Indeed, any member who charges legal tender, rather than the local currency, as compensation for services or goods, breaks a crucial rule (Servet, 1999, p. 59).

Although no one has looked comparatively at the composition of local monetary systems in detail, available descriptions leave the impression that they tend to be socially homogeneous. Internal differences in participation by age and gender (see, e.g., Raddon, 2003) do not significantly qualify that impression. All such systems restrict participation in some regards.

In Germany some *Tauschring* circuits confine their membership to the elderly, the handicapped, foreigners, or women. Others expand their circuit to include whole communities or firms (Pierret, 1999). Even those, however, remain radically delimited as compared to the scope of legal tender.

Local money systems also restrict the commodities they cover. Although the range of goods and services ranges widely, including such items as clothing, farm tools, and food, as well as foreign-language instruction, gym courses, plumbing, gardening, babysitting, and computer support, not all are fit to circulate. For instance, many SEL groups ban transfers of certain goods and services as morally, ecologically, or politically off-limits. Banned commodities include firearms, animals, goods manufactured by third-world exploitation, and in one case a member's book on "how to get rich quick" (Bayon, 1999, pp. 73–74). Bayon reports:

> One of the SEL made an interesting specification concerning massages. An internal document distinguishes erotic massages (growing out of members' personal relations), therapeutic massages (that require the intervention of qualified professionals, eligible for social security reimbursement and exchanges in national currency), and massages designed for general well-being and relaxation. (Bayon, 1999, pp. 73-74)

The first two kinds of massage, according to Bayon, are forbidden, the third acceptable. More generally, this SEL favored treatment by means of alternative medicines.

When it comes to pricing goods and services they exchange, local trading systems commonly reject existing market prices for their own negotiated tariffs. Often the local price reflects the group's greater evaluation of services that, in the members' estimation, the national market undervalues. In a paradoxical turn, for instance, household and caring tasks, typically women's labor excluded or devalued by the mainstream economy, find an appreciative market within the SEL (Helleiner, 2000, p. 44; Raddon, 2003).

What is more, apparently equivalent goods and services fetch different prices depending on the parties' evaluation of the relationship. In a report from the Centre Walras, Etienne Perrot (1999, p. 386) notes: "The personality of the *provider* and the affective dimension of SEL relationships lead the 'client' to pay a friend's price *(prix d'ami)* independent of strict economic calculation." Similarly, Bayon observes:

> We do not set against each other the hours of baby-sitting, or the hours of reading stories to children . . . . It's Jean-Paul my neighbor who watched my child yesterday, it's Hélène who came to read "scary stories" to my young children, etc. At the core of SELs . . . we find chains of exchange and solidarity mixing and interweaving with each other as invisible threads designing the common good. It's Jacques who tells Françoise he needs someone to help him with housework, or precisely Françoise knows Pierre who was helped by Luc, etc. It's people who join in to share chores. (Bayon, 1999, pp. 80-81)

As a result, Bayon continues:

> The structure of "prices" in SEL currency would make an ordinary economist scream. The "same" (but precisely it is not the same) hour of ironing gives us here 50 grains, there, 60 grains, here 40 grains, etc. An oversized new pair of shoes bought by mistake will be given here for 100 grains, there 150 grains. (Bayon, 1999, p. 81)

By the same token, SEL members, according to Bayon, reject prices that seem morally excessive to them, regardless of the amount that the good or service would bring in national currency outside the circuit (see also Raddon, 2003). Even local money systems that peg their currencies to legal tender thus create their own accounting schemes to accommodate setting of values within the membership.

All over the world, then, people are building distinctive social arrangements around parallel monetary systems. Each system begins with a well-marked boundary between inside and outside, differentiates the sorts of transactions that occur inside and outside, uses distinct accounting systems inside and outside, labels and evaluates inside and outside relations differently, and assigns different meanings to the combinations of accounting systems, monetary media, transactions, and relations on either side of the boundary. In so doing, they construct new, powerful, connected categories.

More generally, for each meaningfully distinct category of social relations, people erect a boundary, mark the boundary by means of names and practices, establish a set of distinctive understandings and practices that operate within that boundary, designate certain sorts of economic transactions as appropriate for the relation, bar other transactions as inappropriate, and adopt certain media for reckoning and facilitating economic transactions within the relation (for social boundary processes, see Abbott, 1995; Barth, 1969, 1981; Epstein, 1992; Fuller, 2003; Lamont & Molnar, 2002; Ong, 1996; Sanders, 2002; Tilly, 2005b). All these efforts belong to relational work: establishment of differentiated social ties, their maintenance, their reshaping, their distinction from other relations, and sometimes their termination. They create social boundaries, relations within the boundaries, relations across the boundaries, and meaningful categories distinguishing persons, activities, and relations on different sides of the boundaries.

III. Legal Tenders

Impressively parallel processes occur as people use legal tender. For all the assumption of community money enthusiasts that they are building a distinct world from the crass, insipid, homogenized sphere of legal tender, in fact the same kind of relational work goes on within that other sphere, and has since the invention of money. Ironically, managers of legal tender create a mirror image of local money's categories. They distinguish their genuine money and its economic sphere from corrupt, incomplete, improvised, and inefficient approximations to money. With the backing of a national government, genuine money thus defined takes on the aura of patriotism. As we will see, exactly where the boundary lies and who backs the money become categorical problems with such transnational currency as the euro.

The very creation of uniform national currencies involved an extensive process of social reorganization. Contrary to the presumption that efficient money automatically follows the expansion of markets, national states worked vigorously to impose standardized national forms of money. Starting in the nineteenth century, the US government struggled to replace multiple circulating monies with a uniform currency. It did so by taxing thousands of state-issued paper currencies out of existence, banning foreign currencies; suppressing the private issue of tokens, paper notes, or coins by stores, businesses, churches, and other organizations; and stamping out the personalization of money by individuals (Helleiner, 2003; Zelizer, 1994).

Standardization of money, however, did not proceed smoothly and consensually. Defining American currency became one of the late nineteenth century's most explosive political and social issues. Despite a dramatic post–Civil War increase in people's use of deposits rather than cash, the debates centered on currencies. Were greenbacks "real" money, or did only "hard" metallic money serve as authentic currency? Should gold, as monometallists argued, be the only "true" standard? Or, could silver, as "free silver" proponents maintained, serve as equally sound money? Were notes issued by national banks legitimate? Or, as Greenbackers insisted, was only government-issued money acceptable? These were not merely word games or strictly technical distinctions; the "money question" became a fiercely contested public debate, polarizing social groups and shaping the political process of late nineteenth-century American society.

By the turn of the century, controversy began to wane in the United States. Free-silver proponents lost the 1896 election and the 1900 Gold Standard Act established the gold dollar as the national monetary standard. Within some four decades, the American state had achieved a significant degree of monetary standardization. Not until 1933, however, did Congress formally declare all US coins and currencies to be equal legal tender (Zelizer, 1994, pp. 13–18).

The state moved as well against the personalization of money by individuals. It broadened definitions of counterfeiting and mutilation, pursuing, for instance, the popular late nineteenth-century *trompe l'oeil* paintings of dollar bills. The government even forbade the common late nineteenth-century practice of inscribing coins with sentimental messages, calling that practice "mutilation." After 1909, a law forbidding the mutilation of coins turned the popular "love token" gifts into an illegal currency. As the Supreme Court of Indiana declared in November 1889, the government "has a right to provide a currency for the whole nation, and to drive out all other circulating mediums by taxation or otherwise" (Hancock et al. v. Yaden 366 Supreme Court of Indiana at 372).

It was a losing battle. Although the American state did achieve a significant degree of standardization and monopolization of legal tender, people continually disrupted monetary uniformity, actively creating all sorts of monetary distinctions. In a remarkable parallel to the formation of local monetary communities, people created distinctive uses of legal tender that corresponded to different sets of social relations. They did relational work with legal tender. They did so by a set of earmarking practices: treatments of money that signal the nature of the relationship between the parties to a particular kind of transaction.

Earmarking clearly qualifies as relational work. Techniques of earmarking include three main varieties:

1. Establishing social practices that sort otherwise identical media into distinct categories. Depending on how it is used, when, and most importantly for what type of social relation, the same physically indistinguishable medium (e.g., dollar or a euro) can serve as a wage, a bonus, a tip, a gift, an allowance, charity, or a remittance. Each calls for a different set of routines representing its character.
2. As in the case of local monies, creation of segmented media in the form of tokens, coupons, scrip, chits, food stamps, affinity credit cards, money orders, vouchers, or gift certificates, which are appropriate for restricted sets of relations and transfers, and in many cases are not legal tender within the larger economy.
3. Transformation of selected objects into monetary media, as with cigarettes, postage stamps, subway tokens, poker chips, or baseball cards.

In each case, earmarking calls up its own mental accounting system, for example, separating rent money (kept in a checking account) from gift money (kept in a Christmas Club account). The process of earmarking monies is not only complex and constant but often also highly contested. Disputes arise when parties to an interaction have contradictory understandings of the relationship, when their values clash, or when they are pursuing conflicting interests. They also arise when the parties have adopted different techniques for earmarking, especially when the preferred techniques of one party mean something different and undesirable to the other party.

Such practices connect with psychological work on mental accounting. Studies of the subject generally reject the notion that money is psychologically general, maintaining that instead money involves "multiple symbolizations."

An important literature on mental accounting challenges economists' assumption of fungibility by identifying the ways that individuals distinguish between kinds of money. For instance, people treat windfall income much differently from a bonus or an inheritance, even when the sums involved are identical (see, e.g., Heath & Soll, 1996; Kahneman & Tversky, 1982; McGraw, Tetlock, & Kristel, 2003; Thaler, 1999). Mental accounting turns out to be a psychological earmarking mechanism, in this case a particular treatment of money that fits specific cognitive categories.

Related work points to the behavioral impact of "money illusions" by which people adopt a series of localized conventions for evaluating monetary transactions in different situations rather than translating them into the economists' neutral, fungible medium (see, e.g., Shafir, Diamond, & Tversky, 1997). Political scientist Robert E. Lane (1991) has also documented a wide variety of ways in which Americans think of money as variable, a meaningful symbol of attitudinal feelings such as personal inadequacy, loss of control, shameful failure, security, or need of social approval.

There are two ways—cognitive and relational—of interpreting what is going on with these monetary earmarking practices: two distinguishable yet interdependent processes. One sees monetary variations as mental distinctions or cognitive maps. The other sees monetary differentiation as marking and emerging from distinctive social relations and shared meaning systems. In the latter, money's variations do not just symbolize but in fact serve to construct social relations. They become means of relational work. Thus, social scientists are not simply reporting sophisticated individual budgetary strategies but identifying the significance of monetary practices as outcomes, contents, and origins of social relations. Both processes—cognitive and social—are of course going on. The relational work of establishing legal tender creates social boundaries, relations within the boundaries, relations across the boundaries, and meaningful categories distinguishing persons, activities, and relations on different sides of the boundaries.

IV. The Euro

Across the European Union, the initiation of the euro in 1999 rekindled many of the same struggles over legitimate currencies that had marked the eventually successful nineteenth-century effort of western states to impose national legal tenders (Fishman & Messina, 2006). Along with various forms of electronic money, the euro threatened the precarious monetary monopolies those states had established and incited new versions of earmarking.

Euro promoters took on the delicate task of inventing a currency in order to construct a new transnational economic and political category, what some call Euroland. But unlike national states, euro architects did so without a single political authority backing their efforts. Instead, individual European states have retained their separate sovereignty. This multiplicity of fiscal voices has incited sharp debate among analysts. At one extreme, some experts claim that without a single authority Europe will never achieve an efficient money (Ingham, 2004; McNamara & Meunier, 2002). At the other extreme, observers point out that money has often operated quite well in the absence of any single authority (Cohen, 2004).

Creating the euro's boundary for a zone that now includes 12 nation-states thus poses particular challenges. Some advocates echo arguments resembling local money claims, declaring that the new currency builds European solidarity which, in the long run, will affirm a true European community. In this vein, Élisabeth Guigou, then Europe's Minister for Employment and Solidarity, wrote about the euro in 2002 as "the crowning of 40 years of economic construction and the first element of a European identity" (Guigou, 2002, p. 9).

Similarly intrigued by this possibility, the European Commission's Flash Eurobarometer 2004 public opinion survey of euro users asked respondents whether "Since using the euro, do you personally feel a little more European than before, a little less European than before or would you say that our feeling of being European has not changed?" To that vague question, 78% of respondents said they felt nothing had changed (The Euro, 3 years later, 2004, pp. 40–41).

Dubious about such solidarity reasoning, other official sponsors of the euro emphasize efficiency arguments, notably that the euro facilitates transactions across existing national boundaries. Characteristically, in a 2005 speech advocating the euro to Malta, Joaquín Almunia, European Commissioner for Economic and Monetary Affairs, emphasized the practical benefits of the new currency, including price stability, protection against currency turmoil, reduction of transaction costs for travelers, and comparability of prices (Almunia, 2005). In short, Almunia stressed the euro's improved efficiency rather than its symbolic solidarity.

The European Commission's euro website offers a similar formal response to one of the most frequently asked questions: what are the benefits of the euro? The Commission's answers single out economic advantages, although one item in the list is European identity (Euro, 2005). In either case, analysts stress the creation of a new boundary separating participants in the euro from outsiders. Thus, once again, interaction within and across a boundary generates new connected categories: Euroland and the world outside. Among other things the world outside includes economic zones dominated by the US dollar, the euro's toughest competitor.

Inside Euroland, however, incorporating the euro into their economic transactions poses more personal problems for European consumers. They must decide how to think about economic values expressed in the new currency. In his speech, Almunia identified citizens' "mental or psychological makeover" as "by far the most difficult challenge." Consumer surveys find that what people commonly do is retranslate the euro into their supposedly moribund national currency. The 2004 Flash Eurobarometer Survey shows, for instance, that national currencies remain the "mental benchmark" especially for large, exceptional purchases and more so for women than men.

Even professionals involved in the administration of the euro disclose such mental accounting practices. Emma Bonino, then European commissioner in charge of policy for consumers and their health, said in 1998 that she felt European, yet converted euro prices into "the money I was brought up with, my standard money, my national money, the Italian lire.... For me, ranges of values and memories of prices remain in lire" (Servet, 1998, p. 3). As with state currency, however, earmarking in the case of euro consists of a relational process as well. Surely, many more earmarking practices among users will show up comparable to those studied with national currencies (Dodd, 2005; Kooreman, Faber, & Hofmans, 2004).

Official, top–down earmarking is already in place. Euro banknotes' design, to be sure, symbolizes European unity by carrying a single image unattached to particular nations, anonymous bridges on one side and windows and gateways on the other. But euro coins, while similarly bearing a common European marker on one side, retain a national side. Each country mints its own coins. With the only restriction that it should be surrounded by 12 stars, each nation was free to choose its particular imprint, reproducing national differentiations. Ireland, for example, displayed a Celtic harp on its coins. While Europeans were constructing relationally based categories distinguishing members of the euro zone from outsiders, within that zone both national authorities and individual citizens were using earmarking practices to delineate further us–them subdivisions. They were performing relational work on two boundaries, national and international.

Users of the euro deploy multiple us–them boundaries, from earmarking within the euro zone to the maintenance of the euro/non-euro frontier, to employment of the euro well outside its official territory. Within the zone, as we have seen, people regularly mark off different sets of transactions and relations by means of earmarking practices. At the official boundary, old EU members, Norway and the United Kingdom, defend their sovereignty by refusing the euro any official standing. But outside the European Union, the euro marks off transactions that connect their participants with the euro zone. A 2004 survey by the European Commission reports that across 113 countries on all inhabited continents, 14% had the euro circulating as a parallel currency as against 46% for the US dollar (Survey, 2004, p. 5).

In some parts of Kosovo and Montenegro, according to another EU source, the euro has replaced the German mark as de facto legal tender, while through more official arrangements non-EU members Monaco, Vatican

City, San Marino, Saint-Pierre-et-Miquelon, and Mayotte have adopted locally earmarked versions of the euro (Euro, 2005). Although the dollar still reigns as international currency in many parts of the world, the boundary euro/non-euro is starting to compete with the dollar as the basis of insider/outsider categories. Around and across that boundary, Europeans are performing relational work. They are creating social boundaries; relations within the boundaries; relations across the boundaries; and meaningful categories distinguishing persons, activities, and relations on different sides of the boundaries.

V. Remittances

At first glance, immigrant remittances look like an entirely different world from local money, legal tender, and the euro. Yet immigrants, too, are engaging in social interaction that generates, informs, and then responds to a significant set of connected categories. Their categories also depend on socially maintained boundaries, relations within the boundaries, and relations across the boundaries. They regularly involve mental accounting systems, of which short-term quid pro quo exchanges constitute only one special type. Members of remittance networks complement mental accounting systems with earmarking practices; they establish subdivisions within ostensibly homogeneous media by signaling commitment of different sorts of goods or money to distinct relations and transactions. Finally, they perform unceasing relational work; they invest effort in establishing, terminating, negotiating, and transforming interpersonal relations, and thereby shape boundaries, accounting systems, and categories.

Remittances consist of money and other resources acquired by migrants at their destinations and sent back to their home communities as support for persons and activities. Remittances most often go to family members who have stayed behind or returned, but sometimes also support more distant connections such as priests, politicians, and neighbors. Two different forms of earmarking appear in remittance systems. First, migrants divide their earnings into portions committed to remittances and a remainder for local expense, often living precariously in order to meet their obligations at home: fixing the stove, financing a fiesta, repairing the house, saving for a dowry, and so on.

Second, receiving households commonly perform parallel earmarking, committing migrants' remittances to different activities from local income (for studies of remittance practices, see Amuedo-Dorantes & Pozo, 2005; Conway & Cohen, 1998; Curran & Saguy, 2001; de la Garza & Lowell, 2002; Durand, Parrado, & Massey, 1996; Georges, 1990; Grasmuck & Pessar,

1992; Hirsch, 2003; Hondagneu-Sotelo & Avila, 2002; Julca, 2001; Kurien, 2002; Levitt, 2001a,b; Lucas & Stark, 1985; Mahler, 2001a,b; Menjívar, 2000; Mooney, 2003; Parreñas, 2001; Singh, 2005; Waller Meyers, 1998).

Based on interviews with Hispanic migrants to Miami and Los Angeles in 2002, a Pew Hispanic Center study documents the centrality of remittances to connections between sending and receiving communities. Almost all respondents reported sending remittances to support families back home. Most gave remittances priority over their bills and expenses in the United States. "Before anything," Mexican emigrant respondent Marisela remarked, "I send them the money because they count on it. Then afterwards I pay the bills, my rent, but the first thing I do is send it" (Suro, Bendixen, Lowell, & Benavides, 2002, p. 7).

When it came to basic family expenses back home, most migrants left budgetary control to their families. A Mexican emigrant, Eduardo, told interviewers:

> One part is for savings, the other part for the primary necessities like education. It depends on my wife and the priorities she has. So I go ahead and send the money, and it just goes where she uses it. (Suro et al., 2002, p. 8)

When it came to investments such as buying land, however, remitting emigrants exercised extensive control over the money; they negotiated binding earmarks with their families in the home community. Each of these arrangements clearly involves mental accounting. In each, earmarking concerns budgeting of remitted funds into distinct categories of legitimate expenditure.

Latin American migrants to the United States commonly use wire services to transmit money back home, as a simple search of almost any American city's Latin American neighborhoods for stores with *envios*—remittances— among their advertised wares will verify. Many also use couriers (often known as *viajeros* or travelers) to carry money and other valuables. Finally, migrants who return home for visits regularly carry not only money but also other gifts, including household appliances, as anyone who has ever taken an inexpensive flight from a US airport to the Caribbean or Latin America can testify.

Remittances involve big money. A 2004 United Nations report on international migration shows that during the 1990s remittances passed overseas development assistance as a source of external funds for developing countries; by the early twenty-first century officially counted remittances alone were running about $60 billion per year. Unofficially transmitted money and goods surely added billions more. Remittances have sometimes amounted to more than 60% of international monetary inflows to El Salvador and Nicaragua

(United Nations, 2004, p. 106). In 2002, roughly $27 billion officially sent to Latin America and the Caribbean accounted for about a fifth of the world total of official remittances, and equaled 1.6% of the entire region's gross domestic product (United Nations, 2004, p. 107).

By no means, however, do all long-distance migrants participate actively in remittance systems. Highly educated migrants, for example, often maintain contact with their families of origin without sending significant aid back home. Remittance systems articulate closely with networks through which migrants acquire jobs, housing, and sociability at their destinations. Potential migrants at the origin acquire information and aid connecting them with opportunities at the destination, and returned migrants regularly contribute knowledge and assistance to maintaining the system.

More important for present purposes, relations within remittance systems create strong us–them boundaries: between families of migrants and others at the origin, between migrants and others at the destination, between those migrants who fulfill their obligations and those who default. Defaulters feel the weight of disapproval and exclusion. From the remittance stream's perspective, they form a category of pariahs.

Robert Smith's analysis of Mexican migration to New York City amply illustrates these processes. His 15-year participant observation of the migration stream connecting the Puebla village, he calls Ticuani, to mainly Mexican concentrations within New York documents both creation of a far-reaching remittance network and deep transformation of the network as a result of interaction among people moving back and forth between the two locales (Smith, 2005). By now, roughly 60% of all people born in Ticuani live in the United States, mostly in New York (Smith, 2002, p. 147). Many New York–based Ticuanenses, including those born in New York, actually returned frequently to Mexico and spent significant portions of their time in Ticuani. Modest incomes in New York made it possible to cut fine figures in Mexico.

At the same time, remittances from New York money earners to Ticuanense relatives, building of vacation houses in Ticuani, participation of returning emigrants in public ceremonies, direct intervention of emigrants (whether returned or not) in Ticuani politics, establishment of New York–style youth gangs in Ticuani, and entrusting of New York–born children to their grandmothers in Mexico all help transform social structures connecting New York with Puebla.

These changes have triple effects:

- deeply altering the organization of power and wealth in Ticuani
- reshaping the lives of Ticuanenses in both locales
- creating a new transnational set of interpersonal networks

Without a continuous flow of earnings from mostly modest occupations in New York, the incessantly changing system would collapse. "Remittances," Smith remarks

> are the largest source of income in the region, exceeding even the state funds allocated for the area, according to local politicians. Indeed, almost every peso spent in the Mixteca [Ticuani's region] can be linked to someone washing dishes in New York. Corn vendors make change from thick wads of bills composed of both multicolored pesos and greenbacks. (Smith, 2005, p. 49)

But fed by those resources and by new generations of migrants in both directions, the process sustains boundaries between Ticuanenses and others, shapes relations across those boundaries in both Mexico and the United States, and increases the relative prominence of network segments closely connected to the Ticuanense population in New York.

Smith shows, among other things, that a hometown association operating from New York City regularly intervenes in Ticuani's local affairs to the extent of financing the water supply and backing candidates for public office. Since the 1970s, in fact, many Ticuanense New Yorkers fulfill their village work obligations, or *faenas,* by means of financial contributions channeled to Mexico through a powerful New York–based committee of emigrants. Smith tells the story of accompanying committee members to JFK airport in 1993 as they went off to consult with Ticuani authorities and contractors about a new water system for the village. For this, he reports,

> the largest Ticuani project ever, the Committee raised more than two-thirds of the $150,000 cost of the project, exceeding the Mexican federal, state, and local contributions combined. The Committee has also become involved in Ticuani politics, helping to fashion a set of rules and practices for participating in transnational public life. Fundraising in New York by Ticuanenses has become increasingly important in Ticuani electoral politics. (Smith, 2005, p. 3)

In New York, the Committee had assessed each household in New York or Ticuani it judged able to pay a $300 tax they called a "cooperation," threatening delinquents that their Ticuani houses would not receive water. Almost everyone paid, regardless of how long they had been away from Ticuani (Smith, 2000, p. 212). By competing with local Mexican authorities, the New York Committee's activity was undermining the old structure of local power. It was also converting a segment of the migration-formed trust network into a transnational political institution.

In remittance systems, how do relations, boundaries, and categories interact? Relations between emigrants and households at the origin provide mutual support as well as reinforcing the migrants' longer-term claims on membership in the sending community. Earmarked remittances buttress the crucial relations as they assert the senders' power over those relations. The boundary between faithful remitters and defaulters not only divides upstanding family members from dishonorable exiles but it also separates households that regularly receive support of their migrant members from less fortunate households at the origin.

Reporting on his extensive fieldwork in the Caribbean island of Montserrat as well as in London, Stuart Philpott describes a powerful system of informal controls over remittances from migrants in Great Britain. "Children are impressed," he remarks,

> with the behavior expected from the migrants from a fairly early age. These expectations are implicitly taught in the home through the praise of migrants who send remittances and through the condemnation of the "worthless-minded" kin who do not "notice their families." Stories such as one about the migrant who returned from America with thirty-two trunk loads of gifts for distribution to his family and friends and another about a woman who literally sent her brother a car from America in the days when the only other cars were owned by the wealthiest estate owners, have virtually become moral precepts. (Philpott, 1968, p. 468)

Philpott documents children's trips to the post office in hopes of retrieving money-bearing letters, children's visions of the future in which they emigrate and send back support for their families, complex allocations of money received among family members, reciprocity by sending of homegrown products back to Britain, black magic employed to coerce reluctant remitters—in short, a large array of controls backing up the general understanding that honorable emigrants meet their obligations to family and friends by means of remittances. The obvious consequence: division of emigrants into the two categories of honorable and dishonorable (see also Roberts & Morris, 2003).

Once again, we witness relations generating boundaries and thus forming categories. In remittance systems, relational work pops up everywhere. The relational work of remittances creates social boundaries; relations within the boundaries; relations across the boundaries; and meaningful categories distinguishing persons, activities, and relations on different sides of the boundaries.

VI. Trust Networks

Remittance systems ordinarily incorporate a crucial kind of social arrangement: the trust network. Within all the interpersonal connections that mediate long-distance migration, some stand out by clumping together in relations of mutual trust. In so doing, they establish sharp differences between relations inside and outside the network. The boundary separates people you can trust from people you cannot trust. It establishes us–them categories.

Parallels and overlaps with the social phenomena discussed earlier—local money, legal tenders, the euro, and migrant remittances—will soon become apparent. In trust networks involved in long-distance trade, organization of kinship solidarity, protection of esoteric religious sects, support of international migration, and similar consequential long-term, high-risk activities, participants form us–them boundaries, employ mental accounting systems, adopt earmarking practices, and carry on incessant relational work. In this case, however, the work involves maintenance of trust.

What is trust? We can think of trust as an attitude or as a relationship with practices attached. Here the relationship deserves special attention. Labels such as kinsman, compadre, paisano, fellow believer, and comember of a craft provide a first indication of a trust relationship. But we know a trust relationship more surely by the practices of its participants: If you trust certain people, do not just tell them so; let them take charge of your children's education, lend them your life's savings for investment, take medicines they give you, or help them paint their house on the assumption that they will help you paint yours. If you do not trust them, prove it by doing none of these things, and nothing like them.

Trust consists of placing valued outcomes at risk to others' malfeasance, mistakes, or failures. Trust relationships include those in which people regularly take such risks. Although some trust relationships remain purely dyadic, for the most part they operate within larger networks of similar relationships. Trust networks, then, consist of ramified interpersonal connections, consisting mainly of strong ties, within which people set valued, consequential, long-term resources and enterprises at risk to the malfeasance, mistakes, or failures of others.

How will we recognize a trust network when we encounter or enter one? First, we will notice a number of people who are connected, directly or indirectly, by similar ties; they form a network. Second, we will see that the sheer existence of such a tie gives one member significant claims on the attention or aid of another; the network consists of strong ties. Third, we will discover that members of the network are collectively carrying on major long-term enterprises such as procreation, long-distance trade, workers' mutual aid, practice of an underground religion, or, of course, maintenance of a long-distance migration stream. Finally, we will learn that the configuration of ties within the network sets the collective enterprise at risk to the malfeasance, mistakes, and failures of individual members.

Networks reach into every corner of social life (Watts, 2003, 2004). Social networks include any set of similar connections among three or more social sites. Connections include communication, mutual recognition, shared participation in some activity, flows of goods or services, transmission of diseases, and other forms of consequential interaction. Network sites may be individuals but they can also be organizations, localities, or social positions. A network of connections among people you do not know and who mostly do not know each other brings you your morning newspaper. Another transmits political information. Still others lend invisible structure to flows of money, disease, and linguistic innovation.

Although segments of such networks may overlap with or even constitute trust networks, taken as wholes they do not qualify as trust networks. They do not qualify because their participants do not generally place their major valued collective enterprises at risk to malfeasance, mistakes, or failures by other members of the same networks. In that precise sense, members do not trust each other. Most or all members of trust networks, in contrast, place major valued collective enterprises such as the preservation of their faith, placement of their children, provision for their old age, and protection of personal secrets at risk to fellow members' malfeasance, mistakes, or failures. Accordingly, trust networks constitute only a tiny subset of all networks.

Over thousands of years, nevertheless, ordinary people have committed their major energies and most precious resources to trust networks—not only migration streams, to be sure, but also religious solidarities, lineages, trade diasporas, patron–client chains, credit networks, societies of mutual aid, youth groups, and some kinds of local communities. We participants in kinship and other trust networks usually take them for granted. But they pose important mysteries: how do they maintain cohesion, control, and, yes, trust when their members spread out into worlds rich with other opportunities and commitments?

Their limiting cases, isolated communes and religious communities, seem easier to explain because their very insulation from the world facilitates continuous monitoring, mutual aid, reciprocity, trust, and barriers to exit. But geographically dispersed trust networks somehow manage to produce similar effects, if not usually at the emotional intensities of isolated communities. Maintaining the boundary between "us" and "them" clearly plays an important part in trust networks' continued operation (Tilly, 2005a).

Trust networks figure in many migration streams, especially those organized in continuous chains linking limited origins to limited destinations. In fact, chain-linked long-distance migration provides a privileged laboratory for study of transformations in trust networks. Long-distance migration poses serious risks. These risks dispose potential migrants who do not have extensive professional connections or official sponsors to rely on members of their trust networks for information and advice. The same risks inhibit potential migrants who lack the mediation of trust networks from migrating at all. Instead of a broad distribution across destinations as a function of economic opportunities at those destinations, chain migration channels long-distance moves into a few origin–destination streams; large numbers of people from the same village end up in the same towns or urban neighborhoods thousands of miles away.

Networks persist in the process but change structure and geographic distribution. Since participants generally rely on strong ties to others with whom they are carrying on consequential long-term enterprises and placing those enterprises at risk to the malfeasance, mistakes, or failures of others, the networks in question commonly qualify as trust networks. Chain migration organized around trust networks contributes to the "segmented assimilation" that Portes and Rumbaut (1990, 2001) see as characteristic of recent migration to the United States. Segmented assimilation establishes categorical differences between members and nonmembers of particular migrant streams; ethnic connections and markers persist into the second generation and beyond.

In long-distance migration, mediation of kinfolk repeatedly produces chains in which migrant A facilitates migrant B, migrant B facilitates migrant C, and so on until close ties exist between kin-connected localities at one end of the chain and the other (Tilly, 1990, 2000). Marcelo Borges has reconstructed chain migration from a small, kin-connected cluster of villages in Portugal's southernmost region, Algarve, to the agricultural region of Villa Elisa, Argentina, between La Plata and Buenos Aires. In Villa Elisa, Portuguese immigrants started arriving as agricultural laborers during the 1920s, bought land of their own, and created a viable economic niche as commercial flower gardeners. They married largely within their own population. As is often the case, kinship networks promoted ethnic endogamy.

Borges reports an interview with Francisco, who arrived from Portugal in the early 1930s. Within six years, Francisco had bought land and set himself up as an independent flower grower. At that point, he brought his wife and child to Villa Elisa and started helping other members of his kin group to migrate. Part of his story ran like this:

> First, I asked my sister to come. She came here single. Her husband was my friend. He was single. And I told him—since I had two or three single sisters over there [in Portugal]—that if he wanted one, I would ask her to come. And that's the way it was. So he agreed and I asked ... her to send him her picture so he could get to know her, and I also asked him to send her his picture. And that's the way it was. So he liked her and asked her to come .... He was also Portuguese. He was Algarvian, but from another sitio [hamlet]. (Borges, 2003, pp. 468–469)

Hundreds of transactions on this model formed a Portuguese ethnic community based on Villa Elisa's flower trade. Through just such humble, incremental transactions, trust networks accomplish consequential enterprises—in this case the transplantation and transformation of migrant communities and their economic specialties. In this spectacular case, within Argentina the migration system created mutated versions of the relations, boundaries, and categories that organized social life back in Algarve.

Over the long historical run, kinship—the establishment of publicly recognized ties through combinations of cohabitation and procreation—has no doubt provided the most frequent matrix for the formation of trust networks. Not all kinship networks, by any means, constitute trust networks. Indeed, bilateral lineage systems like those prevailing in most western countries practically forbid that any person's full kinship network could constitute a trust network, if only because it differs in membership from those of the person's father, mother, children, or cousins.

We must distinguish, furthermore, between the formal reckoning of genealogies and the creation of active social relations within the broad framework provided by genealogy. In many kinship systems, for example, adoption and fictive kinship establish binding social ties. In order to qualify as trust networks, kinship connections also require the actual performance of kinship, not the mere establishment of shared ancestry. Katherine Verdery's remarkable ethnography of postsocialist privatization in a Romanian agricultural village traces the judicial and administrative assignment to individuals and families of agricultural plots that had passed through many hands and forms of cultivation since the regime of relatively private property existing before World War II.

Verdery argues that in figuring rights to collectivized property the Romanian government adopted a formal, genealogical conception of rights in land, ignoring for instance who had actually worked various plots under socialism, who had invested care in older former proprietors, and so on. From the government's perspective, any individuals who occupied similar positions within the genealogy—two brothers, two cousins, two aunts—had equal rights to shares in privatizing property over which a household or kin group had a legal claim. That formalistic reasoning clashed with local moral codes. According to Verdery:

> Villagers, however, had not understood kinship that way; for them, it was performative. To be kin meant *behaving* like kin. It meant cooperating to create marriage, baptismal, and death rituals; putting flowers on relatives' graves; helping out with money or other favors; and caring for the elderly (who might not even be one's parents) in exchange for inheriting their land. (Verdery, 2003, p. 165)

To put it in terms, Verdery does not use and might well reject, relations to kin qualified as genuine kinship to the extent that they conformed to the model of trust networks.

Even if whole kinship networks, formally computed, rarely qualify as trust networks, by virtue of cohabitation and procreation, some *segments* of kinship networks often undertake consequential collective enterprises, such as placement of children, and lend themselves to other enterprises such as trade and provision for incompetent persons. In the course of doing so they accumulate resources that remain under their collective control. As age-old struggles over land, cattle, money, and labor power indicate, a kinship network's accumulation of resources then frequently becomes the object of competition between segments of the network, between rival kinship networks, between network members and authoritative organizations seeking to seize resources for support of their own activities.

For villages west of Genoa during the century from 1550 to 1650, Osvaldo Raggio gives us a privileged picture of the interplay between local trust networks and higher-level authorities. Influential families—more exactly, patrilineages—organized their lives in three circles: those of individual households, people who combined a shared family name with recognized kinship, and larger circles of related kin groups. In economic activity, property transfers, political life, and marital strategies, the more extended *parentele* dominated village affairs. With incessant competition for advantage among extended kinship groups and avoidance of higher authorities (including those of the then independent Genovese state), kin groups frequently engaged in feuds, attacking each other's persons and property in round after round of retaliation.

Within the region, feuds ran from small scale to large, building on the fissiparous structure that created kin groups out of households sharing common names and ancestors, but aggregating up the scale to "leagues" and factions incorporating multiple leagues. In mid-sixteenth century, a noble Genovese "captain" bore responsibility for the top–down administration of the town of Chiavari and its dependent political territories. Local people paid his salary. In 1549, captain Ambrosio Rivarola enumerated two major factions that set 71 kin groups in five leagues, on one side, against 20 kin groups in four leagues (Raggio, 1990, pp. 163–168). Although the factions, leagues, and smaller scale kin-based organizations constituted the region's de facto government below the highest levels, they also provided the basis for blood feuds.

Feuds, however, rarely ended without external intervention, either of authoritative kinsmen or of Genovese officials. Often Genovese officials supervised the formation of peacemaking deputations elected from heads of kin groups outside the feud and backed the deputations' authority to craft peace settlements. In the process of feud and settlement, argues Raggio, kin groups not only consolidated their boundaries but also found themselves connecting unintentionally yet firmly to state authorities. As Raggio puts it:

> Like the feud, pacification assumes strong coherence of all relatives with regard to their "principals." Through the negotiations Genovese officials "gave voice" to all parties and legitimized state intervention along with the Prince's authority; but in the same process they legitimized the role of notables and reinforced local forms of social-political organization: *parentele*. (Raggio, 1990, p. 247)

Thus, Genovese trust networks, for all their resort to dissimulation and clientage, depended on backing from the state and yielded a share of their resources in return for state intervention in otherwise murderous conflicts.

In fact, precisely because of their structure trust networks often become vulnerable either to external predation or to externally initiated divide-and-conquer tactics. To the extent that they control visible, desirable resources, such as land, labor power, or commercial wealth, they become objects of envy and greed. As a consequence, leaders of trust networks often engage in countertactics of divide-and-defend with regard to would-be exploiters: playing one ruler off against another.

Of all places, thirteenth-century Galicia, on Spain's west coast, provides surprising documentation. There, the nominal authority of León's king lay thin on the ground, and well-armed local nobles did what they could to gain control over peasant communities, which typically organized around extended kinship systems. Communities themselves had only weak means of military self-defense. Instead of armed resistance, a peasant countertactic consisted of bargaining with powerful monasteries for transfer from royal to ecclesiastical feudal control:

> To offer *amorem y defensa* [love and protection] thus seems to have been a general framework for reciprocity, which in some instances was expressed through additional offers of "help and protection" or "refuge and protection."
>
> Peasants therefore received some sort of guarantee that monastic "defence", "protection", and "love" would offer them support against other social elements that they either objected to or felt threatened by. Such guarantees stabilized the local social system and, as mutual sociability was an objective common to both peasants and their lords, were recognized by both as an indispensable mechanism of reciprocity. (Pastor, Pascua, Rodríguez-López, & Sánchez-León, 2002, p. 287)

Obviously these ties established mutual relations between protectors and protected as well as within the protected community. Less obviously—but more importantly for our purposes—they established boundaries between protégés of different patrons. Once again, they created us–them categories. Once again, they engaged in relational work. Once again, the relational work in question creates social boundaries, relations within the boundaries, relations across the boundaries, and meaningful categories distinguishing persons, activities, and relations on different sides of the boundaries.

VII. Nationalism and Citizenship

It seems a long leap from thirteenth-century Galicia to the politics of nationalism and citizenship. Yet, nationalism and citizenship involve similar processes of relational connection, boundary formation, and categorical creation (Tilly, 1994, 1995). Nationalism is a political program, or rather a complementary pair of political programs, that gained great prominence during the nineteenth century and revived in intensity as empires collapsed during the twentieth century. From the top down, nationalism declares that we who run a state have the right to define that state's culture, to identify its interests, to impose our version of culture and interests on the subject population, and thereby to define the nation. From the bottom up, however, a competitive nationalism asserts that we form a distinct nation, that our rulers are alien or hostile to that nation, and that we, therefore, have a right to our own state. Both programs call for nations to match states—for each nation to have its own state, and each state to have its own distinct nation.

Citizenship connects with nationalism in an interesting way. Citizenship involves establishment of categorically defined (rather than particular) rights and obligations connecting subjects of a given state to that state's agents. Both the top down and bottom up versions of nationalism call for strong citizenship—more precisely, for a certain categorical definition of proper relations between state agents and subjects to prevail across the state's entire range. In the simplest interpretation, always compromised in actual practice, all citizens belong to the nation and all members of the nation become citizens.

Both nationalism and citizenship therefore distinguish a belonging "us" from a great many "them" outside the nation. Anthony Marx has argued, indeed, that all nationalism begins with acts of exclusion. We become us by identifying those who are not us. Marx pursues the development of nationalism by not only analyzing the long-term histories of Spain, France, and England but also making comparisons of South Africa, the United States and Brazil. Marx argues that collective sentiments of commitment to the nation arise through processes of exclusion, directed against those who threaten the nation and/or remain unworthy of inclusion in the nation. They result from relational work at a national scale.

American national identity, Marx claims, formed against the background of African–American slavery, the "us" of white America pitted against the "them" of black America. Similarly but much earlier, according to Marx, Spain developed its relatively weak nationalism through opposition to its domestic Jews and Muslims, France acquired a stronger version of nationalism through opposition to domestic Protestants, and English nationalism swelled in opposition to domestic Catholics. The crucial confrontations, furthermore, occurred on the domestic scene rather than in the international arena. As Marx sums up:

> Rulers came to understand that they could not effectively wage war or diplomacy if they were weakened within by civil or religious conflict, could not then recruit troops, be sure that those troops would remain loyal, and avoid challenges from a "third column" tied to external enemies ... to avoid such difficulties and gain strength, monarchs sought to build national unity and loyalty through domestic religious exclusion. Activists from below did likewise. (Marx, 2003, p. 79)

Thus, popular sentiment and royal will united in opposition to a common enemy.

Marx has put his finger on crucial elements in the formation of both nationalism and citizenship: the drawing and politicization of us–them boundaries, the exclusion of visible others, the foundation of membership on not being something else. In Spain, mobilization against Muslims and Jews, then against their ostensibly Catholic descendants, helped shape prevailing definitions of Spanishness for purposes of nationalism and citizenship. In England, from 1689 to the nineteenth-century political exclusion of non-Anglicans, and especially of Catholics, deeply affected practices of nationalism and citizenship. It created boundaries that still divide Northern Ireland lethally today. Nor were Spain and England alone. During the seventeenth century, French nationalism and citizenship fed on the insistence that the French were not Spanish, not English, and especially not Protestant.

Take another British example. Once the United Kingdom drew the perimeter of full citizenship around well-behaved and propertied adult males on the ground of their greater responsibility for the public weal, the regime opened itself to challenges from other excluded categories of the population, male or female, who had acquired property or could make the case for their own indispensability to the public weal. Working class Chartists of 1838–1848 said as much: we workers allied with merchants and manufacturers in the push for parliamentary reform that brought the great Reform Act of 1832, but the newly enfranchised merchants and manufacturers then closed the door behind them, leaving us workers without full citizenship. This bid to move across the boundary explains the otherwise astonishing concentration of a nineteenth-century workers' movement on purely political reforms: expansion of the suffrage, salaries for members of Parliament, and so on. The People's Charter demanded full citizenship for honest workers—at least if they were male.

Does all this ancient history have any relevance to the operation of nationalism and citizenship today? It has deep relevance. Far from expressing a cumulative sense of common properties alone, citizenship still often comes into being through deliberate exclusion. Macedonian nationalists define Albanians out of the polity, and Islamists seek to deny the unfaithful political rights in mainly Muslim countries. Serbian and Israeli governments distinguish sharply between their strategies of policing in their heartlands and at their edges (Ron, 2003). Once us–them boundaries form, they take on lives of their own as people on either side attach social relations, stories, and daily practices to them.

Citizenship continues to bind people to particular states by means of rights and obligations, which means that shifts of power to transnational or non-state institutions threaten existing patterns of citizenship. Over the next half century, for example, the European Union may actually succeed in making the division between Europeans and non-Europeans blur the petty national distinctions over which Europeans killed each other for three bloody centuries. But both nationalism and citizenship continue to depend on the presence of us–them boundaries, which means they thrive on the exclusion of others. Their very operation creates and depends on powerful political categories. Here, too, relational work creates social boundaries, relations within the boundaries; relations across the boundaries; and meaningful categories distinguishing persons, activities, and relations on different sides of the boundaries.

VIII. Conclusions

Local monies, legal tenders, the euro, migrant remittances, trust networks, nationalism, and citizenship display some unexpected common properties. In all of them, us–them boundaries mark distinct, symbolically charged spheres of social life, relations within boundaries differ significantly from relations across boundaries, but relational work generates and reinforces categories. Despite enormous variation in the criteria of value among these different social phenomena, in all of them shared accounting systems figure as well: obviously in the varieties of money, more subtly in the counting of rights and obligations of trust, nationalism, and citizenship. We could easily extend the same analysis to households, formal organizations, gangs, and many forms of economic cooperation. The general conclusion would remain the same: relations generate and reinforce categories.

To be sure, local monies, legal tenders, the euro, migrant remittances, trust networks, nationalism, and citizenship have their own peculiarities. Trust networks, for example, typically make their rules of entry, exit, and membership much less formal than do the managers of citizenship. Yet our framework helps organize analysis of those peculiarities as well. It calls for disciplined observation and comparison of these elements:

- a boundary
- relations within the boundary
- relations across the boundary
- meaningful categories distinguishing persons, activities, and relations within the boundary from those outside

Put together, the four elements identify a major research program for social scientists: describing change and variation in the four elements, describing interactions among them, and then explaining how those interactions work. Although social scientists use very different terminology from one field to the next, our survey of monies, trust networks, nationalism, and citizenship indicates that many of them are already pursuing a common program.

As for psychology, we hope that professionals in the field will see the implications of our analysis for cognitive processes. At a minimum, our material suggests that relational processes frequently generate and modify us–them categories. These categories then come to seem natural and organize further perceptions of social life. Study of the relational origins of categories looks like a promising site for collaboration between psychologists and social scientists (DiMaggio, 1997; Fiske, 1992; Markman & Gentner, 2001; McGraw & Tetlock, 2005; Niedenthal & Beike, 1997; Ross, Gelman, & Rosengren, 2005; Seeley, Gardner, Pennington, & Gabriel, 2003; Zerubavel, 1991, 1997). Here we have only hinted at three questions of consummate interest to psychologists and social scientists alike:

1. To what extent and how do available categories (or the general properties of all human categories) shape the formation of social relations, for example, by limiting the possible definitions of us–them boundaries?
2. To what extent and how do interacting people come to share similar or identical categories for social relations?
3. What processes produce change in prevailing social boundaries, hence in the categories people use to organize their social lives?

It will take close collaboration between students of cognitive and relational processes to unravel such complex, exciting, fundamental questions.

REFERENCES

Abbott, A. (1995). Things of boundaries. *Social Research, 62*, 857–882.
Almunia, J. (2005). The Euro and the main challenges to achieve convergence. Viewed 7 September 2005. http://europa.eu.int/rapid/pressReleasesAction.do?reference=SPEECH/05/442.
Amuedo-Dorantes, C., & Pozo, S. (2005). On the use of differing money transmission methods by mexican immigrants. *International Migration Review, 39*, 554–576.
Barth, F. (Ed.). (1969). *Ethnic groups and boundaries. The social organization of culture difference* Bergen-Oslo: Universitetsforlaget.
Barth, F. (1981). *Process and form in social life. Selected essays of Fredrik Barth: Volume I.* London: Routledge and Kegan Paul.
Bayon, D. (1999). *Les S.E.L., Systèmes d'échanges locaux, pour un vrai débat*. Levallois-Perret: Yves Michel.
Blanc, J. (2000). *Les Monnaies Parallèles*. Paris: L'Harmattan.
Borges, M. J. (2003). Network migration, marriage patterns, and adaptation in rural portugal and among portuguese immigrants in Argentina, 1870–1980. *History of the Family, 8*, 445–479.
Cohen, B. (2004). *The future of money*. Princeton, N.J.: Princeton University Press.
Conway, D., & Cohen, J. H. (1998). Consequences of migration and remittances for mexican transnational communities. *Economic Geography, 74*, 25–44.
Curran, S. R., & Saguy, A. C. (2001). Migration and cultural change: A role for gender and social networks? *Journal for International Women's Studies, 2*, 54–77.
de la Garza, R. O., & Lowell, B. L. (Eds.). (2002). *Sending money home. Hispanic remittances and community development.* Lanham, MD: Rowman & Littlefield.
DiMaggio, P. (1997). Culture and cognition. *Annual Review of Sociology, 23*, 263–287.
Dodd, N. (2005). Reinventing monies in Europe. *Economy and Society, 34*, 558–583.
Durand, J., Parrado, E. A., & Massey, D. S. (1996). Migradollars and development: A reconsideration of the Mexican case. *International Migration Review, 30*, 423–444.
Epstein, C. F. (1992). Tinkerbells and pinups: The construction and reconstruction of gender boundaries at work. In M. Lamont and M. Fournier (Eds.), *Cultivating differences. Symbolic boundaries and the making of inequality* (pp. 232–256). Chicago: University of Chicago Press.
Euro (2005). The euro: Our currency. Viewed September 6, 2005 http://europa.eu.int/comm/economy_finance/euro/our_currency_en.htm; http://europa.eu.int/comm/economy_finance/euro/world/euro_world_1_en.htm; http://europa.eu.int/comm/economy_finance/euro/world/euro_world_2_en.htm; http://europa.eu.int/comm/economy_finance/euro/world/euro_world_4_en.htm.
Fishman, R. M., & Messina, A. M. (Eds.). (2006). *The year of the euro: The cultural, social, and political import of Europe's common currency.* Chicago: University of Notre Dame Press.
Fiske, A. P. (1992). The four elementary forms of sociality: Framework for a unified theory of social relations. *Psychological Review, 99*, 689–723.
Fuller, S. (2003). Creating and contesting boundaries: Exploring the dynamics of conflict and classification. *Sociological Forum, 18*, 3–30.
Georges, E. (1990). *The making of a transnational community*. New York: Columbia University Press.
Grasmuck, S., & Pessar, P. R. (1992). *Between two islands. Dominican international migration.* Berkeley: University of California Press.

Guigou, É. (2002). Préface. In J.-M. Servet and I. Guérin (Eds.), *Exclusion et Liens Financiers: Rapport du Centre Walras* (pp. 7–10). Paris: Economica.

Hart, K. (1999). *The memory bank: Money in an unequal world.* London: Profile Books.

Heath, C., & Soll, J. B. (1996). Mental budgeting and consumer decisions. *Journal of Consumer Research, 23,* 40–52.

Helleiner, E. (1999). Conclusions—the future of national currencies? In E. Gilbert and E. Helleiner (Eds.), *Nation-states and money: The past, present and future of national currencies* (pp. 215–229). London: Routledge.

Helleiner, E. (2000). Think globally, transact locally: Green political economy and the local currency movement. *Global Society, 14,* 35–51.

Helleiner, E. (2003). *The making of national money: Territorial currencies in historical perspective.* Ithaca: Cornell University Press.

Hirsch, J. S. (2003). *A courtship after marriage.* Berkeley: University of California Press.

Hondagneu-Sotelo, P., & Avila, E. (2002). I'm here but I'm there: The meanings of transnational motherhood. In N. Gerstel, D. Clawson, and R. Zussman (Eds.), *Families at work: Expanding the boundaries* (pp. 139–161). Nashville: Vanderbilt University Press.

Ingham, G. (2004). *The nature of money.* Cambridge, U.K.: Polity.

Julca, A. (2001). Peruvian networks for migration in New York city's labor market, 1970–1996. In H. R. Coerdero-Guzmán, R. C. Smith, and R. Grosfoguel (Eds.), *Migration, transnationalization, and race in a changing New York* (pp. 239–257). Philadelphia: Temple University Press.

Kahneman, D., & Tversky, A. (1982). The psychology of preferences. *Scientific American, 246,* 160–173.

Kooreman, P., Faber, R., & Hofmans, H. (2004). Charity donations and the euro introduction: Some quasi-experimental evidence on money illusion. *Journal of Money, Credit, and Banking, 36,* 1121–1124.

Kurien, P. A. (2002). *Kaleidoscopic ethnicity. International migration and the reconstruction of community identities in India.* New Brunswick, NJ: Rutgers University Press.

Lamont, M., & Molnár, V. (2002). The study of boundaries in the social sciences. *Annual Review of Sociology, 28,* 167–195.

Lane, R. (1991). *The market experience.* New York: Cambridge University Press.

Lets-Linkup (2005). International LETS groups directory. Viewed 26 August 2005. http://www.lets-linkup.com/.

Levitt, P. (2001a). *The transnational villagers.* Berkeley: University of California Press.

Levitt, P. (2001b). Transnational migration: Taking stock and future directions. In A. Portes (Ed.), New research on immigrant transnationalism [Special issue]. *Global Networks: A Journal of Transnational Affairs, 1,* 195–216.

Lucas, R. E. B., & Stark, O. (1985). Motivations to remit: Evidence from Botswana. *Journal of Political Economy, 93,* 901–918.

Mahler, S. J. (2001a). Transnational relationships: The struggle to communicate across borders. *Identities: Global Studies in Culture and Power, 7,* 583–619.

Mahler, S. J. (2001b). Suburban transnational migrants: Long island's salvadorans. In H. R. Cordero-Guzmán, R. C. Smith, and R. Grosfoguel (Eds.), *Migration, transnationalization, and race in a changing New York* (pp. 109–130). Philadelphia: Temple University Press.

Markman, A. B., & Gentner, D. (2001). Thinking. *Annual Review of Psychology, 52,* 223–247.

Marx, A. W. (2003). *Faith in nation. Exclusionary origins of nationalism.* Oxford: Oxford University Press.

McGraw, A. P., & Tetlock, P. E. (2005). Taboo trade-offs, relational framing, and the acceptability of exchanges. *Journal of Consumer Psychology, 15,* 2–15.

McGraw, A. P., Tetlock, P. E., & Kristel, O. V. (2003). The limits of fungibility: Relational schemata and the value of things. *Journal of Consumer Research, 30,* 219–229.

McNamara, K., & Meunier, S. (2002). Between national sovereignty and international power: What external voice for the Euro. *International Affairs, 78*(October), 849–868.

Menjívar, C. (2000). *Fragmented ties. Salvadoran immigrant networks in America.* Berkeley: University of California Press.

Mooney, M. (2003). Migrants' social ties in the US and investment in Mexico. *Social Forces, 81*, 1147–1170.

Niedenthal, P. M., & Beike, D. R. (1997). Interrelated and isolated self-concepts. *Personality and Social Psychology Review, 1*, 106–128.

Ong, A. (1996). Cultural citizenship as subject-making: Immigrants negotiate racial and cultural boundaries in the United States. *Current Anthropology, 37*, 737–762.

Parreñas, R. S. (2001). *Servants of globalization.* Stanford: Stanford University Press.

Pastor, R., Pascua, E., Rodríguez-López, A., & Sánchez-León, P. (2002). *Beyond the market. Transactions, property and social networks in Monastic Galicia 1200–1300.* Leiden: Brill.

Philpott, S. B. (1968). Remittance obligations, social networks and choice among montserratian migrants in Britain. *Man, New Series, 3*, 465–476.

Perrot, E. (1999). La compensation des dettes de SEL. In Jean-Michel Servet (Ed.), *Exclusion et Liens financiers* (pp. 384–391). Paris: Economica.

Pierret, D. (1999). Cercles d'échanges, cercles vertueux de la solidarité. Le Cas de l'Allemagne. *International Journal of Community Currency Research* 3. Viewed 25 July 2003. www.geog.le.ac.uk/ijccr/3no2.html.

Portes, A., & Rumbaut, R. (1990). *Immigrant america. A portrait.* Berkeley: University of California Press.

Portes, A., & Rumbaut, R. (2001). *Legacies: The story of the immigrant second generation.* Berkeley: University of California Press.

Powell, J. (2002). *Petty capitalism, perfecting capitalism or post-capitalism? Lessons from the Argentinian barter network.* Working Paper Series No. 357. Institute of Social Studies, The Hague, Netherlands.

Raddon, M.-B. (2003). *Community and money: Caring, gift-giving, and women in a social economy.* Montreal: Black Rose Books.

Raggio, O. (1990). *Faide e Parentele. Lo Stato Genovese visto dalla Fontanabuona.* Turin: Einaudi.

Rizzo, P. (1999). Réciprocité indirecte et symétrie: l'émergence d'une nouvelle forme de solidarité. In Jean-Michel Servet (Ed.), *Exclusion et liens financiers* (pp. 401–408). Paris: Economica.

Roberts, K. D., & Morris, M. D. S. (2003). Fortune, risk, and remittances: An application of option theory to participation in village-based migration networks. *International Migration Review, 37*, 1252–1281.

Ron, J. (2003). *Frontiers and Ghettos. State Violence in Serbia and Israel.* Berkeley: University of California Press.

Ross, B. H., Gelman, S. A., & Rosengren, K. S. (2005). Children's category-based inferences affect classification. *British Journal of Developmental Psychology, 23*, 1–24.

Sanders, J. (2002). Ethnic boundaries and identity in plural societies. *Annual Review of Sociology, 28*, 327–357.

Schroeder, R. F. H. (2002). Talente Tauschring Hannover (TTH): Experiences of a German LETS and the relevance of theoretical reflections. *International Journal of Community Currency Research* 6. Viewed 25 July 2003. http://www.geog.le.ac.uk/ijccr/vol4-6/6toc.htm.

Seeley, E. A., Gardner, W. L., Pennington, G., & Gabriel, S. (2003). Circle of friends or members of a group? Sex differences in relational and collective attachment to groups. *Group Processes & Intergroup Relations, 6*, 252–263.

Servet, J.-M. (1998). *L'euro au quotidien.* Paris: Desclée de Brouwer.

Servet, J.-M. (Ed.). (1999). *Une Économie Sans Argent: Les Systèmes d'Echange Local.* Paris: Seuil.

Shafir, E., Diamond, P., & Tversky, A. (1997). Money illusion. *The Quarterly Journal of Economics, 112*, 341–374.

Singh, S. (2005). *Sending money home: Money and family in the Indian Diaspora.* Paper presented at the Institute for International Integration Studies Seminar, Trinity College, Dublin, April 13. Viewed October 15, 2005. http://mams.rmit.edu.au/e0eneunbp2w.pdf.

Smith, R. C. (2000). How durable and new is transnational life? Historical retrieval through local comparison. *Diaspora, 9*, 203–232.

Smith, R. C. (2002). Life course, generation, and social location as factors shaping second-generation transnational life. In P. Levitt and M. C. Waters (Eds.), *The changing face of home. The transnational lives of the second generation* (pp. 145–167). New York: Russell Sage Foundation.

Smith, R. C. (2005). *Mexican New York: Transnational worlds of new immigrants.* Berkeley: University of California Press.

Suro, R., Bendixen, S., Lowell, B. L., & Benavides, D. C. (2002). *Billions in motion: Latino immigrants, remittances and banking.* Washington, DC: Pew Hispanic Center and the Multi-lateral Investment Fund Viewed October 13, 2005 http://www.iadb.org/mif/v2/files/nov22b.pdf.

Survey (2004). Survey on the use of euro cash outside the EU. Brussels: European Commission Viewed September 6, 2005. http://europa.eu.int/comm/economy_finance/euro/documents/survey_use_euro.pdf.

Taris, J. (2005). LETS favours. Viewed October 15, 2005. http://www.lets-linkup.com/LETS%20Favours.htm.

Thaler, R. H. (1999). Mental accounting matters. *Journal of Behavioral Decision Making, 12*, 183–206.

The Euro, 3 years later (2004). Flash eurobarometer. European commission. Viewed 7 September 2005. http://europa.eu.int/comm/public_opinion/flash/fl165_euro_en.pdf.

Tilly, C. (1990). Transplanted networks. In V. Yans-McLaughlin (Ed.), *Immigration reconsidered. History, sociology, and politics* (pp. 79–95). New York: Oxford University Press.

Tilly, C. (1994). States and nationalism in Europe 1492–1992. *Theory and Society, 23*, 131–146.

Tilly, C. (Ed.). (1995). *Citizenship, identity and social history.* Cambridge: Cambridge University Press.

Tilly, C. (2000). Chain migration and opportunity hoarding. In J. W. Dacyl and C. Westin (Eds.), *Governance of cultural diversity* (pp. 62–86). Stockholm: CEIFO [Centre for Research in International Migration and Ethnic Relations].

Tilly, C. (2005a). *Trust and rule.* Cambridge: Cambridge University Press.

Tilly, C. (2005b). *Identities, boundaries, and social ties.* Boulder: Paradigm Publishers.

United Nations (2004). Department of economic and social affairs. *World economic and social survey 2004. International migration.* New York: United Nations.

Verdery, K. (2003). *The vanishing hectare. Property and value in postsocialist transylvania.* Ithaca: Cornell University Press.

Waller Meyers, D. (1998). Migrant Remittances to Latin America: Reviewing the Literature. The Tomás Rivera Policy Institute, Working Paper, May. Viewed 5 February 2002. http://www.thedialogue.org/publications/meyers.html

Watts, D. (2003). *Six degrees: The science of a connected age.* New York: Norton.

Watts, D. (2004). The "new" science of networks. *Annual Review of Sociology, 30*, 243–270.

Yen Rivals (2001). The Rising Popularity of Local Currencies. *Trends in Japan*, January 15, 2001. Viewed 25 July 2003. http://www.jinjapan.org/trends00/honbun/tj010115.html

Zelizer, V. A. (1994). *The social meaning of money.* New York: Basic Books.

Zelizer, V. A. (2005). *The purchase of intimacy.* Princeton, NJ: Princeton University Press.

Zerubavel, E. (1991). *The fine line.* New York: Free Press.

Zerubavel, E. (1997). *Social mindscapes: An invitation to cognitive sociology.* Cambridge: Harvard University Press.

LEARNING LINGUISTIC PATTERNS*

Adele E. Goldberg

I. Constructions

Can an understanding of general cognitive processes, such as categorization, shed light on the vexed question of how children come to know the basic grammar of a language? Language has appeared to be too complex and the input too impoverished to be learnable on the basis of the input and general cognitive processes; humans therefore have been thought to bring to the task representations that are specific to language. However, such language-specific representations have been argued to be biologically implausible (Bates & Goodman, 1998; Deacon, 1997; Elman et al., 1996; Sampson, 1997). Moreover, typologists have argued that the idea requires language universals that are empirically unsound (Croft, 2001).

At the same time, recent work has demonstrated that infants are able to extract statistical regularities from the input (e.g., Kuhl, 2000; Saffran, Alsin, & Newport, 1996) and are able to infer intended meanings (Tomasello, 2003). These lines of research offer the possibility that language may ultimately be explicable without resorting to positing innate representations that are specific to language. An analysis of how simple sentence patterns of a language can be learned on the basis of general processes of categorization is suggested in the following paragraph. The issues of *why* children form the generalizations that they do, and more generally, why languages have the generalizations that they have, are also addressed.

---

* The reported work was funded by NSF grant #0613227.

In learning a language, children must generalize over the utterances they hear so that they can creatively produce and understand utterances they have never heard before. One factor that enables language to be used creatively is the existence of strong correlations between formal patterns and the meanings of the utterances in which those formal patterns appear. For example, in English (and many other languages), the double-object or *ditransitive* formal pattern, Subject [Verb Object$_1$ Object$_2$], is associated with the notion of transfer or "giving." This is evident from the fact that, when asked to define a novel verb in the ditransitive context such as that in (1), subjects disproportionately respond that the novel verb means "give" (Ahrens, 1995; Goldberg, 1992).

(1) She mooped him something.   Ditransitive construction

In the case of familiar verbs, the association of the semantics of giving with the ditransitive form is quite strong (see Section VI.B for quantitative analysis). Even when the words in isolation have little or nothing to do with transfer, the overall sentence nonetheless evokes the notion of giving. For example (2a) must be interpreted to mean that Pat baked a cake with the intention of giving the cake to Chris. It cannot be used to mean that Pat baked the cake as a favor for Chris, who was too sick to bake it herself [whereas this is a possible interpretation of the nonditransitive (2b)].

(2a) Pat baked Chris a cake.
(2b) Pat baked a cake for Chris.

The notion of transfer is not reliably associated with *bake* or any of the noun phrases in the sentence: instead it is associated with the formal ditransitive pattern.

TABLE I

CORRESPONDENCES BETWEEN FUNCTION AND FORM

Meaning	Form / Example
X causes Y to receive Z = "give"	Subject V Object Object$_2$
	She mooped him something
X moves (to) Y	Subject V Prep. Phrase
	The truck rumbled down the street
X causes Y to move Z	Subject V Object Prep. Phrase
	She sneezed her tooth across town
X causes Y to become Z	Subject V Object Result. Phrase
	He drank himself silly

Other examples of general correspondences between form and meaning are provided in Table I.

These relations between form and meaning have been variously described as *linking rules* projected from the main verb's specifications (e.g., Bresnan & Kanerva, 1989; Davis, 1996; Dowty, 1991; Grimshaw, 1990; Jackendoff, 1983) as *lexical templates* overlain on specific verbs (Rappaport Hovav & Levin, 1998) or as *constructions*—phrasal form and meaning correspondences—that exist independently of particular verbs (Goldberg, 1995, 2006; Jackendoff, 2002). Construction terminology is used here, but all linguistic and psycholinguistic theories agree that such correspondences between form and meaning exist, whatever the correspondences are called.

II. Can Constructions Be Learned on the Basis of the Input?

A question arises as to where these correspondences come from. Linguists have traditionally argued that they must be hard wired, a part of our genetic endowment which is commonly referred to as "universal grammar" (Baker, 1996; Chomsky, 1957, 1965; Pinker, 1984, 1989). Thus, much previous work on the acquisition of constructions (or linking rules) has focused almost entirely on the question of whether the generalizations that exist in a given language have been acquired at a certain age. Findings using the preferential-looking paradigm have been used to argue that children already have certain linking rules at relatively young ages, the implication being that the linking rules are innate and not learned based on the input (Hirsh-Pasek, Golinkoff, & Naigles, 1996; Naigles, 1990; Naigles, Gleitman, & Gleitman, 1993).

However, a growing number of linguists and psycholinguists, armed with a better understanding of the power of statistical learning and general categorization processes, are taking another look at assumptions about the existence of a universal grammar (Elman et al., 1996; Gomez, 2002; Kuhl, 2000; Saffran, 2001a,b; Saffran & Wilson, 2003; Saffran et al., 1996; Saffran, Johnson, Alsin, & Newport, 1999). Work in this area has demonstrated that domain-general processes can lead to the learning of subtle linguistic generalizations. The majority of this work, however, has focused on the learning of sounds, words, or simple phrase structure rules.

Within the domain of phrasal form–meaning correlations, there have been many demonstrations of the conservative nature of children's early productions with a focus on children's failure to generalize beyond the input until learners have been exposed to a vast amount of data at age 3.5 or older (for summaries see Tomasello, 2000, 2003). The clear implication of this work is that constructions must be learned, since they are acquired so late and in such a piecemeal fashion.

Recent work has been aimed at investigating exactly how children might be able to learn more general form–function pairings from word-specific patterns, but work in this area has only just begun. Childers and Tomasello (2001) is a training study that found a single facilitating factor in the acquisition of the English transitive construction: namely the use of pronouns instead of full NP arguments (cf. also Akhtar, 1999).[1]

Kaschak and Glenberg (2004) have investigated adults' on-line processing of the construction exemplified by *This shirt needs washed*, a construction that was novel to their experimental subjects. They found that speakers were able to read instances of this construction with greater fluency after hearing or reading other instances of the construction. Facilitation was found as well when testing on the same pattern with *wants* after training on *needs*, demonstrating that the facilitation transferred to a related verb. The increased fluency, as measured by shorter reading times, was interpreted to indicate that speakers learned to comprehend the construction; however, the target construction contains familiar words with appropriate inflectional endings and is closely related to familiar expressions such as *This shirt needs to be washed*, with *to be* omitted. There was in fact evidence that subjects were able to comprehend the construction from the outset insofar as they demonstrated increased reading times for semantically inconsistent follow-up sentences even in the initial testing trials.

In an artificial grammar learning task, Gomez (2002) observes that decreasing predictability between adjacent dependencies increases awareness of dependencies between first and third elements. Learning such nonadjacent dependencies is an important prerequisite to learning phrasal constructions insofar as constituents of a construction need not necessarily appear adjacent to one another.

Hudson and Newport (1999) taught adult speakers a toy novel syntax through exposure to sentences that were paired with video clips to provide interpretations. Several different determiners were used in free variation. Adult subjects were then tested on the use of their determiners in production. The experimenters found that subjects failed to regularize (i.e., failed to overgeneralize the use of one determiner) and instead produced the various determiners in roughly the proportions they had heard them used. In an unpublished follow-up study, Hudson and Newport have found that adults do regularize when the alternative determiners each appear with extremely low frequency.

---

[1] Abbott-Smith, Lieven, and Tomasello (2004) attempted to look for other factors that influence the acquisition of the transitive construction, including frequency, semantic similarity, and shared syntactic distribution but found null results.

The majority of work to date has not involved the acquisition of *novel* form–meaning pairings. The target meaning involved has been simple transitivity ("X acts on Y") in the case of previous novel word order studies (e.g., Childers & Tomasello, 2001), identifiabilty (in the case of the determiner study by Hudson & Newport, 1999), or no meaning at all (in the case of artificial grammar learning by Gomez, 2002). That is, these studies do not investigate how it is that a novel meaning comes to be associated with a novel form.

III. Children Can Learn to Map Novel Phrasal Patterns onto Novel Meanings

In recent work, Casenhiser and Goldberg have attempted to address the issue of whether and how novel phrasal form–function pairings could be learned from the input. To this end, a novel construction was created for training in a series of experiments. After witnessing a 3-min training sequence, children and adults were found to be able to extend the pattern beyond their training (Casenhiser & Goldberg, 2005; Goldberg & Casenhiser, in press; Goldberg, Casenhiser, & Sethuraman, 2004).

The meaning assigned to the novel formal pattern was that of APPEARANCE: an entity appears in a location, a novel meaning for English constructions. Subjects watched a set of short video clips in which they saw objects appear in or on various locations within the scene. Each video clip was accompanied by an audio description whose syntactic form was as follows:

(3) noun phrase$_{(theme)}$ noun phrase$_{(location)}$ nonsense verb+o

For example, given a scene in which a spot appears on the king's nose, subjects heard, *The spot the king moopos... The spot the king moopoed.* The entity named by the first noun phrase appeared in the place named by the second noun phrase. In several different manipulations described in this section, children were exposed to 16 instances of the novel construction.

In the training conditions of Casenhiser and Goldberg (2005, Experiment 1) children (mean age 6; 4) heard five different novel verbs in the novel construction. Each scene was repeated exactly twice in each condition. Subjects in the control condition saw the same film but heard no language (Table II).

Following training, a forced-choice comprehension task was administered during which participants were asked to match an audio description to one of two video clips displayed side by side on a computer screen. One scene showed an object appearing in or on a particular location and the other showed the same object interacting with or acting on that location. For example, given

TABLE II

TRAINING STIMULI USED IN CASENHISER AND GOLDBERG (EXPERIMENT 1)[a]

Appearance scene displayed on video	Training condition 1	Control
The rabbit appears on a hat	*The rabbit the hat moopoed*	No sound
The monster wiggles out from under a cloth	*The monster the cloth keeboed*	No sound
The frog drops down onto a box	*The frog the box vakoed*	No sound
The king drops down into a chair	*The king the chair vakoed*	No sound
The sun rises into the sky	*The sun the sky fegoed*	No sound
The queen rolls onto the stage	*The queen the stage sutoed*	No sound
The bug appears onto a table	*The bug the table moopoed*	No sound
The ball rolls into the room	*The ball the room sutoed*	No sound

[a]Eight film clips viewed twice; randomized order constant across subjects; between subjects design.

the audio description *The sailor the pond naifoed*, one scene showed a sailor sailing his boat onto a pond (i.e., he begins off camera and sails into the scene) while the second scene showed the sailor sailing his boat around the pond (while on camera the entire time). The audio description used the novel appearance construction, so the correct answer would be the first scene. The task is reminiscent of the preferential-looking paradigm, the main difference being that our subjects provide an unambiguous behavioral response, pointing to the matching scene instead of simply looking longer at one scene than another.

Results supported the idea that children were able to learn something about the construction, even after minimal exposure. Children in the training conditions significantly outperformed those in the control. The training conditions, but not the control condition, were significantly above chance. (Out of a maximum of 6, mean accuracy in the training conditions was 4.2; mean accuracy in the control condition was 2.9.) The same pattern of results has been found for adults (Goldberg et al., 2004) and in unpublished work on four year olds (Goldberg & Casenhiser, unpublished).

However, there are two issues that must be addressed before firm conclusions can be drawn. First, since all training and test stimuli contained the –*o* suffix on the novel verbs, it is possible that subjects attended only to the –*o* morpheme and did not attend to the novel word order of the construction. In addition, it is possible that the subjects were biased by the training such that they were simply choosing scenes of appearance without attending to any particular aspect of the form of the construction.

To rule out these possibilities, a second study involving children with a mean age of 6; 3, replicated the first study while eliminating the –*o* morpheme from the novel verbs in training and at test (Casenhiser & Goldberg, 2005, Experiment 2). In addition, testing probes were altered as follows: three test items involving the simple transitive construction (<NOUN PHRASE$_{subject}$> <novel verb> <NOUN PHRASE$_{object}$>) were interspersed among three test items using the novel construction (<NOUN PHRASE$_{subject}$> <NOUN PHRASE$_{location}$> <novel verb>). The video clips used at test paired one simple transitive scene and one scene of appearance. For example, given the description *The fireman zats the plane*, participants saw one scene in which the fireman appeared on the scene in the plane and one scene in which the fireman flips the plane over (Table III). Only children who had learned something about both the form and meaning of the construction could distinguish the appearance construction from the transitive construction at test.

Again, results showed that children were able to identify the novel construction and associate it with its meaning of appearance significantly more often after training than in the control condition in which they watched the same video without sound. As expected, subjects in both the experimental and control conditions demonstrated a familiarity with the transitive construction, choosing the transitive scene over the scene of appearance when faced with a novel transitive utterance more often than chance. Thus, while all children displayed an ability to recognize the English transitive construction, only the children who received the training were able to recognize that the novel word order was associated with a meaning of appearance.

Since in this experiment no morphological cue was present—that is, there was no –*o* suffixed to each novel verb—subjects had to learn to distinguish the novel construction from the transitive construction based on word order alone. From these studies, we are tentatively justified in concluding that constructions *can* be learned from the input with minimal training.

TABLE III

Sample Test Items Used in Casenhiser and Goldberg (2005, Experiment 2): Forced-Choice Comprehension Task[a]

Prompt (T: transitive; A: novel appearance construction)	Matching scene	Foil scene
The fireman zats the plane (T)	The fireman flips the plane over	The fireman rides plane onto scene
The king the bed veemos (A)	The king flies into bed from off stage	The king jumps over the bed

[a]Matching scene counterbalanced for L-R presentation.

IV. How Constructions Can Be Learned: A Facilitory Factor

The language input children receive tends to be skewed disproportionately toward a single example or type of example. That is, tokens of individual constructions are typically centered around a small number of words (often a single word), or around a semantic prototype, even when they potentially occur with a much broader range of words or meanings (Brenier & Michaelis, 2004; Cameron-Faulkner, Lieven, & Tomasello, in press; Deane, 2003; Diessel, 2001; Goldberg, 1996, 1999; Hunston & Francis, 1999; Scheibman, 2002; Sethuraman, 2002; Thompson & Hopper, 2001). The verb that accounts for the greatest percentage of tokens for each of five constructions is provided in Table IV (number of verb types is also provided where it is known).

Thus, a single verb regularly accounts for the preponderance of tokens. Zipf long ago noted that highly frequent words account for most linguistic tokens (Zipf, 1935). Although he did not claim that there should be a single most highly frequent word for each clause pattern, nor did Zipf's work prepare us for the fact that a single verb should account for such a lion's share of the tokens. In fact, Gries and Stefanowich have refined the notion

TABLE IV

SKEWING OF CONSTRUCTIONS TOWARD PARTICULAR VERBS

Construction	Precentage of tokens accounted for by *verb:* Total verb types	Corpus/reference
1. Subject V Object	39% *go* (136/353): 39 verb types	Bates et al. (1988) cited by Goldberg, Casenhiser, and Sethuraman (2004)
2. Subject V Object Oblique	38% *put* (99/259): 43 verb types	Bates et al. (1988) cited by Goldberg, Casenhiser, and Sethuraman (2004)
3. Subject V Object Object$_2$	44% *give* (226/517)	Switchboard corpus cited by Bresnan and Nikitina (ms)
4. Subject V one's way Prep. Phrase	20% *make* (235/1177) >50 verb types	Oxford University Press, Lund, Wall Street Journal corpora cited by Goldberg (1999)
5. Subject V Clause	40% *think* (365/926): 8 verb types	Subset of CHILDES (MacWhinney, 2000) cited by Kidd, Lieven, and Tomasello (2005-ms)

of relative frequencies in order to take into account the overall frequencies of the verbs in the language (Stefanowitsch & Gries, 2003). Given that one can expect high-frequency verbs to appear with high frequency, the more relevant question is how frequent are these particular verbs in these particular constructions over and above chance? Stefanowitch and Gries have found that one can never expect a single verb to account for more than 10% of the tokens of any particular nonidiomatic construction, even if the verb is very frequent, because there are so many different verbs: that is, skewing of the magnitude that is found in the data is not expected due to the simple frequencies of the verbs and constructions involved.

Clear motivation exists for speakers to use certain verbs more frequently than others. If we compare, for example, *go* with *amble*, or *put* with *shelve*, it is clear that *go* and *put* are more frequent because they apply to a wider range of arguments and therefore are relevant in a wider range of contexts (Bybee, Perkins, & Pagliuca, 1994; Heine, 1993; Zipf, 1935).

It is *not* claimed that any particular verbs are necessarily the very first verbs uttered. Longitudinal studies have suggested that they might be (Ninio, 1999), but see Campbell and Tomasello (2001) for evidence that they are not always the very first verbs; also see Tomasello and Stahl (2004) for arguments that extreme care must be taken to avoid confusing high frequency with early acquisition when intermittent sampling techniques are used.

As alluded to the preceding paragraph, there were two training conditions used in Casenhiser and Goldberg, Experiment 1. In the BALANCED FREQUENCY TRAINING CONDITION, subjects heard five different novel verbs, each with a relatively low token frequency of 1 or 2 (1-1-2-2-2). The SKEWED FREQUENCY condition was designed to test the hypothesis that children's learning of a novel construction would be aided if a single verb appeared in a disproportionately large number of instances of the novel construction. In the skewed frequency condition, subjects again heard the same five novel verbs, but this time one novel verb had an especially high token frequency of 4, while the other novel verbs were recorded once each (4-1-1-1-1). Each scene was repeated exactly twice in each condition. Any difference among groups can only be attributed to a difference in the linguistic input that subjects were exposed to, as all three conditions watched exactly the same video (Table V).

Results supported the hypothesis: children in the skewed frequency condition performed better than children in the balanced condition. In addition, the balanced frequency condition outperformed the control condition. Mean accuracy in the skewed frequency group was 4.7; in the balanced frequency group, 3.7; and in the control, 2.9 (out of the 6 item test). The finding that the balanced condition outperformed the control condition indicates that skewed frequency facilitates but is not necessary for learning a novel construction. This is important since recent work indicates that there may not

TABLE V

Training Stimuli[a]

	Description heard		
Scene displayed on video	Balanced frequency (2 moopo; 2 vako; 2 suto; 1 keebo; 1 fego)	Skewed frequency (4 moopo; 1 vako; 1 suto; 1 keebo; 1 fego)	Control
The rabbit appears on a hat	The rabbit the hat moopoed	The rabbit the hat moopoed	No sound
The monster wiggles out from under a cloth	The monster the cloth keeboed	The monster the cloth keeboed	No sound
The frog drops down onto a box	The frog the box vakoed	The frog the box moopoed	No sound
The king drops down into a chair	The king the chair vakoed	The king the chair vakoed	No sound
The sun rises into the sky	The sun the sky fegoed	The sun the sky fegoed	No sound
The queen rolls onto the stage	The queen the stage sutoed	The queen the stage sutoed	No sound
The bug appears onto a table	The bug the table moopoed	The bug the table moopoed	No sound
The ball rolls into the room	The ball the room sutoed	The ball the room moopoed	No sound

[a]Eight film clips viewed twice; randomized order constant across subjects; between subjects design.

always be a single token with exceptionally high frequency (Sethuraman & Goodman, 2004).

It is intriguing that very frequent use of one exemplar in a pattern facilitates the learning of the semantics of that pattern. It suggests that after using many sentences with *put* in the Verb Object Locative (VOL) construction as in (4), children come to associate the meaning of *put* with the construction even when the verb is not present as in (5):

(4) She put a finger on that.

(5) He done boots on. (STE, 28 months, Bates, Bretherton, & Snyder, 1988)

The result is that the meaning of roughly "X causes Y to move Z_{loc}" comes to be associated with the Subject Verb Object Oblique$_{path/loc}$ formal pattern. The corpus findings suggest that exactly this sort of tailor-made input is available to language learners for a variety of constructions.

The finding that the mapping between a new phrasal form and meaning pair can be generalized so quickly, with so little input, appears to run counter to a large body of evidence that indicates that children are very conservative learners; that is, children stick closely to the forms they have heard used with particular verbs (Akhtar & Tomasello, 1997; Baker, 1979; Bates & MacWhinney, 1987; Bowerman, 1982; Braine, 1976; Gropen, Pinker, Hollander, Goldberg, & Wilson, 1989; Ingram & Thompson, 1996; Lieven, Pine, & Baldwin, 1997; MacWhinney, 1982; Olguin & Tomasello, 1993; Schlesinger, 1982; Tomasello, 1992, 2000).

It is possible that the difference between conservative learning found in other tasks and in the fast mapping reviewed above is age related, since children are generally most conservative before they are three-and-a-half years old. However, the reason for the conservative learning has been claimed to be that children—and *adults*—operate with a "usage-based" model of language (i.e., a model based on the amount and type of language that is heard used) (Tomasello, 2003). That is, the difference between children and adults has been thought to involve a difference in the amount of experience with the ambient language. Thus, we would not expect to find quicker generalizations in older children than in younger children if they are both exposed to the same amount of input on a novel construction.

Therefore, it seems the difference may well be task dependent. Studies that have documented conservative learning have used a variety of methods including: (i) spontaneous production, (ii) elicited production, and (iii) act-out tasks. These tasks require *recall* of at least aspects of the pairing of form and meaning. Clearly this is true in the case of production, since in order to produce an utterance, the child must be able to recall its form correctly and use it appropriately. In act-out tasks, children are encouraged to act out scenes that they hear verbal descriptions of; this also requires the child to recall the relevant meaning associated with the given form. The task outlined here, on the other hand, only requires that children *recognize* the relevant meaning from among two given alternatives. This is more akin to the preferential-looking paradigm that has been argued in fact to demonstrate early generalizations (Gertner et al., in press; Gleitman, 1994; Naigles & Bavin, 2001) although somewhat controversially (Tomasello, 2000, 2003).

It is possible that the quick learning of the mapping could be taken as an indication that the particular mapping is a part of "universal grammar" and is innately available. A mapping between subject and thing coming to exist, on the one hand, and displaced noun phrase and location on the other, could be added to the set of mapping principles sometimes claimed to be universal. However, I know of no language that has a general mapping that encodes "appearance" in this way. In particular, the mapping violates at least one of the proposed language universals of how arguments are supposed to map to syntactic relations: we would expect that a locative argument should be expressed by an oblique (prepositional phrase) complement (Naigles et al., 1993; Pinker, 1989). Location arguments would require prepositional marking to be considered obliques in English; yet they were simple noun phrases in the experimental stimuli. Thus, given its cross-linguistic rarity, there is no independent reason to believe that the particular generalization learned in the studies reviewed here is innately available.

V. Parallel Facilitory Effect in Nonlinguistic Categorization

The finding that generalization is facilitated when the input is skewed such that one type of example accounts for the lion's share of instances has a strong parallel within nonlinguistic categorization. That is, there is reason to suspect that the learning mechanism is a property of general categorization processes. Elio and Anderson (1984) set up two conditions relevant to the current discussion. In the CENTERED condition, subjects were initially trained on more frequently represented, more prototypical instances, with the study sample growing gradually to include more members of the category. (The study involved descriptions of people belonging to one of two clubs with members' descriptions varying on 5 four-valued dimensions.) In the REPRESENTATIVE condition, subjects were trained on a fully representative sampling from the start. In both conditions, subjects were eventually trained on the full range of instances. Elio and Anderson (1984) demonstrated that the order in which subjects received the more prototypical instances played a role in their learning of the category. In particular, they demonstrated that categories were learned more accurately in the centered condition; the representative condition yielded poorer typicality ratings and accuracy during the test phase on new instances. Elio and Anderson observe, "The superiority of the centered condition over the representative condition suggests that an initial, low-variance sample of the most frequently occurring members may allow the learner to get a 'fix' on what will account for most of the category members" (1984, p. 25).

Gentner likewise notes that processes of analogy required for generalization (her "structural alignment") are facilitated when instances being compared are similar to one another. Gentner, Loewenstein, and Hung (2002-ms) performed an experiment that illustrates this idea: they showed children a particular picture of a Martian to be used as a standard for comparison, and two alternative Martian creatures. The standard Martian and one of the alternatives shared one body part, while the distinct Martian did not. Children were asked, "This one has a *blick*; which one of these has a *blick*?" The results demonstrated that if the two alternatives were highly similar to the standard, children were better able to pick out the relevant shared body part; when they were only weakly similar, finding the body part was more difficult. In addition, Gentner et al. (2002-ms) demonstrated that children who were tested in the high-similarity condition first, were subsequently more successful on the low-similarity items than children who had the same amount of experience with only low-similarity items.

A. EXPERIMENTAL DEMONSTRATION OF THE PARALLEL

Goldberg and Casenhiser (2006) report an experiment with a design parallel to that described for construction learning to test whether the advantage of a single high-frequency exemplar holds in a nonlinguistic task as well. A random dot pattern (with ten dots) was created and used as a prototype; four systematic variations from the prototype pattern were created as well. Subjects in the skewed frequency group saw twice as many instances of the prototype dot pattern as any of the other dot patterns. Subjects in the balanced group were not given this preferential training with the prototype; instead, they saw a more balanced distribution of the prototype pattern in comparison to the other dot patterns. College-aged subjects were tested with a forced-choice task to determine if they were able to distinguish a *new* variation of the prototype from a dot pattern generated randomly. New variations used at test differed from the prototype to the same degree as the variations used in training. The results demonstrate that subjects in the skewed frequency group were significantly more accurate at test than those in the balanced frequency group, thus confirming the suggestion that learning of categories generally is facilitated when a prototype is encountered with skewed frequency as opposed to experience with the same variety of instances, including the prototype, when the prototype does not account for the balance of items.

To summarize, we know that frequency and order of acquisition play key roles in category formation in that training on prototypical instances frequently and/or early facilitates category learning (Bruner, Goodnow, & Austin, 1956; Kruschke, 1996; Maddox, 1995; Nosofsky, 1988). The results obtained with nonlinguistic stimuli are parallel to the results obtained with linguistic stimuli, as described earlier, thus motivating the construal of construction learning as a type of category learning. The novel construction-learning experiments reviewed here combine to indicate that tentative generalizations over items can be made quickly on the basis of little input.

VI. **Why Argument Structure Generalizations Are Learned: What Is the Advantage?**

As many have emphasized, human categorization is generally driven by some functional pressure, typically the need to predict or infer certain properties on the basis of perceived characteristics (Anderson, 1991; Holland, Holyoak,

& Thagard, 1989; Kersten & Billman, 1997; Leake & Ram, 1995; Murphy, 2002; Ross & Makin, 1999; Wisniewski, 1995). That is, cognitive systems do not generalize randomly or completely. In the case of language, the language learner's goal is to understand and to be understood: to comprehend and produce language. There is ample functional pressure to predict meaning on the basis of given lexical items and grammatical characteristics (comprehension); conversely, there is pressure to predict the choice of lexical items and grammatical characteristics given the message to be conveyed (production). Since the sentences the child is learning to understand and produce form an open-ended set, it is not sufficient to simply memorize the sentences that have been heard. The child must necessarily generalize those patterns at least to some extent in order to understand and produce new utterances.

In the following Section VI.A–E, it is argued that the predictive value of constructions encourages speakers to learn them. A second motivation for representing generalized constructions is suggested in Section VI.F, namely that constructions are primed in production.

A. THE PREDICTIVE VALUE OF VERBS IN ARGUMENT STRUCTURE PATTERNS

Generalizing beyond a particular verb to a more general pattern is useful in predicting overall sentence meaning, more useful in fact than knowledge of individual verbs. Goldberg, Casenhiser, and Sethuraman (2005) hypothesize that the predictive value encourages speakers to generalize beyond knowledge of specific verbs to ultimately learn phrasal constructions.

It is clear that constructions are sometimes better predictors of overall meaning than many verbs. For example, when *get* appears with a direct object and prepositional phrase, it conveys caused motion (6); with two postverbal objects, it conveys transfer (7); when *get* appears with a locative complement it conveys motion (8):

(6) Pat got the ball over the fence.

　　Get + VOL pattern → "caused motion"

(7) Pat got Bob a cake.

　　Get + VOO pattern → "transfer"

(8) Pat got into the car.

　　Get + PP → "motion"

Thus, *get* in isolation has low *cue validity* as a predictor of sentence meaning. "Cue validity" is the conditional probability that an object is in a particular category, given that it has a particular feature or cue (Murphy, 1982). Since most verbs appear in more than one construction with corresponding differences in interpretation, speakers would do well to learn to attend to the constructions.

It is possible to quantify the cue validity of verbs and constructions. Both verbs and constructions have the potential to convey the overall event-level interpretation, roughly "who did what to whom." Since this event level interpretation is clearly a *necessary* component of interpretation, it is worth comparing the relative contribution of constructions and verbs at this level. Clearly, in order to arrive at a full interpretation of a sentence, the specifics contributed by only the verb (and its arguments) are required as well.[2]

B. CORPUS EVIDENCE OF THE CONSTRUCTION AS A RELIABLE PREDICTOR OF SENTENCE MEANING

In order to compare the cue validity for overall sentence meaning of verbs and constructions, Goldberg et al. (2005) examined the following two constructions: (Subject) Verb Object Oblique$_{\text{path/loc}}$ and (Subject) Verb Object$_1$ Object$_2$ (VOL and VOO, respectively). Two coders hand-coded each sentence in the Bates corpus (Bates, Bretherton, & Snyder, 1988) on the Child Language Data Exchange System database (CHILDES) (MacWhinney, 1995) by verb, overall meaning, and construction type.

The cue validity for verbs in the formal patterns was determined by calculating how reliably the verbs were used for encoding the meaning that they predominantly displayed in the formal pattern under investigation. In order to determine cue validity across verbs, the weighted average of cue validities of all verbs that can appear in a construction was calculated.

There is a wide variability of cue validities across verbs. In the VOO pattern, a few verbs had perfect cue validities (*feed, give, show, tell*) in our corpus, while other verbs' cue validities were quite low (*fix, get, make*). Again, regardless of the overall cue validity of verbs, this latter fact in itself indicates that attention to the construction's contribution is key to determining who did what to whom.

Cue validity for the formal patterns was determined by considering how many of the instances of the formal pattern conveyed the same overall meaning. This quantity differed depending on how broadly or narrowly

---

[2] Clearly if we compare the contribution of verb and construction to subtle aspects of meaning, involving manner or means, the verb would be more predictive than the construction. This is necessarily true since constructions rarely encode specific meanings: compare "X causes Y to receive Z," the meaning of the ditransitive construction with the meaning of the verbs hand or mail.

the meaning was construed. For example, if transfer is defined literally as involving someone giving something to someone else, then 61% of the VOO utterances encoded transfer. At the same time, if metaphorical instances of transfer were included, a full 94% of instances of the VOO pattern would be classified as involving transfer. Metaphorical instances of transfer include instances such as *She told me a story*; we can generally talk about communication as if it involve physical transfer (e.g., She read the book *to* me; She *offered* a story *to* me; I got the story *from* her). Still, to avoid presupposing that the metaphor is necessarily active in the minds of the speakers, both strict and inclusive criteria are represented in Table VI.

As is evident from Table VI, verbs and constructions had roughly equivalent cue validity as predictors of overall sentence meaning under a strict interpretation of what counts as the same meaning for constructions (comparing .68 and .61 for verbs with .63 and .61 for constructions). Under the more inclusive criteria, constructions are far better predictors of overall sentence meaning than verbs (.85 and .94 for the VOL and VOO patterns, respectively).

What about verbs in other constructions? It may be that verbs are more predictive for some constructions than others. For example, in the simple intransitive construction, the verb used supplies almost all of the lexical content. There is a large difference in sentence meaning between *The vase broke* and *She shouted*. Still, even in these cases, the verbs involved are far from perfect predictors of overall sentence meaning. *Break* can appear both transitively and intransitively—to know whether an agent is known or relevant, one needs to know which construction was used. *Shouted*, too, can be used as a verb of communication (e.g., *She shouted the directions*) or simply a verb of sound emission (e.g., *She shouted for joy*). More research is needed to quantify the cue validity of other constructions.

TABLE VI

COMPARISON OF CUE VALIDITIES OF VERBS AND CONSTRUCTIONS AS PREDICTORS OF OVERALL SENTENCE MEANING

	Cue validity of verbs in the VOL pattern	Cue validity of the formal patterns	
		Strict	Inclusive
VOL (Verb Object Locative)	.68	.63	.85
VOO (Verb Object Object 2)	.61	.61	.94

Calculating cue validities in an existing corpus is a useful way to determine the predictive value of constructions in determining sentence meaning. Another study that was designed to measure the predictive value of constructions is described in the following section.

C. EXPERIMENTAL EVIDENCE FOR CONSTRUCTION AS PREDICTORS OF SENTENCE MEANING

Bencini and Goldberg (2000) performed a sorting study that aimed to compare the semantic contribution of the construction with that of the morphological form of the verb when determining overall sentence meaning. The stimuli were 16 sentences created by crossing 4 verbs with 4 different constructions (Table VII).

Adult subjects were asked to sort these 16 sentences, provided in random order, into 4 piles based on "overall sentence meaning." Subjects could sort equally well by verb: For example, all instances of *throw* (1a–d) being put into the same pile, regardless of construction; or subjects could sort by construction: all instances of, for example, the ditransitive construction (1a, 2a, 3a, and 4a) being put into the same pile. The stimuli were designed to minimize contentful overlap contributed by anything other than the lexical verb. No other lexical items in the stimuli were identical or near synonyms.

TABLE VII
STIMULI FOR SORTING EXPERIMENT

1a. Pat threw the hammer	(VO) Transitive
b. Chris threw Linda the pencil	(VOO) Ditransitive
c. Pat threw the key onto the roof	(VOL) Caused motion
d. Lyn threw the box apart	(VOR) Resultative
2a. Michelle got the book	(VO) Transitive
b. Beth got Liz an invitation	(VOO) Ditransitive
c. Laura got the ball into the net	(VOL) Caused motion
d. Dana got the mattress inflated	(VOR) Resultative
3a. Barbara sliced the bread	(VO) Transitive
b. Jennifer sliced Terry an apple	(VOO) Ditransitive
c. Meg sliced the ham onto the plate	(VOL) Caused motion
d. Nancy sliced the tire open	(VOR) Resultative
4a. Audrey took the watch	(VO) Transitive
b. Paula took Sue a message	(VOO) Ditransitive
c. Kim took the rose into the house	(VOL) Caused motion
d. Rachel took the wall down	(VOR) Resultative

The use of the sorting paradigm is a particularly stringent test to demonstrate the role of constructions. Medin, Wattenmaker, and Hampson (1987) have shown that there is a strong, domain-independent bias toward sorting on the basis of a single dimension, even with categories that are designed to resist such one-dimensional sorts in favor of a sort based on a family resemblance structure (Rosch & Mervis, 1975). One-dimensional sorting has been found even with large numbers of dimensions (Smith, 2001), ternary values on each dimension (Ahn & Medin, 1992), holistic stimuli and stimuli for which an obvious multidimensional descriptor was available (Regehr & Brooks, 1995). The stimuli presented subjects with an opportunity to sort according to a single dimension: the verb. Constructional sorts required subjects to note an abstract relational similarity, involving the recognition that several grammatical functions co-occur. Thus, we would expect verb sorts to have an inherent advantage over constructional sorts.

Nonetheless, results showed that subjects were just as likely to sort by construction as they were to sort according to the single dimension of the morphological form of the verb. If verbs provided equally good cues to overall sentence meaning, there would be no motivation to overcome the preference for one-dimensional sorts. Bencini and Goldberg (2000) hypothesize that constructional sorts were able to overcome the one-dimensional sorting bias to this extent because constructions are in fact better predictors of overall sentence meaning than the morphological form of the verb.

Kaschak and Glenberg (2000) demonstrate that subjects rely on constructional meaning when they encounter nouns used as verbs in novel ways (e.g., *to crutch*). In particular they show that different constructions differentially influence the interpretations of the novel verbs. For example, *She crutched him the ball* (ditransitive) is interpreted to mean that she used the crutch to transfer the ball to him, perhaps using it as one would a hockey stick. On the other hand, *She crutched him* (transitive) might be interpreted to mean that she hit him over the head with the crutch. Kaschak and Glenberg (2000) suggest that the constructional pattern specifies a general scene and that the "affordances" of particular objects are used to specify the scene in detail. It cannot be the semantics of the verb that is used in comprehension because the word form is not stored as a verb but as a noun. Similarly, Kako (2004) finds that subjects' semantic interpretations of constructions and of verbs that fit those constructions are highly correlated, concluding as well that syntactic frames are "semantically potent linguistic entities."

A question arises as to why constructions should be at least as good predictors of overall sentence meaning as verbs. The answer I believe stems from the fact that, in context, knowing the number and type of arguments conveys a great deal about the scene being conveyed. To the extent that verbs encode rich semantic frames that can be related to a number of different basic scenes (Goldberg, 1995), the complement configuration or construction will be as good a predictor of sentence meaning as the semantically richer but more flexible verb.

D. CATEGORY VALIDITY

Recall that cue validity is the probability that an item belongs to a category, given that it has a particular feature: P(cat | feature). We have seen that when the category is taken to be overall sentence meaning, constructions have roughly equivalent cue validity compared with verbs. There is also a second relevant factor. CATEGORY VALIDITY is the probability that an item has a feature, given that the item belongs in the category: P(feature | cat). Thus category validity measures how common or available a feature is among members of a category. The relevant category is again sentence meaning.

As discussed earlier, there is often one verb that accounts for the lion's share of tokens of particular constructions (Goldberg, 1999; Goldberg et al., 2004; Sethuraman, 2002), for example, *put* accounts for many tokens of the caused motion construction, but since the transitive and resultative constructions can also convey caused motion (with verbs such as *send, bring, carry*), the category validity for even *put* is not particularly high. Out of 47 expressions conveying caused motion in the Bates corpus (Bates et al., 1988), 29 involved the verb *put*, resulting in a category validity of .62. Other verbs had far lower category validities. For example, the probability that a sentence with caused motion meaning contained the verb *bring* was only .02, since only 1 of the utterances expressing caused motion used *bring* (1/47).

The average category validity of all verbs that may convey caused motion is equal to $1/n$, where n is the number of verbs that express caused motion. Clearly as the sample size increases, the average category validity for verbs is lowered. When many verbs appear in a particular construction, which is generally the case, the average category validity can approach zero.

Another relevant number is the MAXIMUM CATEGORY VALIDITY, since the maximum category provides an estimate of the category validity associated with the "best guess" of a relevant verb. For example, *put* had the highest category validity of .62 in the Bates corpus (Bates et al., 1988).

The category validity of a construction as a feature of the semantic category caused motion is the probability that the particular construction will be involved, given the interpretation of caused motion. There are generally less than a handful of constructions that express a particular general meaning, and there are certainly far fewer constructions that express a particular meaning than there are verbs that express that meaning. It turns out that both the average category validity and the maximum category were higher for the constructions investigated than they were for the verbs that appear in those constructions (Goldberg et al., 2005).

All things being equal, if two cues have roughly equal cue validity, the higher category validity of one cue will naturally result in a greater reliance on that cue in categorization tasks (Bates & MacWhinney, 1987; Estes, 1986; Hintzman, 1986; Nosofsky, 1988). Thus, constructions are better cues to sentence meaning than verbs insofar as they are as reliable (with equivalent cue validity) and more available (having higher category validity).

E. Languages in Which Verbs Are More Predictive

The verbs in many languages are more restrictive than they are in English, only appearing in constructions that match their meanings. Verbs in Latinate languages, Turkish and Hindi, for example, do not appear in anything like the range of constructions that they do in English even though the verbs often have quite parallel meanings (see, e.g., Narasimhan, 1998). Therefore, it would seem that the verbs in these languages have much higher cue validity than they do in English. And yet it seems unlikely that learners fail to form argument structure constructions in such languages. D. Slobin (personal communication, February 14, 2004) has found in unpublished experimental work that speakers of Turkish readily interpret novel verbs presented in familiar constructions, indicating that speakers are at least able to construct information about an abstract argument structure construction for the purpose of comprehension. The fact that the category validity for constructions is generally higher than that for verbs—insofar as there are more verbs that can be used to convey a particular event frame than there are constructions—may be responsible in part for yielding constructional generalizations.

In addition, there is a second factor that may well play a role in encouraging speakers to form argument structure constructions, even when the cue validity of the verbs in the language is consistently high. This factor involves the phenomenon of CONSTRUCTIONAL PRIMING.

F. Structural Priming and Its Relation to Constructions

A second type of motivation for learning constructions, outlined in this section, is that constructions are primed in production. That is, saying or hearing instances of one grammatical pattern primes speakers to produce other instances of the same. Bock and colleagues (Bock, 1986; Bock & Loebell, 1990; Bock, Loebell, & Morey, 1992) have shown in a number of experimental studies that passives prime passives; ditransitives prime ditransitives, and datives prime datives (cf. also Abbott-Smith, Lieven, & Tomasello, in press;

Bock & Griffin, 2000; Branigan, Pickering, Liversedge, Stewart, & Urbach, 1995a; Chang, Dell, Bock, & Greffin, 2000; Friederici, Schriefers, & Lindenberger, 1998; Hare & Goldberg, 1999; Nicol, 1996; Potter & Lombardi, 1998; Saffran & Martin, 1997; Savage, Lieven, Theakston, & Tomasello, 2003; Scheepers, 2003; Smith & Wheeldon, 2001; Tomasello, 2003; Yamashita, Chang, & Hirose, 2003).

This sort of priming provides a useful tool to investigate the mental representation of linguistic expressions (Bencini, 2002; Branigan et al., 1995). The naturalness of the priming paradigm is supported by the fact that a tendency toward structural repetition occurs in natural unmonitored speech or text (Estival, 1985; Kempen, 1977; Levelt & Kelter, 1982). This suggests that structural priming is not simply a laboratory induced phenomenon, but plays a role in normal sentence production.

Priming has been argued to represent implicit learning in that its effect is unconscious and long lasting (Bock & Griffin, 2000; Chang et al., 2000). Thus, the existence of structural priming may be an important factor underlying the fact that there are generalizations in languages. The same or similar patterns are easier to learn and produce. At the same time, priming of course is not particular to language—repetition of the same motor programs also leads to priming effects.

Bock's original claim was that syntactic tree structures, not constructions with associated meanings, were involved in priming (Bock, 1986, 2001; Bock & Loebell, 1990; Bock et al., 1992). In recent work, the question of whether constructional priming exists has been investigated. That is, can abstract pairings of form with meaning be primed? Chang, Bock, and Goldberg (2003) conducted a simple experiment in which syntactic structure was controlled for, while two different constructions were used as primes. Sample prime and target sentences are given below:

Sample primes:

(9a) She loaded the wagon with hay. ("load with")
(9b) She loaded hay into the wagon. ("load onto")

Sample targets:

(10a) He embroidered the shirt with flowers.
(10b) He embroidered flowers onto the shirt.

Subjects were asked to recall a sentence as it was presented after a short distracter task. Such rapid serial visual presentation (RSVP) tasks have been shown to allow priming effects (Potter & Lombardi, 1998). If semantics matters in priming then we should see "load-with" structures priming other "load-with" structures significantly more than "load-onto" structures. In fact this is exactly what was found. Also, as predicted by constructional

TABLE VIII

Examples of "Object-Raising" and "Object-Control" Sentences

a. She believed it to be raining	Object raising
b. He knew there to be men on the roof	Object raising
c. She persuaded him to leave the room	Object control
d. He asked her to be there	Object control

priming, subjects produced significantly more load-onto types of sentences after load-onto type primes than after load-with primes.

The constructional priming found cannot be wholly attributed to an overlap in prepositions, since "load-onto" sentences used a variety of prepositions including *over, onto, into, around,* and *on.* Moreover, Griffin and Weinstein-Tull (2003) have shown that "object-raising" sentences prime other object-raising sentences more than "object-control" sentences, despite a lack of any shared morphology. As illustrated in Table VIII, object-raising sentences are sentences in which the direct object noun phrase does not bear a semantic relation directly to the verb but instead is only related indirectly as the semantic subject of the verb phrase complement. As the DO of object-raising sentences need not bear a semantic relation directly to the verb, it may in fact be nonreferential (as *it* and *there* are in a and b in Table VIII).

The fact that priming was found for object-raising sentences by other object-raising sentences suggests priming of the form–function pairing: constructional priming; the results are unexpected if only formal cues were taken into account, since both object-raising and object-control constructions arguably have the same form. See also Hare and Goldberg (1999) for further evidence of form–function priming. To summarize, constructions can be primed, which implies that the level of generalization involved in argument structure constructions is a useful one to acquire.

VII. Motivating the Particular Form–Function Pairings That Exist in Languages

What are the cross-linguistic generalizations about how arguments are linked to syntactic positions, and why do they exist if the generalizations are learned on the basis of the input? Some linguists have claimed the existence of impressive universals in how arguments are expressed; however, such universals are typically claimed to hold only of some underlying level of syntactic representation. A growing number of theorists have raised critical objections to positing such underlying levels (for discussion see Goldberg, 2006); without such underlying levels, the true universals are far fewer. Moreover, the universals that exist are often straightforwardly accounted for by general cognitive, attentional, and processing factors (Croft, 2001; Goldberg, 2006; Hawkins, 2004). Let us consider one such example.

Dowty (1991) proposed linking generalizations that are now widely cited as capturing the observable (i.e., surface) cross-linguistic universals in how arguments are linked to syntactic relations. He observed that in simple active clauses, *if* there is a subject and an object, *and if* there is an agent-like entity and an "undergoer" then the agent is expressed by the subject, and the undergoer is expressed as a direct object. Roughly, arguments that are volitional, sentient, causal, or moving are agent-like, while arguments that undergo a change of state, are causally affected or stationary are considered undergoers.

The generalization is fairly modest. It implicitly allows for languages in which the notion of "subject" does not play a central role and, in fact, many languages primarily rely on a notion of "topic" rather than "subject." Moreover, since the generalization only holds of active clauses, it allows for the fact that the passive construction only optionally expresses an agent argument, and when the agent is expressed, it appears as a nonsubject oblique (e.g., a prepositional phrase). A fair generalization, nonetheless, can be rephrased as follows:

(1) The Salient Participants in Prominent Slots (SPPS) Generalization
    Actors and undergoers are generally expressed in prominent syntactic slots. (Goldberg, 2004)

The SPPS generalization in (1) also accounts for the fact that an agent argument without an undergoer and an undergoer without an agent are also expressed in a prominent syntactic positions; finally, this generalization has the added advantage that it follows directly from well-documented aspects of our general attentional biases.

Humans' attention is naturally drawn to agents, even in nonlinguistic tasks. For example, visual attention tends to be centered on the agent in an event, during and after an action is performed (Robertson & Suci, 1980). Infants as young as 9 months have been shown to attribute intentional behavior to even inanimate objects that have appropriate characteristics (e.g., motion, apparent goal-directedness) (Csibra, Gregely, Biró, Koós, & Brockbank, 1999); infants habituated to a scene in which a computer-animated circle jumped over an obstacle and contacted another circle, expected the first circle to take a direct route when the obstacle was removed from the scene. Children as young as 16 months can distinguish intentional versus accidental actions (Carpenter, Akhtar, & Tomasello, 1998). Thus, the characteristics of agents (volition, sentience, and movement) are closely attended to by prelinguistic infants in visual as well as linguistic tasks.

The undergoer in an event is generally the endpoint of some sort of force (Croft, 1991; Langacker, 1987; Talmy, 1976). Endpoints are generally better attended to than onsets in both nonlinguistic and linguistic tasks. For example, Regier and Zheng (2003) note that subjects are better able to discriminate between events that have distinct endpoints than distinct onsets; in addition, subjects use a wider range of more specific verbs to describe endpoint-focused actions (such as putting a key in a lock) than onset-focused actions (such as taking a key out of a lock) (see also Landau, 2003).

The tendency to attend closely to one particular type of endpoint, that of change of state, begins as early as 6 months. Woodward's (1998, 1999) studies demonstrate that 6-month-old infants attend more to changes of state than to changes of motion without corresponding state-change. Jovanovic et al. (in press) replicated Woodward's study and also demonstrated that 6-month-old infants attend to changes of state even if the means of achieving the change of state is unfamiliar (in this case a pushing-over effect is caused by means of a hand outstretched, palm outward) (see also Bekkering, Wohlschlager, & Gattis, 2000; Csibra et al., 1999). It has been hypothesized that *effects* of actions are the key elements in action representations both in motor control of action and in perception (Prinz, 1990, 1997).

Thus the observation that agents and undergoers tend to be expressed in prominent slots follows from general facts about human perception and attention. For a fuller discussion of proposed universals and the issues that arise, see, for example, Croft (2001) and Goldberg (2004, 2006, Chapter 9).

VIII. Conclusions

How do learners go from the specific to the general? There is a good deal of evidence in the field of nonlinguistic categorization that information both about specific exemplars and generalizations over exemplars are learned on the basis of experience (Anderson, 1971; Murphy, 2002; Nosofsky, 1988; Posner & Keele, 1968; Ross & Makin, 1999; Ross, Perkins, & Tenpenny, 1990). The same is true in the case of language, at the phonological and morphological levels (e.g., Bybee, 1985; Kuhl, 2000) and at the level of argument structure and phrasal patterns as well (see Goldberg, 2006; Tomasello, 2003 for overviews).

Recent experimental work has demonstrated that a high-frequency exemplar facilitates accurate linguistic generalization, that is, holding overall type and token frequency constant, learners are better able to generalize when one type accounts for a large proportion of the tokens (Casenhiser & Goldberg, 2005; Goldberg et al., 2004). It seems that the high-frequency instance acts as an anchor point for the generalization. Similar results have been found in nonlinguistic categorization as well (Elio & Anderson, 1984; Goldberg & Casenhiser, 2006).

These findings are potentially far-reaching since the language input children receive tends in general to be skewed disproportionately toward a single example or type of example. That is, tokens of individual constructions are typically centered around a small number of words or around a semantic prototype, even when they potentially occur with a much broader range of words or meanings.

Beyond the question of how learners generalize to the constructional level is the issue of why they generalize beyond their item-specific knowledge. As reviewed here, it may well be that the generalizations are advantageous because the construction has roughly equivalent cue validity as a predictor of overall sentence meaning as the morphological form of the verb and has much greater category validity. That is, the construction is at least as reliable and much more available. Moreover, given the fact that many verbs have quite low cue validity in isolation, attention to the contribution of the construction is essential.

Motivating constructional generalizations in a different way is the simple fact that hearing or producing a particular construction makes it easier to produce the same construction. Instead of learning a myriad of unrelated constructions, speakers do well to learn a smaller inventory of patterns in order to facilitate on-line production.

Work investigating how linguistic generalizations can be learned on the basis of statistical regularities in the input has only just begun. But the parallels with nonlinguistic categorization are quite striking and hold out the promise that we may well be able to ultimately account for the complexities of language by relating them to findings in nonlinguistic domains.

REFERENCES

Abbott-Smith, K., Lieven, E., & Tomasello, M. (2004). Training 2;6-year-olds to produce the transitive construction: The role of frequency, semantic similarity and shared syntactic distribution. *Developmental Science, 7,* 48–55.

Ahn, W.-K., & Medin, D. L. (1992). A two-stage model of category construction. *Cognitive Science, 16,* 81–121.

Ahrens, K. (1995). The Mental Representation of Verbs. UC San Diego: Ph.D. Dissertation.

Ahrens, K., & Swinney, D. (1995). Participant roles and the processing of verbs during sentence comprehension. *Journal of Psycholinguistic Research, 24,* 533–547.

Akhtar, N. (1999). Acquiring word order: Evidence for data-driven learning of syntactic structure. *Journal of Child Language, 26*, 339–356.

Akhtar, N., & Tomasello, M. (1997). Young children's productivity with word order and verb morphology. *Developmental Psychology, 33*, 952–965.

Anderson, J. R. (1991). The adaptive nature of human categorization. *Psychological Review, 98*, 409–429.

Anderson, S. R. (1971). On the role of deep structure in semantic interpretation. *Foundations of Language, 6*, 197–219.

Baker, C. L. (1979). Syntactic theory and the projection problem. *Linguistic Inquiry, 10*, 533–581.

Baker, M. (1996). On the structural positions of themes and goals. In J. Rooryck and L. Zaring (Eds.), *Phrase structure and the lexicon* (pp. 7–34). Dordrecht: Kluwert.

Bates, E., & Goodman, J. (1998). Grammar form the lexicon. In B. MacWhinney (Ed.), *The emergence of language* (pp. 197–212). Hillsdale, NJ: Lawrence Erlbaum Associates.

Bates, E., & MacWhinney, B. (1987). Competition, variation, and language learning. In Brian MacWhinney (Ed.), *Mechanisms of language acquisition* (pp. 157–193). Hillsdale, NJ: Lawrence Erlbaum Associates.

Bates, E., Bretherton, I., & Snyder, L. (1988). *From first words to grammar: Individual differences and dissociable mechanisms*. New York: Cambridge University Press.

Bekkering, F., Wohlschlager, A., & Gattis, M. (2000). Imitation of gestures in children is goal-directed. *Quarterly Journal of Experimental Psychology, 53A*, 153–164.

Bencini, G. M. L. (2002). The representation and processing of argument structure constructions. Ph.D. thesis, University of Illinois.

Bencini, G. M. L., & Goldberg, A. E. (2000). The contribution of argument structure constructions to sentence meaning. *Journal of Memory and Language, 43*, 640–651.

Bock, K. J. (1986). Syntactic persistence in language production. *Cognitive Psychology, 18*, 355–387.

Bock, K. J., & Griffin, Z. M. (2000). The persistence of structural priming: Transient activation or implicit learning? *Journal of Experimental Psychology-General, 129*, 177–192.

Bock, K. J., & Loebell, H. (1990). Framing sentences. *Cognition, V*, 1–39.

Bock, K. J., Loebell, H., & Morey, R. (1992). From conceptual roles to structural relations: Bridging the syntactic cleft. *Psychological Review, 99*, 150–171.

Bowerman, M. (1982). Reorganizational processes in lexical and syntactic development. In E. Wanner and L. R. Gleitman (Eds.), *Language acquisition: The state of the art* (pp. 319–346). New York: Cambridge University Press.

Braine, M. D. S. (1976). *Children's first word combinations* (Vol. 4(1)). Monographs of the Society for Research in Child Development.

Branigan, H. P., Pickering, M. J., Liversedge, S. P., Stewart, A. J., & Urbach, T. P. (1995). Syntactic priming: Investigating the mental representation of language [Nov]. *Journal of Psycholinguistic Research, 24*, 489–506.

Brenier, J., & Michaelis, L. A. (2005). Optimization via syntactic amalgam: Syntax-prosody mismatch and copula doubling. *Corpus Linguistics and Linguistic Theory, 1*, 45–88.

Bresnan, J., & Kanerva, J. M. (1989). Locative inversion in Chichewa: A case study of factorization in grammar. *Linguistic Inquiry, 20*, 1–50.

Bruner, J. S., Goodnow, J. J., & Austin, G. A. (1956). *A study of thinking*. New York: Wiley.

Bybee, J. (1985). *Morphology: A study of the relation between meaning and form*. Amsterdam: John Benjamins Publishing Company.

Bybee, J., Perkins, R., & Pagliuca, W. (1994). *The evolution of grammar: Tense, aspect, and modality in the languages of the world*. Chicago: University of Chicago Press.

Cameron-Faulkner, T., Lieven, E., & Tomasello, M. (2003). A construction based analysis of child directed speech. *Cognitive Science, 27*, 843–873.

Campbell, A. L., & Tomasello, M. (2001). The acquisition of english dative constructions. *Applied Psycholinguistics, 22*, 253–267.
Carpenter, P., Akhtar, N., & Tomasello, M. (1998). Fourteen-through 18-month-old infants differentially imitate intentional and accidental actions. *Infant Behavior and Development, 21*, 315–330.
Casenhiser, D., & Goldberg, A. E. (2005). Fast mapping of a phrasal form and meaning. *Developmental Science, 8*(6).
Chang, F., Bock, K. J., & Goldberg, A. E. (2003). Do thematic roles leave traces in their places? *Cognition, 90*, 29–49.
Chang, F., Dell, G. S., Bock, K., & Griffin, Z. M. (2000). Structural priming as implicit learning: A comparison of models of sentence production [Mar]. *Journal of Psycholinguistic Research, 29*, 217–229.
Childers, J. B., & Tomasello, M. (2001). The role of pronouns in young children's acquisition of the english transitive construction. *Developmental Psychology, 37*, 739–748.
Chomsky, N. (1957). *Syntactic structures*. The Hague: Mouton.
Chomsky, N. (1965). *Aspects and the theory of syntax*. Cambridge: MIT Press.
Croft, W. (1991). *Syntactic categories and grammatical relations: The cognitive organization of information*. Chicago: Chicago University Press.
Croft, W. (2001). *Radical construction grammar*. Oxford: Oxford University Press.
Csibra, G., Gergely, G., Biró, S., Koós, O., & Brockbank, M. (1999). Goal-attribution and without agency cues: The perception of "pure reason" in infancy. *Cognition, 72*, 237–267.
Davis, T. (1996). Linking and the hierarchical lexicon. Ph.D. dissertation, Stanford: linguistics department.
Deacon, T. (1997). *The symbolic species: The co-evolution of language and the brain*. New York: W. W. Norton.
Deane, P. (2003). Co-occurrence and constructions. In L. Lagerweft, W. Spooren, and L. Degand (Eds.), *Determination of information and tenor in texts: Multidisciplinary approaches to discourse*. Amsterdam: Stichting Neerlandistiek, and Muenster: Nodus Publikationen.
Diessel, H. (2001). The Development of Complex Sentence Constructions in English. A Usage-Based Approach. University of Leipzig. Habilitation thesis.
Dowty, D. (1991). Thematic proto-roles and argument selection. *Language, 67*, 547–619.
Elio, R., & Anderson, J. R. (1984). The effects of information order and learning mode on schema abstraction. *Memory and Cognition, 12*, 20–30.
Elman, J., Bates, E., Johnson, M., Karmiloff-Smith, A., Parisi, D., & Plunkett, K. (1996). *Rethinking innateness: A connectionist perspective on development*. Cambridge, MA: MIT Press.
Estes, W. K. (1986). Array models for category learning. *Cognitive Psychology, 18*, 500–548.
Estival, D. (1985). Syntactic priming of the passive in English. *Text, 5*, 7–21.
Friederici, A. D., Schriefers, H., & Lindenberger, U. (1998). Differential age effects on semantic and syntactic priming [Dec]. *International Journal of Behavioral Development, 22*, 813–845.
Gentner, D., Loewenstein, J., & Hung, B. T. (2002-ms). *Comparison facilitates learning part names*.
Gertner, Y., Fisher, C., & Eisengart, J. (in press). Learning words and rules: Abstract knowledge of word order in early sentence comprehension. *Psychological Science*.
Gleitman, L. (1994). The structural sources of verb meanings. In Paul Bloom (Ed.), *Language acquisition: Core readings* (pp. 174–221). Cambridge: MIT Press.
Goldberg, A. E. (1992). The inherent semantics of argument structure: The case of the English ditransitive construction. *Cognitive Linguistics, 3*, 37–74.
Goldberg, A. E. (1995). *Constructions: A construction grammar approach to argument structure*. Chicago: Chicago University Press.

Goldberg, A. (1996). Optimizing constraints and the persian complex predicate. *Linguistic Society, 22*, 132–146.
Goldberg, A. E. (1999). The emergence of argument structure semantics. In B. MacWhinney (Ed.), *The emergence of language*. Lawrence Erlbaum Publications Hillsdale, NJ.
Goldberg, A. E. (2004). But do we need universal grammar? *Cognition, 94*(1), 77–84.
Goldberg, A. E. (2006). *Constructions at work: The nature of generalization in language*. Oxford: Oxford University Press.
Goldberg, A. E., & Casenhiser, D. (2006). Learning argument structure constructions. In E. Clark and B. F. Kelly (Eds.), *Constructions in acquisition*. Stanford: Center for the Study of Language and Information.
Goldberg, A. E., & Casenhiser, D. (unpublished). *Four year olds demonstrate fast mapping of phrasal forms and meanings*. Princeton University.
Goldberg, A. E., Casenhiser, D., & Sethuraman, N. (2004). Learning argument structure generalizations. *Cognitive Linguistics, 14*, 289–316.
Goldberg, A. E., Casenhiser, D., & Sethuraman, N. (2005). The role of prediction in construction-learning. *Journal of Child Language, 32*(2), 407–426.
Gomez, R. (2002). Variability and detection of invariant structure. *Psychological Science, 13*, 431–436.
Griffin, Z. M., & Weinstein-Tull, J. (2003). Conceptual structure modulates structural priming in the production of complex sentences. *Journal of Memory and Language, 49*, 537–555.
Grimshaw, J. (1990). *Argument structure*. Cambridge, MA: MIT Press.
Gropen, J., Pinker, S., Hollander, M., Goldberg, R., & Wilson, R. (1989). The learnability and acquisition of the dative alternation in english. *Language, 65*, 203–257.
Hare, M., & Goldberg, A. E. (1999). *Structural priming: Purely syntactic?* Paper presented at Proceedings of the Cognitive Science Society.
Hawkins, J. A. (2004). *Efficiency and complexity in grammars*. Oxford: Oxford University Press.
Heine, B. (1993). *Auxiliaries: Cognitive forces and grammaticalization*. New York: Oxford University Press.
Hintzman, D. L. (1986). "Schema abstraction" in a multiple-trace memory model. *Psychological Review, 93*, 411–428.
Hirsh-Pasek, K., Golinkoff, R. M., & Naigles, L. (1996). Young children's use of syntactic frames to derive meaning. In K. Hirsh-Pasek and R. M. Golinkoff (Eds.), *The origins of grammar: Evidence from early language comprehension* (pp. 123–158). (vol.) Cambridge, MA: MIT Press.
Holland, J. H., Holyoak, K. J., & Thagard, R. E. R. (1989). *Induction: Processes of inference, learning and discovery*. Cambridge, MA: MIT Press.
Hudson, C. L., & Newport, E. (1999). *Creolization: Could adults really have done it all?* Paper presented at the Proceedings of the 23rd Annual Boston University Conference on Language Development, Boston.
Hunston, S., & Francis, G. (1999). *Pattern grammar. A corpus-driven approach to the lexical grammar of english*. Studies in Corpus Linguistics 4. (pp. xii, 289). Amsterdam: John Benjamins.
Ingram, D., & Thompson, W. (1996). Early syntactic acquisition in german: Evidence for the modal hypothesis. *Language, 72*, 97–120.
Jackendoff, R. (2002). *Foundations of language*. Oxford: Oxford University Press.
Kako, E. (2005). The semantics of syntactic frames. *Language and Cognitive Processes*.
Kaschak, M. P., & Glenberg, A. M. (2000). Constructing meaning: The role of affordances and grammatical constructions in sentence comprehension. *Journal of Memory and Language, 43*(3), 508–529.
Kaschak, M. P., & Glenberg, A. M. (2004). This construction needs learned. *Journal of Experimental Psychology: General, 133*, 450–467.

Kempen, G. (1977). Conceptualizing and formulating in sentence production. In S. Rosenberg (Ed.), *Sentence production: Developments in research and theory* (pp. 259–274). Hillsdale, NJ: Erlbaum.

Kersten, A. W., & Billman, D. (1997). Event category learning. *Journal of Experimental Psychology: Learning, Memory and Cognition, 23*, 638–658.

Kidd, E., Lieven, E., & Tomasello, M. (in press). Examining the contribution of lexical frequency and working memory to the acquisition of syntax. *Cognitive Development*.

Kruschke, J. K. (1996). Base rates in category learning. *Journal of Experimental Psychology: Learning, Memory and Cognition, 22*, 3–26.

Kuhl, P. (2000). A new view of language acquisition. *Proceedings of the National Academy of Sciences of the United States of America, 99*(22), 11850–11857.

Landau, B. (2003). *Starting at the end: The importance of goals in spatial language and spatial cognition.* Paper presented at Conference on Spatial Language and Spatial Cognition, Baltimore, Maryland.

Langacker, R. W. (1987). *Foundations of cognitive grammar* (Vol. I). Stanford, CA: Stanford University Press.

Leake, D. B., & Ram, A. (1995). Learning, goals, and learning goals: A perspective on goal-driven learning. *Artificial Intelligence Review, 9*, 387–422.

Levelt, W., & Kelter, S. (1982). Surface form and memory in question answering. *Cognitive Psychology, 14*, 78–106.

Lieven, E. V. M., Pine, J. M., & Baldwin, G. (1997). Lexically-based learning and early grammatical development. *Journal of Child Language, 24*, 187–219.

MacWhinney, B. (1982). Basic syntactic processes. In S. A. Kuszaj, II (Ed.), *Language development* (Vol. Syntax and Semantics vol. 1, pp. 73–136). New Jersey: Lawrence Erlbaum Associates.

MacWhinney, B. (1995). *The CHILDES project: Tools for analyzing talk.* Hillsdale, NJ: Lawrence Erlbaum Associates.

Maddox, W. T. (1995). Base-rate effects in multidimensional perceptual categorization. *Journal of Experimental Psychology: Learning, Memory and Cognition, 21*, 288–301.

Medin, D. L., Wattenmaker, W. D., & Hampson, S. E. (1987). Family resemblance conceptual cohesiveness, and category construction. *Cognitive Psychology, 12*, 242–279.

Murphy, G. L. (1982). Cue validity and levels of categorization. *Psychological Bulletin, 91*, 174–177.

Murphy, G. L. (2002). *The big book of concepts.* Cambridge: MIT Press.

Naigles, L. R. (1990). Children use syntax to learn verb meanings. *Journal of Child Language, 17*, 357–374.

Naigles, L. R., & Bavin, E. L. (2001). *Generalizing novel verbs to different structures: Evidence for the early distinction of verbs and frames.* Paper presented at the BU Conference of Language Acquisition, Boston.

Naigles, L. R., Gleitman, L., & Gleitman, H. (1993). Children acquire word meaning components from syntactic evidence. In E. Dromi (Ed.), *Language and cognition: A developmental perspective* (vol. 5, pp. 104–140). New Jersey: Ablex Publishing.

Narasimhan, B. (1998). The encoding of complex events in hindi and english. Doctoral dissertation, Boston University.

Nicol, J. L. (1996). Syntactic priming [Dec]. *Language and Cognitive Processes, 11*, 675–679.

Ninio, A. (1999). Pathbreaking verbs in syntactic development and the question of prototypical transitivity. *Journal of Child Language, 26*, 619–653.

Nosofsky, R. (1988). Similarity, frequency and category representations. *Journal of Experimental Psychology: Learning, Memory and Cognition, 14*, 54–65.

Olguin, R., & Tomasello, M. (1993). Twenty-five-month-old children do not have a grammatical category of verb. *Cognitive Development, 8*, 245–272.

Pinker, S. (1984). *Language learnability and language development.* Cambridge, MA: Harvard University Press.
Pinker, S. (1989). *Learnability and cognition: The acquisition of argument structure.* Cambridge, MA: MIT Press.
Posner, M. I., & Keele, S. W. (1968). On the genesis of abstract ideas. *Journal of Experimental Psychology, 77,* 353–363.
Potter, M. C., & Lombardi, L. (1998). Syntactic priming in immediate recall of sentences [Apr]. *Journal of Memory and Language, 38,* 265–282.
Prinz, W. (1990). A common coding approach to perception and action. In O. Neumann and W. Prinz (Eds.), *Relationships between perception and action: Current approaches* (pp. 167–201). Berlin: Springer Verlag.
Prinz, W. (1997). Perception and action planning. *European Journal of Cognitive Psychology, 9,* 129–154.
Rappaport Hovav, M., & Levin, B. (1998). Building verb meanings. In M. Butt and W. Geuder (Eds.), *The projection of arguments: Lexical and Compositional factors* (pp. 97–134). Stanford, CA: CSLI Publications.
Regehr, G., & Brooks, L. R. (1995). Category organization in free classification: The organizing effect of an array of stimuli. *Journal of Experimental Psychology: Learning, Memory and Cognition, 21,* 347–363.
Regier, T., & Zheng, M. (2003). *An attentional constraint on spatial meaning.* Paper presented at Proceedings of the 25th Annual Meeting of the Cognitive Science Society, Boston, MA.
Robertson, S. S., & Suci, G. J. (1980). Event perception in children in early stages of language production. *Child Development, 51*(1), 89–96.
Rosch, E., & Mervis, C. B. (1975). Family resemblances: Studies in the internal structure of categories. *Cognitive Psychology, 7,* 573–605.
Ross, B. H., & Makin, V. S. (1999). Prototype versus exemplar models. *The concept of cognition.* Cambridge, MA: MIT Press.
Ross, B. H., Perkins, S. J., & Tenpenny, P. L. (1990). Reminding-based category learning. *Cognitive Psychology, 22,* 460–492.
Saffran, E. M., & Martin, N. (1997). Effects of structural priming on sentence production in aphasics. *Language and Cognitive Processes, 12,* 877–882.
Saffran, J. R. (2001a). The use of predictive dependencies in language learning. *Journal of Memory and Language, 44,* 493–515.
Saffran, J. R. (2001b). Words in a sea of sounds: The output of infant statistical learning. *Cognition, 81,* 149–169.
Saffran, J. R., & Wilson, D. P. (2003). From syllabus to syntax: Multilevel statistical learning by 12-month-old infants. *Infancy, 4,* 273–284.
Saffran, J. R., Alsin, R., & Newport, E. L. (1996). Statistical learning by 8-month-old infants. *Science, 274,* 1926–1928.
Saffran, J. R., Johnson, E. K., Alsin, R., & Newport, E. L. (1999). Statistical learning of tone sequences by human infants and adults. *Cognition, 70,* 27–52.
Sampson, G. (1997). *Educating eve: The language instinct debate.* New York: Cassell.
Savage, C., Lieven, E., Theakston, A., & Tomasello, M. (2003). Testing the abstractness of children's linguistic representations: Lexical and structural priming of syntactic constructions in young children [Nov]. *Developmental Science, 6,* 557–567.
Scheepers, C. (2003). Syntactic priming of relative clause attachments: Persistence of structural configuration in sentence production [Oct]. *Cognition, 89,* 179–205.
Scheibman, J. (2002). *Point of view and grammar: Structural patterns of subjectivity in american english conversation.* Amsterdam: Benjamins.

Schlesinger, I. M. (1982). *Steps to language: Toward a theory of language acquisition.* Hillsdale, NJ: Lawrence Erlbaum Associates.

Sethuraman, N. (2002). The acquisition of verbs and argument structure constructions, Linguistics, UCSD dissertation.

Sethuraman, N., & Goodman, J. (2004). Children's monstery of the transitive construction. Paper presented at the Stanford Child Language Research Forum, Stanford, CA.

Smith, L. B. (2001). Importance of overall similarity of objects for adults' and children's classifications. *Journal of Experimental Psychology: Human Perception and Performance, 7*, 811–824.

Smith, M., & Wheeldon, L. (2001). Syntactic priming in spoken sentence production—an online study [Feb]. *Cognition, 78*, 123–164.

Stefanowitsch, A., & Gries, S. T. (2003). Collostructions: Investigating the interaction between words and constructions. *International Journal of Corpus Linguistics, 8*, 209–243.

Talmy, L. (1976). Semantic causative types. In M. Shibatani (Ed.), *Syntax and semantics 6: The grammar of causative constructions.* New York: Academic Press.

Thompson, S. A., & Hopper, P. J. (2001). Transitivity, clause structure and argument structure: Evidence from conversation. In J. L. Bybee and P. J. Hopper (Eds.), *Frequency and the emergence of linguistic structure* (pp. 27–60). Amsterdam: John Benjamins.

Tomasello, M. (1992). *First verbs: A case study of early grammatical development.* Cambridge: Cambridge University Press.

Tomasello, M. (2000). Do young children have adult syntactic competence? *Cognition, 74*, 209–253.

Tomasello, M. (2003). *Constructing a language: A usage-based theory of language acquisition.* Cambridge, MA: Harvard University Press.

Tomasello, M., & Stahl, D. (2004). Sampling children's spontaneous speech: How much is enough? *Journal of Child Language.*

Wisniewski, E. J. (1995). Prior knowledge and functionally relevant features in concept learning. *Journal of Experimental Psychology: Learning, Memory and Cognition, 21*, 449–468.

Yamashita, H., Chang, F., & Hirose, Y. (2003). *Pure order priming: Structural priming in Japanese.* Paper presented at CUNY.

Zipf, G. K. (1935). *The psycho-biology of language.* Boston: Houghton Mifflin.

UNDERSTANDING THE ART OF DESIGN: TOOLS FOR THE NEXT EDISONIAN INNOVATORS

Kristin L. Wood and Julie S. Linsey

I. Motivation and Overview

The ability to invent, create, and innovate is at the very core of engineering and product development. It provides a forum for designers to apply creativity and contribute their personal flair. It also represents the time when technology is chosen or developed to fulfill customer and societal needs. While this core ability is well recognized and acknowledged, significant research questions exist regarding our understanding of invention and creation as part of the design and product development process. This chapter investigates a sector of these research questions, focusing on the area of concept creation and its relationships to informational categories. A working hypothesis of this investigation is that category decomposition and representation (i.e., categorization) provide the scaffolding of innovative concept development for products. For the real-world problems encountered by engineers, it is this scaffolding that deserves significant attention as an interdisciplinary area of inquiry by the research fields of engineering and psychology.

A. Edisonian Design

Few of us can imagine life without electricity, light bulbs, computers, or many of the other modern marvels we take for granted each and every day. What genius developed such things? Can the creation of such art forms be taught?

Fig. 1. A snapshot of "Edisonian invention."

Do such inventive ideas strike like a bolt of lightning? Why do some people seem prone to moments of insight and inspiration? When we think of these underlying questions of invention, Thomas Edison comes to mind as the symbol for inventive success.

Figure 1 illustrates, emblematically, the inspirations of Thomas Edison. Edison is one of the most prolific inventors in US history with over a 1000 patents (Dyer, Martin, & Meadowcroft, 1929). Most people associate him with the invention of the incandescent light bulb (even though he was one of many inventors to work on this device). Edison was the first to build from, combine, and further develop previous research into a practical device (Baldwin, 1995). A practical, electrically powered light bulb was just a tip of his influence on our world. He invented not only a practical light bulb but also the necessary power distribution system and related lighting systems for carrying it into everyday life.

To many, invention appears to be a mysterious art in which individuals are either naturally gifted in or not. Even today Edison remains an icon in this mysterious world of invention with researchers seeking to uncover his genius. Currently, the Thomas A. Edison Papers, a research center at Rutgers University, seeks to increase the availability of millions of documents related to Edison and his work (*The Thomas A. Edison Papers*, 2005). As indicated by these documents, some information exists regarding the process Edison used to approach design and more has been inferred based on academic study. Edison's authorized biography describes his now well-known trial-and-error method for invention. His famous statement, "Genius is one percent inspiration and 99 percent perspiration," is quoted regularly (Dyer et al., 1929). Beyond mere trial and error, Edison also built his invention upon the scientific knowledge of the day. Edison began each project with a thorough study of the available literature from which he based his experimentation (Dyer et al., 1929). The trial-and-error approach for design development is useful when scientific guidance is inadequate but is a very time consuming and expensive process. This approach with its inherent limitations supplements the design process today.

Other details of Edison's approach to design are known. He frequently based designs for a new device on products he had previously seen or developed. For example, he used his knowledge of telegraph circuitry to assist in the development of the practical light bulb (Baldwin, 1995). From his first marketable invention, a voting machine, he learned the value of developing inventions that people wanted and were willing to buy (Dyer et al., 1929). Currently, this process is more commonly referred to as customer-centered product development or "voice of the customer." Some of Edison's approaches to design are known at a high level but the details of how he was able to achieve such success, in many cases, are unavailable. For example, how was Edison able to perceive connections between the design of various devices when other inventors who had access to similar knowledge were unable to develop such devices? This question, and its numerous variants, represents the allure that creativity and invention have on the human psyche.

But is this question unfathomable? Is it possible to probe Edisonian inspiration and create teachable principles, not to replace the human in the art of design (i.e., creativity) but to enable and enhance the innate abilities of all humans as designers? Research in the fields of psychology and engineering design, over the last two decades, indicates an affirmative answer to this question. The process of product development can be strongly influenced by a systematic approach developed through scientific study (Hubka & Eder, 1996; Otto & Wood, 2001; Pahl & Beitz, 1996; Ullman, 2003; Ulrich & Eppinger, 2000). Design methods and the related research are based on studying, characterizing, and categorizing the characteristics of exceptional engineering designs, the resulting industrial products or processes, and the ways in which designers categorize the design problems to arrive at innovations. Through a number of different research approaches, a large number of design methods have been developed to change the so-called "fuzzy front end of product development" into a more predictable, systematic process that can be learned. In this chapter, we explore these developments, focusing on the relationships to categorization. This exploration creates a foundation for teachable methods of invention, setting the stage for the next generation of Edisonian innovators.

B. Enhancing the Art of Design: Classification and Categorization

At the core of contemporary design methods is the categorization (or classification) of information. By definition, classification is the act or method of distributing into a class or category according to characteristics. Synonymously, categorization is the basic cognitive process of arranging into classes or categories. Teachable design methods rely heavily on classification as a general method and categorization as the supporting cognitive process. Categories, that is, general classes of ideas, terms, or things that mark divisions or coordinations within a conceptual scheme, enable abstractions to search for ideas and concepts. Categories facilitate the representation of vast quantities of information into manageable sets. Categories allow for reasoning, combinatorics, and genesis beyond the possibilities enumerated by the elemental ideas or terms of the categories themselves.

Within this contextual framework, we explore the use of categorization in product design and development. We first examine the process of product development and its various stages. We then investigate, more fully, the concept generation phase of product development, considering first the representations of information followed by methods for utilizing these representations to create ideas. These investigations lead to a discussion of important research questions in concept generation and their inherent interdisciplinary nature in engineering and psychology.

II. A Product Development and Concept Generation Process

Figure 2 shows a number of consumer products. These products illustrate the variety produced from product development processes. Figure 2A, for example, pictures a General Motors EV-1 automobile. This vehicle demonstrates the need for flexibility in products to adapt to changing technology. It also illustrates, as with all automobiles, the need for feature variety, depending on the desires of the consumer. Some groups of consumers will be willing to pay for attractive features. Their threshold of added cost correlates with the value they associate with a given feature such as interior materials,

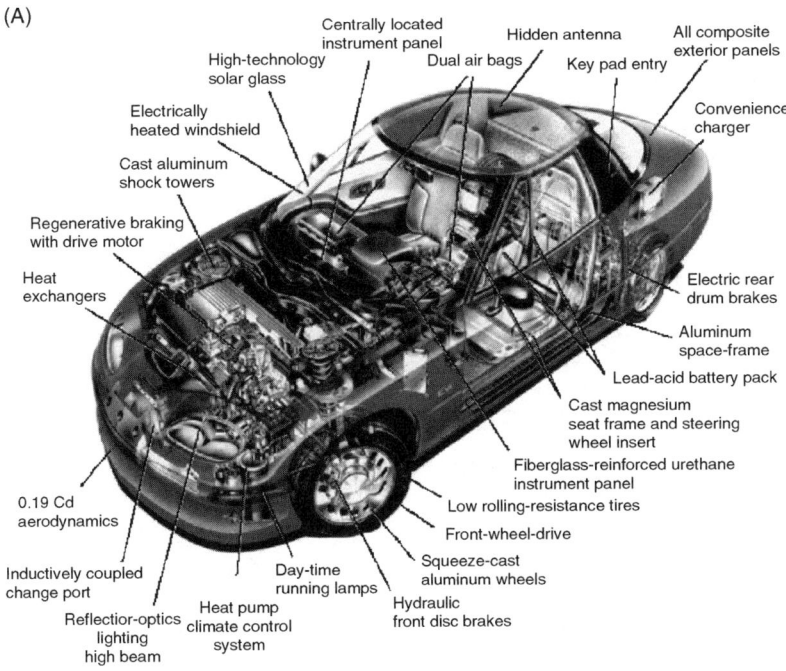

General motors' EV-1

Fig. 2. A range of products illustrating innovations in a variety of markets (Otto & Wood, 2001, 2005).

(B)

Personalized nike shoes
(color, emblems, soles)
(Nike, 2004)

(C)

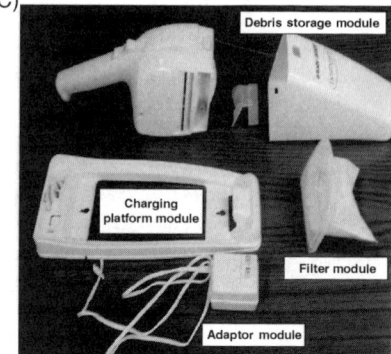

Dustbuster cordless vacuum (B&D)
DB250C (Rajan et al., 2003, 2005)

(D)

B&D VersaPac product
family

(E)

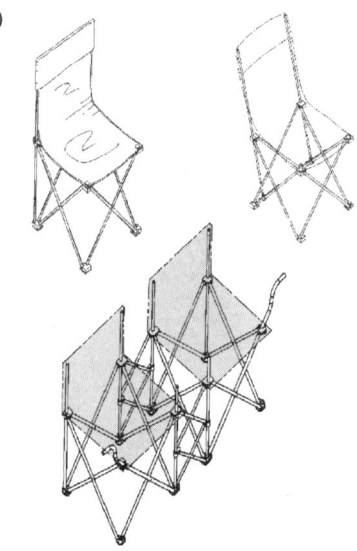

Foldable chair products: single,
reclining, and dual (US Patents
D432,823, 2000; 6,231,119, 2001a;
6,241,311, 2001b; 6,296, 304, 2001c)

Fig. 2. *continued*

console functionality, and alloy wheel designs (Piller, Reichald, Moslein, & Lohse, 2000; Pine, 1993; Reichwald, Piller, & Möslein, 2000).

Figure 2B–E illustrate four products of smaller scale than the GM EV-1 automobile. Nike ID shoes provide flexibility to the customer in terms of color choice, customized emblems (such as college names, symbols, and mascots), and choice of sole designs. The Black and Decker (B&D) Dustbuster product illustrates a modular design. Feature changes to one module, in future evolutions or product portfolios, may have little effect on other modules. The B&D VersaPac product represents a product family. Multimodal customer needs are addressed with a common product platform. And the foldable chair products illustrate the direct evolution of a single chair to a reclining and dual chair product. These product evolutions include added features with little or no changes to the original product architecture.

The product development processes employed to create the products shown in Fig. 2 require a complex set of tasks. There are tasks of creating, understanding, communicating, testing, and persuasion. At its highest level, we characterize any product development process with three phases: *understand the opportunity, develop a concept,* and *implement a concept.* Figure 3 illustrates this three-phased process (Otto & Wood, 2001, 2005).

The first phase of product development encompasses all activities needed to make the decision to launch a new product development effort. The second phase encompasses all activities to make the decision on what the product will be. The final phase encompasses all activities to make every product consistently work well. After the final product development phase, the product is ready to be manufactured. In reality, these phases overlap and are complex; yet, they help us to categorize the efforts needed to develop a product, and like all categorizations, there are counterexamples and the boundaries are fuzzy.

A product development process, as illustrated in Fig. 3, can be thought of as a sequence of parallel and serial *activities* or steps to be completed. Within any phase, there are concurrent development activities. Mechanical design proceeds in parallel with electrical design in parallel with software code development and with industrial design. To ensure compatibility of these activities, many companies force the periodic "assembling" of the product as it stands at a given point in time, along with its associated forecasted systems that remain uncertain (such as production, distribution, and so on). This assembly process is executed to obtain a better picture of the design as it is evolving, to evaluate that preliminary system, and, to freeze parts of the design. Thus, some development decisions are made final at this point

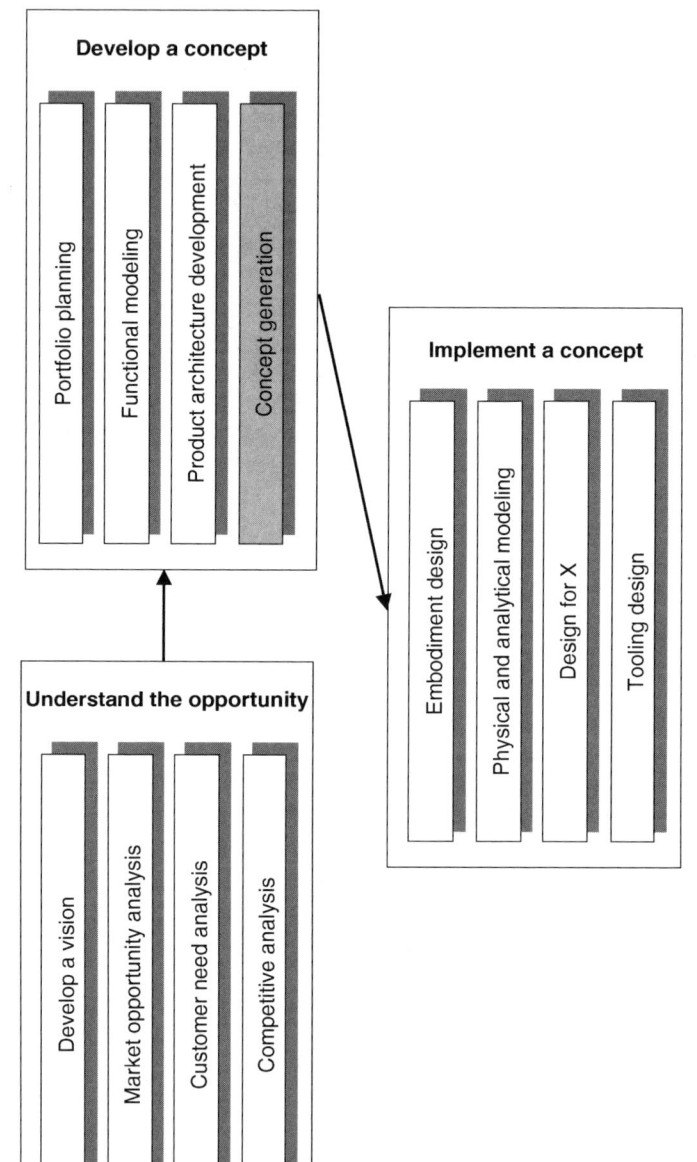

Fig. 3. A product development process.

in time, such as general layout, user operation/interface, control, suppliers, and so on.

A. UNDERSTANDING THE OPPORTUNITY

The first phase of product development, "Understand the Opportunity," is characterized with four activities. This first step in a product development process often entails the creation of a vision for a new product. What product do we wish were in the market? What is difficult with the current product we use? Why does it not do something we want it to? How do we wish to impact society with an invention? The answers to these questions are visions for a new product.

Visions are the driving force in understanding market opportunities. Everyone has an idea for a new product, every user has thoughts on how they wish their devices would work better, every CEO has a vision for command of a market, and every research scientist has a vision for how their technology can be applied. The question is whether any vision can be transformed into a successful realization. Can it be developed and implemented into a product at a worthwhile profit? The first part of this question is the market opportunity. The revenue that might be extracted by a new product from a market has to be estimated. In today's competitive environment, the estimated price and volume that a market will carry is always the starting point.

Having completed a market analysis and made a decision to proceed to develop a new product, a development team next must analyze and understand the needs and desires of a customer population. To obtain this understanding, we must think about the customer population statistically. One obvious way is to determine the average response of the customer population on any set of criteria and call this average the response of the average customer. Similarly, we can consider the difficult, hard to achieve levels mentioned in the responses of the customer population that occur out at the tails of the customer distribution. These two customer levels are important for a design team to consider.

Another categorization of the customer population is to consider the different use patterns that the customer population exhibits. For companies operating in global markets, where the design is for customers in many different countries, climates, and economies, geographical breakdowns are often effective. Socioeconomic categories are also often effective such as characterizations by income, gender, marital status, and age. The point is to have a clear customer-need-based description (demographics) of the market segment or segments that are to be met by a new product.

Yet another categorization that a design team should consider is to characterize the customer population by lead-lag usage. That is, for products with rapidly changing technology, one can find a fraction of the customer population that is always on the leading-edge use of the product. These persons use the product in a way that the rest of the customer population will also exhibit in a few years or so. These *lead-customers* are important for a design team to identify and to open a line of communication. For example, university students are lead users of computer network technology; they are on-line most often and develop new uses for network technology such as the first weather reporting sites, the first online camera pictures, the first site to report when a coke machine is empty, and so on. Now, weather information and traffic pictures are common on the web. From one perspective, developing product technology that merely satisfies these customers will in turn simultaneously delight the average customer.

B. Developing a Concept

Having clarified all available information, including the customer needs, how a product must fit into the market and the cost range that defines the product, the design team can work to meet these expectations. The first activity in this effort ("Developing a Concept") is to design a set of general market specifications for the product. This activity must be undertaken with respect to the portfolio architecture, that is, the complementary set of products, the company has to offer.

Understanding the portfolio architecture, customer needs, and competition orients a design team toward the generation of a new concept. One of the first tasks in concept generation is to determine what the product must do to supply the customer satisfaction, independent of how it is implemented. This task entails the execution of functional modeling.

Functionally, all products *do something*. Products, therefore, accept "inputs" and operate to produce "outputs," the desired performance. We can model any product, assembly, subassembly, or component as a *system*, with inputs and outputs that traverse a system boundary. The essence of such a model is the need-function-form definition of engineering design, where our focus here is on translating the customer needs for a product to the product functions.

A functional model describes the inputs, outputs, and transformations that must happen for a product to work. For most products, there are several possible groupings for subsets of these functions into physical subassemblies. Developing the interfaces in the product embodies the product architecting process.

Product architecting, at a basic level, starts the creation of effective *layouts* of components and subsystems: where different tasks are completed by subsets of the product, how they complete them, how the subsystems interact, how the subsystems are divided and interfaced. If we look a little closer at the act, itself, of creating product architecture, it is apparent that the focus is on transforming product function to product form.

There exist two general categories of architecture types: product and portfolio. Portfolio architectures relate to a group or family of products. Design strategies revolve around whether to, how to, and the form of sharing components among the products in a portfolio. Product architecture, on the other hand, relates to a specific product layout. In this category, strategies for product design revolve around the product's market and performance.

The functional model and alternative product architectures set the stage for very effective concept engineering. Here, a product development team generates many concepts for implementing the functional specification. The activity of concept generation is one of the hallmarks of engineering design. It provides a forum for designers to apply creativity and contribute their personal flair. It also represents the time when technology is chosen or developed to fulfill the customer needs.

In this sense, the imaginary clay of product development is molded during concept generation. Artistic skills must be brought to bear that will allow us to shape the clay according to the direction of our inner-eye, experience, and knowledge. Tools are also needed to remove portions of the clay, to wet and reshape it, to spin it into new forms, and to add features that will appeal to customers. These tools enhance the creativity of the designers, resulting in a broad range of concepts for a product vision.

After interactively generating concepts to meet a market opportunity, the concepts must be narrowed and refined to a portfolio of concept offerings or a single-concept entity. This process is known as concept selection. An industrial concept selection process is a team-based decision-making effort. Generally, concept selection is a critical point in a product development process. It might be that there is no clear solution concept that should be pursued; different members of the team may have strong opinions on different solutions, and incorrect decisions can be costly.

The concept selection process at this stage must deal with this uncertainty. The process is focused on clearly articulating differences in understanding among team members, forming common definitions, and expanding the options considered due to these differences in understanding. The ultimate goal of this process is team buy-in and consensus. When the process is implemented, a design team will have agreement on the concept to pursue, each member will understand why they changed their mind to the collective consensus, and each member will be supportive of their change in position. If the team does not reach this state of consensus, the team will understand exactly why there remains a difference in opinion and have agreement on what must be further analyzed to resolve the issue. In such a case, the concept selection will then be completely determined by the results of this analysis.

C. IMPLEMENTING A CONCEPT

Having selected a concept, it must be implemented for the final phase of product development. Much of this activity is *embodiment engineering*, where a chosen concept is given form through specification of components to purchase, specifications of parts to manufacture, and specifications for their assembly into the product.

One important aspect of embodiment is *modeling*, or the testing of new implementation ideas by physical construction—building it—or by analysis—numerically modeling it. Modeling is typically understood in terms of explaining physical phenomena in the rich tradition of the physical sciences. In product development, we do not want to explain physical phenomena, we want to develop a novel product that will delight customers, fulfill our dreams, satisfy our ethical responsibilities, and make money. Therefore, we must consider modeling in the real-world context—the product development process—and demonstrate how it supports design decision-making.

Methods to actually make models of the physical processes in a product are often difficult to initiate and evolve for effective decision-making. When appropriately developed, these methods assist in constructing mathematical models of customer needs in terms of variables a design team can change, using the customer needs, functional model, and generated concepts. Based on the developed performance metrics that reflect customer needs, designers must use these metrics to select a preferred design configuration. Experimental methods help to explore different configuration alternatives and to construct performance models. Methods of optimization also assist in studying the developed models and to help a design team select values for specific configuration variables.

In addition to the many performance-related metrics of a product, a design team has additional engineering specification that their product must meet. These specifications are the discussion of the various *Design-for-X* methods, where *X* is one of these requirements. For example, *design for manufacturing and assembly* methods are applied to ensure the ease of manufacturing and assembly of a product. *Design-for-the-environment* methods, likewise, ensure a product uses minimal impact materials and operations.

At the end of this phase, a working preproduction prototype exists. Often, production planning and manufacturing process design are also underway. These activities represent the final point in the development, resulting in

D. Product Development and Categorization

Figure 4 illustrates example outcomes of a product developed following this product development process. This product is an assistive guitar for persons with disabilities (Krager, Moody, Qureshi, Porlier, & Singh, 2005). Automated instruments provide an avenue for teaching basic instrument lessons and for appreciating the musical sounds produced by the instrument. In the case of the automated assistive guitar, a modular architecture is developed, separating strumming, fretting, picking, and guitar attachment into distinct subsystems. These modules provide the ability to focus on particular actions of playing a guitar while automating other actions. For example, strumming with a particular rhythm or cadence may be actuated within the modular guitar system while the operator slides the fretting mechanism to learn or play different chords. The operator(s) may also change picks, adjust strumming speeds, or change particular guitars within the device. The operator may also, optionally, position the guitar in height and orientation on a stand.

The product development process, illustrated by this assistive guitar product, includes a number of instances where categorization assists and enhances the designers' abilities. As an example, consider the phase of "Understanding the Opportunity." As discussed earlier, a key aspect of this stage is the determination of customer needs. Customer needs provide a basis for an engineering specification for the product vision. Specifications, in turn, assure that a product has measurable targets for meeting the vision.

In creating these specifications, a number of product requirements are latent. These latent needs are unspoken expectations of the customers (such as every product is expected to be durable and safe), requirements legislated by the government, or attributes that are prescribed by standards organizations (such as ISO—International Standards Organization or ANSI—American National Standards Institute). To create a complete product specification, categories of requirements assist and direct the designers' efforts. Table I shows a useful set of categories developed by Franke (1975) for the specification creation process. These categories were developed by Franke (1975) as part of a scientific study of industrial product development. They guide the cognitive development of specifications by leading the designer to the key areas that describe a product and its development. These categories also provide a guidepost for determining the sufficiency of a product specification.

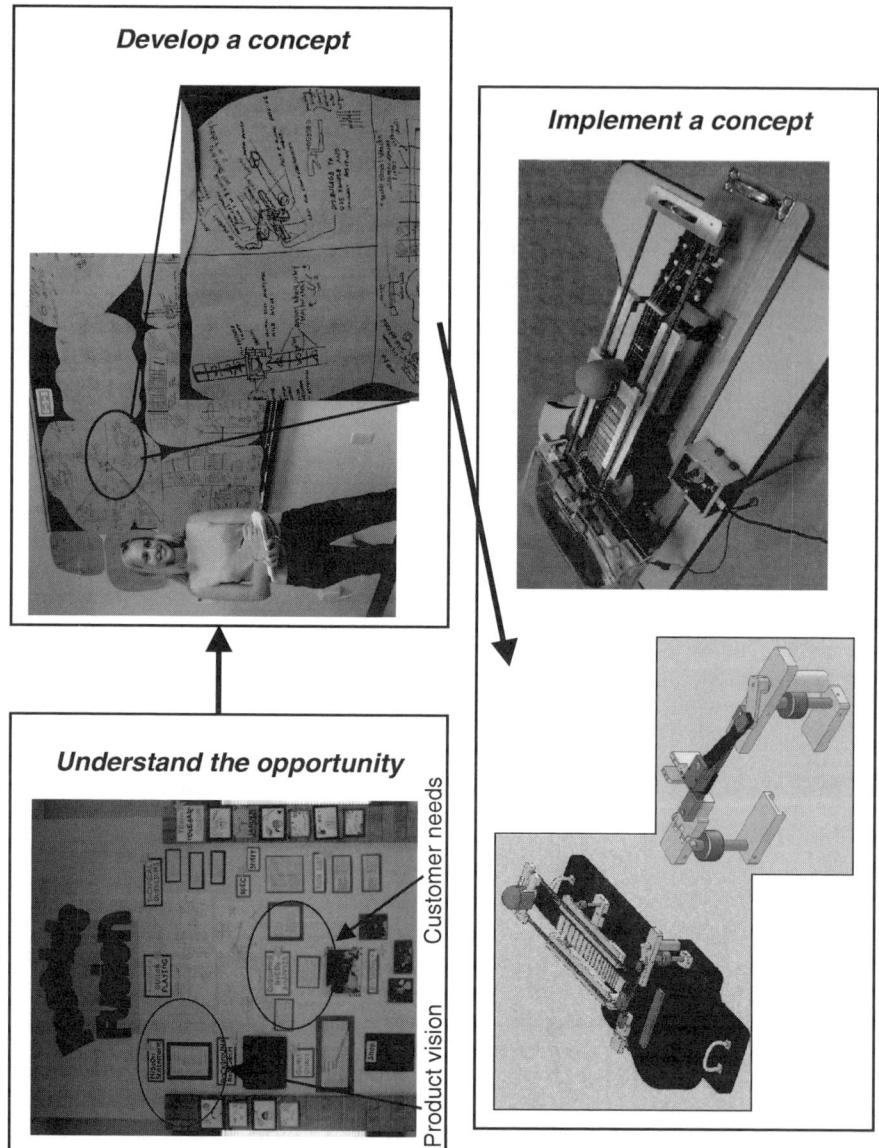

Fig. 4. Assistive guitar product created for persons with disabilities, following the product development process of Fig. 3.

TABLE I

CATEGORIES FOR SEARCHING AND DECOMPOSING SPECIFICATIONS
(FRANKE, 1975)

Specification category	Category description
Functional	Primary functional requirements for what a product is to do
Geometry	Dimensions, space requirements, ...
Kinematics	Type and direction of motion, velocity, ...
Forces	Direction and magnitude, frequency, load imposed by, energy type, efficiency, capacity, conversion, temperature
Material	Properties of final product, flow of materials, design for manufacturing
Signals	Input and output, display
Safety	Protection issues
Ergonomics	Comfort issues, human interface issues
Production	Factory limitations, tolerances, wastage
Quality control	Possibilities for testing
Assembly	Set by design for manufacturing (DFM) or special regulations or needs
Transport	Packaging needs
Operation	Environmental issues such as noise
Maintenance	Servicing intervals, repair
Costs	Manufacturing costs, materials costs
Schedules	Time constraints

III. The Scaffolding of Concept Generation: Category Representations

Building on this model of product development, our attention now focuses on the area of concept creation and its relationships to informational categories. Contemporary research in engineering design shows clear ties that categorization provides a potential scaffolding for innovative concept development of products. Categorization in concept generation is the decomposition and representation of "idea generators." Idea generators are abstractions of artifacts that provide the mechanism by which a designer will identify a concept solution or analogy. Categories of idea generators include many possibilities such as textual labels, functional descriptions, functional diagrams, generalized engineering parameters, artifact sketches, and metaphorical physical artifacts (such as representative products, components of products, or subsystems of products). We explore typical categories of idea generators here, beginning with functional descriptions and diagrams.

A. FUNCTION, FUNCTION CATEGORIES, AND FUNCTION DIAGRAMS

What is a "function?" A function of a product is a statement of a clear, reproducible relationship between the available input and the desired output of a product, independent of any particular form. More generically, function is the action for which an artifact is particularly fitted or employed, or what an artifact is to be used for.

To illustrate the meaning of product functions, Fig. 5 shows an example consumer product and an example subsystem of an automobile. The product, in this case a cordless screwdriver, is opened to reveal its internal structure. Functional labels are also included to describe the purpose of the various product components and regions of the product. These functions, as represented by the labels, capture what the product does at an elemental level. These functions operate collectively to meet the purpose of the product system. In the case of the cordless screwdriver, the purpose is to tighten and loosen threaded fasteners.

Over the last 20 years, new methods for engineering design have emerged that focus, as part of the product development process, on the mapping of customer needs to functional descriptions. These descriptions are then used to generate and select sets of technologies that satisfy the underlying functional requirements (Akiyama, 1991; Hundal, 1990; Miles, 1972; Otto & Wood, 2001; Pahl & Beitz, 1996). Functional descriptions of this type (Fig. 5) have a number of intrinsic advantages:

- Concentration is on "what" has to be achieved by a new concept or redesign and not "how" it is to be achieved. By so doing, a component- and

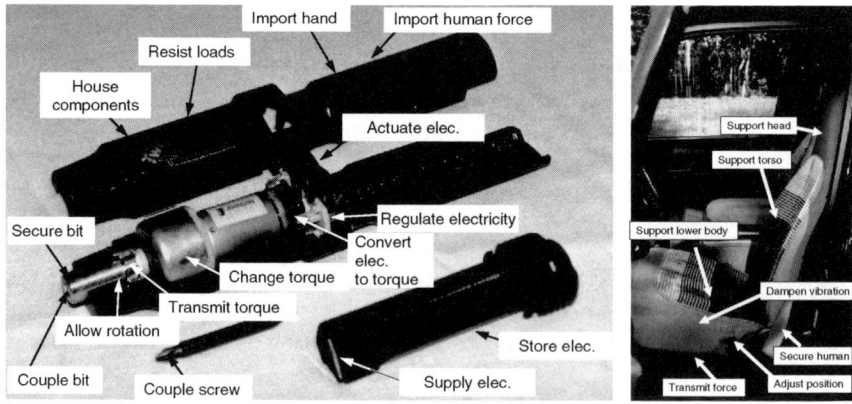

Fig. 5. Example consumer products with functional labels.

form-independent expression of the design task may be achieved to comprehensively search for solutions.
- Functional modeling provides a basis for organizing the design team, tasks, and process. To the extent that functions of the product are independent, design-process activities may be chosen according to the independent product "chunks." The interactions between the functional elements provide the required key communications needed among the concurrent design activities. Interfacing specifications can be readily developed.
- Functions or sets of functions may be derived or generated directly from customer needs. These functions define clear boundaries to associate assemblies or subassemblies of the final design solutions. These boundaries provide a basis for seeking modular concepts.
- Creativity may be enhanced by the ability to decompose problems and manipulate partial solutions. By first decomposing a design task into its functional elements, solutions to each element are more apparent due to the reduction of complexity and extraneous information.
- Functional modeling provides a natural forum for abstracting a design task. Many levels of functional abstractions may be created from a very high-level single function statement to alternative detailed functional statements for a design's subsystems. Through abstraction, a design team may search for the "real" problem being solved, while minimizing biases.
- By mapping customer needs first to function and then to form, more solutions may be systematically generated to solve the design problem. "If one generates one idea it will probably be a poor idea; if one generates twenty ideas, one good idea might exist for further development" (Ullman, 1996).
- Needs mapped to function and then to form promote set-based concurrent engineering processes (Sobek & Ward, 1996). Set-based concurrent engineering processes are the simultaneous development of products across the different disciplines involved in product development (such as mechanical engineering, industrial design, or electrical engineering). Feasible regions of technology may be explicitly defined based on functional requirements not implicitly. Trade-offs may also be explored in parallel among a wide array of radical and known solutions since a common functional description is driving the design effort directly from the voice of the customer.

There are various methods for classifying functions. Based on a careful empirical study of various products, Table II shows a general classification of functions. These classes represent basic or atomic functions that can be solved with a basic artifact, where the given synonyms are equivalent to the classes. Basic functions, in this sense, operate on flows (of energy, materials, or signals) in a product to produce a desired performance

TABLE II

Function Classes, Basic Functions, and Synonyms

Class (primary)	Secondary	Tertiary	Synonyms (correspondents)
Branch	Separate		Isolate, sever, disjoin
		Divide	Detach, *isolate*, release, sort, split, disconnect, subtract
		Extract	Refine, filter, purify, percolate, strain, *clear*
		Remove	Cut, drill, lathe, polish, sand
	Distribute		Diffuse, dispel, disperse, dissipate, diverge, scatter
Channel	Import		Form entrance, *allow*, input, *capture*
	Export		Dispose, eject, *emit*, empty, *remove*, destroy, eliminate
	Transfer		Carry, deliver
		Transport	Advance, lift, move
		Transmit	Conduct, convey
	Guide		Direct, shift, steer, straighten, switch
		Translate	Move, relocate
		Rotate	Spin, turn
		Allow DOF	*Constrain*, unfasten, unlock
Connect	Couple		Associate, connect
		Join	Assemble, fasten
		Link	Attach
	Mix		Add, blend, coalesce, combine, pack
Control magnitude	Actuate		Enable, initiate, start, turn-on
	Regulate		Control, equalize, limit, maintain
		Increase	*Allow*, open
		Decrease	Close, delay, interrupt
	Change		Adjust, modulate, *clear*, demodulate, invert, normalize, rectify, reset, scale, vary, modify
		Increment	Amplify, enhance, magnify, multiply
		Decrement	Attenuate, dampen, reduce
		Shape	Compact, compress, crush, pierce, deform, form
		Condition	Prepare, adapt, treat
	Stop		End, halt, pause, interrupt, restrain
		Prevent	Disable, turn-off
		Inhibit	Shield, insulate, protect, resist
Convert	Convert		Condense, create, decode, differentiate, digitize, encode, evaporate, generate, integrate, liquefy, *process*, solidify, transform
Provision	Store		Accumulate
		Contain	*Capture*, enclose
		Collect	Absorb, consume, fill, reserve
	Supply		Provide, replenish, retrieve

TABLE II *continued*

Class (primary)	Secondary	Tertiary	Synonyms (correspondents)
Signal	Sense		Feel, determine
		Detect	Discern, perceive, recognize
		Measure	Identify, *locate*
	Indicate		Announce, show, denote, record, register
		Track	Mark, time
		Display	*Emit*, expose, select
	Process		Compare, calculate, check
Support	Stabilize		Steady
	Secure		*Constrain*, hold, place, fix
	Position		Align, *locate*, orient
	Overall increasing degree of specification →		

(Hirtz, Stone, McAdams, Szykman, & Wood, 2002; Stone & Wood, 1999, 2000).

In addition to the function classes, basic flow classifications are needed. Functions operate on flows through products to produce a desired result. Three flow classes of materials, energy, and signals form the general categories of flows. These flow classes may be further decomposed into elemental flows as shown in Table III. Within each class, flows are separated into basic flows. In practice, a basic flow description is formed from a basic word plus the class it belongs to.

Using the categorization of functions and flows in Tables II and III, we may state a design problem as a functional description. Consider, for example, a design problem with applications in third world countries. ThinkCycle (Thinkspace: Peanut Sheller, 2004) is a web site facilitating distributed design collaboration to meet the needs of underserved communities. An example problem stated on ThinkCycle is to design a device to quickly shell peanuts for use in places like Haiti and West African countries (Table IV). The current solution to this problem is to shell the peanuts by hand, and no electrical energy sources are available. Customer needs for the peanut sheller are low cost, easy to manufacture, quickly shelling a large quantity of peanuts, and the device must remove the shell with minimal damage to the peanuts. A corresponding functional description might be stated as "import energy" to the system, "break the shell," and "separate the peanut from the shell." This description employs the categorization of functions and flows as stated in Tables II and III. Idea generators, in the form of these functional descriptions, provide a construct for the cognitive search of concepts.

TABLE III

Flow Classes (of Energy, Materials, or Signals), Basic Flows, and Synonyms

Class (primary)	Secondary	Tertiary	Synonyms (correspondents)
Material	Human		Hand, foot, head
	Gas		Homogeneous
	Liquid		Incompressible, compressible, homogeneous,
	Solid	Object	Rigid-body, elastic-body, widget
		Particulate	
		Composite	
	Plasma		
	Mixture	Gas-gas	
		Liquid-liquid	
		Solid-solid	Aggregate
		Solid-Liquid	
		Liquid-Gas	
		Solid-Gas	
		Solid-Liquid-Gas	
		Colloidal	Aerosol
Signal	Status	Auditory	Tone, word
		Olfactory	
		Tactile	Temperature, pressure, roughness
		Taste	
		Visual	Position, displacement
	Control	Analog	Oscillatory
		Discrete	Binary
Energy	Human		
	Acoustic		
	Biological		
	Chemical		
	Electrical		
	Electromagnetic	Optical	
		Solar	
	Hydraulic		
	Magnetic		
	Mechanical	Rotational	
		Translational	
	Pneumatic		
	Radioactive/nuclear		
	Thermal		
	Overall increasing degree of specification →		

TABLE IV

Design Problem: "Peanut Sheller"

Design problem	Design a device to quickly shell peanuts for use in places like Haiti and West African countries.
Customer needs	1. Low cost 2. Easy to manufacture 3. Quickly shelling of a large quantity of peanuts 4. Remove the shell with minimal damage to the peanuts
Functions	1. Import energy 2. Break the shell 3. Separate the peanut from the shell

TABLE V

Design Problem: "Art Enabling Device for Persons with Disabilities"

Design problem	A device needs to be designed to allow children with severe physical disabilities to create art projects. The children have very limited motor skills. They cannot hold items such as a paint brush. The device needs to be actuated by simple electrical devices such as the large switch shown on the left. Teachers will set up the device for the students to use. The device must be safe and easy to use.
Customer needs	1. Easy to create art with very limited motor skills 2. Very easy to operate 3. Simple operation with the push of large buttons or other simple devices 4. The art medium (e.g., paint, glue, glitter, and/or markers) device should not make a large mess and needs to be easy to clean up
Functions	1. Contain art medium such as paint, glue, glitter, and/or markers 2. Position the art medium over the paper 3. Dispense the art medium onto the paper 4. Hold paper in place

Tables V and VI illustrate two further examples of design problems and their conversions to functional descriptions. In the first case, a device is needed for assisting persons with disabilities create works of art with different art media. The second case focuses on a portable device to wash one's hands and brush one's teeth in a dorm room setting where a sink is unavailable. Both problem descriptions include functional descriptions based on function and flow categories. Concepts may be generated within these categorical descriptions.

TABLE VI
Design Problem: "Dorm Room Washing Device"

Design problem	Design a portable device for a dorm room to allow you to wash your hands, your dishes, and brush your teeth in your dorm room. Your dorm room does not have a sink
Customer needs	1. Easy to wash your hands 2. Convenient and sanitary to wash dishes 3. Convenient to brush your teeth 4. Easily portable
Functions	1. Contain water 2. Heat the water 3. Dispense water to object 4. Dispose of or store the dirty water

With the basic descriptions listed, basic solutions will most likely result. Open research questions include what is the appropriate level of functional description (granularity), what types of functional elements should be used (basic, advanced, expansive), and how many functional elements should be used as a starting point?

An alternative representation of function for product development problems is the use of diagrams. Using the language of the functional basis, designers can describe a system using a connected set of functions and flows. An example of a functional model (diagram) for a subsystem of an extraterrestrial probe is shown in Fig. 6 (Linsey, Van Wie et al., 2005b). This functional model represents the design problem of collecting rock samples from the Martian surface. Input flows of energy, materials, and signals are converted to desired results (outputs) through functional elements. These functional elements and their connections abstract the design problem as idea generators for the product development team.

Figure 7 shows another example of a functional model (diagram) for a device to cook popcorn. Again, input flows of energy (electricity), materials (popcorn kernels and butter), and signals are converted to the desired output of hot, buttered popcorn. Functional models, of this form, can be implemented as catalysts during conceptual design to promote creative generation of concepts. The functional elements and connections lead to cognitive search paths for elemental solutions. This search for solutions may focus on the redesign and evolution of a current product or technology, or, alternative, the search for solutions to an original creation of a design artifact.

The functional model of the popcorn popper can support numerous avenues for creative design. At an elementary functional level, a designer may

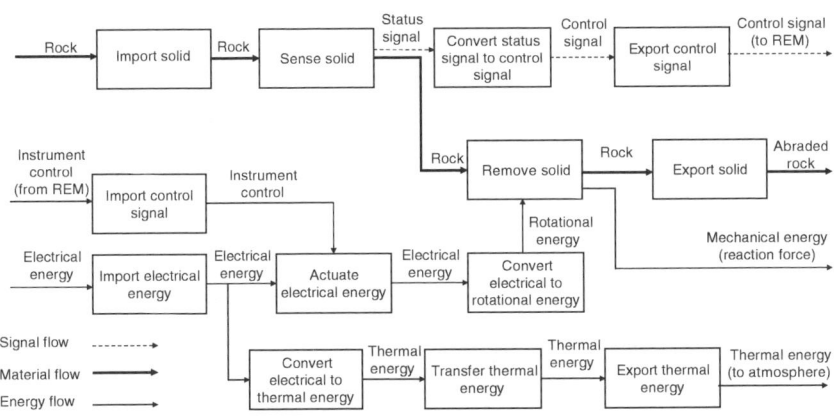

Fig. 6. NASA Martian rover with rock probe (Courtesy of NASA) and a corresponding rock probe functional diagram.

focus the idea generation process on a single function such as "fluidize the popcorn." Possible solutions including gravity, static electricity, forced air, the natural convection of air, forced water, or the natural convection of steam. Functional models also highlight likely modules within the product. From Fig. 7, an engineer who is familiar with functional modeling can see that the functions of "capture air," "store air," and "move air" are a good candidate set of functions for a single module within this product. The popcorn popper of Fig. 7 implements this modular design feature. Functional models can also show the required ordering of particular functions or highlight places where

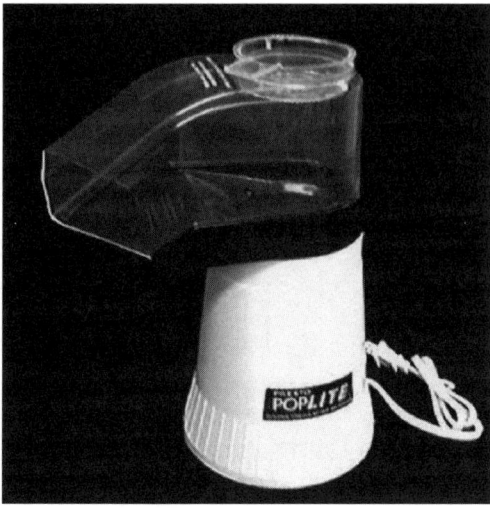
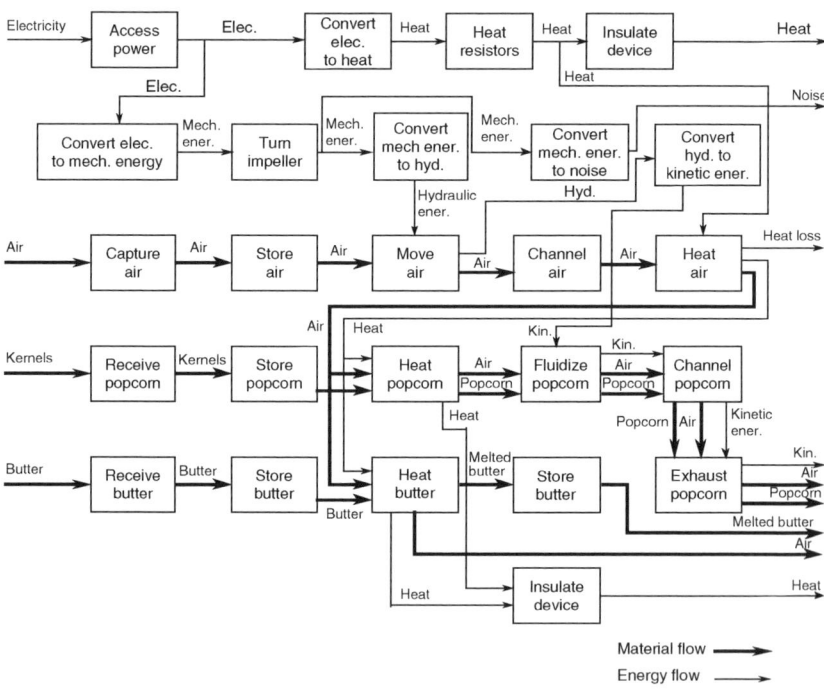

Fig. 7. Hot-air popcorn popper and a corresponding functional diagram.

this ordering may be altered. By inspecting the functional diagram, an engineer may consider the ordering of "move air," "channel air," and then "heat air." If the order was instead "heat air," "channel air," and "move air," the solution would be to use natural convection to heat and move the air eliminating the need for a fan within the device. This solution will not work for popcorn but might work for other substances.

B. GENERALIZED ENGINEERING PARAMETERS

The *Theory of Inventive Problem Solving* (TIPS) was developed by Genrikh S. Altshuller in the former USSR, beginning in the late 1940s (Altshuller, 1984; Domb, 1998; Fey & Rivin, 1996; Ivanov, 1994; Sushkov, Mars, & Wognum, 1995). The basis of this theory is the discovery that patterns exist in patent claims, many of them based on the same working principles. Building on this discovery, Altshuller collaborated with an informal collection of academic and industrial colleagues to study patents and search for the patterns that exist (Sushkov et al., 1995). Hundreds of person-years were devoted to this effort, and thousands to millions of patents have been studied, resulting in the insight that patents may be classified into five categories. The first two categories were designated as "routine design," meaning that they do not exhibit significant innovations beyond the current technology. These categories are "basic parametric advancement" and "change or rearrangement in a configuration." The last three categories, on the other hand, represent designs that included inventive solutions. These three categories are "identifying conflicts (contradictions) and solving them with known physical principles," "identifying new principles," and "identifying new product functions and solving them with known or new principles."

Based on these categories and patent studies, Altshuller (1984) observed a number of trends in historical invention. Some of the key observations, in the context of product design, include the following:

• Evolution of engineering systems (products) develops according to the same patterns, independent of the engineering discipline or product domain. These patterns may be used to predict the trends of future evolutions in a product domain. They may also be used to direct the search for new concepts.

• Conflicts (or contradictions) in the parameters of a design are the key drivers for product invention. Principles for eliminating conflicts are universal across product domains. Application of these principles implies that compromise is unacceptable.

• The systematic application of physical effects aids invention since a particular product team does not know all physical knowledge.

These insights led Altshuller (1984) to focus his attentions on inventive problem solving for cases where design conflicts exist. Design conflicts, or contradictions, exist when parameters of the design problem have a negative correlation. Improvement in one parameter of the design problem will lead, typically to the deterioration in another parameter. For example, if a design problem seeks to have a durable solution, but one that is also lightweight, durability will compete with the weight of the device. Typical solutions to design problems will create a compromise to durability and weight, in this case. These types of solutions provide neither lightweight nor durable characteristics. Instead, an innovative solution is needed that breaks the conflict and creates solutions that satisfy weight and durability issues.

Altshuller categorized types of engineering parameters from the patent studies so that conflicts could be represented and stated for innovative solution. Table VII shows the generalized parameters for the TIPS. Pairs of these parameters lead to statements of conflicts. For example, let us consider the design problem of creating a device to iron clothes. A natural conflict in this problem is to have a lightweight device (ergonomics) but one that also applies a suitable force to clothing so that wrinkles may be removed. Using the TIPS generalized engineering parameters, this conflict may be restated as "force versus weight of moving object." This representation in the categories of

TABLE VII

Generalized Engineering Parameters for Describing Design Conflicts

1. Weight of moving object
2. Weight of stationary object
3. Length of moving object
4. Length of stationary object
5. Area of moving object
6. Area of stationary object
7. Volume of moving objec
8. Volume of stationary object
9. Velocity
10. Force
11. Stress or pressure
12. Shape
13. Stability of object's composition
14. Strength
15. Duration of action generalized by moving object
16. Duration of action generalized by stationary object
17. Temperature
18. Brightness
19. Energy consumed by moving object
20. Energy consumed by stationary object
21. Power
22. Energy loss
23. Substance loss
24. Information loss
25. Waste of time
26. Quantity of a substance
27. Reliability
28. Accuracy of measurement
29. Manufacturing precision
30. Harmful actions affecting the design object
31. Harmful actions generated by the design object
32. Manufacturability
33. User friendliness
34. Repairability
35. Flexibility
36. Complexity of design object
37. Difficulty to control or measure
38. Level of automation
39. Productivity

generalized parameters may now be used to seek innovative solutions using design principles identified for such conflicts. We explore this type of design principle solution in Section IV.

C. PHYSICAL PRINCIPLE CLASSIFICATION

Physical classifying schemes are categories of high-level physical principles or geometry. They direct the development of concepts by stimulating thoughts in the designers that may not have been considered in a purely intuitive approach. By choosing a category, a product development team can focus on the generation of concepts in a particular technological area or specific line of thought (Pahl & Beitz, 1996).

Table VIII lists example classification schemes for generating concepts. The classifications range from geometry to form properties, and they include subtopics to refine the search. These classifications are chosen to facilitate identification and combination of essential solution characteristics of a product.

To use a classification scheme, the design team focuses on the primary product functions and architecture. A matrix is then formed, listing the product functions as rows and the columns as solutions to these functions according to the categories chosen from Table VIII. Each category is then systematically considered, where the search for solution exists for each category.

As a basic application of this directed-search method, Fig. 8 shows the solutions to the product function of "store energy." The classifying scheme is "energy types," and the headings for this scheme are mechanical (motion), hydraulic (fluid), electrical, and thermal. These ideas may be integrated into an alternative design for a product that needs a "store energy" function.

D. TEXTUAL IDEA GENERATORS

Another type of category representation is textual idea generators. Textual idea generators may be applied to redirect the search for ideas during concept generation. The categories are derived based on studies of idea generation and cognitive initiators.

Table IX lists a number of idea generators that may be used as part of concept generation. They may be used by a group or by an individual. These idea generators help to breakdown conceptual blocks by refocusing the group or individual along a different train of thought. To apply the generators, a keyword or activity is stated, followed by a questioning period about the keyword or activity (Otto & Wood, 2001).

TABLE VIII

Classifying Schemes for Generating Concepts (Pahl & Beitz, 1996)

Class	Heading/category	Examples
Working geometry		
	Type	Point, line, surface, body
	Shape	Curve, circle, ellipse, hyperbola, parabola
		Triangle, square, rectangle, pentagon, hexagon, octagon
		Cylinder, cone, rhombus, cube, sphere
		Symmetrical, asymmetrical
	Position	Axial, radial, tangential, vertical, horizontal. Parallel, sequential
	Size	Small large, narrow, broad, tall, low
	Number	Undivided, divided
		Simple, double, multiple
Working motions		
	Type	Stationary, translational, rotational
	Nature	Uniform, nonuniform, oscillating
		Planar or 3D
	Direction	x-y-z or about x-y-z
	Magnitude	Velocity, acceleration
	Number	One, several, composite movements
Basic material properties		
	State	Solid, liquid, gaseous
	Behavior	Rigid, elastic, plastic, viscous
	Form	Solid bodies, grains, powder, dust
Basic structural properties		
	Joints	Rigid, rotational, sliding
	Alignment	Horizontal, vertical, angled, truss
	Loading Conditions	Tension, compression, bending, torsion, and shear

E. Physical Principle Diagrams

Beyond the textual idea generators, in common language questions or physical principle classifications, we may also consider diagrammatic representations of physical principles. An example, from the domain of mechanical engineering, is *force flow analysis*.

Force flow analysis is a systematic method for facilitating directed product evolution through identification of opportunities for possible component

Type of energy / Principle	Mechanical	Hydraulic	Electrical	Thermal
1	Flywheel J, ω (rot.)	Hydraulic reservoir a. Bladder b. Piston c. Membrane (pressure energy)	Battery V	Mass m, s, $\Delta\theta$
2	Moving mass m (trans.)	Liquid reservoir h	Capacitor (elec. field)	Heated liquid
3	m, h (pot. energy)	Flowing liquid	Magnet (magn. field)	Super heated steam
4	Metal spring F,d (elasticity)			
5				
6				

Fig. 8. Example of classifying schemes to generate concepts for the function "store energy," adapted from Pahl and Beitz (1996).

combinations in products from the domain of mechanical effort transmissions (Greer, Jensen, & Wood, 2004; Greer, Wood, Jensen, & Wood, 2002; Jensen et al., 2000; Lefever, 1995; Lefever & Wood, 1996; Otto & Wood, 2001). The term mechanical effort transmission is defined to be any device that transmits mechanical force or torque. Force flow analysis uses a force flow diagram to model the transfer of effort (force or torque) through the components of a product. The effort flow diagram is a semantic network composed of nodes and links that are described using the fundamentals of graph theory. The nodes represent the components of the product, while the links represent the interfaces between the components. Whenever possible, force flow diagrams are configured in such a manner that they mimic the general topology of the product. A force flow diagram maps the flow of effort from the input interface(s), through all the affected components, then to the output interface(s).

TABLE IX

Textual Idea Generator Categories for Probing Questions

Idea generator category	Questions or application
Make analogies	What analogies exist in nature? What analogous products exist in any product domain? How do these products solve the same product functions?
Wish and wonder	What if . . .?
Sketch/use physical models (e.g., Tinker Toys or Lego's)	What would an idea look like? How does this model satisfy the function? What can we change?
Eliminate or minimize?	If we remove a feature, how does the device perform? What can we use to replace the feature? What if a feature was smaller? What should I omit? Should I divide it? Split it up? Separate it into different parts? Understate? Streamline? Make miniature? Condense? Compact? Subtract? Delete? Can the rules be eliminated?
Substitute	What can be substituted? Who else? What else? Can the rules be changed? Other ingredient? Other material? Other process or procedure? Other power? Other place? Other approach? What else instead?
Combine	Can we combine purposes? How about an assortment? How about a blend? An alloy? Combine units? What other article or device could be merged with this?
Adapt	What else is like this? What other idea does this suggest? Does the past offer a parallel? What could I copy? Whom could I emulate? What idea could I incorporate? What other process could be adapted?
Modify or magnify	What can be magnified, made larger, or extended? What can be exaggerated? Overstated? What can be added? More time? Stronger? Higher? How about greater frequency? Extra features? What can add extra value? What can be duplicated? How could I carry it to a dramatic extreme? Convert a round action to straight? How can this be altered for the better? What can be modified? Is there a new twist? Change meaning, color, motion, sound, odor, form, or shape? Change name? What changes can be made in the plans? In the process? In the marketing?
Put to other uses (repackage an old idea)	What else can this be used for? Are there new ways to use as is? Other uses if modified? What else could be made form this? Other extensions? Other markets?
Reverse or rearrange	What other arrangements might be better? Interchange components? Other pattern? Other layout? Other sequence? Change the order? Transpose cause and effect? Change pace or schedule? Can I transpose positive and negative? What are the opposites? What are the negatives? Should I turn it around? Up instead of down? Consider it backwards? Reverse roles? Do the unexpected?
What if the product function changes gender?	Feminine and masculine features? What are their opposites?

Interfaces are a critical element in effort flow analysis. An interface is defined as:

> A spatial region where there exists energy and/or material flow between components or between a component and the external environment.

This definition does not include information such as spatial or structural aspects. Force flow analysis focuses on the energy flow, one of the fundamental functional flows: material, energy, and information (Table III). While a complete description of an interface is important, the goal is simply to describe the existence and fundamental nature of interfaces in real designs.

In force flow analysis, all the information about the product is captured in the interface description. At a minimum, this information consists of the type of relative motion, the direction of the effort flow, and the operation with which the effort is associated. The interfaces are characterized based on the type of relative motion that exists between connected components. Table X captures the permutations of possible relative motion types as well as the naming convention adopted to describe each possibility. Because this relative motion set spans all possible combinations of relative motion in mechanical transmissions, and because the members of this set are orthogonal, the set is referred to as a *basis for relative motion* in force flow analysis.

Four flow classifications are now possible. We define these classifications (links) as follows:

"N-Link": No relative motion either at the interface or between the components.
"C-Link": Relative motion between the components only.
"R-Link": Relative motion both at the interface and between components.
"I-Link": Relative motion at the interface only.

TABLE X

RELATIVE MOTION PERMUTATIONS IN FORCE FLOW REPRESENTATION

Classification of force flow and relative motion types	Relative motion location	
Link type	Between interfaces	Between components
N-Link	0	0
C-Link	0	1
R-Link	1	1
I-Link	1	0

In the context of this classification, Fig. 9A and B illustrates the force flow diagram of a staple remover product (diagram is superimposed on the physical layout of the device). Notice that the force flow diagram shows an input hand force that flows through the components of the staple remover product. This input force is transformed by the device to remove a staple that secures a group of papers or other materials.

The flow labels of Table X are listed on the force flows between components for the staple remover. These labels provide indicators, or idea generators, for improving the product in terms of component combination. Guidelines may be applied to direct the component combination and identify opportunities for improvement. Figure 10 shows an example result of this process, where a one-piece, integrally molded staple remover product results. This new product configuration includes a compliant hinge between the two hand grips and embodies an innovative concept from the force flow analysis. A further example of innovation from force flow analysis is the application to an umbrella product. Figure 11 shows a scaled prototype of a one-piece umbrella mechanism. This mechanism uses compliance and living-hinges to replace the cumbersome and high part-count linkage subsystems of traditional umbrellas. These opportunities were suggested through the categorization of flow links as part of force flow analysis.

IV. Basic Concept Generation Methods: Transforming Representation to Physical Layouts

Concept generation, as described here, is the divergent development of many alternatives solutions to a design problem, where the focus is on innovation, structural layout, and function satisfaction. A convergent strategy is adopted once a breadth of ideas is formed. This ensuing strategy provides a means of converging to a single solution (or finite portfolio of solutions) that will ultimately be the product in the marketplace.

Concept generation methods may be classified, broadly, into two categories: *intuitive* and *directed*, Fig. 12 (Otto & Wood, 2001). The intuitive category relates to the methods that focus on idea generation from within an individual or group of individuals. The intent of such methods is to remove barriers to divergent thinking so that new connections and features in a product may be visualized. By removing these barriers, the environment of idea generation may be filled with conditions that promote creativity. Directed methods, on the other hand, use a systematic, step-by-step, approach to searching for a solution. These methods rely on technical information, expertise, and guidelines to seek solutions to technical problems.

Understanding the Art of Design

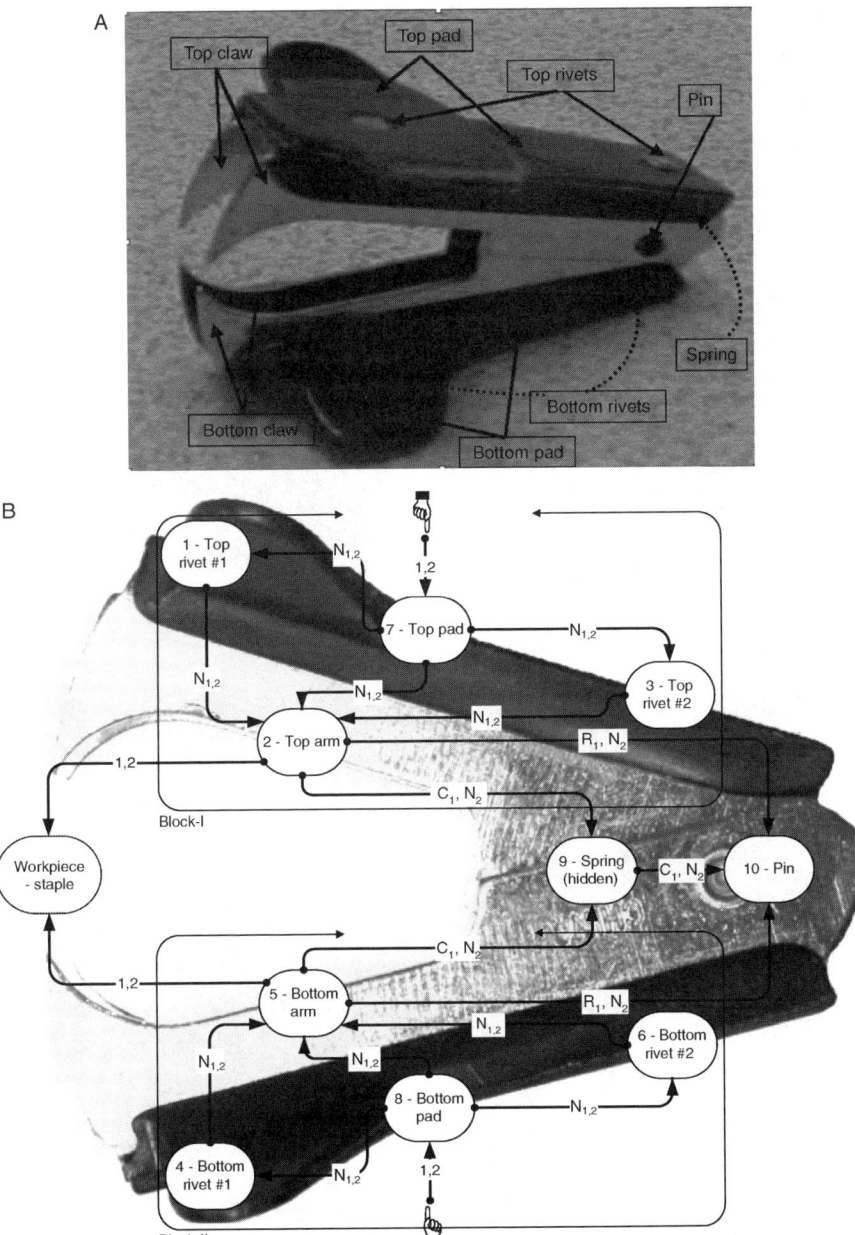

Fig. 9. (A) Schematic for a staple remover product. (B) Force flow diagram of a staple remover product.

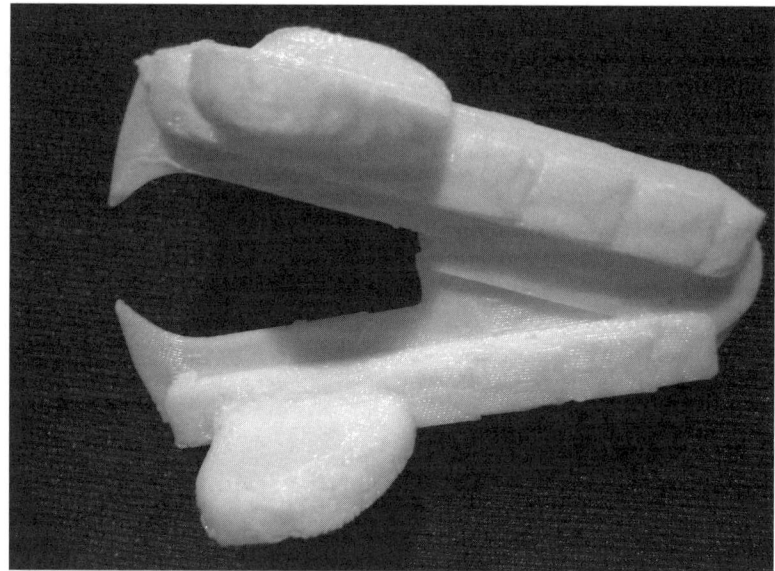

Fig. 10. Evolved stapler product with reduced components.

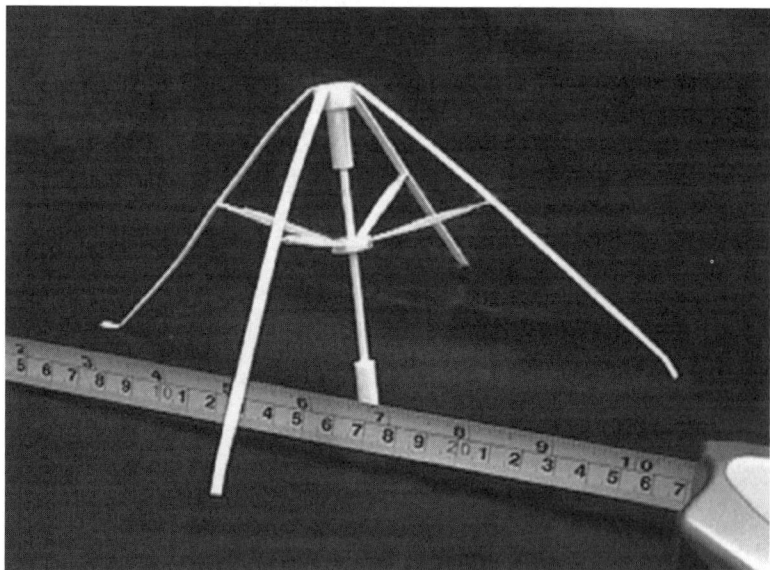

Fig. 11. Example application result of force flow diagrams: a "one-piece umbrella."

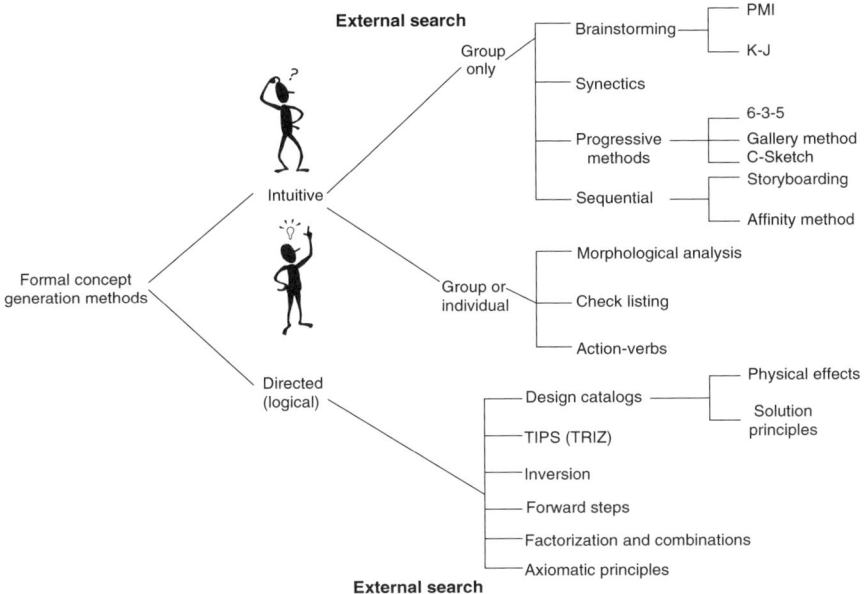

Fig. 12. A classification of concept generation methods.

Ideally, they force solutions to be determined along a particular path, even though the final solution is not readily apparent at the outset. As such, these methods balance the technical and technological information available with the make up of the design team or the work environment.

In the remainder of this section, we study a range of concept generation methods (Adams; 1986; DeBono, 1967; Gryskiewicz, 1999; Michalko, 1991, 2001; Ulrich & Eppinger, 2004; Utterback, 1996). These methods employ the categorization and category representations of Section III to create form solutions to product design and development problems. Representations, such as functional descriptions, functional diagrams, conflicts represented with generalized parameters, textual classification of physical principles, and force flow diagrams, are the inputs to concept generation methods. The initial phases of design, which include conceptual design, have been shown to have the most significant impact on the cost of a product (Römer, Weißhahn, & Hacker, 2001). Effective concept generation methods that utilize the scaffolding of category representations have the potential to enhance designers' abilities in these initial product development phases.

A. Osborn's Brainstorming and Mind Mapping

Brainstorming (Osborn, 1957) is an intuitive method of generating concepts. It focuses on product function and architecture, where an individual or team members communicate ideas verbally during a set period of time. All team members are encouraged to be open and uninhibited during the initial sessions of brainstorming. There is no need to strictly adhere to product specifications but instead to focus on the needs of a product, as embodied in categorical representations, such as a functional description, functional diagram, and so on.

The overall aim of brainstorming is to obtain several concepts that might work as solution principles to a piece of the design problem. Ideally, the search is comprehensive, where no solution is left unmentioned. Of course, this comprehensive requirement will never be satisfied, but the team (or individual) does the best it can. A breadth of solutions is desired.

The primary advantage of brainstorming is the ability of a set of individuals to collectively build on each other to generate ideas that would not arise individually. (The group is greater than the sum of the individual parts.) Team members will *piggyback* and *leapfrog* each other. Piggybacking creates building block-ideas to words, body language, statements, and concepts stated by a team member. Responses to team member's statements include relations, inversions, tangential or partial changes, antonyms, synonyms, and so on. Leapfrogging, on the other hand, results in divergent or discontinuous jumps in the responses. Each team member brings different expertise, skills, experience, and personality to a group effort of piggybacking and leapfrogging. Brainstorming taps into this diversity to create, quickly, a large number of high-level solutions.

Disadvantages of the method include a number of factors. The "right idea" may not come at the "right time." There is no guarantee. Group conventions may sidetrack or inhibit original ideas. The team may be distracted by a misdirected focus, or certain team members may dominate the discussion. Likewise, the team that is assembled for a given session might not be open to new ideas. This situation will tend to condone only known solutions with a self-prophesizing result.

Even though these disadvantages exist, brainstorming is a powerful technique for generating concepts. A committed team creates ideas together (that are *not* judged at the time of the session) and that possibly triggers further ideas.

One effective way to enhance a brainstorming session to generate a greater breath of ideas is by using *mind mapping*. Here, the brainstorming facilitator starts with a clean sheet of paper, writes the problem statement (e.g., functional description) in the center of the paper, and draws a box around it.

Then, as ideas are generated to solve the problem, they are recorded quickly, say with two or so words, with circles drawn around them. Each new idea to solve the initial problem is connected to the original problem statement.

As an idea is refined, or as an idea sparks another idea, these ideas are connected to the idea that sparked them. Ideas that are all basically the same concept should branch out of the originally proposed concept. Entirely different concepts should have their own branches emanating from the problem statement.

If the problem statement is refined into a new one, this new form can be recorded by entering a new problem statement and drawing a box around it. Problem statements in boxes distinguish the concepts in circles. The new problem statement should be connected to the concept that sparked the reformulated or refined statement by a directed arrow. Typically, some concepts introduce categories that then are brainstormed upon. Mind maps help a facilitator visualize this process, as the mind map will show a single well-fielded branch or category. These categories greater enhance the piggybacking process.

As an example of brainstorming with mind mapping, consider the peanut shelling problem described in Table IV. Figure 13 shows the results of a brainstorming session utilizing the functional description of the problem. Notice in the figure that a number of abstract categories of solutions emerged from the session. These categories were explored fully during brainstorming, resulting in a great breadth of textual solutions.

B. BRAINSKETCHING, C-SKETCH, 6-3-5, AND GALLERY METHODS

A number of drawbacks exist in the traditional brainstorming method. These drawbacks may be classified according to two primary factors: idea generation may be dominated by a small number of team members or by an over zealous facilitator and brainstorming usually relies on an oral, verbal, or textual means of communication. The first factor creates an atmosphere that squelches participation by members, resulting in fewer ideas being generated. The second factor only provides one media for expressing concepts. The execution of fuller written descriptions and sketches are usually not employed.

Alternative methods to address these deficiencies are known as the *Gallery, C-Sketch, Brainsketching, and "6-3-5" methods*, also known as *brain-writing methods*. The Gallery method combines periods of sketching with periods of discussion. C-Sketch focuses strictly on sketches as the media for creating concepts. The Brainsketching method recommends sketches, in addition to key words and short descriptions. "6-3-5" adds a set of process

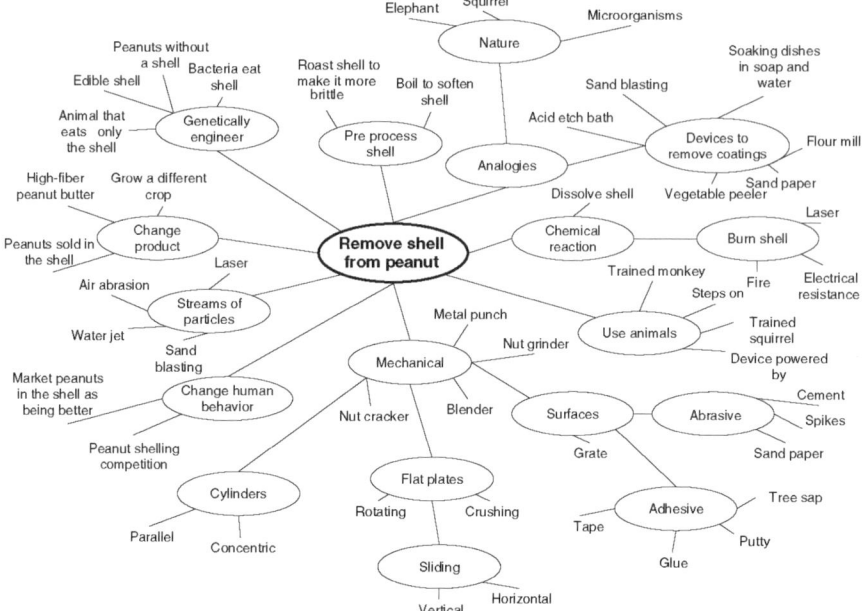

Fig. 13. Mind map of the peanut shelling design problem (Table IV).

steps to Brainsketching to improve concept generation (Otto & Wood, 2001; Pahl & Beitz, 1996; Rohrbach, 1969; Shah, 1998; VanGundy, 1988).

We focus our discussion here on what we call the modified "6-3-5" approach emphasizes sketching but within the context of the original "6-3-5" method. The modified "6-3-5" approach uses the following guidelines and process steps. Team members are arranged around a table, usually a circular table to provide continuity. Six ("6") members in the team are ideal; however, the number of participants can range from 3 to 8 members. Each member sketches three ("3") ideas for the product functions, architecture, or overall configuration under consideration. Usually the top five product functions with respect to the customer needs are considered. Fifteen to thirty concepts typically result from the process in a period of 25–35 min. The ideas may initially be restricted to each individual product function, not combinations of them, or the overall layout drawings from the product architecture analysis. Alternatively, other category representations, as described in Section III, are used to initiate the modified "6-3-5" approach. After developing solution principles for each primary product function, modified "6-3-5" approach is repeated to aggregate the principles into integrated concept variants. Again, 25–35 concepts typically result.

After each member of the concept generation team spends T minutes of work on the initial concepts, the paper is passed to the right around the table. The team members now have T more minutes to add an additional idea to the paper and to modify and extend the ideas from the previous team members. This timed process continues until all sheets of paper have been added/modified by each team member (total of 35–60 min, typically).

The passing of the papers through one cycle is known as a "round." The method encourages a total of five ("5") rounds (spaced in time) to refine and combine ideas. The "5" rounds represent the last designation in the modified "6-3-5" method.

A number of guidelines help to achieve success from the "6-3-5" method. There should be no verbal communication until a cycle (round) is completed. By restricting verbal communication, no one member can dominate the concept generation process. Traditional brainstorming may be implemented after a few "6-3-5" sessions so that team members will be able to interact and spur ideas through fruitful communications.

Besides this guideline, the focus of the modifications during the passing of ideas should be on advancing the ideas not negative criticism. As a team member views a pictorial idea, the visual image should be used as a catalyst for imagination. Unintentional product features will be viewed from quick sketches since team members are prevented, initially, from describing the intent of their sketches (beyond labels and a concise statement). Sketches are the preferred mode for expressing concepts.

As an illustration of modified "6-3-5" approach, consider the design of a peanut shelling device described in Table IV. Before concept generation, systematic methods result in significant data and category representations to be used for creating concept variants. These data, in part, include organized customer needs, a functional model, an assessment of the product architecture, and benchmarking information.

Applying brainsketching to this problem, Fig. 14 shows an iteration of the modified "6-3-5" method. This figure shows the first three concepts generated by one individual of the product development team. Figure 15 then illustrates the results of the next subround of the process, where the concept paper from the first individual is passed to a team member. Notice from Figs. 14 and 15 that a rich set of initial solutions result from sketching as applied to the functional description of Table IV. Variety and creative solutions are emerging to the problem. The sketched results from modified "6-3-5" approach result in unexpected interpretation from a team member. These sketches also show practical potential due to the inherent geometry shown in sketches.

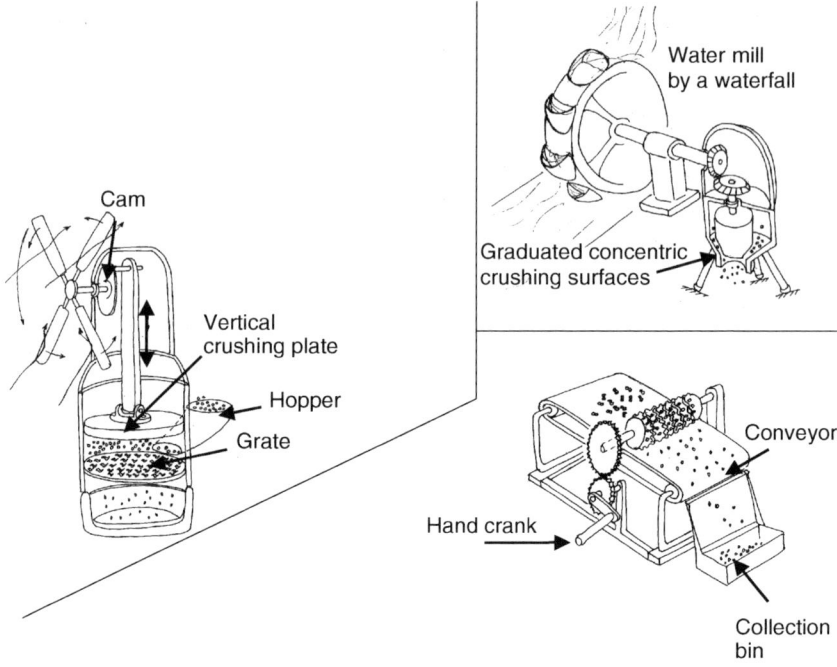

Fig. 14. First phase of modified "6-3-5" method: application to the peanut shelling design problem (Table IV).

C. ENGINEERING EMPIRICAL RESULTS AND CATEGORIZATION

There are numerous studies on variations of Osborn's brainstorming (Mullen, Johnson, & Salas, 1991) and computer-based brainstorming (Fjermestdad & Hiltz, 1998), but little data exists on the other previously mentioned techniques (Gryskiewicz, 1988; Paulus & Yang, 2000). Within engineering design, there is growing interest in exploring and improving idea generation methods (Lewis, Sadosky, & Connolly, 1975; Linsey, Green, Murphy, Wood, & Markman, 2005a; Shah, 1998; Shah, Vargas-Hernández, Summers, & Kulkarni, 2001; Van der Lugt, 2000, 2002; Vidal, Mulet, & Gómez-Senent, 2004). One of the main differences between "6-3-5" or C-Sketch is the number of ideas any one person can use for inspiration at a given time.

Two group idea generation studies within engineering explored how the number of ideas a participants can view at a given time affects the idea generation process (Linsey et al., 2005a; Shah et al., 2001). Linsey, Green et al. used a factorial experiment to directly measure the effects of displaying all the ideas on a wall in front of a group gallery style (similar to Gallery

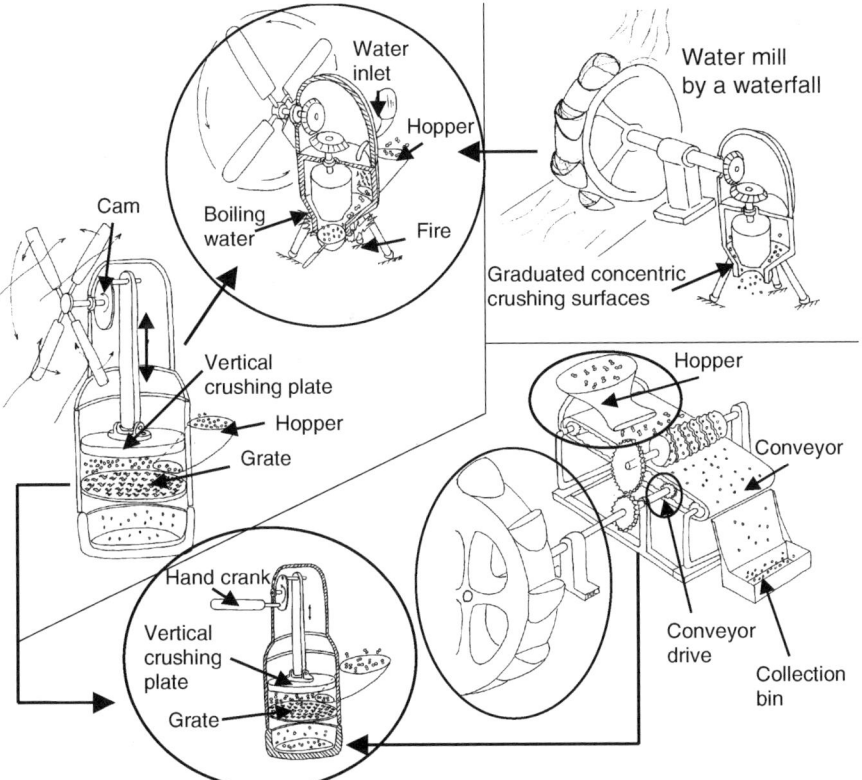

Fig. 15. Second phase of the "6-3-5" method: application to the peanut shelling design problem (Table IV).

method) as compared to allowing each participant to rotationally view a subset of all ideas (similar to "6-3-5" or C-Sketch). The second factor used in the Linsey, Green et al. experiment controlled how the participants could communicate: written words only, sketches only, or a combination of written words and sketches. This experiment showed rotational viewing of a subset of ideas resulted in a greater quantity of nonredundant ideas. This effect was significant when the conditions containing "sketches only" were removed, Fig. 16. Data from the "sketches only" conditions showed a very different pattern of results likely due to the poor quality of sketches produced by the engineering undergraduates. Without any verbal annotations, the sketches alone were difficult to interpret.

Shah et al. (2001) also investigated a set of techniques that vary the proportion of ideas displayed to the participants. In this study, the complete

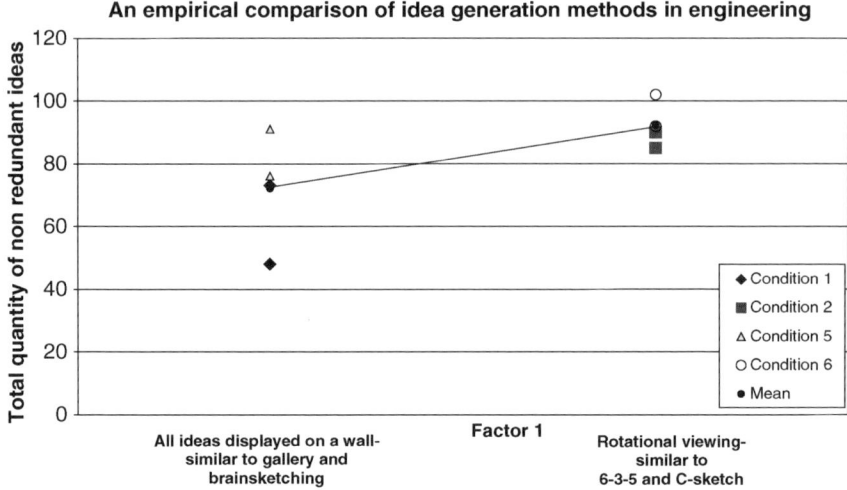

Fig. 16. Results from an empirical comparison of idea generation methods.

techniques of C-Sketch, "6-3-5," and Gallery method were studied in their entirety, coupling the representation of ideas with the method for displaying ideas. C-Sketch (sketches with rotational viewing) outperformed Gallery method for the novelty and variety of ideas generated and was similar for the quality of ideas. Gallery method produced ideas with greater quality, novelty, and variety than "6-3-5" (written words with rotational viewing). Quantity of idea results was not given.

Ward's work (1995) presents an interesting hypothesis for some of the results being seen from group concept generation studies in engineering. Ward (1995) has shown that categorization plays a critical role when developing new ideas. His work also illustrates the limitations categorization can place on creative idea generation. It is possible that by allowing participants to view a greater number of ideas during an idea generation session they tend to categorize the problem in a particular way thus limiting the number of ideas generated. Linsey, Green et al. believed the reduction in ideas due to gallery style viewing was caused by participants paying less attention to the ideas but the hypothesis based on Ward's work cannot be ruled out.

Other empirical results present interesting phenomena (Bays & Leifer, 1996; Fricke, 1996; Goldschmidt, 1996, 1998; Ho, 2001; Stauffer & Ullman, 1988; Waldron & Waldron, 1988). Categorization of a design problem as innovative has been shown to lead to design fixation. Senior mechanical engineering students were shown to fixate on designs with certain characteristics, whereas industrial design students did not fixate on innovative designs in either the mechanical realm or industrial design (Jansson & Smith, 1991; Purcell & Gero, 1996).

D. THEORY OF INVENTIVE PROBLEM SOLVING

Using the TIPS' generalized engineering parameters (Table VII), a straightforward process may be developed for generating concepts. The (simplified TIPS) process begins with a functional description or other representations. From the functional description (in addition to benchmarks, engineering specifications, product architecture, and other data), conflicts are identified in the design task. These conflicts are then stated as contradictions in the *generalized parameters*, or *engineering parameters*, where a generalized parameter is a controllable variable or set of variables that embody a physical effect in a product. Design principles are then applied to suggest ways in which the conflict may be resolved. The resulting concepts are refined with known physical effects and analogies to existing solutions. The final step is to refine the concepts, from the principles and effects, into a concrete geometry.

Tables XI and XII provide necessary data to execute this simplified TIPS process. Table VII lists the 39 generalized parameters for describing product performance metrics. Tables XI and XII list the TIPS' design principles with corresponding definitions. The generalized parameters and design principles are derived from the large quantity of patents studied as part of TIPS. For a design problem categorized as a conflict (with the generalized parameters), applicable design principles are chosen that represent typical inventive solutions to the conflict.

As an example application, let us consider the evolution of an iron product for smoothing the wrinkles from clothing. An important function of an iron is to transfer force to the clothing to aid in removing wrinkles. It is equally important to import the human hand and reduce the force on the user (comfortable use). The conflict is straightforward; we desire a heavy iron to remove wrinkles, but we do not want a heavy iron due to the impact on ergonomics.

Stated in generalized parameters (Table VII), the conflict is with regard to the force (#10) versus weight of moving object (#2). Using a matrix (not shown) that relates the conflict to the common solutions principles, the conflict of force and weight of moving object leads to the TIPS' principles of "8, 1, 37, 18" for application to the design problem. Reviewing each of these design principles in Tables XI and XII, it is suggested that a counterweight be added, that the design be divided into independent parts (mass of iron versus user interface), that thermal expansion be added, or that mechanical vibration (such as resonance, piezovibration, ultrasonics, or electromagnetic vibrations) be added to the concept. These suggestions may lead to a levered

TABLE XI

TIPS' Design Principles (1–20) to Solve Engineering Conflicts

1	Principle of segmentation	Divide the object into independent parts that are easy to disassemble, increase the degree of segmentation as much as possible
2	Principle of removal	Remove either the disturbing part or the necessary part from the object
3	Principle of local quality	Change the object's or environment's structure from homogeneous to nonhomogeneous. Let different parts of the object carry different functions
4	Principle of asymmetry	Make object asymmetrical or increase asymmetry
5	Principle of joining	Merge homogeneous objects or those intended for contiguous operations
6	Principle of universality	Let one object perform several different functions. Remove redundant objects
7	The nesting principle	Place one object inside another, which in turn is placed in a third, and so on, or, let an object pass through a cavity into another
8	Principle of counterweight	Attach an object with lifting power or use the interactions with the environment, for example, aerodynamic lift
9	Principle of preliminary counteraction	Perform a counteraction to the desired action before the desired action is performed
10	Principle of preliminary action	Perform the required action before it is needed, or set up the objects such that they can perform their action immediately when required
11	Principle of introducing protection in advance	Compensate for the low reliability of an object by introducing protections against accidents before the action is performed
12	Principle of equipotentiality	Change the conditions such that the object does not need to be moved up or down in the potential field
13	Principle of opposite solution	Implement the opposite action of what is specified. Make a moving part fixed and the fixed part mobile. Turn the object upside down
14	Principle of spheroidality	Switch from linear to curvilinear paths, from flat to spherical surfaces, and so on. Make use of rollers, ball bearings, spirals. Switch from direct to rotating motion. Use centrifugal force
15	Principle of dynamism	Make the object or environment able to change to become optimal at any stage of work. Make the object consist of parts that can move relative to each other. If the object is fixed, make it movable
16	Principle of partial or excessive action	If 100% is unobtainable, try for slightly less or slightly more

TABLE XI *continued*

17	Principle of moving into a new dimension	Increase the object's degree of freedom. Use a multilayered assembly instead of a single layer. Incline the object or turn it on its side. Use the other side of an area
18	Use of mechanical vibrations	Make the object vibrate. Increase the frequency of vibration. Use resonance, piezovibrations, ultrasonic, or electromagnetic vibrations
19	Principle of periodic action	Use periodic or pulsed actions, change periodicity. Use pauses between impulses to change the effect
20	Principle of uninterrupted useful effect	Keep all parts of the object constantly operating at full power. Remove test or set up runs

TABLE XII

TIPS' DESIGN PRINCIPLES (21–40) TO SOLVE ENGINEERING CONFLICTS

21	Principle of rushing through	Carry out a process or individual stages of a process at high speed
22	Principle of turning harm into good	Use harmful factor to obtain a positive effect. Remove a harmful factor by combining it with other harmful factors. Strengthen a harmful factor to the extent where it ceases to be harmful
23	The feedback principle	Introduce feedback. If there already is feedback, change it
24	The go between principle	Use an intermediary object to transfer or transmit the action. Merge the object temporarily with another object that can be easily taken away
25	The self-service principle	The object should service and repair itself. Use waste products from the object to produce the desired actions
26	The copying principle	Instead of unavailable. Complicated or fragile objects use a simplified cheap copy. Replace an object by its optical copy, make use of scale effects. If visible copies are used, switch to infrared or ultraviolet copies
27	Cheap short life instead of expensive longevity	Replace an expensive object that has long life with many cheap objects having shorter life
28	Replacement of a mechanical pattern	Replace a mechanical pattern by an optical, acoustical, or odor pattern. Use electrical, magnetic, or electromagnetic fields to interact with the object. Switch from fixed to movable fields changing over time. Go from unstructured to structured fields
29	Use of pneumatic or hydraulic solutions	Use gaseous or liquid parts of an object instead of solid parts

continues

TABLE XII *continued*

30 Using flexible membranes and fine membranes	
31 Using porous materials	Make the object porous or use porous elements, for example, inserts, covers, and so on. If the object is already porous, fill the pores in advance with some useful substance
32 The principle of using color	Change the color or translucency of an object or its surroundings. Use colored additives to observe certain objects or processes. If such additives are already used, employ luminescence traces
33 The principle of homogeneity	Interacting objects should be made of the same material or material with identical properties
34 The principle of discarding and regenerating parts	Once a part has fulfilled its purpose and is no longer necessary, it should automatically be discarded or disappear, for example, evaporate, or change its shape. Parts that become useful after a while should be automatically generated
35 Changing the aggregate state of an object	Change state, for example, solid to liquid. Use pseudostates and intermediary states, for example, elastic solid bodies
36 The use of phase changes	Use phenomena occurring in phase changes, for example, use of volume changes, heat dissipation, and so on
37 Application of thermal expansion	Use expansion or contraction of materials by heat. Use materials with different thermal expansion coefficients
38 Using strong oxidation agents	Replace air with enriched air or replace enriched air with oxygen. Treat the air or oxygen with ionizing radiation. Use ionized oxygen. Use ozone
39 Using an inert atmosphere	Replace the normal environment with an inert one or a vacuum
40 Using composite materials	Switch from homogeneous materials to composites

counterweight in the first case, a foot operated sandwich iron in the second case, and water spray in the third case.

For the last design principle, mechanical vibration may be added with an eccentric weight that would increase the force into the clothing, while reducing the carrying weight of the iron. This solution creates a conflict, however, since the user, during the operation of the iron, will also feel the vibration forces over clothing. Adding a vibration absorber between the hand and the vibration source in the clothing may solve this conflict. Alternatively, a different vibration source can be applied that may vibrate the clothing near its resonance frequency using low input amplitudes. An example would be to use ultrasonics or piezovibrations of water molecules or fabric particles within the clothing. These applications of generalized parameter categories and TIPS principles demonstrate potential outcomes of the concept generation process, perhaps indicating the next generation of clothes iron.

E. DESIGN-BY-ANALOGY

Design-by-analogy, analogies to nature, analogous products, and design reuse, are noted methods for conceptual design (e.g., French, 1996; Gordon, 1961; Hacco & Shu, 2002; Otto & Wood, 2001; Pahl & Beitz, 1996; Pugh, 1991). Visual or functional similarity can be found based in these methods. Figure 17 illustrates a number of interesting design-by-analogy examples, such as a lamp, being aesthetically similar to the shape of a flower or a hydra. The Sydney Opera housed is also based on a visual similarity to the yachts in the surrounding harbor (Craig, 2001). Analogy can also lead to innovative functional designs. An analogy based on a snake resulted in an innovative product, the snake lamp (Giesecke, 2004). As a new device is developed, it is frequently based on previous products that serve a similar function. When the first train

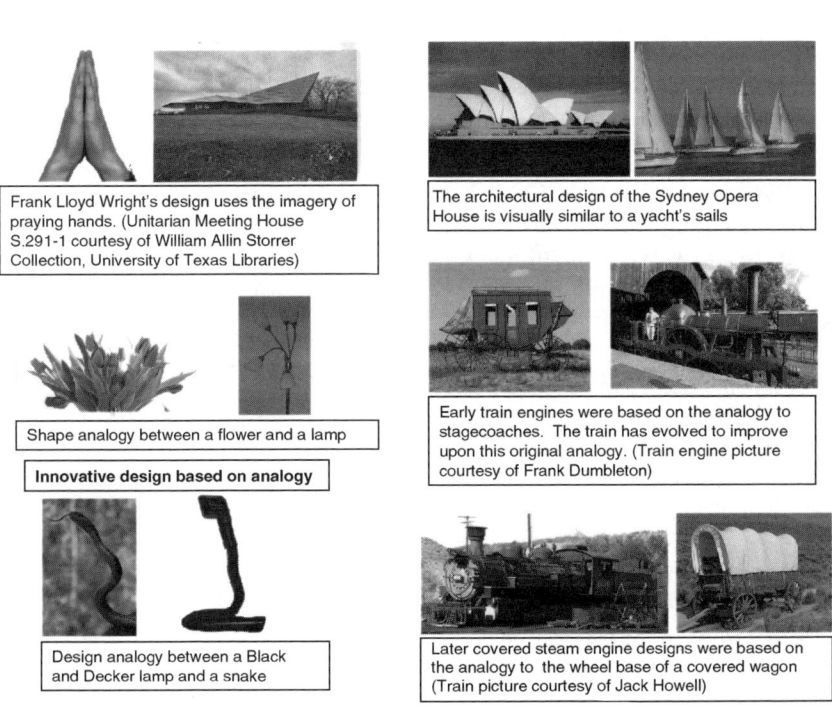

Fig. 17. Examples of design-by-analogy.

engines were developed, they were based on an analogous product, the stage coach (Ward, 1995).

In psychology, three areas of substantial research form a solid foundation for understanding design-by-analogy: analogical reasoning, naïve physics, and reasoning with diagrams. A significant amount of work has been carried out in psychology to understand the cognitive processes people use for creating and understanding analogies (e.g., Blanchette & Dunbar, 2000, 2001; Dunbar, 1997; Elio & Anderson, 1981; Falkenhainer, Forbus, & Gentner, 1989; Gentner, Holyoak, & Kokinov, 2001; Gentner & Markman, 1997; Gentner, et al., 1997; Holyoak & Thagard, 1989; Hummel & Holyoak, 1997; Namy & Gentner, 2002; Sieck, Quinn, & Schooler, 1999). This work demonstrates that people are able to find similarities between domains on the basis of shared relationships among components. Notice that this description of what defines an analogy is domain general. Consistent with this description, most research has focused on factors that influence reasoning by analogy in a domain-general way (Markman & Gentner, 2001).

Design in an engineering context also requires understanding of domain-specific reasoning processes. Psychology recognizes the importance of understanding the domain-specific processes that create representations, but much less work has been devoted to understanding these processes because they require focusing on the content of particular domains (Chalmers, French, & Hofstadter, 1992). There has been some work in cognitive science on naïve physics, which seeks to understand how people reason about the world around them with inaccurate and incomplete models of the physics (e.g., Forbus, 1984; Kuipers, 1994; White & Frederiksen, 1990; Williams, Hollan, & Stevens, 1983). An important contribution from naïve physics to our work is the understanding that humans are good at reasoning qualitatively about the physical world and predictions. The work in this area also demonstrates that reasoning is difficult when the particular quantitative values of ratios between quantities are important for reasoning. By understanding the cognitive process and the areas where humans need assistance, better methods can be developed to support design-by-analogy in product development. A third relevant area of research is on reasoning with diagrams. This work has brought about a number of insights including a set of guidelines for developing suitable and useful diagrams (e.g., Cheng, 2002; Hegarty & Just, 1993; Hegarty, Meyer, & Narayanan, 2002; Novick & Hurley, 2001; Pedone, Hummel, & Holyoak, 2001; Stenning, 2002).

Consider an example method to illustrate design-by-analogy. This method uses the concepts of functional models and classification (McAdams, Stone, & Wood, 1998, 1999, 2000). Functional models map input flows of energies, materials, and signals (information) to the corresponding output states. Such models were extended to formal representations known as *functional and flow bases* (Tables II and III). These bases are a formal classification language, which represent the range of functions and flows that occur in products or inventions. Based on the functions and the customer needs of a given product, analogous and nonobvious products can be explored. A case study of a pickup winder for a guitar is shown in Fig. 18 (McAdams & Wood, 2000). A pickup is an electromagnetic device with thousands of small-gauge wire windings as part of an electric guitar. Obvious analogies for the pickup winder include a fishing reel and a bobbin winder on a sewing machine. In addition to the obvious analogies, the functional and flow bases also showed an electric vegetable peeler as being a similar product. The analogy to a vegetable peeler leads to an innovative design (prototype shown in Fig. 18).

F. INSIGHTS FOR ENGINEERING FROM THE CATEGORIZATION LITERATURE

Current psychological research into categorization provides important insight, guidance, and empirical support for current design methods and future research. The research explores a variety of problems including open-ended idea generation (e.g., Ward, 1995), analysis in physics (e.g., Chi, Feltovich, & Glaser, 1981) and algebra (e.g., Hinsely, Hayes, & Simon, 1978). This research has not been applied directly to practical engineering problems but has explored the typical types of problems engineers face. Much of the applicable literature focuses on comparing experts and novices in a particular area thus offering deeper understanding of the cognitive processes of engineers (experts). Categorization is an important process in problem solving. The research supplies insights into the superior performance of expert problem solvers (e.g., Chi et al., 1981; Proffitt, Coley, & Medin, 2000). Experts solving physics problems often begin with a qualitative analysis (Chi et al.,1981). This strategy is likely to be true of engineers. The expertise of an engineer is frequently within a small area of engineering such as a particular discipline of engineering (i.e., mechanical) and a particular area (i.e., mechanics of materials) or industry (i.e., automotive). Variation in the type of expertise and experience level changes how items and problems are categorized (e.g., Chi et al., 1981). Experts often categorize problems based on deep structural similarities as opposed to irrelevant contextual similarities (i.e., Chi et al., 1981). Experts will use contextual information when surface similarities coexists with deep structural similarities thus aiding the processes (Blessing, & Ross, 1996). In addition to experience, categorization can be influenced by goals with organization around the ideals for a particular category (Barsalou, 1985; Lynch, Coley, & Medin, 2000; Medin, Lynch, Coley, & Atran, 1997).

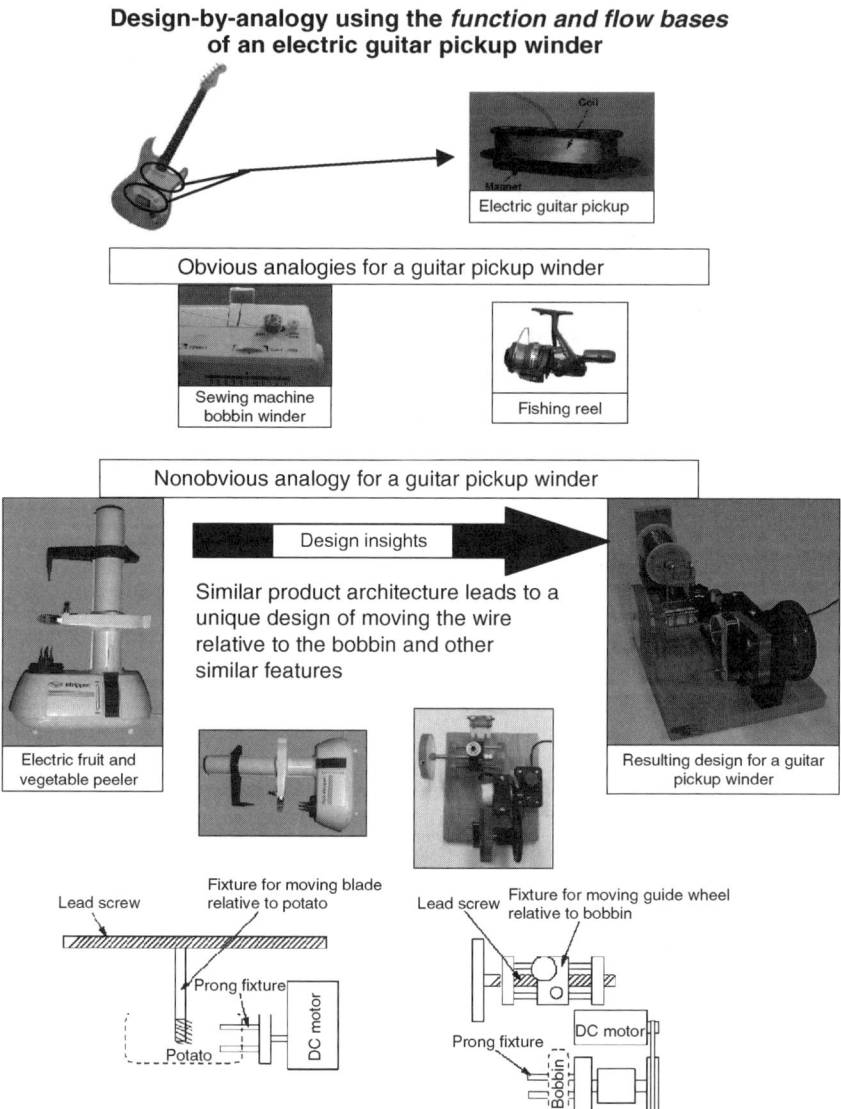

Fig. 18. A nonobvious design analogy between a pickup winder and an electric vegetable peeler resulting from functional models and formalisms known as functional and flow bases.

Ward's work (1995) shows that the categorization of a problem tends to structure the solutions and thus limit the solution space deemed appropriate. Corollary concepts exist in idea generation techniques such as Progressive Abstractions, Reversals, Why Method and Assumption Reversals (VanGundy, 1988), which seek to illicit and validate various assumptions (limitations) being made during the idea generation process.

V. Discussion and "Golden Nuggets"

We have explored categories and their representations in enhancing the generation of concepts for product development or engineering design problems. The representations discussed in this chapter provide the scaffolding for redescribing design problems for innovation access. The corresponding concept generation methods employ these descriptions to realize the form solutions to real-world, societal problems. These form solutions need only be engineered and implemented in their respective marketplaces.

By no means have we covered all possible representation schemes or types of categorization. Many implicit and explicit representations exist in the literature of concept generation. We have likewise not documented the hundreds of reported concept generation methods in the open literature. Many methods exist, and numerous variants of these methods are advocated to assist in the development of innovations in various marketplaces.

Assuming, however, that the categories, their representations, and the associated concept generation methods are illustrative and illuminating, we have a basis for discussion and analysis. The focus of our discussion here is on the postulation of open research questions. Consider the following research questions, generated from the topical coverage of this chapter:

- What is the range of different representations of categorization?
- What level and type of information should be categorized to enhance the art of design?
- What is the minimal information to create these enhancements?
- Are other types of representations of greater utility? How can physical artifacts and "props" be used as alternative representations? Does the flaring of other senses besides visual or auditory lead to enhancements in idea creation?
- What are the roles of colors, tactile discriminates, and personal style in the creation process?
- How are categorical representations to be used, most effectively, in conjunction with concept generation techniques?
- What order of concept generation techniques will lead to the greatest breadth and diversity of potential solutions?

- Can the outcomes of one-concept generation method be used as the seeds for another or a sequence of other-concept generation methods?
- How do we measure, accurately and repeatably, generated concepts to *real-world* engineering problems for their uniqueness, variety, potential, and practical implementation?
- What is the role of computation or computer-assisted tools in category representation and implementing concept generation methods?
- What pedagogical advancements are needed to utilize categorization, representations, and their employment in concept generation? How can personality typing be used to advance the teaching of concept generation? What is the role of hands-on activities in learning concept generation methods?
- What forms of analogical representation are most useful for innovative design?
- What are the fundamental and underlying principles that make analogies useful to a designer?
- What benefits are there to physical models in design-by-analogy? Why do engineers use them? What types of problems do they highlight? How do they assist designers in visualizing analogies, and what limitations do they add? What is the effect on design-by-analogy of a static model compared to a dynamic model or a full working mock-up?
- What are the effects of different manipulative media in the idea generation process? Which ones lead to design fixation, and which ones are most beneficial for concept development?

We end here with these open research questions. While we hope that the discussions of product development, category representations, and concept generation methods are thought provoking and a genesis for collegial debate, the research questions are the fundamental result of this chapter. They are motivated by current literature and the technical material of this chapter. They represent opportunities to advance our understanding of the art of design. They represent future challenges and collaborations between the fields of engineering and psychology. They embody the potential for learnable principles for designers to become the next Edisonian contributors.

Acknowledgments

The work reported in this document was made possible, in part, by the University of Texas at Austin College of Engineering, and the Cullen Trust Endowed Professorship in Engineering No. 1. We wish to acknowledge Dr. Art Markman of the Department of Psychology at The University of Texas. Our discussions with Dr. Markman in the area of design-by-analogy have been illuminating and his expertise in cognitive psychology has greatly enhanced our vision in this area. We also wish to acknowledge the contribution of Vikramjit Singh for his assistant in the development of the graphics for this chapter. Any opinions, findings, or recommendations are those of authors and do not necessarily reflect the views of the sponsors.

REFERENCES

Adams, J. L. (1986). *Conceptual blockbusting: A guide to better ideas.* Reading, MA: Addison-Wesley.

Akiyama, K. (1991). *Function analysis: Systematic improvement of quality performance.* Cambridge, MA: Productivity Press.

Altshuller, G. S. (1984). *Creativity as an exact science.* Luxembourg: Gordon and Breach Publishers.

Baldwin, N. (1995). *Edison inventing the century.* New York: Hyperion.

Barsalou, L. W. (1985). Ideals, central tendency, and frequency of instantiation as determinants of graded structure in categories. *Journal of Experimental Psychology: Learning, Memory, & Cognition, 11*(4), 629–654.

Bays, V., & Leifer, L. J. (1996). Understanding information management in conceptual design. In N. Cross, H. Christiaans, and K. Dorst (Eds.), *Analyzing design activity* (pp. 151–168). Chichester, UK: John Wiley & Sons.

Blanchette, I., & Dunbar, K. (2000). How analogies are generated: The roles of structural and superficial similarity. *Memory & Cognition, 28*(1), 108–124.

Blanchette, I., & Dunbar, K. (2001). Analogy use in naturalistic settings: The influence of audience, emotion, and goals. *Memory & Cognition, 29*(5), 730–735.

Blessing, S. B., & Ross, B. H. (1996). Content effects in problem categorization and problem solving. *Journal of Experimental Psychology: Learning, Memory, & Cognition, 22*(3), 792–810.

Chalmers, D. J., French, R. M., & Hofstadter, D. R. (1992). High-level perception, representation, and analogy: A critique of artificial intelligence methodology. *Journal of Experimental & Theoretical Artificial Intelligence, 4,* 185–211.

Cheng, P. C. H. (2002). Electrifying diagrams for learning: Principles for complex representational systems. *Cognitive Science, 26,* 685–736.

Chi, M. T. H., Feltovich, P. J., & Glaser, R. (1981). Categorization and representation of physics problems by experts and novices. *Cognitive Science, 5,* 121–152.

Craig, D. L. (2001). Perceptual simulation and analogical reasoning in design. ProQuest Digital Dissertations, Georgia Institute of Technology.

DeBono, E. (1967). *New think: The use of lateral thinking in the generation of new ideas.* New York: Basic Books.

Domb, E., & Slocum, M. (Eds.) (1998). *The TRIZ Journal.* Retrieved from http://www.triz-journal.com/

Dunbar, K. (1997). How scientists think: On-line creativity and conceptual change in science. In T. B. Ward, S. M. Smith, and J. Vaid (Eds.), *Creative thought: An investigation of conceptual structures and processes* (pp. 461–493). Washington, DC: American Psychological Association.

Dyer, F. L., Martin, T. C., & Meadowcroft, W. H. (1929). *Edison: His life and inventions.* New York and London: Harper & Brothers Publishers.

Elio, R., & Anderson, J. R. (1981). The effects of category generalizations and instance similarity on schema abstraction. *Journal of Experimental Psychology: Human Learning and Memory, 7*(6), 397–417.

Falkenhainer, B. F., Forbus, K. D., & Gentner, D. (1989). The structure mapping engine: Algorithm and examples. *Artificial Intelligence, 41*(1), 1–63.

Fey, V., & Rivin, E. (1996). TRIZ: A new approach to innovative engineering and problem solving. *Target, Association for Manufacturing Excellence, 12*(4), 7–13.

Fjermestdad, J., & Hiltz, S. R. (1998). An assessment of group support systems experimental research: Methodology and results. *Journal of Management Information Systems, 15*(3), 7–149.

Forbus, K. D. (1984). Qualitative process theory. *Artificial Intelligence, 24*, 85–168.

Franke, H.-J. (1975). Methodische schritte beim klaren konstruktiver aufgabenstellungen. *Konstruktion, 27*, 395–402.

French, M. (1996). *Conceptual design*. London, UK: Springer-Verlag.

Fricke, G. (1996). Successful individual approaches in engineering design. *Research in Engineering Design—Theory, Applications and Concurrent Engineering, 8*(3), 151–165.

Gentner, D., & Markman, A. B. (1997). Structural alignment in analogy and similarity. *American Psychologist, 52*, 45–56.

Gentner, D., Brem, S., Ferguson, R., Wolff, P., Markman, A. B., & Forbus, K. (1997). Analogy and creativity in the works of Johannes Kepler. In T. B. Ward, S. M. Smith, and J. Vaid (Eds.), *Creative thought: An investigation of conceptual structures and processes* (pp. 403–459). Washington, DC: American Psychological Association.

Gentner, D., Holyoak, K. J.,, & Kokinov, B. (Eds.) (2001). *The analogical mind*. Cambridge, MA: The MIT Press.

Giesecke, F. (2004). *SnakeLight™, Case Study*. Retrieved January, 2004, from http://cwx.prenhall.com/bookbind/pubbooks/giesecke/chapter0/deluxe.html.

Goldschmidt, G. (1996). The designer as a team of one. In N. Cross, H. Christiaans, and K. Dorst (Eds.), *Analyzing design activity* (pp. 65–92). Chichester, UK: Wiley.

Goldschmidt, G. (1998). Contents and structure in design reasoning. *Design Issues, 14*(3), 85–100.

Gordon, W. (1961). *Synectics*. New York, NY: Harper & Row.

Greer, J., Jensen, D., & Wood, K. (2004). Effort flow analysis: A methodology for directed product evolution. *Journal of Design Studies, 25*(2), 103–214.

Greer, J., Wood, J., Jensen, D., & Wood, K. L. (2002). Guidelines for product evolution using effort flow analysis: Results of an empirical study. *ASME Design Theory and Methodology Conference, September 2002*.

Gryskiewicz, S. (1999). *Positive turbulence: Developing climate for creativity, innovation, and renewal*. San Francisco: Jossey-Bass.

Gryskiewicz, S. S. (1988). Trial by fire in an industrial setting: A practical evaluation of three creative problem-solving techniques. In K. Gronhaug and G. Kaufmann (Eds.), *Innovation: A cross-disciplinary perspective* (pp. 205–232). Oslo, Norway: Norwegian University Press.

Hacco, E., & Shu, L. H. (2002). Biomimetic concept generation applied to design for remanufacture. In *Proceedings of the DETC 2002, ASME 2002 Design Engineering Technical Conferences and Computer and Information in Engineering Conference*. Montreal, QuebecCanada.

Hegarty, M., & Just, M. A. (1993). Constructing mental models of machines from text and diagrams. *Journal of Memory and Language, 32*, 717–742.

Hegarty, M., Meyer, B., & Narayanan, N. (2002). *Diagrammatic representation and inference*. London: Springer.

Hinsely, D. A., Hayes, J. R., & Simon, H. A. (1978). From words to equations: Meaning and representation in algebra word problems. In P. A. Capenter and M. A. Just (Eds.), *Cognitive processes in comprehension*. Hillsdale, NJ: Erlbaum.

Hirtz, J., Stone, R., McAdams, D., Szykman, S., & Wood, K. (2002). A functional basis for engineering design: Reconciling and evolving previous efforts. *Journal of Research in Engineering Design, 13*(2), 65–82.

Ho, C.-H. (2001). Some phenomena of problem decomposition strategy for design thinking: differences between novices and experts. *Design Studies, 22*(1), 27–45.

Holyoak, K. J., & Thagard, P. (1989). Analogical mapping by constraint satisfaction. *Cognitive Science, 13*, 295–355.

Hubka, V., & Eder, W. E. (1996). *Design science: Introduction to the needs, scope and organization of engineering design knowledge*. Berlin: Springer-Verlag.

Hummel, J. E., & Holyoak, K. J. (1997). Distributed representations of structure: A theory of analogical access and mapping. *Psychological Review, 104*(3), 427–466.

Hundal, M. (1990). A Systematic method for developing function structures, solutions, and concept variants. *Mechanical Machine Theory, 25*(3), 243–256.

Ivanov, G. (1994). *Creative formulas, or how to invent*. (in Russian). Russia: M. Prosvenia Publishing.

Jansson, D., & Smith, S. (1991). Design fixation. *Design Studies, 12*(1), 3–11.

Jensen, D. D., Greer, J. L., Wood, K. L., & Nowack, M. L. (2000). Force flow analysis: Opportunities for creative component combination. *ASME International Mechanical Engineering Congress and Expo,* Orlando, FL.

Krager, J., Moody, C., Qureshi, A., Porlier, J., & Singh, V. (2005). Automated assistive guitar: Orchestrating technology integration in music therapy. *Proceedings of the RESNA (Rehabilitation Engineering Society of North America) Annual Conference,* June 2005.

Kuipers, B. (1994). *Qualitative reasoning: Modeling and simulation with incomplete knowledge*. Cambridge, MA: The MIT Press.

Lefever, D. (1995). *Integrating design for assemblability techniques and reverse engineering*. Master's Thesis, The University of Texas, Austin, Texas.

Lefever, D., & Wood, K. (1996). Design for assembly techniques in reverse engineering and redesign. *Proceedings of ASME DETC DTM '96,* Irvine, CA.

Lewis, A. C., Sadosky, T. L., & Connolly, T. (1975). The effectiveness of group brainstorming in engineering problem solving. *IEEE Transactions on Engineering Management, EM-22*(3), 119–127.

Linsey, J. S., Green, M. G., Murphy, J., Wood, K. L., & Markman, A. B. (2005a). Collaborating to success: An experimental study of group idea generation techniques. *Proceeding of ASME Design Theory and Methodology Conference 2005,* Long Beach, CA.

Linsey, J. S., Van Wie, M., Green, M. G., Wood, K. L., & Stone, R. (2005b). Functional representations in conceptual design: A first study in experimental design and evaluation. *Proceedings of 2005 American Society for Engineering Education Annual Conference,* Portland, OR.

Lynch, E. B., Coley, J. D., & Medin, D. L. (2000). Tall is typical: Central tendency, ideal dimensions, and graded category structure among tree experts and novices. *Memory & Cognition, 28*(1), 41–50.

Markman, A., & Gentner, D. (2001). Thinking. *Annual Review of Psychology, 52*, 223–247.

McAdams, D. A., Stone, R. B., & Wood, K. L. (1998). Understanding product similarity using customer needs. *Proceeding of the DETC'98, 1998 ASEM Design Engineering Technical Conferences,* Atlanta, GA.

McAdams, D. A., Stone, R. B., & Wood, K. L. (1999). Functional interdependence and product similarity based on customer needs. *Research in Engineering Design, 11*, 1–19.

McAdams, D. A., & Wood, K. L. (2000). Quantitative measures for design by analogy. *Proceedings of the DETC'00, 2000 ASME Design Engineering Technical Conferences,* Baltimore, MD.

Medin, D. L., Lynch, E. B., Coley, J. D., & Atran, S. (1997). Categorization and reasoning among tree experts: Do all roads lead to Rome? *Cognitive Psychology, 32*(1), 49–96.

Michalko, M. (1991). *Thinkertoys: A handbook of business creativity*. Berkley, CA: Ten Speed Press.

Michalko, M. (2001). *Cracking creativity: The secrets of creative genius*. Berkley, CA: Ten Speed Press.

Miles, L. D. (1972). *Techniques of value analysis and engineering*. New York: McGraw-Hill.

Mullen, B., Johnson, C., & Salas, E. (1991). Productivity loss in brainstorming groups: A meta-analytic integration. *Basic and Applied Social Psychology, 12*(1), 3–23.

Namy, L. L., & Gentner, D. (2002). Making a silk purse out of two sow's ears: Young children's use of comparison in category learning. *Journal of Experimental Psychology: General, 131*(1), 5–15.

Nike, ID Individually Designed (2004). Retrieved 2004, from http://www.nikeid.com

Novick, L. R., & Hurley, S. M. (2001). To matrix, network, or hierarchy: That is the question. *Cognitive Psychology, 42*(2), 158–216.

Osborn, A. (1957). *Applied imagination*. New York, NY: Scribner.

Otto, K. N., & Wood, K. L. (2001). *Product design: Techniques in reverse engineering, systematic design, and new product development*. NY: Prentice-Hall.

Otto, K. N., & Wood, K. L. (2005). *Product design: Techniques in reverse engineering, systematic design, and new product development*. Beijing:Pearson Education Asia Limited and Publishing House of Electronics Industry, Simplified Chinese Edition.

Pahl, G., & Beitz, W. (1996). *Engineering design—A systematic approach* (2nd ed.). London: Springer.

Paulus, P. B., & Yang, H. C. (2000). Idea generation in groups: A basis for creativity in organizations. *Organizational Behavior and Human Decision Processes, 82*(1), 76–87.

Pedone, R., Hummel, J., & Holyoak, K. (2001). The use of diagrams in analogical problem solving. *Memory & Cognition, 29*(2), 214–221.

Piller, F. T., Reichald, R., Möslein, K., & Lohse, C. (2000). Broker Models for Mass Customization. *Proceedings AMCIS,* Long Beach, CA.

Pine, B. J. (1993). *Mass customization: The new frontier in business competition*. Boston, MA: Harvard Business School Press.

Proffitt, J. B., Coley, J. D., & Medin, D. L. (2000). Expertise and category-based induction. *Journal of Experimental Psychology: Learning, Memory, & Cognition, 26*(4), 811–828.

Pugh, S. (1991). *Total design*. New York, NY: Addison-Wesley Publishers.

Purcell, A. T., & Gero, J. S. (1996). Design and other types of fixation. *Design Studies, 17*(4), 363–383.

Rajan, P., Van Wie, M., Campbell, M., Wood, K., & Otto, K. (2005). An empirical foundation for product flexibility. *Design Studies, 26*(4), 405–438.

Rajan, P. K., Van Wie, M., Otto, K., Wood, K., & Campbell, M. (2003). Design for flexibility—measures and guidelines. *International Conference on Engineering Design ICED 2003.*

Reichwald, R., Piller, F. T., & Möslein, K. (2000). Information as a critical success factor for mass customization. *ASAC-IFSAM 2000 Conference,* Montreal, Quebec, Canada.

Rohrbach, B. (1969). Kreativ nach regeln—Methode 635, eine neue technik zum lösen von problemen. *Absatzwirtschaft, 12,* 73–75.

Römer, A., Weißhahn, G., & Hacker, W. (2001). Effort-saving product representations in design—results of a questionnaire survey. *Design Studies, 22*(6), 473–490.

Shah, J. J. (1998). Experimental investigation of progressive idea generation techniques in engineering design. *Proceedings of the DETC'98, 1998 ASME Design Engineering Technical Conferences,* Atlanta, GA.

Shah, J. J., Vargas-Hernández, N., Summers, J. S., & Kulkarni, S. (2001). Collaborative Sketching (C-Sketch)—An idea generation technique for engineering design. *Journal of Creative Behavior, 35*(3), 168–198.

Sieck, W. R., Quinn, C. N., & Schooler, J. W. (1999). Justification effects on the judgment of analogy. *Memory & Cognition, 27*(5), 844–855.

Sobek, D., & Ward, A. (1996). Principles from Toyota's set-based concurrent engineering process. *Proceedings of the ASME Design Theory and Methodology Conference,* Irvine, CA.

Stauffer, L. A., & Ullman, D. G. (1988). Comparison of the results of empirical studies into the mechanical design process. *Design Studies, 9*(2), 107–114.

Stenning, K. (2002). *Seeing reason: Image and language in learning to think.* New York: Oxford University Press.

Stone, R., & Wood, K. (1999). Development of a functional basis for design. *Proceeding of DETC'99, 1999 ASME Design Engineering Technical Conferences,* Las Vegas, Nevada.

Stone, R., & Wood, K. (2000). Development of a functional basis for design. *Journal of Mechanical Design, 122*(4), 359–370.

Sushkov, V., Mars, N., & Wognum, P. (1995). Introduction to TIPS: Theory for creative design. *Journal of AI Engineering, 9*(3), 177–189.

ThinkSpace: Peanut Sheller. (2004). Retrieved March 2004, from http://www.thinkcycle.org/tcspace/tspace?tspace_id=41963

The Thomas A. Edison Papers. (2005). Retrieved August 27, 2005, from http://edison.rutgers.edu/andhttp://edison.rutgers.edu/about.htm

Ullman, D. G. (1996). *The mechanical design process* (2nd ed.). New York: McGraw-Hill.

Ullman, D. G. (2003). *The mechanical design process* (3rd ed.). New York: McGraw-Hill.

Ulrich, K. T., & Eppinger, S. D. (2000). *Product design and development* (2nd ed.). Boston and New York: Irwin McGraw-Hill (http://www.ulrich-eppinger.net).

Ulrich, K. T., & Eppinger, S. D. (2004). *Product design and development.* Boston and New York: McGraw-Hill.

Unitarian Meeting House S.291-1. (1947). William Allin Storrer Collection, The Alexander Architectural Archive, The University of Texas Libraries, The University of Texas at Austin.

Utterback, J. (1996). *Mastering the dynamics of innovation.* Boston: Harvard Business Press.

Van der Lugt, R. (2000). Developing a graphic tool for creative problem solving in design groups. *Design Studies, 21,* 505–522.

Van der Lugt, R. (2002). Brainsketching and how it differs from Brainstorming. *Creativity & Innovation Management, 11*(1), 43–54.

VanGundy, A. B. (1988). *Techniques of structured problem solving* (2nd ed.). New York, NY: Van Nostrand Reinhold Company.

Vidal, R., Mulet, E., & Gómez-Senent, E. (2004). Effectiveness of the means of expression in creative problem-solving in design groups. *Journal of Engineering Design, 15*(3), 285–298.

Waldron, M. B., & Waldron, K. J. (1988). A time sequence study of a complex mechanical system design. *Design Studies, 9*(2), 95–106.

Ward, T. B. (1995). What's old about new ideas? In S. M. Smith, T. B. Ward, and R. A. Finke (Eds.), *The creative cognition approach* (pp. 157–178). Cambridge, MA: The MIT Press.

White, B. Y., & Frederiksen, J. R. (1990). Causal model progressions as a foundation for intelligent learning environments. *Artificial Intelligence, 42*(1), 99–157.

Williams, M. D., Hollan, J. D., & Stevens, A. L. (1983). Human reasoning about a simple physical system. In D. Gentner and A. L. Stevens (Eds.), *Mental models* (pp. 131–153). Hillsdale, NJ: Lawrence Erlbaum Associates.

Zheng, E. (October 31, 2000). Seat and back support for collapsible chair. *U.S. Patent No. D432,823.*

Zheng, E. (May 15, 2001a). Foldable dual-chair. *U.S. Patent No. 6,231,119.*

Zheng, E. (June 5, 2001b). Support ring for holding a fabric seat on inclined frame tube. *U.S. Patent No. 6,241,311.*

Zheng, E. (October 2, 2001c). Inclined back support arrangement for folding furniture. *U.S. Patent No. 6,296,304.*

CATEGORIZING THE SOCIAL WORLD: AFFECT, MOTIVATION, AND SELF-REGULATION

Galen V. Bodenhausen, Andrew R. Todd, and Andrew P. Becker

I. Introduction

Categorization lies at the heart of social perception. In order to form an impression of others, we interpret their behavior in terms of the trait categories it exemplifies. Then, based on the cluster of traits that we have inferred, we may categorize social targets into broader types. This bottom–up pathway to social impressions is complemented by a top–down pathway in which perceptually given characteristics (e.g., sex, race, and so on) serve as a basis for category identification, leading to the derivation of trait inferences and behavioral expectations based on stored generic knowledge about the category. Most social impressions result from a mixture of such theory-driven and data-driven processes, but categories inevitably provide the scaffold for the entire enterprise. Perhaps because early social psychological theory was much more influenced by the Gestalt psychologists than by the behaviorists, notions of cognitive representation and categorization have long been integral to theories of social psychology (e.g., Krech & Crutchfield, 1948; Scheerer, 1954). A half century ago, Allport (1954) championed the role of categorization in normal social functioning. Allport wrote at length about man's "normal and natural tendency to form generalizations, concepts, categories, whose content represents an oversimplification of his world of experience" (p. 27), and he argued that such categories can be "rational," in that they are reasonably well calibrated to social reality, or they can be "irrational," in that they reflect hearsay, fantasy, or ego-defensive needs as opposed to any kernel of truth. Allport forcefully linked prejudice to this latter type of category.

Is the process of categorizing people in any sense fundamentally different from the process of categorizing nonsocial objects? This question has been posed periodically (e.g., Hastie & Carlston, 1980; Lingle, Altom, & Medin, 1984; Markus & Zajonc, 1985; Wattenmaker, 1995, 2000), with varying conclusions. From the standpoint of the basic cognitive operations involved in categorization per se, there seems to be little basis for expecting important differences (Hastie & Carlston, 1980). However, there may nevertheless be a variety of ways in which these basic categorization processes are modified by interactions with other mental systems, in particular those invoking "hot" affective and motivational concerns. Moreover, the stimuli that form the input for social categorization may be much more complex than with other kinds of categorization (Lingle et al., 1984). By taking these issues into account, research on social categorization may provide insights about category use *in situ* that might be missed if researchers restrict their investigations to the categorization of the relatively simple kinds of nonsocial stimuli that form the basis of much prior research. Although affording valuable possibilities of stimulus control within the laboratory environment, such research may overlook important dynamics of how the mind functions in its everyday ecological context.

In this chapter, we review recent research on social categorization, emphasizing a variety of issues that reflect potentially important differences between social and nonsocial cognition. We begin by presenting a basic model of how categories operate in social perception, focusing in particular on the problems posed by the complexity of social stimuli. Then, we investigate some of the motivational and affective influences that moderate the functioning of these basic operations. In light of these considerations, we then revisit the question of what, if anything, is "special" about social categorization.

II. A Schematic Model of Social Categorization

There is no shortage of potential bases for social categorization. We can and do categorize people on the basis of their demographic attributes, social roles, personality types, and body shapes, among others. Decades of research has shown that when we categorize individuals in terms of their social identities, stereotyping and prejudice can follow (see Dovidio, Glick, & Rudman, 2005; Schneider, 2004). However, most of this research has been conducted from the perspective of a particular form of bias (e.g., racism or sexism), and the studies have been conducted in a manner that focused the perceiver's attention on single, particular identity dimensions. In doing so, researchers have often side-stepped a very fundamental question. Specifically,because a given individual could potentially be categorized in any number of distinct ways (e.g., occupation, sex, race, sexual orientation, religion, and so on), how do the various facets of a person's identity contribute to social impressions? Are multiple categories invoked and used, or does social perception tend to orient itself around a small subset of the available contenders? If the latter, what mechanisms are involved in the category selection process? Although nonsocial objects are generally also multiply categorizable, humans are likely among the most richly multidimensional stimuli we ever think about, so these questions are pressing ones for an understanding of social perception.

Figure 1 provides a schematic overview of our basic theoretical model, which starts with a consideration of category identification and selection and then characterizes how selected social categories can bias subsequent reactions to the target person. We use the term "biased response" here not in a pejorative sense but merely to designate that the selected category (or categories) substantially influence the response process. (Whether such biases are considered to be desirable or not is a topic to which we will later return.) Given that alternative bases for categorization can imply very different kinds of bias, our first concern lies in understanding how particular categories capture the focus of the perceiver's attention. As previously noted, in many laboratory studies, stimulus information about a target is constrained such that one might know little or nothing about the target's social identity other than a particular focal dimension (e.g., his/her gender). In real life, however, we assume that multiple bases for social categorization are likely to be perceptually available in many contexts. We further assume that only a small subset of these available categories will typically be influential in subsequent social perception. In many cases, a single category may dominate

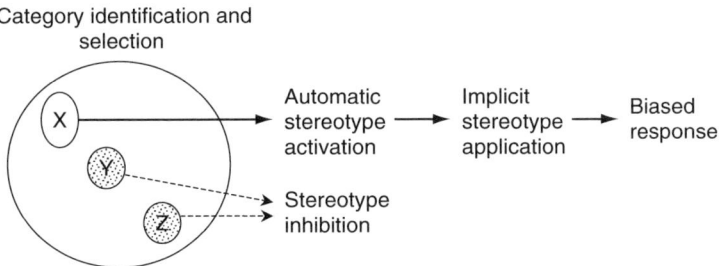

Fig. 1. Schematic model of social categorization.

the social perception process in the sense that it serves as the primary basis for organizing one's mental representation of the social target. This *category dominance hypothesis* (Bodenhausen & Macrae, 1998; Macrae & Bodenhausen, 2000) derives from an assumption that efficient and coherent social impressions are increasingly elusive as the number of considered identity dimensions increases. Different identities might support contradictory inferences (e.g., the categories "female" and "lawyer" may yield different expectations about kindness and nurturance), and unless there is a pressing desire for extremely finely tuned, accurate impressions, the more streamlined impression afforded by a dominant category may suffice for the perceiver's purposes.

In Fig. 1, a set of possible categorical identities (X, Y, & Z), all relevant to the same target, are perceptually available (or readily retrievable from memory, in the case of previously encountered targets). For example, if the target of social perception were Eddie Murphy, some possible categorical identities would include "African Americans," "Comedians," or "Rich People." The category dominance hypothesis posits that when thinking about him, not all of these categories will be simultaneously active; rather, only a subset will be guiding perception, inference, and response to the target. The model assumes that all detectable bases for categorization are initially activated, but it is the first one to reach a critical threshold of activation that will come to dominate a perceiver's reaction to Mr. Murphy. By virtue of winning this horse race, the dominant category becomes the focus of subsequent processing as activation spreads through the relevant category representation to the associated traits (or stereotypes) that are applicable to category members. The losers of the horse race, however, are assumed not merely to be passively neglected but rather to be actively inhibited; as the mental system "tunes in" to the dominant impression, it simultaneously "tunes out" distracting, irrelevant, or otherwise competing representations (Bodenhausen & Macrae, 1998; Macrae, Bodenhausen, & Milne, 1995).

Within such a model, a key question of course is what determines the dominant category. Several relevant factors have been shown to give a particular category the edge in its race to capture the social perception process. Categories that are normatively rare are, by their nature, distinctive and attention grabbing and therefore influential in social perception and judgment (Nelson & Miller, 1995). The immediate social context can also make particular identities distinctive, even if they are very commonplace in a broader sense. For example, being the only woman in a room otherwise full of men will make the category female salient when thinking about this target (see McGuire, McGuire, Child, & Fujioka, 1978). The behavior of a social target will also tend to recruit categorizations that accord with his or her observed behavior, based on the perceiver's beliefs about relevant category norms, a phenomenon termed "normative fit" (Turner, Oakes, Haslam, &

McGarty, 1994). For example, if we observe an Asian woman eating rice with chopsticks, her ethnicity may be more salient than her gender; however, if the same woman were breast-feeding an infant, her gender would likely be more salient than her ethnicity. The social situation and the behavior of the target are often likely to bias the perceiver's attention toward contextually meaningful social identities (e.g., Barden, Maddux, Petty, & Brewer, 2004; Wittenbrink, Judd, & Park, 2001). Finally, research by Patalano, Chin-Parker, and Ross (2006) shows that categories that provide the greatest degree of coherence among the observed characteristics of a target tend to dominate inference making. Coherence is said to exist when the observed features sensibly go together within a common causal model or theory, as, for example, when a common underlying causal factor explains the range of observed properties (Ahn, 1998; see also Wittenbrink, Hilton, & Gist, 1998). If a particular category provides this kind of structural coherence to features that are evident in a target, that category is likely to dominate over other bases for categorization in generating inductive inferences.

Dispositional and transient characteristics of the perceiver are also important in influencing category dominance. Some categories may be chronically accessible for particular perceivers. For instance, persons who are high in racial prejudice are likely to use race as a dominant category consistently when ethnic minority group members are encountered as opposed to age group, occupation, gender, and so on (Stangor, Lynch, Duan, & Glass, 1992). Chronic or momentary goals may also orient attention to particular social identities (Bruner, 1957; Srull & Wyer, 1986). Additionally, the perceiver's recent experiences are likely to temporarily enhance the accessibility of particular categories (Wyer & Srull, 1989). Having recently read a newspaper article about an instance of alleged racial discrimination, for example, might orient the perceiver to focus more on the ethnicity of subsequently encountered targets than (s)he otherwise would have done. Each of these factors would be expected to produce enhanced activation of particular categories, giving them an advantage in the race to impressional dominance.

What happens when a category achieves dominance? As depicted in Fig. 1, the model holds that category selection results in the cognitive activation of stereotypes associated with the category. For example, if a target's sex dominates then gender stereotypes will be activated in working memory. This process of stereotype activation is automatic in the sense that it is assumed to happen very rapidly, efficiently, and without any conscious intention. Once activated, stereotypic concepts can exert a range of influences on subsequent information processing. They can bias attention toward stereotypically expected behavior (e.g., Bodenhausen, 1988) and lead perceivers to interpret ambiguous behavior as stereotype-consistent (Sagar & Schofield, 1980). For example, Hugenberg and Bodenhausen (2003) showed that, among racially prejudiced European Americans, ambiguous facial displays of Black targets were more readily interpreted as hostile than closely matched displays of White targets. Social behavior commonly contains a degree of ambiguity, and perceivers rely on the most cognitively accessible concepts to disambiguate its meaning (Wyer & Srull, 1989). Once activated, stereotypes serve this function too. We assume that these processes of stereotype application are typically implicit, in the sense that people are not consciously aware of the relevant processes; they only experience the output of those processes. Thus, rather than feeling that their impressions are based on suppositions and inferences derived from the target's social group, perceivers experience their impressions as "given," the mere registration of seemingly objective facts about the target. In this sense, stereotypes are self-validating: by implicitly assimilating ambiguous input to stereotypic expectancies, perceivers subjectively experience stereotype confirmation without realizing the role their own minds have played in constructing this seemingly confirmatory evidence. Of course, assimilation is not the only possible function of activated stereotypic knowledge. If the observed behavior or characteristics of the target do not fit with stereotypic expectancies then judgments are often contrasted away from the stereotypic standard, producing more extreme, counter-stereotypic impressions (e.g., Biernat, 2003). In either case, though, the impression is biased by the activation of stereotypes.

This very brief summary provides an overview of the basic assumptions we have made about the ways social categories inform social perceptions, judgments, and behaviors. The main contrast we have drawn, so far, between social categorization and categorization of other stimuli resides in our assumption that people are more multifaceted than many other types of stimuli, and this multipotentiality requires a cognitive system that can navigate the complexity and still yield meaningful impressions. We have postulated a system that, working behind the scenes, produces streamlined, coherent impressions by activating stereotypes associated with dominant categories while simultaneously inhibiting rival bases for categorization. As we previously noted, another potentially important difference between social and nonsocial categories may lie in the generally greater extent to which the former interact with strong motivational and affective forces. In the remainder of the chapter, we will consider the roles that motivation and affect may play in moderating the basic processes depicted in Fig. 1.

III. Motivational Influences

A. The Varieties of Motivational Influence

Psychologists have postulated the existence of dozens of drives, motives, and needs that putatively energize and direct behavior and cognition. Given the vital role played by motivation in person perception (e.g., Dunning, 2001), it is necessary to understand which of these various motivational forces matter the most in moderating social categorization. Although a variety of conceptual schemes have been proposed to describe the basic human motives (for recent examples, see Fiske, 2004; Woike & McAdams, 2004), there is no clear consensus. We focus our attention on four of the motivational themes that have emerged most consistently in the social psychological literature—motivations encompassing (a) the desire for knowledge and understanding, (b) the desire for a positive self-image, (c) the desire for the approval of others, and (d) the desire to express a personally meaningful value system (for similar taxonomies, see Kunda & Spencer, 2003; Smith, Bruner, & White, 1956).

One set of motivational concerns has been labeled "epistemic motives" (e.g., Ford & Kruglanski, 1995), which concern the desire for an effective understanding of the social world. Obviously, the desire to understand the social world is the root motivation underlying social perception. We form impressions of others in our quest to understand and predict the environments that we must navigate in our social lives. Beyond this basic desire for understanding, one can examine a variety of more specific motives that determine preferences for how such knowledge is acquired. Among the variables that have been explored under this rubric, need for closure (Kruglanski & Webster, 1996) is perhaps the most well studied. Individuals who are high in the need for closure desire rapid, unambiguous, and orderly understandings of the world. Kruglanski's research shows that among persons who are high in the need for closure, rigid stereotypic thinking is relatively commonplace because these kinds of impressions yield a sense of an orderly, predictable, and manageable social world. Such persons should be particularly unlikely to consider multiple bases for categorizing social targets, focusing instead on a dominant category that maximizes efficient, clear-cut impression formation (Kruglanski & Freund, 1983).

The motivation to view oneself in a positive light has also been studied extensively. The arsenal of cognitive strategies that people employ in order to view themselves in a positive light is truly diverse and creative (e.g., Kwan, John, Kenny, Bond, & Robins, 2004). For example, this motive can be satisfied by venerating people who provide positive feedback and vilifying those who question our merit or goodness. To venerate the praise-giver, one may selectively attend to categorical identities that connote competence while simultaneously inhibiting categories that could possibly undermine the praise-giver's credibility. On the other hand, being on the receiving end of criticism may lead one to denigrate the critic so as to deflect this personal threat. In this case, categories that challenge the critic's competence may be activated while those that augment the critic's competence would be actively inhibited. Sinclair and Kunda (1999) documented this phenomenon in a series of studies. For example, after completing a fictitious interpersonal skills questionnaire, participants received either positive or negative (false) feedback on their performance from either a Black doctor or a White doctor (both male). Results indicated that participants who received positive feedback from the Black doctor exhibited not only heightened activation of concepts associated with doctors (e.g., "medical") but also heightened inhibition of concepts stereotypically associated with Blacks (e.g., "violent"). In contrast, participants receiving negative feedback from the Black doctor showed exactly the opposite pattern; that is, they exhibited heightened activation of concepts associated with Blacks and inhibition of concepts associated with doctors.

In a similar vein, Fein, Spencer, and their colleagues (Fein & Spencer, 1997; Spencer, Fein, Wolfe, Fong, & Dunn, 1998) have shown that people who have experienced an external threat to their self-worth (e.g., negative performance feedback on an intelligence test) are especially likely to activate and apply negative stereotypes to others, presumably in an effort to gain an ego boost by feeling superior. In fact, after being given the opportunity to disparage a stereotyped target, threatened participants did indeed exhibit greater increases in self-esteem than their unthreatened counterparts (Fein & Spencer, 1997). Unlike Sinclair and Kunda's (1999) Black doctor, the stereotyped targets in the Fein and Spencer (1997) study were in no way connected to the negative feedback received by participants. Thus, it seems that after receiving a blow to their otherwise positive self-concept, perceivers seek to disparage even out-group members who are "innocent bystanders," and they gain self-esteem benefits from doing so. Even when cognitively distracted, ego-threatened individuals still manage to find sufficient cognitive resources to activate stereotypes about an incidentally presented out-group target (Spencer et al., 1998). It seems clear that the need for positive self-regard can exert a potent moderating effect on processes of category identification and stereotype activation in social perception. Indeed, social identity theory (Tajfel & Turner, 1986) is founded on the assumption that perceivers are motivated to view their own groups as superior to other groups. The process of (negative) stereotype application represents a principal means for satisfying this motive.

Research on the consequences of our desire for social acceptance and the approval of others also has a long history (Baumeister & Leary, 1995). In the realm of social perception, one relevant question concerns whether there are socially acceptable and socially unacceptable ways of thinking about the social world. If certain ways of looking at the world elicit opprobrium, one might be highly motivated to avoid these taboo impressions. Consider the following proposition: "It is just plain wrong to rely on stereotypes in forming impressions of others." The twentieth century undoubtedly witnessed a shift toward such a norm; in regard to many social groups, prejudice and stereotyping are now generally seen as detestable (see Oskamp, 2000). To the extent that one has any inclination toward stereotypic impressions, this sea change would be expected to exert a powerful counterforce. However, Devine (1989) has argued that, because of the residue of prejudice and discrimination that still exists in our lately more egalitarian culture, most people still tend to have automatic stereotypic responses as a result of cultural conditioning. To the extent that such reactions have also become culturally demonized, people may often be very motivated to avoid categorical reactions to many social out-groups. When rooted in a desire to avoid the disapproval of others, this motive has been called *external* motivation to control prejudice (Plant & Devine, 1998). It is external in the sense that it hinges on the approval or disapproval of others. Having a conditioned, automatic inclination toward using a particular category to understand one's experiences, but feeling an acute pressure *not* to use this category, creates an interesting cognitive dilemma that may result in stereotyping and prejudice being camouflaged in the form of rationalizations that appear to provide socially acceptable, ostensibly nonstereotypic reasons for responding to out-group targets in essentially stereotypic ways (Dovidio & Gaertner, 2004).

As described thus far, this cognitive dilemma reflects a schism between personal inclinations and social conventions. A similar dilemma can arise due to an intrapersonal schism. A fourth important motivational force is our desire to hold and express meaningful values (e.g., Schwartz, 1996). The rise of culture norms proscribing stereotypes and prejudice occurred because many individuals in our society sincerely and personally endorse egalitarian values (Schuman, Steeh, Bobo, & Krysan, 1997). To the extent that such values are held dear, people will want to enact and express them. As such, there is often also an *internal* motivation to avoid prejudice (Plant & Devine, 1998).

Having a strong internal motivation to control prejudice, based on personal values rather than fear of others' disapproval, does not necessarily guarantee that unwanted stereotypic thoughts will not arise in one's mind. Indeed, several models of person perception (e.g., Bargh, 1999; Devine, 1989) assume that stereotypes are highly likely to be automatically activated upon perception of a category member. These models generally assume that automatic stereotype activation is generated by an associative mental system that is distinct from the propositional reasoning system wherein personal values are articulated and their implications are understood (see Gawronski & Bodenhausen, in press; Strack & Deutsch, 2004). However, there is evidence suggesting that truly low-prejudiced perceivers (i.e., those for whom egalitarian values are self-defining) in fact do activate "taboo" categorical knowledge less readily than their more prejudiced counterparts (Kawakami, Dion, & Dovidio, 1998; Lepore & Brown, 1997; Wittenbrink, Judd, & Park, 1997). In these studies, participants were subliminally presented with a verbal category label (e.g., *Black*), after which the activation of stereotypic concepts (e.g., *poor*) was assessed. Results generally indicate that lower-prejudice individuals are less likely than individuals higher in prejudice to activate stereotypic concepts automatically in response to the category label, despite sharing essentially identical levels of explicit knowledge regarding the stereotypes of the social group in question.

Recent research conducted by Moskowitz and colleagues (Moskowitz, Gollwitzer, Wasel, & Schaal, 1999; Moskowitz, Salomon, & Taylor, 2000) provides complementary evidence that the presence of social out-group members can trigger the activation of egalitarian concerns among those persons who are committed to egalitarian values. That is, egalitarian motives appear to be activated when relevant out-group members are encountered, influencing subsequent information-processing dynamics. In these studies, participants were preselected based on their degree of endorsement of egalitarianism, and it was predicted that chronic egalitarians, for whom concepts like *social justice* and *equality* are self-defining, would exhibit preconscious control of stereotype activation. Nonchronics, on the other hand, were predicted to activate stereotypes upon perceiving relevant group members. Indeed, participants with a chronic motivation to be egalitarian did evince decreased stereotype activation in comparison to nonchronics, and they also exhibited increased activation of egalitarian concepts (i.e., *equality, fairness, tolerance*) following African American face primes. Nonchronics, who do not consider egalitarian concepts to be particularly self-defining, failed to show this same pattern. What is more, the increased activation of egalitarian concepts among chronic egalitarians was found only when these concepts were preceded by African American face primes, suggesting that participants' internalized egalitarian personal standards were only activated when a relevant cue (i.e., a Black face) was present.

B. Self-Regulation of Social Perception

These considerations suggest the need for a modification of the basic model presented in Fig. 1. Because motivational factors can exert such marked moderating effects on social categorization, the process cannot really be understood without factoring in the extent to which perceivers may effortfully modify their automatic tendencies (cf. Brewer, 1988; Fiske & Neuberg, 1990). For internal and/or external reasons, perceivers seek to regulate their own cognitive processes to produce palatable or permissible results. A modification of our basic model, reflecting this reality, is provided in Fig. 2.

In order for an individual to exert control over stereotypic thoughts and deeds, motivation is only one of the critical factors. Given a motivation to avoid stereotypes, it is also necessary that the individual be aware of the

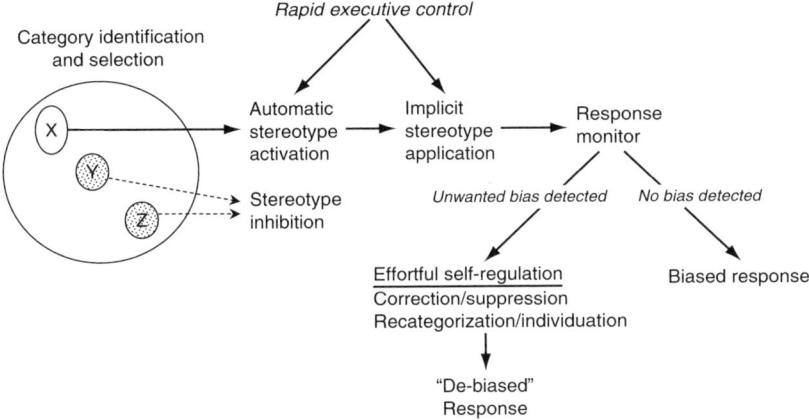

Fig. 2. Expanded model of social categorization.

potential emergence of this bias (e.g., Strack & Hannover, 1996). As we have argued, stereotyping typically operates in an implicit, background manner, and vigilance is required to detect its occurrence. In addition, because self-regulation is thought to be effortful and resource dependent, sufficient attentional capacity is needed to complement the motivational desire for egalitarianism (for a review, see Bodenhausen, Macrae, & Sherman, 1999). Insufficient attentional resources are assumed to result in self-regulatory failure (e.g., Posner & Rothbart, 2000). When these interdependent preconditions of motivation, awareness, and attentional capacity are in place, the basic, automatic processes of social categorization may be modified by the perceiver's self-regulatory efforts.

As shown in Fig. 2, we assume that when properly motivated, perceivers monitor their initial responses to a social target, checking for the presence of unacceptable thoughts. Essentially, this response monitor acts as a discrepancy detector. It is functionally similar to Carver and Scheier's (1990) *comparator* in that its purpose is to signal the perceiver when there is a discrepancy between the current state and a more desired state. Of particular interest is the fact that, when working to prevent unwanted mental outputs, this monitoring process must necessarily involve the activation of these very same unwanted mental contents (Wegner, 1994), which serve as the criterion for evaluating one's (tentative) impressions. That is, we cannot determine whether or not our impressions are free of stereotypic bias without activating some representation of the stereotypic content for comparison purposes. If a discrepancy is detected between the desired state (lack of stereotypic content) and the actual state, self-regulatory strategies are deployed in an effort to bring the actual state in line with the desired state.

Monteith (Monteith, 1993; Monteith & Voils, 2001) has posited a self-regulation model of prejudice reduction. According to her model, acting in a manner that is inconsistent with one's egalitarian standards elicits guilt and compunction, which then spark correction attempts to reduce the inconsistency and to eliminate the negative affect. More recently, Monteith and colleagues (Monteith, Ashburn-Nardo, Voils, & Czopp, 2002) have posited an associative mechanism whereby perceivers are able to form a link between the cues that elicit guilt (e.g., the presence of a stereotyped group member) and the processes causing the guilt (e.g., automatic stereotype activation). Over time, and through these associations, cues may come to act as a warning signal that self-discrepant responding is possible, and the implementation of self-regulatory strategies ensues.

Once perceivers are aware of the potential for stereotypic bias, and assuming they have ample attentional resources at their disposal, any one of a variety of regulatory strategies can be deployed. One such strategy involves making direct adjustments to overt responses in the opposite direction of the presumed bias (Wegener & Petty, 1997; Wilson & Brekke, 1994). On first glance, this *stereotype correction* approach seems like a promising strategy for regulating unwanted stereotypic influences on impressions and judgments. However, unless perceivers are particularly adept at detecting the magnitude and direction of their bias, they are vulnerable to both under- and overcorrection (Petty & Wegener, 1993).

A second self-regulatory strategy involves an active attempt to prevent stereotypic thoughts from ever entering into consciousness. While *stereotype suppression* may also be an intuitively appealing strategy, attempting to control one's thoughts may have unintended effects. According to Wegner's (1994) model of mental control, thought suppression initiates two distinctive mental processes: a *monitoring process* that searches consciousness for the presence of the unwanted thought, and an *operating process* that focuses one's attention on something other than the unwanted thought (i.e., a distracter) when the unwanted thought is detected. Because the operating process is effortful and requires cognitive capacity for its successful execution, it can be undermined by cognitive load or a relaxation of suppression intentions. On the other hand, the monitoring process, once engaged, works effortlessly and continuously in its search for the to-be-suppressed thought. Because, as previously noted, the monitoring process necessarily requires the activation of the unwanted thought as the basis of the search criterion, the thought gets repeatedly primed, ironically causing it to become much more accessible (Macrae, Bodenhausen, Milne, & Jetten, 1994). Consequently, should the operating process get short-circuited, the unwanted thought may reach a level of hyperaccessibility, and a *rebound* effect may occur. That is, the unwanted thought may exert an even greater influence on thoughts and behaviors than if no suppression attempt were ever made in the first place (e.g., Galinsky & Moskowitz, 2000; Macrae et al., 1994). Taken together, the available studies paint a rather bleak picture for stereotype suppression as a self-regulatory strategy. Nevertheless, with sufficient cognitive resources and persistence in their intentions to suppress, perceivers may be able to successfully control the unwanted influences of stereotypes (for a review, see Monteith, Sherman, & Devine, 1998).

Another strategy involves changing the basis of one's impression from a taboo category to some more socially acceptable category (*recategorization*). For example, if while forming an impression of a Black doctor one detects the emergence of racial stereotypes, one could try to shift the focus of one's impression to the other salient (occupational) category. Although still based on stereotypes, such an impression would likely be palatable because the generally positive stereotypes about doctors are considered far more "permissible" than common racial stereotypes. Another version of recategorization is provided by Gaertner and Dovidio's (2000) common in-group identity model, which maintains that if members of different groups come to see themselves as members of a single, superordinate group, thoughts and actions concerning former out-group members should begin to resemble those regarding the in-group. Applied to the present context, if perceivers detect unwanted stereotypic biases in their initial impressions, they may seek out and emphasize categorical identities that the target shares with them, focusing on what they have in common. Encountering an ethnic minority group member, for example, the person could focus on a shared national identity ("we're all Americans") as a strategy for minimizing stereotypic bias. Note that this strategy involves changing one's salient *self*-categorization as well as the category applied to the target. Research confirms that perceivers are willing and able to undergo these kinds of identity shifts when they suit their current purposes (Mussweiler, Gabriel, & Bodenhausen, 2000). The important point is that, given the multifaceted nature of social identity, it will commonly be possible to find converging identities with most targets, forming a basis for feelings of intragroup kinship rather than intergroup alienation.

A final strategy, *individuation*, involves the differentiation of individuals based on their unique attributes. In essence, this strategy defies the principle of category dominance and instead relies upon the simultaneous consideration of multiple identity dimensions. Thus, one thinks about a target not merely in terms of her ethnicity, but also her sex, occupation, personality traits, food preferences, and any other characteristics that might be salient. Any one of these characteristics could form the basis for a categorical response (women, teachers, introverts, chocolate-lovers, and so on), but when simultaneously considered, simplistic generalizations about these categories are likely to give way to more complex, integrated impressions that reconcile contradictions and produce a relatively unique, personalized impression that is unlikely to be dominated by unwanted stereotypic notions. The effectiveness of this strategy is clearly constrained by the amount of information available about the target. In a minimal encounter with a target, we might not be able to discern much more than basic demographic identities, so rich, individuated impressions reflecting the person's relatively unique combination of social categories would not be possible. Ample research suggests that individuation is an outcome that occurs only when accuracy motivation is high and cognitive resources are ample (for a review, see Bodenhausen et al., 1999).

All of the preceding self-regulatory strategies can be characterized as being largely effortful and cognitively taxing. However, we do not rule out the possibility that self-regulation may be executed more automatically as well. According to Bargh's (1990) automotive model, a temporary goal can become a chronic, relatively automatic one if it is frequently and consistently pursued. The repeated pairing of the goal (e.g., to be egalitarian) with a goal-triggering stimulus (e.g., the presence of a stereotyped group member) may result in the goal being automatically activated upon exposure to that stimulus (Bargh & Gollwitzer, 1994). Over time, one may no longer need to consciously initiate goal pursuit rather the mere presence of a goal-triggering stimulus will suffice.

Recent evidence has begun to confirm that inhibition of stereotypic biases can indeed occur at a relatively automatic level (e.g., Amodio et al., 2004; Conrey, Sherman, Gawronski, Hugenberg, & Groom, 2005). For example, Amodio et al. (2004) examined event-related potentials associated with unwanted racial bias. In a task adapted from Payne (2001), they presented participants with Black and White faces as primes (for 200 ms), followed by the brief presentation of a picture of an object, which was either a gun or a tool. The task was simply to correctly classify the object (as either a gun or a tool). Stereotypic bias would be reflected in a greater tendency to misidentify a tool as a gun following a Black (versus White) prime. Such errors were relatively commonplace, confirming the importance of stereotypes in automatic aspects of social perception, and when they occurred, they were associated with an error-related negativity (ERN) brainwave generated in the anterior cingulate, consistent with the activation of a response conflict detector (see MacDonald, Cohen, Stenger, & Carter, 2000). The rapidity of these ERNs suggests extremely quick detection of unwanted racial biases. Moreover, participants who consistently showed the strongest ERNs were more likely to exercise greater control in performing the task (as indicated by process-dissociation parameter estimates). Overall, these findings suggest that neural systems can very rapidly detect unwanted racial bias and recruit controlled processes in an effort to counteract this bias. Although these efforts at control are imperfect (at least under the rapid-response requirements of the

Payne weapons/tools paradigm), they do indicate that rapid deployment of control processes occurs, in a way that does not appear to be conscious and effortful, as implied by the Bargh's automotive model. For this reason, we include in Fig. 2 a recognition that executive control processes can act on implicit aspects of social categorization directly and independently of the effortful processes that we highlighted earlier. It is clear that, in both automatic and effortful ways, motivation exerts a potent influence on the activation, use, and inhibition of social categories.

IV. Affective Influences

We have also argued that social categories are different from nonsocial categories in that they are intimately bound up with affect. The social world is an affective world. There are at least three distinct senses in which affect could bear on social categorization (Bodenhausen, Mussweiler, Gabriel, & Moreno, 2001). The first two are forms of *integral affect*, which characterizes situations in which the social category itself is directly implicated in an emotional experience (Bodenhausen, 1993). In *chronic integral affect*, the affective state arises directly from the category. That is, thinking about the category, or its members, directly creates feelings such as anger, fear, guilt, joy, or some other emotional reaction. In *episodic integral affect*, an affective state arises within the context of an interaction with the members of a social category; it may (or may not) differ markedly from the chronic feelings associated with the group. For example, one might be generally fearful of Arabs but have an extraordinarily positive interaction with an Arab person. In such a case, the episodic integral affect would be different in valence from the chronic affect. Finally, there is *incidental affect*, which covers instances in which preexisting affective states that originated from unrelated sources are present when the members of a social category are encountered.

The emergence of chronic integral affect presupposes that a particular categorization has already occurred, so this type of affect should have little bearing on initial category selection, but it might exert an influence on the subsequent stages of the model depicted in Fig. 2. As previously noted, feelings such as empathy and guilt might increase the likelihood that people are vigilant for unwanted stereotypic influences, leading to a greater likelihood that they will engage in self-regulatory strategies designed to eliminate such influences (Monteith, 1993). The interaction of chronic and episodic integral affect is likely to be particularly important for subsequent modification of initial categorical reactions. In the previous example of a highly positive interaction with a member of an otherwise fear-eliciting group, it is possible that this kind of experience will lead to incremental changes in the chronic integral affect that is elicited by the group. More immediately, the mismatch in affective reactions may play a particularly important role in eliciting recategorization. In particular, the chapter on intergroup contact suggests that positive episodic integral affect may be particularly important in changing stereotypes and prejudices (Jones, 1997; Tropp & Pettigrew, 2005), and they may accomplish this salutary effect by promoting recategorization of out-group targets into broader and more inclusive social categories (Dovidio, Gaertner, & Loux, 2000).

Although the forms of affect that are integral to social stimuli constitute one of the commonly invoked bases for arguing that categorization of social stimuli is different from categorization of nonsocial stimuli, in fact most of the available evidence examining the relationship between affect and social categorization has focused on incidental affect. There is substantial and growing evidence that incidental affective states can influence all of the stages in our schematic model.

A. CATEGORY SELECTION AND STEREOTYPE ACTIVATION

There are several reasons to suppose that affective states can influence which categories come to dominate social perception. One possibility is that affective states may lead perceivers to focus on aspects of a target stimulus that are in some way affectively congruent with the perceiver's subjective state. This *affective resonance hypothesis* would propose, for example, that an anxious person would be more likely to emphasize the ethnic identity of a Black athlete because this identity is associated with cultural stereotypes of dangerousness and threat, whereas the occupational identity of the target (associated with positive emotion and enjoyment—depending perhaps on the team affiliation of the player) would be emphasized by individuals who are feeling positive. The resonance hypothesis accords with prior research showing that individuals better remember information that matches their mood at the time the information is encoded (e.g., Bower, Gilligan, & Monteiro, 1981; Bower & Mayer, 1985). Such findings indicate that attention tends to be directed toward affect-congruent stimuli in a heterogeneous stimulus set. If so, then perhaps it will also be directed toward the most affectively congruent attributes of a single, compound stimulus. Although this notion is perhaps intuitively compelling, there is to date very limited evidence bearing on its validity. The majority of the research on affective influences on social cognition has utilized paradigms in which the stimulus person's identity is highly constrained (e.g., only gender information is available), rendering the question of category selection irrelevant. Moreover, much research conducted since Bower's seminal investigations has failed to replicate a mood-congruency pattern in memory or judgment; many researchers have thus concluded that automatic mood-congruent retrieval effects currently lack compelling support (Matthew & Wells, 1999; Wyer, Clore, & Isbell, 1999).

While the notion of mood congruency has generally not panned out in social perception research, alternative ideas have proven more fruitful. In particular, a range of empirical findings support the idea that moods and emotions can influence which strategies perceivers use in construing the social environment (e.g., Bless, 2001; Clore, Gasper, & Garvin, 2001; Schwarz, 2001). The basic idea is that emotional states trigger response tendencies that directly influence cognition and action systems (e.g., Frijda, 1988). Emotional states typically occur in reaction to particular kinds of situations and events (e.g., loss elicits sadness, danger elicits fear, insult elicits anger, and so on), and this view holds that an emotion carries with it a readiness to respond in ways that are generally appropriate for the classes of situations that trigger the emotion. For example, fear is thought to mobilize rapid responses and to narrow the focus of attention to the most dominant informational cues present in the environment (Easterbrook, 1959; Eysenck, 1992). Extrapolating from these ideas, one might propose that feeling anxious or fearful would orient social perceivers toward the most generally dominant social categories—the basic categories that are used most habitually—rather than unusual or lower-frequency categories. By considering the response tendencies that are associated with various discrete emotions, one might generate a range of predictions concerning processes of category selection in social perception.

Recent studies by Hugenberg, Bodenhausen, Becker, and Perrott (2005) examined the influence of anxiety and happiness on category selection when multiply categorizable targets were presented to social perceivers. Participants in one study first underwent a happy, anxious, or neutral mood induction involving a series of short films. Then, as part of an ostensibly unrelated study, they were presented with one of two multiply categorizable targets, either a Black doctor (i.e., negatively valenced demographic category, positively valenced occupational category) or a female lawyer (positive demographic category, negative occupational category). Participants contemplated these targets under the guise of a study on the formation of impressions via the Internet; they viewed a series of personal websites, including the critical one in which the multiply categorizable target was presented (with both pictorial and verbal descriptions conveying the category memberships). After viewing the critical website, participants performed a lexical decision task (LDT) designed to test the accessibility of the two categories that applied to the target. For example, for the Black doctor, some of the words in the LDT were categorical associates of "doctor" and some were category associates of "Blacks," while others were unrelated to the category (pronounceable nonwords were of course also included as stimuli in the task). Results showed that, compared to participants in a neutral condition, participants in both happy and anxious conditions exhibited enhanced accessibility (i.e., faster responses) for demographic categories (African American and woman) and inhibited (i.e., below-baseline) access to the occupational categories (doctor and lawyer); no mood-congruency effects were found. Hugenberg et al. interpreted this finding in terms of a "back-to-basics" hypothesis, which holds that certain affective states lead people to focus more on the most basic, frequently used social categories (e.g., demographic identities) at the expense of less basic categories. A rationale for this hypothesis was already presented for the case of anxiety. A somewhat different rationale leads to the same prediction for happiness. Specifically, happiness can be thought of as a safety signal that indicates that energy (and cognitive resources) can be conserved because there are no pressing problems to solve. Moreover, positive affect may confer a sense of confidence in one's most immediate first reactions (Bodenhausen, Kramer, & Süsser, 1994a). As such, the mind can run on "autopilot," relying on the most basic, dominant patterns of thought (e.g., Bless, 2001), unless there is some intrinsic enjoyment to be had by engaging in more effortful or creative cognitive activity, which seems unlikely in this "Internet Impressions" study. Thus, this study provides evidence that the selection of basic-level categories is a variable that is subject to affective biases.

The studies by Hugenberg et al. (2005) document a moderating effect of affective states on category selection along a *horizontal* dimension (i.e., alternative, non-nested social categories). Affective states might also influence category selection along a *vertical* dimension (i.e., nested, sub- to superordinate categories). Clore et al. (2001) propose that positive affect promotes more global processing that may imply attention to higher, more abstract levels of stimulus identity. On the other hand, sad affective states are posited to induce a local-processing focus that may imply more attention to low-level, subordinate levels of stimulus identity. A series of studies that show affective influences on global versus local processing supports a general link between positive affect and more global attentional processing (Fredrickson & Branigan, 2005; Gasper, 2004; Gasper & Clore, 2002), but these studies did not specifically examine social categorization. Research that did specifically investigate the effects of positive mood on levels of social categorization (Dovidio, Gaertner, Isen, Rust, & Guerra, 1998) has confirmed that positive affect leads to the selection of more inclusive categories. However, there is a limiting condition on this effect. Specifically, the bias toward superordinate category selection when in a positive mood does not take place when the information being categorized is itself negative (Isen, Niedenthal, & Cantor, 1992).

Although there is a great deal remaining to be learned, it seems increasingly clear that a perceiver's subjective affective state can bias the aspects of a social target's multidimensional identity that capture attention and form the basis for organizing the perceiver's impressions and reactions. This bias is evident even when the affective experience has its origins in situations entirely unrelated to the subsequently encountered target.

B. STEREOTYPE APPLICATION AND EXPRESSION

Assuming that a given category is selected for emphasis in social perception, one can still ask to what extent affective states might moderate the likelihood of its application to the target (and subsequent expression in overt responses). A fair amount of evidence bearing on this possibility has accumulated. The "feelings as information" model (Schwarz, 2001) provides a generally effective account for the bulk of the findings. This model assumes a linkage between moods and information-processing tendencies. The key idea is that mood provides information about what kind of strategy is required to manage the current situation effectively. Happy moods signal that all is well, and one can go with one's dominant, initial reactions. Sadness, in contrast, signals that the situation is problematic, and cautious, more detailed deliberation is warranted. Consistent with this line of thinking, prior research on persuasion has shown that happy people are more likely to change their minds on the basis of quick, heuristic processes (such as the presence of a high-status communicator), whereas sad people are more likely to change their minds on the basis of more effortful, systematic processes (specifically, detailed scrutiny of the argumentation; see Bless, Bohner, Schwarz, & Strack, 1990; Mackie & Worth, 1989). Applied to the present context, the somewhat counterintuitive implication of this line of thinking is that happy people should be more likely to apply and express activated stereotypic concepts, whereas sad people should be more likely to scrutinize their initial reactions closely and modify them in ways that will often minimize the influence of stereotypes.

Bodenhausen, Sheppard, and Kramer (1994b) reported several studies in which participants were placed in a good mood (depending on the particular study, by music, facial feedback, or recalling idiosyncratic personal memories of happy times) and then asked to make decisions about cases of alleged legal infractions. The defendant in these cases was either stereotypically associated with the offense (e.g., a student athlete accused of cheating on an exam) or not (a nondescript student accused of cheating on an exam). Across all studies, happy moods were associated with greater stereotyping. Specifically, the stereotypic offender was judged more likely to be guilty than a nonstereotypic offender with otherwise identical case evidence, reflecting greater stereotype application. This pattern was equally evident irrespective of arousal levels; excited, energetic happiness produced the same pattern as calm, serene happiness. The only exception to this pattern occurred when participants were first told that they would have to be able to justify their decisions about the case. Under this condition, happy participants were particularly unlikely to apply stereotypes. Thus, the effects of happiness appear to have little to do with the *ability* to avoid stereotypic influences because happy people quite readily did avoid such influences when motivated by the pressure of accountability. Instead, it appears that happiness simply engenders a readiness to go with one's dominant initial impression, unless some other motivation overrides this readiness. Similar effects have since been reported by several other researchers (e.g., Bless, Schwarz, & Kemmelmeier, 1996; Park & Banaji, 2000).

The effects of sadness have also been fairly extensively examined. In a paradigm very similar to Bodenhausen, Kramer and Süsser (1994a), Bodenhausen, Sheppard and Kramer (1994b) showed that sad people were no more likely than those in a neutral mood to apply and express stereotypes. Other research suggests that sad people may even be less likely to rely on general social categories than people in a neutral mood (e.g., Edwards & Weary, 1993; Weary & Gannon, 1996) because they prefer a more cautious, detail-oriented style of information processing that goes well beyond the first, dominant reactions that arise. Lambert, Khan, Lickel, and Fricke (1997) showed that sad people are more likely to engage in correction of stereotypic biases (but only when such biases were perceived to be inappropriate). These findings collectively indicate that sad people are generally less likely to apply and express stereotypes than their happy counterparts.

The "feelings-as-information" approach has generally focused on valence as the key factor dictating the impact of feelings on information-processing strategies: positive moods lead to more cursory processing while negative moods lead to more extensive processing. While the previously described literature confirms this claim, it is noteworthy that the only variety of negative affect considered was sadness. One might well wonder whether the more effortful and detail-oriented style of sad or mildly depressed people would apply equally to angry or fearful individuals. In fact, there are both conceptual and empirical reasons to doubt that this is so. As previously noted, Hugenberg et al. (2005) developed a rationale for expecting anxious people to rely on dominant response tendencies, based in part on the well-established notion that anxiety and fear are linked to the mobilization of rapid responses via the sympathetic nervous system. Because these states are linked to situational threats to one's well-being, they do signal a problem that might benefit from careful consideration: however, deliberation may be a luxury that one cannot afford when in a dangerous situation (unlike sad situations). In the speed-accuracy tradeoff of human evolution, it appears that fear has tipped the balance toward speedy responses. And indeed, the limited available evidence does indicate that anxiety is associated with greater application and expression of stereotypes (Baron, Inman, Kao, & Logan, 1992; Wilder, 1993; but see Curtis & Locke, 2005). For example, Baron et al. had individuals who were high in dental anxiety complete a measure of stereotyping while they waited for a dental procedure (which they expected would be performed by a novice dentist). Under these conditions, stereotyping was more pronounced compared to nonanxious patients.

Besides anxiety/fear and sadness, there is also some evidence bearing on anger's effects on stereotyping. Like anxiety, anger is an emotion that occurs in agonistic contexts, and it tends to produce an urgent impulse to respond. Quite intuitively, anger and rage are not associated with careful deliberation but with impulsive action (see Berkowitz, 1993). Corresponding to this fairly self-evident claim is evidence that anger is associated with reliance upon more simplistic, cognitive shortcut strategies (Lerner, Goldberg, & Tetlock, 1998), including stereotyping (Bodenhausen et al., 1994b). Interestingly, however, this tendency appears to be equally true regardless of whether the simplistic cognitive strategy produces a negative or a positive judgment. That is, incidental anger did not necessarily lead to negative judgments. Even when a cognitive shortcut implied a positive judgment, angry people were more likely to utilize it than those in a neutral (or sad) mood (Bodenhausen, et al., 1994b).

One last negative emotion that deserves mention is guilt. As we previously noted, Devine (1989) and Monteith (1993) emphasize the idea that guilt, when specifically linked to one's own reliance on stereotypes and prejudice, is an important motivator of efforts to avoid or correct for such biases. Experimental inductions of guilt have supported this claim. Son Hing, Li, and Zanna (2002) had participants who had previously revealed evidence of racial prejudice (on an implicit measure) complete a hypocrisy induction in which they wrote an essay about how important it was to avoid racial bias. Participants in the hypocrisy condition were also asked to write about times when they had behaved in a racially prejudiced way; in a control condition, this confession was not required. At a later point in time, the participants completed a behavioral measure of discrimination against a racial out-group. Results confirmed that the hypocrisy induction did create feelings of guilt, and that those who felt guilty also ended up subsequently showing less discrimination against the out-group, reflecting inhibition of the racial attitudes and stereotypes that had previously been evident. Thus, guilty affect can influence the expression of stereotypes, presumably by motivating the additional effort required to go beyond initial impressions that are likely to be tinged with implicit stereotype application (see also Pedersen, Beven, Walker, & Griffiths, 2004).

Emotion thus appears to be bound up in a variety of ways with the unfolding of social perception. It influences which categories will be applied to a target, and it influences how likely the perceiver is to stop with a largely category-based (stereotypic) impression or to invoke more effortful information-processing strategies that go beyond stereotypic generalizations. Old-fashioned notions of an antagonism between rationality and emotionality do not seem very adequate for capturing the complexity of the interaction between the feeling system and the thinking system. If we want to understand how the thinking system works, especially in the affectively rich context of social life, emotion must be a fully integrated part of the story.

V. Identification-Based Affect, Motivation, and Inference

We have argued that social categorization must be understood as intimately connected to motivation and emotion. Although in practice social stimuli may be generally more likely to invoke motivational concerns and affective reactions than the relatively more sterile nonsocial stimuli that are often employed in categorization research, there is little reason for assuming that nonsocial cognition cannot also be influenced by and infused with motivation and affect as well. While the study of social categorization invites particular attention to these connections, one cannot reasonably assume that they are not found in nonsocial domains as well. We also noted that social stimuli are often more complex and multifaceted than the nonsocial stimuli presented in research on categorization, and this makes the nature of social categorization relatively more uncertain. Again, while it may be generally true that people are much more complex than most other stimuli we encounter, it is also true that the categorization of nonsocial stimuli can also be uncertain as they can also be multifaceted (e.g., Malt, Ross, & Murphy, 1995; Murphy & Ross, 1994; Ross & Murphy, 1996). In these respects, the case for major qualitative differences between social categorization and the categorization of nonsocial stimuli remains relatively unconvincing.

However, there may yet be one respect in which social categorization is more meaningfully distinct from other kinds of categorization. Specifically, in social categorization, it is possible for the perceiver to *identify* with the target of categorization in a way that is generally unlikely to occur with nonsocial objects. Although the prospects are dim for my ability to identify with an oak tree or an ashtray, I might, under at least some circumstances, be able to identify with virtually any person I might be contemplating. At the personal level, this identification involves empathizing with the target and taking his or her perspective, which might influence how the person is categorized and stereotyped. Moreover, once a person is categorized as belonging to "my group," then a social level of identification emerges in which commonalities are emphasized and differences minimized (Turner et al., 1994). Perhaps the most critical fact about social categorization is the fact that, by imposing a particular categorical identity on another person, we are, implicitly or explicitly, invoking a social identity that either includes or excludes ourselves; this process carries with it particularly potent motivational and affective consequences that influence how social perception unfolds. In this section, we explore the implications of this unique aspect of social categorization.

Beginning in infancy, it is clear that most people have the capacity to empathize with other people (and perhaps some animals), "putting themselves in the shoes" of social targets (Davis, 1994; Kohlberg, 1976; Mead, 1934). There is abundant evidence attesting to the prosocial benefits that can be gleaned from imagining the thoughts, feelings, and experiences of others, including an increased interest in their welfare (Batson, Chang, Orr, & Rowland, 2002; Clore & Jeffery, 1972), heightened attention to the unjust treatment of stigmatized groups (Finlay & Stephan, 2000), more inclusive categorical representations of others and their social groups (Davis, Conklin, Smith, & Luce, 1996), and decreased stereotype activation and application (Galinsky & Moskowitz, 2000). With respect to the latter two, it has been suggested that adopting the perspective of another individual leads people "to perceive that they themselves and members of the other group share a common humanity and a common destiny" (Stephan & Finlay, 1999, p. 735). Although perhaps melodramatically phrased, this insight is appropriate to the kinds of dramatic shifts in social perception that can be evident when empathy is felt for the members of otherwise negatively stereotyped or despised social categories. Perspective taking is instrumental in altering the way in which social targets are represented cognitively because focusing on the unique attributes of individual targets, or focusing on the similarities between the target and the perceiver, reduces the salience of intergroup boundaries. As previously noted, perceiving a target as belonging to a different group is sufficient, in and of itself, to motivate discriminatory responses toward the target (e.g., Tajfel & Turner, 1986). Reducing intergroup boundaries should therefore substantially reduce the possibility that targets will be perceived by reference to negative stereotypes associated with their out-group status.

The power of empathy is sometimes so substantial that not only might a target's out-group status be minimized but also it might actually be converted to in-group status. That is, feelings of empathy may result in social targets being recategorized within a common in-group identity (Gaertner & Dovidio, 2000) with subsequent impressions becoming more "self-like" rather than stereotype based. Recent research by Galinsky and Moskowitz (2000) found that college students showed decreased activation of stereotypic concepts associated with the elderly (e.g., *dependent, stubborn, forgetful*) after writing an essay about a day in the life of an elderly person. Galinsky and Moskowitz argue that taking the perspective of a target causes the perceiver's mental representation of that target to merge with his or her own self-representation (cf., Aron, Aron, Tudor, & Nelson, 1991). By extension, if the target's social group membership is salient, this "self-other merging" may actually lead to an "in-group-out-group merging" (Cialdini, Brown, Lewis, Luce, & Neuberg, 1997; Davis et al., 1996).

An alternative but related possibility is that perspective taking reduces stereotype activation through its amplification of self-focus, which, in turn, enhances the efficiency of self-regulatory processes (Carver & Scheier, 1981). That is, as a perceiver actively imagines how he or she would feel if put in the target's situation, the perceiver's level of self-awareness is likely to escalate. This heightened self-focus may be sufficient to trigger self-regulatory processes including the regulation of undesirable stereotypes (Macrae, Bodenhausen, & Milne, 1998). Current work in our lab is examining the extent to which heightened self-focus mediates prejudice reduction following perspective taking.

There are other important questions about the role of empathy in social perception that remain to be addressed. For example, while the literature is replete with instances in which adopting a target's psychological perspective has proven to be effective at "smoothing the cogs of social interaction and fostering social bonds" (Galinsky, Ku, & Wang, 2005, p. 110), the majority of this research has induced perspective taking via explicit instructions. Consequently, it remains an empirical question under which conditions perceivers spontaneously take the perspective of a stereotyped group member in the absence of explicit instructions from an experimenter.

The literature reviewed earlier makes it clear that empathy can provide a basis for cognitively including the social target within the in-group, producing fundamental shifts in how the person is evaluated and mentally represented. The reverse process also holds: perceiving a person to be a fellow in-group member produces positive feelings and a sense of shared characteristics (e.g., Simon, Pantaleo, & Mummendey, 1995; Smith, Coates, & Walling, 1999). The ability to project properties from the self onto to others who are perceived to be members of the same in-group (Robbins & Krueger, 2005) is another aspect of social categorization that is unlikely to find many analogs in the realm of nonsocial categorization.

VI. Conclusions

Research on the categorization of people leads to a range of research questions that one might be much less inclined to pursue if one studied the categorization of nonsocial objects. The inherent complexity of human beings, affording multiple bases for categorization of any particular social target, raises questions about how categories are selected under conditions of uncertainty. The social world is where we commonly experience our most important life outcomes, so a range of motivational forces come to bear on the categorization process in social perception. Additionally, we argue that the emotional stakes are commonly higher in the contemplation of social, as compared to nonsocial, stimuli. These realities of social perception have led to a wide range of research on the motivational and affective contexts of everyday cognition. However, it is clearly the case that one could readily investigate these same issues in nonsocial domains. Uncertainty, motivated preferences, or emotional reactions surely exist in other domains of categorization too, but the social context compels the investigation of these issues, because of their centrality to interpersonal life.

What may be unique to social categorization and perception is the particular set of motives and emotions that are associated with identification with a target that is being categorized. The categories that are brought to bear on nonsocial objects (with the exception of certain broad categories such as "animals," "things that move," or "things found on Earth") are almost never ones that include the perceiver. In the social domain, imposed categories carry very important information based on whether they include or exclude the perceiver. Inclusion implies similarity and solidarity, while exclusion implies a divide that can foster mistrust and the presumption of differences (e.g., Miller & Prentice, 1999). These emotions and motivations are intrinsic to the categorization process itself, and they ultimately constitute the fundamental difference between social and nonsocial categorization.

Social categorization is a topic of importance in social psychology because it is assumed to guide and influence social interaction. In Fig. 2, we sketched out our view of how categories come to bias social responses. The connections between social categorization and behavior lead to another issue that is probably not widespread in nonsocial domains: self-scrutiny of categorization processes and outcomes. The connections between social categorization and social justice are hard to escape in modern society. Moral and deontic considerations govern basic processes of categorization in the social domain in powerful ways. As Allport (1954) knew, to understand social categorization requires not only understanding the basic, "rational" processes that govern generalizations of all kinds but also to investigate the "irrational" motives and emotions that bias the formation and use of these generalizations, producing impressions that sometimes reflect and reproduce a range of cultural injustices. In the post–civil rights era, it is clear that many social perceivers are aware of this danger, and they engage in self-regulatory processes designed to produce acceptably egalitarian social perceptions and behavior. The basic mechanisms of categorization thus must be situated within the contexts of culture and history, if their operation in the social domain is to be fully illuminated.

REFERENCES

Ahn, W. (1998). Why are different features central for natural kinds versus artifacts? The role of causal status in determining feature centrality. *Cognition, 69,* 135–178.

Allport, G. W. (1954). *The nature of prejudice.* Reading, MA: Addison-Wesley.

Amodio, D. M., Harmon-Jones, E., Devine, P. G., Curtin, J. J., Hartley, S. L., & Covert, A. E. (2004). Neural signals for the detection of unintentional race bias. *Psychological Science, 15,* 88–93.

Aron, A., Aron, E. N., Tudor, M., & Nelson, G. (1991). Close relationships as including other in the self. *Journal of Personality and Social Psychology, 60,* 241–253.

Barden, J., Maddux, W. W., Petty, R. E., & Brewer, M. B. (2004). Contextual moderation of racial bias: The impact of social roles on controlled and automatically activated attitudes. *Journal of Personality and Social Psychology, 87,* 5–22.

Bargh, J. A. (1990). Automotives: Preconscious determinants of thought and behavior. In E. T. Higgins and R. M. Sorrentino (Eds.), *Handbook of motivation and cognition* (Vol. 2, pp. 93–130). New York: Guilford.

Bargh, J. A. (1999). The cognitive monster: The case against the controllability of automatic stereotype effects. In S. Chaiken and Y. Trope (Eds.), *Dual process theories in social psychology* (pp. 361–382). New York: Guilford.

Bargh, J. A., & Gollwitzer, P. M. (1994). Environmental control of goal-directed action: Automatic and strategic contingencies between situations and behavior. In W. D. Spaulding (Ed.), *Integrative views of motivation, cognition, and emotion* (pp. 71–124). Lincoln, NE: University of Nebraska Press.

Baron, R. S., Inman, M. L., Kao, C. F., & Logan, H. (1992). Negative emotion and superficial social processing. *Motivation and Emotion, 16,* 323–346.

Batson, C. D., Chang, J., Orr, R., & Rowland, J. (2002). Empathy, attitudes and action: Can feeling for a member of a stigmatized group motivate one to help the group. *Personality and Social Psychology Bulletin, 28,* 1656–1666.

Baumeister, R. F., & Leary, M. R. (1995). The need to belong: Desire for interpersonal attachments as a fundamental human motivation. *Psychological Bulletin, 117,* 497–529.

Berkowitz, L. (1993). Towards a general theory of anger and emotional aggression: Implications of the cognitive-neoassociationistic perspective for the analysis of anger and other emotions. In R. S. Wyer, Jr. and T. K. Srull (Eds.), *Perspectives on anger and emotion: Advances in social cognition* (Vol. 6, pp. 1–46). Hillsdale, NJ: Erlbaum.

Biernat, M. (2003). Toward a broader view of social stereotyping. *American Psychologist, 58,* 1019–1027.

Bless, H. (2001). Mood and the use of general knowledge structures. In L. L. Martin and G. L. Clore (Eds.), *Theories of mood and cognition: A user's guidebook.* Mahwah, N J: Erlbaum.

Bless, H., Bohner, G., Schwarz, N., & Strack, F. (1990). Mood and persuasion: A cognitive response analysis. *Personality and Social Psychology Bulletin, 16,* 311–345.

Bless, H., Schwarz, N., & Kemmelmeier, M. (1996). Mood and stereotyping: The impact of moods on the use of general knowledge structures. In M. Hewstone and W. Stroebe (Eds.), *European review of social psychology* (Vol. 7, pp. 63–93). New York: Wiley.

Bodenhausen, G. V. (1988). Stereotypic biases in decision making and memory: Testing process models of stereotype use. *Journal of Personality and Social Psychology, 55*, 726–737.
Bodenhausen, G. V. (1993). Emotions, arousal, and stereotypic judgments: A heuristic model of affect and stereotyping. In D. M. Mackie and D. L. Hamilton (Eds.), *Affect, cognition, and stereotyping* (pp. 13–37). San Diego, CA: Academic Press.
Bodenhausen, G. V., & Macrae, C. N. (1998). Stereotype activation and inhibition. In R. S. Wyer, Jr. (Ed.), *Stereotype activation and inhibition: Advances in social cognition* (Vol. 11, pp. 1–52). Mahwah, NJ: Erlbaum.
Bodenhausen, G. V., Kramer, G. P., & Süsser, K. (1994a). Happiness and stereotypic thinking in social judgment. *Journal of Personality and Social Psychology, 66*, 621–632.
Bodenhausen, G. V., Sheppard, L. A., & Kramer, G. P. (1994b). Negative affect and social judgment: The differential impact of anger and sadness. *European Journal of Social Psychology, 24*, 45–62.
Bodenhausen, G. V., Macrae, C. N., & Sherman, J. S. (1999). On the dialectics of discrimination: Dual processes in social stereotyping. In S. Chaiken and Y. Trope (Eds.), *Dual-process theories in social psychology* (pp. 271–290). New York: Guilford Press.
Bodenhausen, G. V., Mussweiler, T., Gabriel, S., & Moreno, K. N. (2001). Affective influences on stereotyping and intergroup relations. In J. P. Forgas (Ed.), *Handbook of affect and social cognition* (pp. 319–343). Mahwah, NJ: Erlbaum.
Bower, G. H., & Mayer, J. D. (1985). Failure to replicate mood-dependent retrieval. *Bulletin of the Psychonomic Society, 23*, 39–42.
Bower, G. H., Gilligan, S. G., & Monteiro, K. P. (1981). Selectivity of learning caused by affective states. *Journal of Experimental Psychology: General, 110*, 451–473.
Brewer, M. B. (1988). A dual-process model of impression formation. In T. K. Srull and R. S. Wyer, Jr. (Eds.), *A dual-process model of impression formation: Advances in social cognition* (Vol. 1, pp. 1–36). Hillsdale, NJ: Erlbaum.
Bruner, J. S. (1957). On perceptual readiness. *Psychological Review, 64*, 123–152.
Carver, C. S., & Scheier, M. F. (1981). The self-attention-induced feedback loop and social facilitation. *Journal of Experimental Social Psychology, 17*, 545–568.
Carver, C. S., & Scheier, M. F. (1990). Principles of self regulation. In E. T. Higgins and R. Sorrentino (Eds.), *Handbook of motivation and cognition* (Vol. 2, pp. 3–52). New York: Guilford.
Cialdini, R. B., Brown, S. L., Lewis, B. P., Luce, C., & Neuberg, S. L. (1997). Reinterpreting the empathy-altruism relationship: When one into one equals oneness. *Journal of Personality and Social Psychology, 73*, 481–494.
Clore, G. L., & Jeffery, K. M. (1972). Emotional role playing, attitude change, and attraction toward a disabled person. *Journal of Personality and Social Psychology, 23*, 105–111.
Clore, G.L, Gasper, K., & Garvin, E. (2001). Affect as information. In J. P. Forgas (Ed.), *Handbook of affect and social cognition* (pp. 121–144). Mahwah, NJ: Erlbaum.
Conrey, F. R., Sherman, J. W., Gawronski, B., Hugenberg, K., & Groom, C. (2005). Separating multiple processes in implicit social cognition: The quad-model of implicit task performance. *Journal of Personality and Social Psychology, 89*, 469–487.
Curtis, G. J., & Locke, V. (2005). The effect of anxiety on impression formation: Affect-congruent or stereotypic biases? *British Journal of Social Psychology, 44*, 65–83.
Davis, M. H. (1994). *Empathy: A social psychological approach*. Boulder, CO: Westview Press.
Davis, M. H., Conklin, L., Smith, A., & Luce, C. (1996). Effect of perspective taking on the cognitive representation of persons: A merging of self and other. *Journal of Personality and Social Psychology, 70*, 713–726.
Devine, P. G. (1989). Stereotypes and prejudice: Their automatic and controlled components. *Journal of Personality and Social Psychology, 56*, 5–18.

Dovidio, J. F., & Gaertner, S. L. (2004). Aversive racism. In M. P. Zanna (Ed.), *Advances in experimental social psychology* (Vol. 36, pp. 1–52). Amsterdam: Elsevier.

Dovidio, J. F., Gaertner, S. L., Isen, A. M., Rust, M., & Guerra, P. (1998). Positive affect, cognition, and the reduction of intergroup bias. In C. Sedikides, J. Schopler, and C. A. Insko (Eds.), *Intergroup cognition and intergroup behavior* (pp. 337–366). Mahwah, NJ: Erlbaum.

Dovidio, J. F., Gaertner, S. L., & Loux, S. (2000). Subjective experiences and intergroup relations: The role of positive affect. In H. Bless and J. P. Forgas (Eds.), *The message within: The role of subjective experience in social cognition and behavior* (pp. 340–371). New York: Psychology Press.

Dovidio, J. F., Glick, P., & Rudman, L. A. (Eds.) (2005). *On the nature of prejudice: Fifty years after Allport.* Malden, MA: Blackwell.

Dunning, D. (2001). On the motives underlying social cognition. In A. Tesser and N. Schwarz (Eds.), *Blackwell handbook of social psychology: Intraindividual processes* (pp. 348–374). Malden, MA: Blackwell.

Easterbrook, J. A. (1959). The effect of emotion on cue utilization and the organization of behavior. *Psychological Review, 66,* 183–201.

Edwards, J. A., & Weary, G. (1993). Depression and the impression-formation continuum: Piecemeal processing despite the availability of category information. *Journal of Personality and Social Psychology, 64,* 636–645.

Eysenck, M. W. (1992). *Anxiety: The cognitive perspective.* Hove: Lawrence Erlbaum Associates.

Fein, S., & Spencer, S. J. (1997). Prejudice as self-image maintenance: Affirming the self through derogating others. *Journal of Personality and Social Psychology, 73,* 31–44.

Finlay, K. A., & Stephan, W. G. (2000). Improving intergroup relations: The effects of empathy on racial attitudes. *Journal of Applied Social Psychology, 30,* 1720–1737.

Fiske, S. T. (2004). *Social beings: A core motives approach to social psychology.* New York: Wiley.

Fiske, S. T., & Neuberg, S. L. (1990). A continuum model of impression formation, from category-based to individuating processes: Influence of information and motivation on attention and interpretation. In M. P. Zanna (Ed.), *Advances in experimental social psychology* (Vol. 23, pp. 1–74). New York: Academic Press.

Ford, T. E., & Kruglanski, A. W. (1995). Effects of epistemic motivations on the use of accessible constructs in social judgment. *Personality and Social Psychology Bulletin, 21,* 950–962.

Fredrickson, B. L., & Branigan, C. (2005). Positive emotions broaden the scope of attention and thought-action repertoires. *Cognition & Emotion, 19,* 313–332.

Frijda, N. H. (1988). The laws of emotion. *American Psychologist, 43,* 349–358.

Gaertner, S. L., & Dovidio, J. F. (2000). *Reducing intergroup bias: The common ingroup identity model.* New York: Psychology Press.

Galinsky, A. D., & Moskowitz, G. B. (2000). Perspective-taking: Decreasing stereotype expression, stereotype accessibility, and in-group favoritism. *Journal of Personality and Social Psychology, 78,* 708–724.

Galinsky, A. D., Ku, G., & Wang, C. S. (2005). Perspective-taking and self-other overlap: Fostering social bonds and facilitating social coordination. *Group Processes & Intergroup Relations, 8,* 109–124.

Gasper, K. (2004). Do you see what I see? Affect and visual information processing. *Cognition & Emotion, 18,* 405–421.

Gasper, K., & Clore, G. L. (2002). Attending to the big picture: Mood and global versus local processing of visual information. *Psychological Science, 13,* 34–40.

Gawronski, B., & Bodenhausen, G. V. (in press). Associative and propositional processes in evaluation: An integrative review of implicit and explicit attitude change. *Psychological Bulletin*.

Hastie, R., & Carlston, D. E. (1980). Theoretical issues in person memory. In R. Hastie, T. M. Ostrom, E. B. Ebbesen, R. S. Wyer, Jr., D. L. Hamilton, and D. E. Carlston (Eds.), *Person memory: The cognitive basis of social perception* (pp. 1–53). Hillsdale, NJ: Erlbaum.

Hugenberg, K., & Bodenhausen, G. V. (2003). Facing prejudice: Implicit prejudice and the perception of facial threat. *Psychological Science, 14*, 640–643.

Hugenberg, K., Bodenhausen, G. V., Becker, A. P., & Perrott, D. A. (2005). *Affective states influence category selection in person perception*. Unpublished manuscript.

Isen, A. M., Niedenthal, P. M., & Cantor, N. (1992). An influence of positive affect on social categorization. *Motivation and Emotion, 16*, 65–78.

Jones, J. M. (1997). *Prejudice and racism* (2nd ed.). New York: McGraw-Hill.

Kawakami, K., Dion, K., & Dovidio, J. (1998). Racial prejudice and stereotype activation. *Personality and Social Psychology Bulletin, 24*, 407–416.

Kohlberg, L. (1976). Moral stages and moralization: The cognitive–developmental approach. In T. Lickona (Ed.), *Moral development and behavior* (pp. 31–53). New York: Holt, Rinehart & Winston.

Krech, D., & Crutchfield, R. S. (1948). *Theory and problems of social psychology*. New York: McGraw-Hill.

Kruglanski, A. W., & Freund, T. (1983). The freezing and unfreezing of lay-inferences: Effects on impressional primacy, ethnic stereotyping, and numerical anchoring. *Journal of Experimental Social Psychology, 19*, 448–468.

Kruglanski, A. W., & Webster, D. M. (1996). Motivated closing of the mind: "Seizing" and "freezing." *Psychological Review, 103*, 263–283.

Kunda, Z., & Spencer, S. J. (2003). When do stereotypes come to mind and when do they color judgment? A goal-based theoretical framework for stereotype activation and application. *Psychological Bulletin, 129*, 522–544.

Kwan, V. S. Y., John, O. P., Kenny, D. A., Bond, M. H., & Robins, R. W. (2004). Reconceptualizing individual differences in self-enhancement bias: An interpersonal approach. *Psychological Review, 111*, 94–110.

Lambert, A. J., Khan, S. R., Lickel, B. A., & Fricke, K. (1997). Mood and the correction of positive versus negative stereotypes. *Journal of Personality and Social Psychology, 72*, 1002–1016.

Lepore, L., & Brown, R. (1997). Category and stereotype activation: Is prejudice inevitable? *Journal of Personality and Social Psychology, 72*, 275–287.

Lerner, J. S., Goldberg, J. H., & Tetlock, P. E. (1998). Sober second thought: The effects of accountability, anger, and authoritarianism on attributions of responsibility. *Personality and Social Psychology Bulletin, 24*, 563–574.

Lingle, J. H., Altom, M. W., & Medin, D. L. (1984). Of cabbages and kings: Assessing the extendability of natural object concept models to social things. In R. S. Wyer, Jr. and T. K. Srull (Eds.), *Handbook of social cognition* (1st ed. Vol. 1, pp. 71–117). Hillsdale, NJ: Erlbaum.

MacDonald, A. W., Cohen, J. D., Stenger, V. A., & Carter, C. S. (2000). Dissociating the role of dorsolateral prefrontal cortex and anterior cingulate cortex in cognitive control. *Science, 288*, 1835–1837.

Mackie, D. M., & Worth, L. T. (1989). Processing deficits and the mediation of positive affect in persuasion. *Journal of Personality and Social Psychology, 57*, 27–40.

Macrae, C. N., & Bodenhausen, G. V. (2000). Social cognition: Thinking categorically about others. *Annual Review of Psychology, 51*, 93–120.

Macrae, C. N., Bodenhausen, G. V., Milne, A. B., & Jetten, J. (1994). Out of mind but back in sight: Stereotypes on the rebound. *Journal of Personality and Social Psychology, 67*, 808–817.

Macrae, C. N., Bodenhausen, G. V., & Milne, A. B. (1995). The dissection of selection in person perception: Inhibitory processes in social stereotyping. *Journal of Personality and Social Psychology, 69*, 397–407.

Macrae, C. N., Bodenhausen, G. V., & Milne, A. B. (1998). Saying no to unwanted thoughts: Self-focus and the regulation of mental life. *Journal of Personality and Social Psychology, 74*, 578–589.

Malt, B. C., Ross, B. H., & Murphy, G. L. (1995). Predicting features for members of natural categories when categorization is uncertain. *Journal of Experimental Psychology: Learning, Memory, and Cognition, 21*, 646–661.

Markus, H., & Zajonc, R. B. (1985). The cognitive perspective in social psychology. In G. Lindzey and E. Aronson (Eds.), *Handbook of social psychology* (3rd ed., pp. 137–230). New York: Random House.

Matthews, G., & Wells, A. (1999). The cognitive science of attention and emotion. In T. Dalgleish and M. Power (Eds.), *Handbook of cognition and emotion* (pp. 171–192). New York: Wiley.

McGuire, W. J., McGuire, C. V., Child, P., & Fujioka, T. (1978). Salience of ethnicity in the spontaneous self-concept as a function of one's ethnic distinctiveness in the social environment. *Journal of Personality and Social Psychology, 36*, 511–520.

Mead, G. H. (1934). *Mind, self, and society.* Chicago: University of Chicago Press.

Miller, D. T., & Prentice, D. A. (1999). Some consequences of belief in a group essence: The category divide hypothesis. In D. A. Prentice and D. T. Miller (Eds.), *Cultural divides: Understanding and overcoming group conflict.* New York: Russell Sage Foundation.

Monteith, M. J. (1993). Self-regulation of prejudiced responses: Implications for progress in prejudice reduction efforts. *Journal of Personality and Social Psychology, 65*, 469–485.

Monteith, M. J., & Voils, C. I. (2001). Exerting control over prejudiced responses. In G. B. Moskowitz (Ed.), *Cognitive social psychology: The Princeton symposium on the legacy and future of social cognition* (pp. 375–388). Mahwah, NJ: Erlbaum.

Monteith, M. J., Sherman, J. W., & Devine, P. G. (1998). Suppression as a stereotype control strategy. *Personality and Social Psychology Review, 2*, 63–82.

Monteith, M. J., Ashburn-Nardo, L., Voils, C. I., & Czopp, A. M. (2002). Putting the brakes on prejudice: On the development and operation of cues for control. *Journal of Personality and Social Psychology, 83*, 1029–1050.

Moskowitz, G. B., Gollwitzer, P. M., Wasel, W., & Schaal, B. (1999). Preconscious control of stereotype activation through chronic egalitarian goals. *Journal of Personality and Social Psychology, 77*, 167–184.

Moskowitz, G. B., Salomon, A. R., & Taylor, C. M. (2000). Preconsciously controlling stereotyping: Implicitly activated egalitarian goals prevent the activation of stereotypes. *Social Cognition, 18*, 151–177.

Murphy, G. L., & Ross, B. H. (1994). Predictions from uncertain categorizations. *Cognitive Psychology, 27*, 148–193.

Mussweiler, T., Gabriel, S., & Bodenhausen, G. V. (2000). Shifting social identities as a strategy for deflecting threatening social comparisons. *Journal of Personality and Social Psychology, 79*, 398–409.

Nelson, L. J., & Miller, D. T. (1995). The distinctiveness effect in social categorization: You are what makes you unusual. *Psychological Science, 6*, 246–249.

Oskamp, S. (Ed.) (2000). *Reducing prejudice and discrimination.* Mahwah, NJ: Erlbaum.

Park, J., & Banaji, M. R. (2000). Mood and heuristics: The influence of happy and sad states on sensitivity and bias in stereotyping. *Journal of Personality and Social Psychology, 78,* 1005–1023.

Patalano, A. L., Chin-Parker, S., & Ross, B. H. (2006). The importance of being coherent: Category coherence, cross-classification, and reasoning. *Journal of Memory and Language, 54,* 407–424.

Payne, B. K. (2001). Prejudice and perception: The role of automatic and controlled processes in misperceiving a weapon. *Journal of Personality and Social Psychology, 81,* 181–192.

Pedersen, A., Beven, J., Walker, I., & Griffiths, B. (2004). Attitudes toward indigenous Australians: The role of empathy and guilt. *Journal of Community & Applied Social Psychology, 14,* 233–249.

Petty, R. E., & Wegener, D. T. (1993). Flexible correction processes in social judgment: Correcting for context-induced contrast. *Journal of Experimental Social Psychology, 29,* 137–165.

Plant, E. A., & Devine, P. G. (1998). Internal and external motivation to respond without prejudice. *Journal of Personality and Social Psychology, 75,* 811–832.

Posner, M. I., & Rothbart, M. K. (2000). Developing mechanisms of self-regulation. *Development and Psychopathology, 12,* 427–441.

Robbins, J. M., & Krueger, J. (2005). Social projection to ingroups and outgroups: A review and meta-analysis. *Personality and Social Psychology Review, 9,* 32–47.

Ross, B. H., & Murphy, G. L. (1996). Category-based predictions: Influence of uncertainty and feature associations. *Journal of Experimental Psychology: Learning, Memory, & Cognition, 22,* 736–753.

Sagar, H. A., & Schofield, J. W. (1980). Racial and behavioral cues in black and white children's perceptions of ambiguously aggressive acts. *Journal of Personality and Social Psychology, 39,* 590–598.

Scheerer, M. (1954). Cognitive theory. In G. Lindzey (Ed.), *Handbook of social psychology* (1st ed., pp. 91–142). Reading, MA: Addison-Wesley.

Schneider, D. J. (2004). *The psychology of stereotyping.* New York: Guilford.

Schuman, H., Steeh, C., Bobo, L., & Krysan, M. (1997). *Racial attitudes in America: Trends and interpretations* (2nd ed.). Harvard University Press: Cambridge, MA.

Schwartz, S. (1996). Value priorities and behavior: Applying a theory of integrated value systems. In C. Seligman, J. M. Olson, and M. P. Zanna (Eds.), *The psychology of values: The Ontario symposium* (Vol. 8, pp. 1–24). Hillsdale, NJ: Erlbaum.

Schwarz, N. (2001). Feelings as information: Implications for affective influences on information processing. In L.L. Martin & G.L. Clore (Eds.) *Theories of Mood and Cognition: A user's guidebook.* Mahweh, N J: Erlbaum.

Simon, B., Pantaleo, G., & Mummendey, A. (1995). Unique individual or interchangeable group member? The accentuation of intragroup differences versus similarities as an indicator of the individual self versus the collective self. *Journal of Personality and Social Psychology, 69,* 106–119.

Sinclair, L., & Kunda, Z. (1999). Reactions to a black professional: Motivated inhibition and activation of conflicting stereotypes. *Journal of Personality and Social Psychology, 77,* 885–904.

Smith, E. R., Coates, S., & Walling, D. (1999). Overlapping mental representations of self, ingroup, and partner: Further response time evidence and a connectionist model. *Personality and Social Psychology Bulletin, 25,* 873–882.

Smith, M. B., Bruner, J. S., & White, RW. (1956). *Opinions and personality.* Wiley: New York.

Son Hing, L. S., Li, W., & Zanna, M. P. (2002). Inducing hypocrisy to reduce prejudicial responses among aversive racists. *Journal of Experimental Social Psychology, 38,* 71–78.

Spencer, S. J., Fein, S., Wolfe, C. T., Fong, C., & Dunn, M. A. (1998). Automatic activation of stereotypes: The role of self-image threat. *Personality and Social Psychology Bulletin, 24*, 1139–1152.

Srull, T. K., & Wyer, R. S., Jr. (1986). The role of chronic and temporary goals in social information processing. In R. M. Sorrentino and E. T. Higgins (Eds.), *Handbook of motivation and cognition* (Vol. 1, pp. 503–549). New York: Guilford.

Stangor, C., Lynch, L, Duan, C., & Glass, B. (1992). Categorization of individuals on the basis of multiple social features. *Journal of Personality and Social Psychology, 62*, 207–218.

Stephan, W. G., & Finlay, K. (1999). The role of empathy in improving intergroup relations. *Journal of Social Issues, 55*, 729–743.

Strack, F., & Deutsch, R. (2004). Reflexive and impulsive determinants of social behavior. *Personality and Social Psychology Review, 8*, 220–247.

Strack, F., & Hannover, B. (1996). Awareness of influence as a precondition for implementing correctional goals. In P. M. Gollwitzer and J. A. Bargh (Eds.), *The psychology of action: Linking cognition and motivation to behavior* (pp. 579–596). New York: Guilford Press.

Tajfel, H., & Turner, J. C. (1986). The social identify theory of intergroup behavior. In S. Worchel and W. G. Austin (Eds.), *Psychology of intergroup relations* (pp. 7–24). Chicago: Nelson-Hall.

Tropp, L. R., & Pettigrew, T. F. (2005). Differential relationships between intergroup contact and affective and cognitive dimensions of prejudice. *Personality and Social Psychology Bulletin, 31*, 1145–1158.

Turner, J. C., Oakes, P., Haslam, S. A., & McGarty, C. (1994). Self and collective: Cognition and social context. *Personality and Social Psychology Bulletin, 20*, 454–463.

Wattenmaker, W. D. (1995). Knowledge structures and linear separability: Integrating information in object and social categorization. *Cognitive Psychology, 28*, 274–328.

Wattenmaker, W. D. (2000). Domains and knowledge effects: Strategies in object and social classification. *American Journal of Psychology, 113*, 405–429.

Weary, G., & Gannon, K. (1996). Depression, control motivation, and person perception. In P. M. Gollwitzer and J. A. Bargh (Eds.), *The psychology of action: Linking cognition and motivation to behavior*. New York: Guilford Press.

Wegener, D. T., & Petty, R. E. (1997). The flexible correction model: The role of naive theories of bias in bias correction. In M. P. Zanna (Ed.), *Advances in experimental social psychology* (Vol. 29, pp. 141–208). Mahwah, NJ: Erlbaum.

Wegner, D. M. (1994). Ironic processes of mental control. *Psychological Review, 101*, 34–52.

Wilder, D. A. (1993). The role of anxiety in facilitating stereotypic judgments of outgroup behavior. In D. Mackie and D. L. Hamilton (Eds.), *Affect, cognition, and stereotyping: Interactive processes in group perception* (pp. 87–109). San Diego: Academic Press.

Wilson, T. D., & Brekke, N. (1994). Mental contamination and mental correction: Unwanted influences on judgments and evaluations. *Psychological Bulletin, 116*, 117–142.

Wittenbrink, B., Judd, C. M., & Park, B. (1997). Evidence for racial prejudice at the implicit level and its relationships with questionnaire measures. *Journal of Personality and Social Psychology, 72*, 262–274.

Wittenbrink, B., Hilton, J. L., & Gist, P. L. (1998). In search of similarity: Stereotypes as naïve theories in social categorization. *Social Cognition, 16*, 31–55.

Wittenbrink, B., Judd, C. M., & Park, B. (2001). Spontaneous prejudice in context: Variability in automatically activated attitudes. *Journal of Personality and Social Psychology, 81*, 815–827.

Woike, B., & McAdams, D. (2004). Motives. In V. J. Derlega, B. J. Winstead, and W. H. Jones (Eds.), *Personality: Contemporary theory and research* . (3rd ed., pp. 156–189). Belmont, CA: Wadsworth.

Wyer, R. S., Jr., & Srull, T. K. (1989). *Memory and cognition in its social context.* Hillsdale, NJ: Erlbaum.

Wyer, R. S., Jr., Clore, G. L., & Isbell, L. (1999). Affect and information processing. In M. P. Zanna (Ed.), *Advances in experimental social psychology* (Vol. 31, pp. 1–77). New York: Academic Press.

RECONSIDERING THE ROLE OF STRUCTURE IN VISION

Elan Barenholtz and Michael J. Tarr

I. Introduction

How do we recognize complex objects? The problem of recognition can be summarized as determining how perceptual mechanisms map infinitely varying two-dimensional images into representations of a finite set of three-dimensional objects. Both learning and memory are intrinsic to this process; learning because inferences must be made about the regularities in the way objects vary across examples, and memory because theories of object recognition are in essence theories of how objects are instantiated as long-term visual representations. Thus, any account of the visual recognition of complex objects is an account of how observers learn about and remember the visual world.

In this chapter, we consider some fundamental arguments in favor of *structure*–the encoding of objects on the basis of features and their relations–in mental representations and apply them to the particular challenges of visual object recognition. Structural accounts can be distinguished from what we will term pure "holistic" accounts such as simple template and some view-based models. These latter approaches achieve recognition by *globally* matching an incoming input whole cloth to some stored representation that does not distinguish individual features or their relations (e.g., Lades et al., 1993)—perhaps after performing some global transformation on the input or model (e.g., Uilman, 1989). According to these theories no individual features are differentiated; a match between an incoming image and a stored image is registered based on global similarity across a homogeneous input space—that is, each individual unit can play the same role as any other. Structural accounts can also be contrasted with pure "featural" accounts, which encode and recognize objects on the basis of some set of localized features but without *explicitly* encoding the position or relations among these features— that is, a "bag of features" (Mel, 1997).

It is important to point out that the term structure as we are using it here refers only to the question of whether relations and features are encoded separately—an issue that is orthogonal to the specific nature of the features or relations themselves. However, the term has also sometimes been recruited (perhaps inappropriately) in the empirical debate as to whether human object recognition is viewpoint dependent/viewpoint invariant (Biederman & Bar, 1999; Biederman & Gerhardstein, 1995; Hayward & Tarr, 2000; Tarr & Bülthoff, 1995). In these contexts, "structural" has been synonymous with viewpoint invariance, presumably because theories supporting invariance directly consider the properties of three-dimensional volumetric primitives. Indeed, the position of the second author of this chapter has often been mistakenly interpreted as antistructuralist because of his support for the claim that recognition shows viewpoint dependency. However, for the second author at least, the debate about viewpoint dependency was always about the nature of the *features* encoded in object representations (e.g., Geons or view-dependent local features) not about structural versus image-based accounts.[1] That is, image-based object representations were (and are) construed as collections of local, view-dependent image features that *may* or *may not be* related to one another in a structural manner (e.g., Edelman & Intrator, 2003; Tarr & Bülthoff, 1998). In other words, viewpoint-dependent features and volumetric features are *both* consistent with a structural architecture as we are defining it here. Consequently, the second author has taken issue with accounts of his view that paint it as "template-like" or "holistic" in the most simplistic sense (Hummel, 2000).

Intuitions about the critical role of relational information have played a part in a number of influential theories of visual object recognition (Biederman, 1987; Marr & Nishihara, 1978). According to both of these proposals, objects are represented and recognized on the basis of a set of generic volumetric (three-dimensional) primitives and their (explicit) spatial relationships. However, the focus of these theories—along with most other theories of recognition, including our own—has been on determining the

[1] The second author remembers a long and pleasant poolside conversation at the first VisionScienceS meeting in which he and Irv Biederman came to a rapprochement, agreeing that our core difference of opinion what the nature of the features in the representation.

nature of the molar features used by the visual system not on the nature of the spatial relations between such features. For example, Biederman's (1987) "Recognition-By-Components" model is quite specific about its vocabulary of three-dimensional primitives—Geons. In contrast, it makes only a brief mention of the way in which these features are related to one another and it eschews any strong theoretical justification for which relations are included, instead relying more on correspondence with verbalizable predicates, such as "on top of." The empirical research supporting these theories follows a similar pattern: the evidence for (and against) particular feature types is extensive, while the evidence for any explicit representation of relational information is somewhat sparse.

To some extent, this lack of data may be due to an inherent difficulty in establishing evidence for structure: by definition, structural representations require that features and their relations can vary independently; however, without *a priori* knowledge about what constitutes a visual feature there is no way to determine whether a particular experimental manipulation affects only one property and not the other. This "chicken-and-egg" problem raises serious challenges in examining structure directly and has not been successfully dealt with in the experimental literature. Instead, the primary strategy has been to use "likely" features that are chosen by the experimenter based on their plausibility. For example, the primary source of evidence for structural recognition concerns facial recognition in which the set of basic features are nameable parts of the face (e.g., eyes, nose) whose spacing is manipulated by translating the individual features in the image (for an example of attempts to leverage linguistic intuitions to study visual relations, see Hayward & Tarr, 1995). However, there are a number of models of recognition that include higher-order features that include more than one nominal part in a single feature (Ullman, Vidal-Naquet, & Sali, 2002; Zhang & Cottrell, 2005) in which case altering the spacing between the basic parts actually changes the features themselves.

One of the best pieces of evidence for structural models in visual recognition is text reading. Recent empirical evidence suggests that word recognition depends on identifying letters as opposed to recognizing the word holistically as a single pattern. Pelli, Farell, and Moore (2003) showed that words are unreadable unless their individual *letters* can be recognized independently. This means that words are recognized on the basis of constituent features, in this case letters; in addition, since we can quickly and efficiently distinguish between different words consisting of the same letters (e.g., "bat" ≠ "tab"), word identification clearly depends on representing the relations between these features. However, while this is an evidence for a form of structural recognition, it is unclear to what extent reading is representative of more general recognition; unlike other visual features, letters are initially learned as individual, separable symbols that contribute to a whole on the basis of their phonetic referents and there appear to be regions of visual cortex specialized for letter processing (Cohen et al., 2000). In other words, they are explicitly structural in a way that other visual objects are not.

In recent years, the pendulum seems to have swung away from structural accounts to more image-driven theories of recognition. In particular, a number of theories in the computational and neuroscience literature have been proposed (Edelman, 1993; Riesenhuber & Poggio, 1999; Wallis & Rolls, 1997) that rely on a features-only strategy in which the features consist of image patches. Importantly, according to these theories the relations between individual features is not explicitly encoded, only the presence of a feature (in the location it happens to be) is considered as evidence. In this chapter, we reconsider a number of theoretical reasons why encoding features as *well* as some set of relations (i.e., structure) can be computationally advantageous. First, we attempt to define structure in its most general form as it has been defined within other domains of cognition and consider the application to visual recognition. Then we consider a number of varieties of structural theories of recognition and their potential application to specific problems in recognition. In addition, we consider some evidence—both experimental and also based on simple demonstrations—for structural representations in visual recognition.

II. Defining Structure

Structural accounts of recognition are those in which the identification of a visual object depends on both a set of features and the relations between those features within some representational space. Clearly, according to this definition, there are a large variety of potential theories that may be described as structural. "Features" in the visual domain can mean just about anything: image patches, object parts, or particular image properties (e.g., luminance), while "relations" between these features are any comparison between a set of individuated features. A meaningful feature refers to a property of a spatially localized region in an image; that is, it cannot be a global property of the entire image since relations can only be defined between two or more features. For the purposes of the discussion here, we will focus primarily on *spatial* relations between features, sometimes referred to as *configural* information. However, the general arguments we put forward can be applied to other forms of relational encoding as well.

A. Structure as Compositionality

The idea that the identification of a complex whole is dependent on some set of constituent features as well as their relations are related to the more general concept of *compositionality* (Fodor, 1975; Fodor & Pylyshyn, 1988). In general, we may say that some complex object X is *composed* of some units $a,b,c...$ *if and only if* the identity of X as X is contingent on the identities a,b,c and their relations within a space. For example, a grammatical sentence (in English) is composed of words since its grammaticality depends on the property of the words (i.e., their lexical category) and the relations between them (word order). A critical point to compositionality is that the properties of the units are defined *independently* of the composition. For example, the lexical category of the words does not change as a function of its place within the sequence (although some words belong to multiple categories). This latter property is central to compositionality since it allows for new compositions to be generated without new "emergent" properties that must be learned independently.

Compositionality is defined with regard to the assignment of some *property* to a complex entity such as a label, a meaning, or a referent. For visual recognition, a compositional approach is one in which the identification of some object—that is, corresponding to a specific name or category—depends on the object's features *and* their relations. Thus, it is not enough for the visual system to *extract* structure from visual input in a bottom-up manner (Markman, 1999; Marr & Nishihara, 1978); the assignment of a given property must be conditional on that structure. This is a critical distinction to keep in mind when considering evidence for structure in recognition. The primate visual system is clearly able to extract and represent structural information, for example, spatial relations, at a wide variety of scales. This is obviously true for images that contain multiple objects (we can describe, based on visual input, whether the cat is on the mat or the mat is on the cat). In addition, there is a great deal of evidence that the visual system naturally parses unitary objects into smaller units or "parts." Recent research on figure-ground assignment (Barenholtz & Feldman, in press), symmetry detection (Baylis & Driver, 1994), category learning (Goldstone, 2000; Schyns & Rodet, 1998), the movement of attention (Barenholtz & Feldman, 2003), and the perception of transparency (Singh & Hoffman, 1998) have all suggested a division of shapes into distinct parts.

However, the ability and/or propensity to parse scenes into objects and parts and extract structural information is not the same thing as recognizing objects *on the basis* of their structure. There is a significant body of empirical (Markman, 1999) and theoretical (Feldman, 2003a,b) support for structural information in visual grouping. Hinton (1979) demonstrated that mental imagery does include structural information without explicitly addressing how features come to be related to one another. But imagery is not recognition. For example, there is no doubt that we extract the eyes, nose, and mouth from a viewed face (and can potentially use such information in imagining a face); however, this does not rule out the possibility that identifying an image as a face or recognizing a particular individual proceeds holistically—based, for example, on a template model of an entire face in which individual features are not differentiated (e.g., see Zhang & Cottrell, 2005).

Consider the following example: there is a natural tendency to see the large letter "M" in Fig. 1 as being constructed from smaller units—"H"s (such "hierarchical" letters have been used extensively in research concerning local versus global processing; e.g., Navon, 1977). However, we would not say that the "M" is *composed* of "H"s—even though we can clearly discern these nominal "features"—because the identity of the larger pattern as an "M" does not depend on the smaller units being identified as "H"s. For example, if the "H"s were interchanged with some other letter or blurred so as to be unrecognizable, this would not affect the identity of the "M." Alternatively, even if there is a structural description of an object inherently, this does not mean that the visual system employs it for recognition. For example, the square in Fig. 2 can be parsed into an arbitrary set of possible "features" with varying degrees of psychological plausibility. And, unlike the previous example, the identity of the square as such depends on the properties of these features as well as their configuration. However, it is unlikely that the visual system actually uses most of these structural descriptions (and might use none) in identifying squares.

This distinction between "available" structure and what we are calling compositional structure is important to keep in mind when considering evidence for structure in recognition. For example, Hummel (2000) argues against view-based theories of recognition based on the observation that we are able to compare images, such as the right and left images in Fig. 3, in a way that suggests structural encoding (e.g., we would say that both are formed by the same units, a circle and a triangle in different relations).

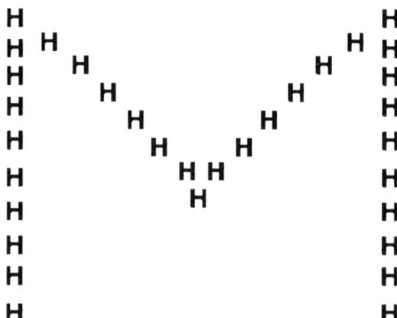

Fig. 1. An "M" built out of "H"s but not *composed* of "H"s.

Reconsidering the Role of Structure in Vision

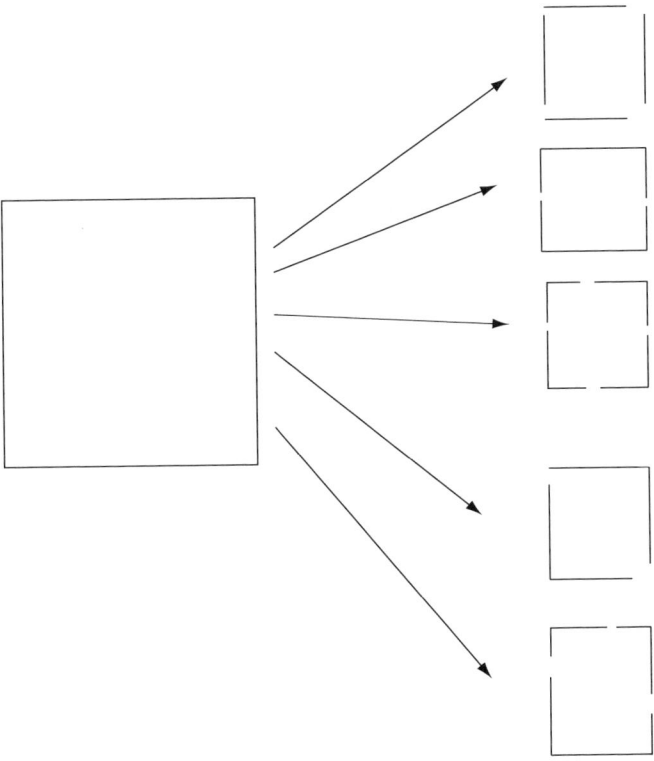

Fig. 2. Parsing a square into arbitrary "features."

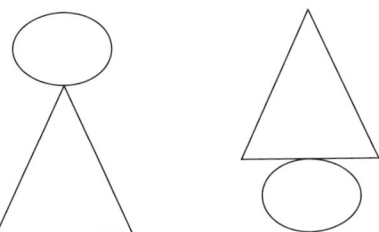

Fig. 3. Adapted from Hummel (2000). The same two features in different configurations.

However, this ability to extract and describe structural information in one context does not necessarily mean that this structure is used to assign a label or category—that is, the process of object recognition. Similarly, in another recent paper, Arguin and Saumier (2004) provide evidence that structural representations are used in a visual search task. Specifically, search is observed to be more difficult when a target shares either parts *or* spatial configurations with distracters. However, visual search—finding a predefined target amongst similar distracters—makes very different processing demands as compared to *de novo* recognition. For example, object recognition is highly underconstrained in that you are unlikely to know *in advance* what you are looking at; even given some scene schema, the potential number of possible objects in enormous. In contrast, visual search typically predefines a single, unique, target and all an observer need to do is extract features from the image that disambiguate it from everything else in the scene. Thus, evidence for structure in one case is not necessarily evidence for structure in the other.

B. THE IMPORTANCE OF FEATURES IN STRUCTURAL REPRESENTATIONS

An obvious issue arises with regard to the "M" in Fig. 1: even if the particular shape of the smaller units (i.e., "H"s) is not critical to the identification of the "M," successful recognition is ultimately dependent on the relations among *some* set of smaller units. Thus, the "M" might still be viewed as being composed of smaller features and their spatial relations. Along the same lines, all of visual recognition might be considered to be trivially compositional because it ultimately depends on the activation of localized units (i.e., ganglion cell receptive fields) whose relative position is clearly critical in encoding and recognizing an object (Edelman, 1993). In particular, the retina and downstream neural layers are organized spatiotopically such that proximity of activation on the retina reflects two-dimensional proximity in the real world. Moreover, it is clear that this structure is utilized by the visual system (to argue otherwise would be silly). A similar argument could be made for the presence of structure with regard to a template model that depends on the activity of individual receptors. However, it is our contention that these examples do not constitute genuine compositionality because these features, independent of their configuration, do not constrain the possible space of objects; *any* object can give rise to a response in almost any specific ganglion receptive field or photoreceptor. The locations that these units encode are only useful in that they contribute to larger patterns of activation based on the information across multiple units.

In other words, meaningful structural accounts, like pure feature-based accounts, require that the identity of the features be critical to the identity of the complex object. This can be captured by stating that in a structural representation both the features and the relations must contain diagnostic *information*. Information (in Shannon's sense) is a measure of the amount of uncertainty that is removed on the basis of some particular datum.

The information (or more precisely "self information," also called the "surprisal") of an individual datum is defined as the negative log of the probability of that datum's occurrence. For example, the result of a fair coin toss carries a certain amount of information because there is uncertainty between two possible outcomes ($\log_2(1/0.5) = \log_2(2) = 1$ bit), while the outcome of a dice roll carries more information because there are six possible outcomes ($\log_2(1/(1/6)) = \log_2(6) = 2.585$ bit).

With regard to recognition or categorization of an image, this construal of information can be used to measure the extent to which the presence of specific features and configurations constrain the space of possible objects in the world that may give rise to that image. For example, given a homogenous distribution of objects,[2] a high information feature would be one that only occurs in the presence of a small number of the objects—and thus whose presence eliminates a large number of potential objects—while a low information feature would be one that occurs in a larger number of objects—and thus whose presence eliminates a smaller number of potential objects. Thus, a visual feature that is common to *all* objects contains *no* information. The activation of any individual photoreceptor, while encoding some property of the distal stimulus, contains almost no information vis-à-vis recognition since nearly *any* object can presumably generate that activation under the right circumstances. A similar argument may apply to the oriented blobs that are characteristic of the receptive field responses in V1 neurons. Although these could potentially serve as candidate features in compositional system (Bienenstock, Geman, & Potter, 1997, treat oriented linelets as the basis of a compositional system) according to the requirement that individual features contain information, this seems unlikely in that virtually any object in the world that is free to move in space can produce a particular oriented edge. Thus, V1 may not be engaged in genuine "feature" extraction but instead may be functioning as a form of filtering that reduces redundancy in the image by only permitting certain patterns of activation to be further processed (Barlow, 1959) or encoding the statistics of natural images using Markov random fields (Black & Roth, 2005). This might simply serve to push the homogeneous input space—that is, in which any unit can play the same role as any other—higher up in the system rather than serving as a genuine compositional feature set.

Of course, just as the features in a structural representation must contain information, so must the relations among features. This means that for some

---

[2] Strictly speaking, the information of a feature measures the probability of its occurrence, which depends both on the number of objects that contain that feature and the probability of the occurrence of those objects; a feature that is specific to a small set of objects that are themselves very common can still have a low information value. However, the rule for a homogeneous distribution described here will, on average, be true.

property to be based on compositional structure, it cannot be derived solely on the basis of the identity of the features alone. For example, if the presence of nose, eyes, and mouth in an image are sufficient evidence to decide that an image contains a face, than the identity "face" is not structural. In other words, in a compositional encoding, information is "shared" among the separable dimensions of feature-type and feature configuration. As we will discuss later, an important outcome of this is that the set of features needed to define a particular object will be more *generic* when configural information is included.

III. Why Be Structural?

The computational utility of compositional structure has been considered in depth with regard to a number of cognitive domains, and in particular, with respect to language. A compositional architecture allows you to generate arbitrary constructions based on a limited set of starting units, a property referred to as *productivity* (Fodor & Pylyshyn, 1988). For example, natural language speakers are able to produce a theoretically infinite set of different grammatical sentences. Since it is not possible to learn every sentence in a language individually, speakers must have access to a compositional system consisting of a finite set of units (words) and rules for ordering them (syntax). By applying composition rules recursively, an infinite set of possible grammatical structures can be produced. Inversely, any grammatical sentence can be parsed into its constituent units and grammatical structure. A rigorous treatment of compositional linguistics was first proposed by Chomsky who showed that a formal language can be described (i.e., every sentence in the language can theoretically be generated) by a set of production rules and a finite set of symbols. While Chomsky's program relates exclusively to grammaticality, the idea of compositionality has been extended to the semantics of language and to our general cognitive capacities. For example, Fodor (1975) argues that thought itself is compositional, based in part on the observation that our mental capacity is open-ended (productive) in much the same way that language is, since we can understand and maintain beliefs about an infinite number of propositions (Fodor & Pylyshyn, 1988).

Is visual recognition productive in the same manner as thought and language? Despite some authors' suggestions to this effect (Edelman & Intrator, 2003), we believe that, strictly speaking, visual recognition is inherently nonproductive. Productivity refers to the capacity to generate or understand *new* compositions in which the set of known units are composed in a way that has not been encountered before (e.g., a novel sentence) but which can be understood based on our knowledge of the constituent units and the composition rules. This capacity to understand new compositions, even those that are superficially radically different from those that have been encountered before is at the heart of Fodor and Pylyshyn's (1988) challenge to noncompositional architectures such as connectionism.[3] Object recognition, on the other hand, consists of determining that some viewed object contains the *same* (or nearly the same) compositional structure (i.e., a specific set of units and their relations) as one that has been viewed before, in order to assign that object to some predetermined category or label. There is no sense in which we are able to recognize some *new* composition of features except insofar as they are similar to some learned composition, an inherently nonproductive form of processing.

Instead, the utility of structural encoding is that it vastly increases the representational capacity of some restricted set of features—an argument cited by Biederman (1987) for using a limited collection of Geons plus spatial relations in his model. A structureless, feature-based approach can be described as representing each object in terms of an unordered set of features (e.g. $\{A,B,D\} = \{D,B,A\} = \{B,A,D\}$). Given a set of N unique features (i.e., the same feature cannot appear more than once in a given object) the number of possible representations is the number of subsets minus one or $2^n - 1$. Assuming that the *position* of the features is informational however (i.e., the sets are ordered so that $\{A,B\}$ is distinguished from $\{B,A\}$), the number of possible objects is $\sum(k = 1:n)n!/(n-k)!$, where n is the number of features. For example, with 6 features you can represent 63 distinct objects based on a feature-only approach. If the sets are ordered, you can represent 1956 objects *based on the same set of features*. In other words, the category defined by the visual features can be further delineated on the basis of configural information. Of course, this number only reflects serial order which is analogous to allowing the encoding of left-of and right-of relations; it would grow more quickly in a spatial coordinate system that encodes above or below and *much* more quickly in an absolute coordinate system that measures distances between features. The potential utility of the increased capacity is twofold. First, it allows you to represent a much larger number of objects on the basis of the same set of features. This allows for a more economical representational system when the encoding cost of the features is higher than the encoding cost of the relations. Second, it allows you to capitalize on structural information that is already present in the image—information that pure feature-based strategies discard—in order to perform recognition when the features themselves might not be diagnostic.

---

[3] Whether such properties are actually consistent or inconsistent with such architectures remain an open question in our minds.

To see this, we identify two broad classes of structural encoding that carry different potential utility for recognition: *category-specific* and *category-generic* structure. Category-specific structure is the application of structural information to a set of features that are bound to a particular category. For example, a given class of objects (e.g., elephants) may contain a unique set of visual features (e.g., big ears, trunk) that is common across multiple exemplars of that category. Moreover, these features may be specific to the particular category and be shared across all the members of that category. These features may be extracted *after* the initial identification has taken pace (e.g., based on a holistic strategy) or they may be the basis of the original identification (i.e., cases where the features, independent of their relations are diagnostic for the category).

Category-generic structure refers to structural information applied to a set of features that are common across multiple categories. For example, Biederman's (1987) theory relies on a small number of primitives to represent virtually all complex objects. As discussed earlier, features in a compositional representation must contain information; however, they do not need to contain as *much* information as in a strictly feature-based representation because the configural properties contain information as well. This means that the set of features used to identify an object can be less precise, that is, more generic, when structure is included. This provides two potential benefits. First, the total set of features used to recognize all objects can be much smaller because the same set of features can be reused to represent multiple objects. Note that this benefit applies even if one construes features as localized receptive field responses. Our best guesses about neural coding suggest that there is only a limited repertoire of selectivities within the primate visual system (Logothetis & Sheinberg, 1996); thus, it behooves vision theorists to account for how these relatively simple neural codes may be combined to represent the wide range of objects we encounter and recognize. Second, utilizing structure may allow recognition to proceed in cases where the features in the image are *inherently* "generic"—due, for example, to image noise, occlusion, or a rotation in depth. What follows is an attempt to define the particular role(s) of these two notions of structure in somewhat more detail.

A. CATEGORY-SPECIFIC STRUCTURE

Category-specific structure can be viewed as a form of "features-plus" encoding since it involves imposing configural information over a set of features that may already be diagnostic for a category. Feature-only representations are, in and of themselves, appealing for several reasons. Most feature-based strategies capitalize on the redundancy across images of objects in a particular category in order to identify a member of that category (e.g., Ullman et al.,

2002). For example, the category "faces" may depend on the presence of nose, eyes, and mouth, which are visually similar across different examples of the category. Recognizing objects based on features, rather than whole images, carries a number of likely benefits. First, the number of potential stored images is smaller than in purely holistic systems—in which each object is stored as a unique image or set of images—since multiple objects can be represented on the basis of the same set of features.[4] Second, extraneous information can be ignored and attention may be paid only to informative features. This allows feature-based strategies to overcome image variability and effectively generalize across different images. For example, while different houses vary considerably from one another in terms of their global appearance, doors and windows tend to be fairly similar across houses. This means that in theory, you might be able to recognize a wide variety of images as houses, despite their large differences, on the basis of a small number of shared stored features.

However, feature-plus (i.e., structural) encodings provide a number of potential benefits beyond feature-only encoding. Ignoring relational information between features limits the power of a representational system in several ways. First, feature-based strategies may *overgeneralize* in cases where features are present but in the wrong configuration. For example, an image may contain two different objects that contain the diagnostic features of some third object. In addition, feature-based strategies are also limited in terms of the number of differentiated objects they can distinguish; to the extent that some class of objects is defined on the basis of some particular set of features, members *within* that category cannot be distinguished from one another. Instead, further delineation within a class defined by some set of features requires a new set of features (e.g., contrast the local features used to categorize faces as faces used by Ullman et al., 2002, with the more global features used to individuate faces used by Zhang & Cottrell, 2005).

Category-specific structural approaches can serve to overcome these problems. Overgeneralization is dealt with by *constraining* the possible space of images containing the appropriate features to those in which the appropriate relations hold between features (e.g., Amit & Geman, 1997). Structural encoding allows you to define relations with varying degrees of specificity.

---

[4] Although this claim might appear contrary to the "multiple-views" approach advocated by the second author (Tarr, 1995), this theory actually makes a case for "views" as sets of viewpoint-dependent features, not holistic entities or templates. Indeed, Perrett, Oram, and Ashbridge's (1998) "evidence-accumulation" model over multiple local features has been our preferred explanation for why systematic effects of viewpoint are observed in visual recognition tasks (Tarr, 2003).

For example, encoding configuration in terms of "coarse" or qualitative relations (such as discussed earlier) rather than in terms of specific metrical distances allows for a great deal of generalization flexibility while still preserving certain basic constraints. Alternatively, relations can be defined in a more sophisticated fashion based on the typical variability within a category. For example, we recently conducted a series of experiments in which subjects judged pairs of objects to be more similar when that were produced by *articulating* their parts in a physically plausible manner—rotated around their intersection or "joint" with the object—as compared to other objects consisting of the same parts but articulated in a nonbiological manner—rotated around the part's endpoint (Fig. 4). These results suggest a means of achieving recognition, that is, "invariant to articulations." Critically, this approach depends on explicitly modeling the spatial relations between object parts.

Category-specific structure also allows much higher representational power on the basis of the same feature set. As is well known from the categorization literature, a given object can belong to many hierarchically arranged categories, for example, the same object can be identified as an animal, as a

Fig. 4. The two bottom shapes represent valid (left column) and nonvalid (right column) articulations of a part of the top object. In the valid articulation, the part rotates around the endpoint where the part joins the "body"; in the nonvalid articulation, the part rotates around an endpoint on the opposite side.

bird, as a duck, and as Daffy Duck (e.g., Rosch, Mervis, Gray, Johnson, & Boyes-Braem, 1976). To the extent that some set of features is diagnostic for a particular category, it cannot distinguish *between* members of that category. Category-specific structure can serve to "push down" the same set of features into more specific categories by imposing configural information over the shared set of features. This sort of structural encoding will typically rely on a metric (or "second order") encoding that allows you to define specific distances between features, rather than rough topological relations. This can dramatically reduce encoding cost for differentiating between members of a class of visually similar objects; even though there will always be some encoding cost to specifying the relations themselves, this will usually be much smaller than the cost of establishing new features for each new partition.

The most extreme examples of the potential economy of relational encoding are cases in which an observer may want to distinguish between *every* member of a particular class of similar objects in order to perform individual-level recognition (e.g., face recognition). In a feature-only system, each individual must be distinguished on the basis of a new feature, a clearly inefficient strategy when these are computationally costly features such as images. Relational information imposed on the original set of generic features, however, can provide the needed differentiation without introducing new features. For example, in Zhang and Cottrell (2005) informative spatial relations between parts are handled by creating larger noncompositional features. In our view, regardless as to whether this works or not, this is highly inefficient in that you may potentially need to create new features for each object to be recognized. A more efficient strategy is to actually encode the relations between *generic* features across the class that are potentially most informative with regard to individuation within that class. An example of this kind of discriminatory ability is so-called perceptual expertise (Bukach, Gauthier, & Tarr, in press)—the ability of experts to distinguish between members of a visually homogeneous object class at a specific (e.g., species or individual) level which untrained observers cannot distinguish reliably. Of course, the most prominent example of perceptual expertise in the visual domain is face recognition; different faces are visually similar to one another as compared with other objects, in part because they typically contain the same basic parts (eyes, nose, mouth, and so on), these features tend to be visually similar to one another across faces, and they appear in the same qualitative configuration across faces. That is why, as mentioned earlier, generic features (e.g., equating across individual noses) can serve as an effective strategy for detection. However, to the extent that the features are generic, they will not be able to distinguish between individual faces. A structural account—one that differentiates between individual faces on the basis of spacing between the features—on the other hand, could theoretically encode many different faces on the basis of this same set of features and their relations.

This reasoning suggests that facial recognition—as opposed to face detection—is particularly well adapted to a structural recognition strategy. There is a sizable body of evidence that has been taken to suggest that facial recognition—as opposed to face detection—relies on structural encoding (Gauthier & Tarr, 2002; Maurer, Le Grand, & Mondloch, 2002; Tanaka & Farah, 1993; although see Riesenhuber et al., 2004). For example, in Tanaka and Farah's (1993) study, changing the horizontal position of the eyes affected the recognition of the nose and recognition of face parts in isolation was poorer than the recognition of the same parts embedded in the appropriate face. Both of these effects are consistent with the idea that the representation of an individual face includes spatial relations between parts; consequently, perturbing those relations or removing them altogether hinders recognition. Of course, although it is not our favored explanation, both effects would also be found if faces were encoded as unitary templates or as collections of large features (e.g., one feature encompassing both the nose and the eyes; Zhang & Cottrell, 2005). Thus, such results, although consistent with structural models, do not actually provide definitive evidence for such models. Similarly, one of the most often cited pieces of evidence for configural coding in face recognition—the "face inversion effect" (Yin, 1969)—may also be explained by the poorer match to larger *viewpoint-dependent* features or by the disruption of the processing of structural information. More specifically, the face inversion effect is typically defined as disproportionately (relative to nonface objects) poorer performance for both encoding and recognizing faces when inverted 180° in the picture plane. If the particular configural relations used to support individual face identification are view dependent, for example, "above" or anchored relative to gravitational upright then picture-plane inversions will disrupt one's ability to derive such relations. Alternatively, if the eyes, nose, and mouth are encoded as one large feature then rotated versions of faces will necessarily produce mismatches between input images and such global features. Furthermore, such higher-order features will typically contain less symmetry around the horizontal axis as compared to "standard" features (e.g., eyes and mouths which are typically fairly symmetrical around the horizontal axis), making it more likely that larger features would be susceptible to inversion effects.

There are other reasons to question whether these and related results actually provide support for structure in face recognition. First, the generality of the distinction between "featural" and "configural" processing in terms of the face inversion effect has been disputed based on both psychophysical and computational grounds (Riesenhuber, Jarudi, Gilad, & Sinha, 2004). Second, there are important questions concerning the interpretation of some of these results and their relation to "everyday" face recognition. For example, a subset of studies demonstrating the use of configural information relies on a task in which pairs of highly similar images are compared after a brief interval, the subject's task is judging whether the two faces are the same or different (Le Grand, Mondloch, Maurer, & Brent, 2001; Maurer, Le Grand, & Mondloch, 2002). These face stimuli (e.g., "Jane" and her sister; Le Grand et al., 2001) would probably be judged as being the same individual by a naïve or casual observer. Thus, it is possible that observers in these studies are converging on a structural strategy—explicitly using spacing information—that is not engaged in typical facial recognition.

Finally, a potential red herring in these studies is that they often assume *a priori* that the features of a face are confined to nameable parts such as the eyes, nose, and mouth and that the spacing between them can be manipulated without changing the features of the face. For example, in Tanaka and Farah's (1993) study, they used stimuli consisting of simple "MacAMug" line drawings, containing contour information only for eyes, nose, and mouth; no surface texture or albedo (surface reflection) information was shown. Yet, as already discussed, plausible theories of facial recognition will almost certainly include features that encompass several of these "basic" features (Riesenhuber et al., 2004; Zhang & Cottrell, 2005) to form "higher order" features (e.g., a single feature could contain an eye and part of the nose), as well as surface information (Moore & Cavanagh, 1998; Vuong, Peissig, Harrison, & Tarr, 2005). In either case, line drawings of nameable face parts alone would constitute degraded stimuli, potentially prompting idiosyncratic strategies.

B. CATEGORY-GENERIC STRUCTURE

Category-specific structure refers to cases in which the set of features is bound to a particular category. This presents the possibility that such features are extracted *after* category membership has been determined. For example, as mentioned earlier, it is possible for the extraction of the eyes, nose, and mouth of a face to take place *after*—and even be dependent on— the identification of the image as a face. Conversely, in the case of category-generic structure, it is possible that structural information can be utilized in order to determine category membership in the first place, based on much more generic features that are in and of themselves *not* diagnostic for any category. That is, structural information exclusively defines category membership, regardless of local feature appearance. Evidence for this kind of structural encoding can be found in a number of very simple examples. First, consider the case of the "smiley face" emoticon (Fig. 5A) which can easily be recognized on the basis of very sparse features. It is very clear that a strategy

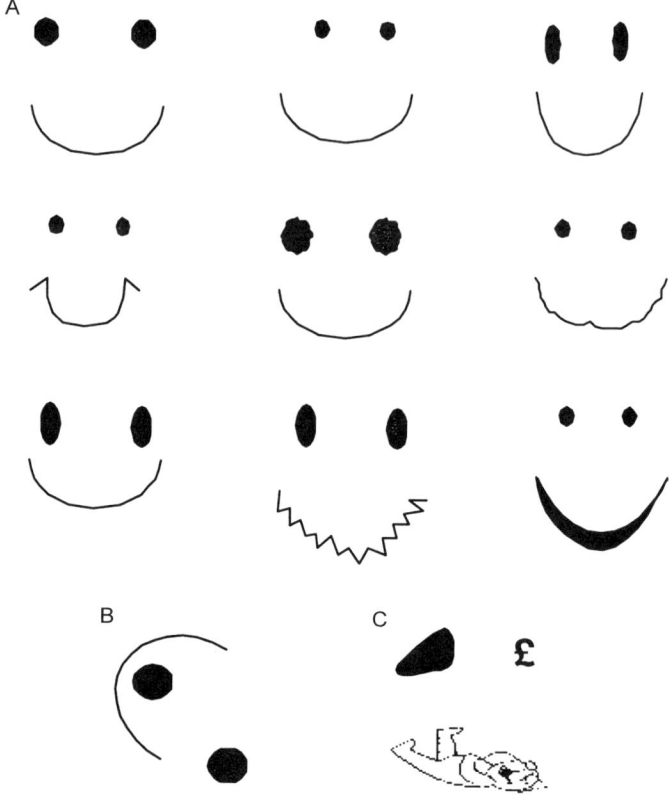

Fig. 5. (A) Valid smiley faces. (B) A scrambled smiley face. (C) A valid face configuration with bad features.

operating purely on the basis of the localized features in this image will not recognize the image as a face (the features are simply dots and curved contours). Such features, even taken together, contain very little information as they are consistent with almost an infinite set of objects. For example, the image in Fig. 5B contains the same features but is clearly *not* a face; the configuration of the features clearly matters. However, configuration is not the *only* thing that matters; as Fig. 5C makes obvious, not just *any* features in the appropriate configuration constitute a smiley face either. As required in our construal of structural representations, both the features and their relations appear to be critical. However, the range of potential features is very large and does not appear to be specific to particular objects. Of course, one might counter that our ability to recognize such images might depend on a template-like representation in which both the appearance of local features and their relations matter. However, this alternative becomes somewhat less plausible when considering the wide variety of images—some of which you have probably never encountered before—that still look like a smiley face. As mentioned earlier, holistic or pure template representations are typically poor at generalizing to novel images.

Another counterargument to this particular example is that a smiley face is a highly stylized image and recognizing it may be more like interpreting *symbols* in a manner akin to text reading (which, as discussed earlier, is most likely structural) than to object recognition. However, the same basic phenomenon can be demonstrated for other, less familiar types of images a well. For example, it is easy to recognize the various images in the left-hand column of Fig. 6 (two faces and a pair of stylized people). However, as

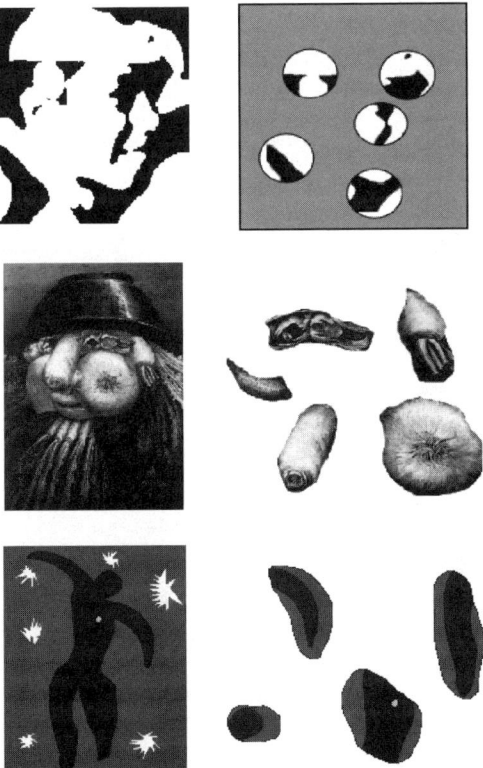

Fig. 6. The left column shows three easily recognizable objects. The right column shows that they are unrecognizable by features alone.

should be clear from the images in the right-hand column, the individual local features of these images are *not* recognizable outside of the configural context of the entire image (try inverting the page to produce a similar effect for the left-hand images).

Like the smiley face images, these examples pose a challenge to pure feature-based accounts. In particular, it does not appear likely that a local feature-matching scheme would arrive at the "correct" interpretation of the individual features in these examples (i.e., the one that you ultimately end up with after recognizing the whole). However, as with the smiley faces, you cannot arbitrarily replace these features with others—such as one vegetable with another (i.e., shape does matter)—and retain the same identity, just as you cannot replace the letters of a word and retain the same word. Instead, we suggest that functionally generic features, such as those in Fig. 6, do help to constrain the possible space of objects in the image but do not single out a unique object or part (e.g., the fact that it is a leek serving as the nose is irrelevant; on the other hand, it is an elongated cylindrical shape—replacing it with a mango would probably not work). For example, as illustrated in Fig. 7 the circular feature is a candidate for many different parts (e.g., a wheel, an eye) while the elongated oval feature may be a candidate for other parts (e.g., a dish antenna, a mouth). In a pure feature-based account any

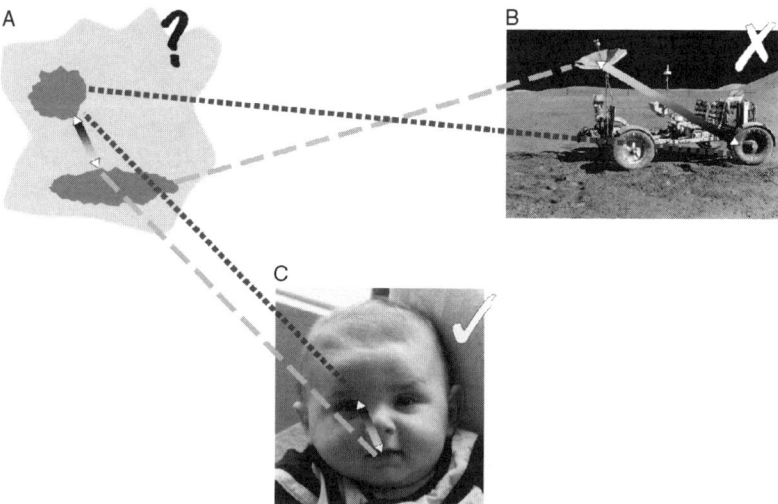

Fig. 7. (A) An ambiguous object containing generic features. (B) A potential match that contains the same features but in a different configuration. (C) A potential match that contains the same features in the same configuration. It is the structural information that distinguishes between these two candidates.

hypothesis for the identity of the entire object is likely to be based on the joint probability of the co-occurrence of these parts, given some object in the distal scene. For highly generic features, this calculation would be unlikely to yield the correct answer with any reliability since many objects are likely to match the generic features (Fig. 7B). However, in a structural encoding scheme, the hypothesized object would be the one that maximizes the probability of that set of features *and* their particular configuration (Fig. 7C). This provides additional constraint that may serve to identify the object with greater accuracy (e.g., Amit & Geman, 1997). This configural weighting could be instantiated in one of several ways. For example, in a "global" method, the goal would be to choose the *object* label that maximizes the likelihood of observing the features and their relations. The face in Fig. 7C might be chosen because the class "faces" maximizes the probability of these generic features in this particular configuration. Alternatively, a "local" method might have the goal of choosing, on a feature-by-feature basis, the individual object *parts* that maximize the likelihood of those features taking into account their occurrence in the image relative to *the position of other features*. This calculation could be realized by treating the features as interacting weights—for instance, as a Markov random field (Geman & Geman, 1984) in which individual features influence others based on their local spatial proximity or relational probabilities calculated over extended spatial ranges (Roth & Black, 2005). In such a scenario, the final object label would "emerge" based on the weightings of the local, interacting, features. The face in Fig. 7C might be chosen because eye and mouth are likely interpretations of the generic features given their spatial relationship. Regardless of whether local or global methods are used, the key point is that relational information may provide the leverage to achieve robust recognition based on generic features.

IV. Conclusions

It is our contention that the primate visual system is "built" to represent structure at multiple levels of processing. That is, from retinal processing to scene understanding, information about both what things are and where they there are is represented in one form or another. What is less clear is whether structural information in a truly compositional form is utilized in accomplishing the "holy grail" of visual abilities, recognition. Structural object representations once seemed like an obvious approach to recognition, yet even nominally structural models have emphasized the nature of features at the expense of a clearer explication of structural codes. At the same time, a number of challenges to such models have stymied the development of better-specified theories of structure in both theoretical and experimental work. In the end, the particular features of the representation may be less crucial than the implementations of structure in successful models of visual recognition. At a minimum, simply relying on features, without their relational information, amounts to ignoring highly valuable information that is readily available to the visual system. As we have discussed, such information can serve to economize visual encoding by allowing the same set of features to be used far more flexibly as well as supporting robust recognition under conditions where feature-based strategies are likely to fail. Thus, our view is that the advantages of including structure are such that the question is not really *whether* structure is critical to object recognition but rather *how* structure is represented in a manner that makes visual recognition possible in the first place.

Acknowledgment

This research was supported by NGA Award #HM1582-04-C-0051 to both authors.

References

Amit, Y., & Geman, D. (1997). Shape quantization and recognition with randomized trees. *Neural Computation, 9*, 1545–1588.

Arguin, M., & Saumier, D. (2004). Independent processing of parts and of their spatial organization in complex visual objects. *Psychological Science, 15*, 629–633.

Barenholtz, E., & Feldman, J. (2003). Visual comparisons within and between object-parts: Evidence for a single-part superiority effect. *Vision Research, 43*(15), 1655–1666.

Barenholtz, E., & Feldman, J. (in press). Determination of visual figure and ground in dynamically deforming shapes. *Cognition*.

Barlow, H. B. (1959). Sensory mechanisms, the reduction of redundancy, and intelligence. In "The mechanisation of thought processes." London: Her Majesty's Stationery Office.

Baylis, G. C., & Driver, J. (1994). Parallel computation of symmetry but not repetition in single visual objects. *Visual Cognition, 1*, 377–400.

Biederman, I. (1987). Recognition-by-components: A theory of human image understanding. *Psychological Review, 94*, 115–147.

Biederman, I., & Bar, M. (1999). One-shot viewpoint invariance in matching novel objects. *Vision Research, 39*, 2885–2899.

Biederman, I., & Gerhardstein, P. C. (1995). Viewpoint-dependent mechanisms in visual object recognition: Reply to Tarr and Bülthoff (1995). *Journal of Experimental Psychology: Human Perception and Performance, 21*(6), 1506–1514.

Bienenstock, E., Geman, S., & Potter, D. (1997). Compositionality, MDL priors, and object recognition. In M. C. Mozer, M. I. Jordan, and T. Petsche (Eds.), *Advances in Neural Information Processing Systems*, (Vol. 9). Cambridge, MA: MIT Press.

Black, M. J., & Roth, S. (2005). *The Receptive Fields of Markov Random Fields.* Paper presented at Cosyne, Salt Lake City, UT, March 17–20.

Bukach, C., Gauthier, I., & Tarr, M. J. (2006). Beyond faces and modularity. *Trends in Cognitive Sciences, 10*, 159–166.
Cohen, L., Dehaene, S., Naccache, L., Lehericy, S., Dehaene-Lambertz, G., Henaff, M. A., et al. (2000). The visual word form area: Spatial and temporal characterization of an initial stage of reading in normal subjects and posterior split-brain patients. *Brain, 123*(Pt. 2), 291–307.
Edelman, S. (1993). Representing three-dimensional objects by sets of activities of receptive fields. *Biological Cybernetics, 70*, 37–45.
Edelman, S., & Intrator, N. (2003). Towards structural systematicity in distributed, statically bound visual representations. *Cognitive Science, 27*, 73–109.
Feldman, J. (2003a). What is a visual object? *Trends in Cognitive Sciences, 7*(6), 252–255.
Feldman, J. (2003b). Perceptual grouping by selection of a logically minimal model. *International Journal of Computer Vision, 55*(1), 5–25.
Fodor, J. A. (1975). *The language of thought*. Cambridge, MA: MIT Press.
Fodor, J., & Pylyshyn, Z. (1988). Connectionism and cognitive architecture: A critique. *Cognition, 28*, 3–71.
Gauthier, I., & Tarr, M. J. (2002). Unraveling mechanisms for expert object recognition: Bridging brain activity and behavior. *Journal of Experimental Psychology: Human Perception and Performance, 28*(2), 431–446.
Geman, S., & Geman, D. (1984). Stochastic relaxation, Gibbs distributions, and the Bayesian restoration of images. *IEEE Transactions on Pattern Analysis and Machine Intelligence, 6*, 721–741.
Goldstone, R. L. (2000). Unitization during category learning. *Journal of Experimental Psychology: Human Perception and Performance, 26*(1), 86–112.
Hayward, W. G., & Tarr, M. J. (1995). Spatial language and spatial representation. *Cognition, 55*, 39–84.
Hayward, W. G., & Tarr, M. J. (2000). Differing views on views: Comments on Biederman & Bar (1999). *Vision Research, 40*, 3895–3899.
Hinton, G. (1979). Some demonstrations of the effects of structural descriptions in mental imagery. *Cognitive Science, 3*, 231–250.
Hummel, J. E. (2000). Where view-based theories break down: The role of structure in shape perception and object recognition. In E. Dietrich and A. Markman (Eds.), *Cognitive dynamics: Conceptual change in humans and machines* (pp. 157–185). Hillsdale, NJ: Lawrence Erlbaum.
Lades, M., Vorbruggen, J. C., Buhmann, J., Lange, J., von der Malsburg, C., Wurtz, R. P., et al. (1993). Distortion invariant object recognition in the dynamic link architecture. *IEEE Transactions on Computers, 42*, 300–311.
Le Grand, R., Mondloch, C. J., Maurer, D., & Brent, H. P. (2001). Early visual experience and face processing. *Nature, 410*(6831), 890 (Correction *Nature* 412, 786).
Logothetis, N. K., & Sheinberg, D. L. (1996). Visual object recognition. *Annual Review of Neuroscience* (Vol. 19, pp. 577–621). Palo Alto, CA: Annual Reviews.
Markman, A. B. (1999). *Knowledge representation*. Mahwah, NJ: Lawrence Erlbaum.
Marr, D., & Nishihara, H. K. (1978). Representation and recognition of the spatial organization of three dimensional structure. *Proceedings of the Royal Society of London B, Biological Sciences, 200*, 269–294.
Maurer, D., Le Grand, R., & Mondloch, C. J. (2002). The many faces of configural processing. *Trends in Cognitive Sciences, 6*(6), 255–260.
Mel, B. (1997). SEEMORE: Combining color, shape, and texture histogramming in a neurally inspired approach to visual object recognition. *Neural Computation, 9*, 777–804.
Moore, C., & Cavanagh, P. (1998). Recovery of 3D volume from 2-tone images of novel objects. *Cognition, 67*(1–2), 45–71.

Navon, D. (1977). Forest before the trees: The precedence of global features in visual perception. *Cognitive Psychology, 9*, 353–383.

Pelli, D. G., Farell, B., & Moore, D. C. (2003). The remarkable inefficiency of word recognition. *Nature, 423*(6941), 752–756.

Perrett, D. I., Oram, M. W., & Ashbridge, E. (1998). Evidence accumulation in cell populations responsive to faces: An account of generalisation of recognition without mental transformations. *Cognition, 67*(1,2), 111–145.

Riesenhuber, M., & Poggio, T. (1999). Hierarchical models of object recognition in cortex. *Nature Neuroscience, 2*(11), 1019–1025.

Riesenhuber, M., Jarudi, I., Gilad, S., & Sinha, P. (2004). Face processing in humans is compatible with a simple shape-based model of vision. *Proceedings of the Royal Society of London B, Biological Sciences, 271*(Suppl. 6), S448–S450.

Rosch, E., Mervis, C. B., Gray, W. D., Johnson, D. M., & Boyes-Braem, P. (1976). Basic objects in natural categories. *Cognitive Psychology, 8*, 382–439.

Roth, S., & Black, M. J. (2005, June). Fields of experts: A framework for learning image priors. Paper presented at the IEEE Conference on Computer Vision and Pattern Recognition (CVPR), (Vol. 2, pp. 860–867).

Schyns, P. G., & Rodet, L. (1998). Categorization creates functional features. *Journal of Experimental Psychology: Learning, Memory, and Cognition, 23*(3), 681–696.

Singh, M., & Hoffman, D. (1998). Part boundaries alter the perception of transparency. *Psychological Science, 9*, 370–378.

Tanaka, J. W., & Farah, M. J. (1993). Parts and wholes in face recognition. *Quarterly Journal of Experimental Psychology, 46A*, 225–245.

Tarr, M. J. (1995). Rotating objects to recognize them: A case study of the role of viewpoint dependency in the recognition of three-dimensional objects. *Psychonomic Bulletin and Review, 2*(1), 55–82.

Tarr, M. J. (2003). Visual object recognition: Can a single mechanism suffice? In M. A. Peterson and G. Rhodes (Eds.), *Perception of faces, objects, and scenes: Analytic and holistic processes* (pp. 177–211). Oxford, UK: Oxford University Press.

Tarr, M. J., & Bülthoff, H. H. (1995). Is human object recognition better described by geon-structural-descriptions or by multiple-views? *Journal of Experimental Psychology: Human Perception and Performance, 21*(6), 1494–1505.

Tarr, M. J., & Bülthoff, H. H. (1998). Image-based object recognition in man, monkey, and machine. *Cognition, 67*(1–2), 1–20.

Ullman, S. (1989). Aligning pictorial descriptions: An approach to object recognition. *Cognition, 32*, 193–254.

Ullman, S., Vidal-Naquet, M., & Sali, E. (2002). Visual features of intermediate complexity and their use in classification. *Nature Neuroscience, 5*, 682–687.

Vuong, Q. C., Peissig, J. J., Harrison, M. C., & Tarr, M. J. (2005). The role of surface pigmentation for recognition revealed by contrast reversal in faces and Greebles. *Vision Research, 45*(10), 1213–1223.

Wallis, G., & Rolls, E. T. (1997). Invariant face and object recognition in the visual system. *Progress in Neurobiology, 51*(2), 167–194.

Yin, R. K. (1969). Looking at upside-down faces. *Journal of Experimental Psychology, 81*(1), 141–145.

Zhang, L., & Cottrell, G. W. (2005). Holistic processing develops because it is good. In B. G. Bara, L. Barsalou, and M. Bucciarelli (Eds.), *Proceedings of the 27th annual cognitive science conference*. Mahwah: Lawrence Erlbaum.

CONVERSATION AS A SITE OF CATEGORY LEARNING AND CATEGORY USE

Dale J. Barr and Edmundo Kronmüller

I. The Importance of Setting in Categorization Research

The many categorization decisions that people make in everyday life are not performed in isolation but are embedded in some setting—for example, driving a car, shopping at the supermarket, or participating in a conversation. The notion of "setting" can be broadly construed to include both the informational environment in which categorization decisions are made and the specific task in which the categorizer is engaged. This includes assumptions about what information the environment presents to the individual categorizer, whether the environment contains of other individuals that can supply information or that must adapt their categorizations to one another, where the categories come from, how the learner determines which categories are relevant in a given situation, and the goals dictated by the structure of the ongoing task.

Despite the importance of setting, categorization research has tended to study categorization in the abstract, where the goal of categorization is to learn the categories themselves (for a broad critique of this approach, see Markman & Ross, 2003). However, even this "decontextualized" approach to categorization assumes a kind of setting, albeit one that is highly idealized. Consider the standard category learning experiment. In such an experiment, participants are given the goal of learning a category or set of categories that have been predefined by the experimenter. Before the experiment begins, participants are told the labels for the various categories that they will be learning. There is a learning phase in which participants view stimuli and are either told the appropriate categorization or they must classify the instance themselves and learn from the feedback that is provided. The process repeats itself until the learner reaches some performance criterion.

What kind of setting is idealized here? Essentially, it is one that resembles many pedagogical settings in which a novice learns a set of preexisting categories from an expert teacher. In such a setting, the goal of learning is for the novice to acquire a set of preexisting categories. The expert ostensibly defines the category by exposing the novice to a variety of examples and labeling each one. The learner acquires the categories in social isolation and is not required to share information or adapt to other people in the environment.

Although this idealized expert-novice setting is one that has guided research on categorization for decades, there are many other settings involving category learning and category use. In this chapter, we focus on one very important setting—conversation—and discuss aspects of conversational settings that raise new challenges for existing theories of categorization as well as pose new questions about the development and use of categories.

II. Categorization Processes in Conversation

Conversation is undoubtedly one of the primary settings of category learning and category use. It is a principal setting of category learning: children acquire many of their concepts through face-to-face interactions with caretakers and with their peers. It is also a major setting for category use: People spend a large portion of their lives in conversation with other people, and these conversations invariably involve numerous categorizations of entities and situations.

A. REFERENCE AS A KIND OF CATEGORIZATION

Of the many aspects of language use that would fall under the rubric of categorization (e.g., identifying words or phonemes, telling whether a sentence is intended literally or metaphorically, engaging in conceptual combination to interpret a complex noun phrase), one is especially critical—referential communication. Reference involves relating language to the world. In reference, the goal of categorization is to establish joint attention on some entity (henceforth, the referent) with an interlocutor. The referent of an act of categorization can be a particular entity in the world (e.g., A *shark* was seen off the coast of Malibu) or an entire class of objects (e.g., The *shark* is a creature that lives in the ocean).

Using language to refer to an object is, essentially, a kind of categorization (Brown, 1958). Most clearly, when a speaker points at a referent and asserts, *that is a shark*, the speaker is asserting the referent's membership in the category designated by the label *shark*. However, categorization assertions are more often presupposed than explicitly conveyed. Thus, even a simple definite description, such as *the shark*, implicitly asserts that the referent is a member of the category conventionally designated by the label *shark* (Russell, 1905). The label used in speech can be seen as a kind of "pointer" to an underlying category to which the referent is said to belong. Most categorization research can be said to have accepted the "labeling as categorization" hypothesis, given that the vast majority of studies signal category membership to the learner through the use of a symbolic label.

An alternative to viewing labeling as a kind of categorization would be to view it as a kind of "social mnemonic" that allows people to share attention to an object without bearing the strong entailments involved in nonlinguistic categorization. If this were the case, however, then any label that I choose to refer to an object—dog, animal, creature, living thing—should not matter as long as it uniquely identifies the referent for the listener. Yet by choosing one label over another, one makes relevant different properties associated with the category. It would be quite odd for me to ask a friend to take care of the *creature* in my apartment while I am away, even if the label *creature* would uniquely designate my dog for the listener (Cruse, 1977). Even metaphorical language that is not literally true (e.g., my job is a jail) can be viewed as a special kind of categorization, where the topic ('job') is placed into a category of which the vehicle ('jail') is a prototypical exemplar (Glucksberg & Keysar, 1990). Thus, the topic inherits prototypical properties of this category exemplified by the vehicle (e.g., something that is constraining, authoritarian, or unpleasant).

B. STRATEGIES FOR REFERENT CATEGORIZATION

Language offers different strategies for categorizing referents. One strategy is to use proper names, but proper names have limited generality, since they are typically only used to denote people and places (and sometimes pets or even cars). Another strategy involves use of pronouns (he, she, it) and demonstratives (this, that). These items are typically used to refer to entities that are easily accessible due to recent mention in the discourse or that are salient in the current physical context (Ariel, 1988; Gundel, Hedberg, & Zacharski, 1993). Compared to common nouns, pronouns and demonstratives have little semantic content and depend strongly on the context for interpretation.

In this chapter, we focus on categorizations that use definite descriptions—a noun phrase using the article "the" and a phrase that describes the referent. The simplest definite description involves mentioning the name of a category to which the referent belongs. The lexicon of a language provides a rich, ready-made system of distinctions for classifying referents. This system is characterized by a hierarchical organization that makes it possible to classify referents at various levels of specificity: superordinate, basic, and subordinate. For example, it is possible to classify one and the same object as a *vehicle*, as a *car*, or as a *Ferrari*. However, sometimes a simple lexical classification is inadequate to distinguish a referent from a set of contextually available alternatives (Olson, 1970). For example, the categorization *the man* is likely to fail to designate the intended referent whenever there is another entity in the context that also fits that description (i.e., another man). Under such circumstances, speakers will typically find it necessary to further specify the referent by using modifiers that come before or after the head noun. For example, *the old man sitting on the bench* is a description that involves modifiers both before and after the noun *man*. Such a description can be considered a kind of "goal-derived" category (Barsalou, 1991) that is formed on the spot for the purpose of individuating a referent from the set of contextually given alternatives. The possibility of creating such ad hoc categories gives language users unlimited flexibility in how a referent is to be categorized.

C. Overview of the Chapter

Thus far, we have characterized reference in a way that would not seem to pose significant problems for the standard view of categorization. Yet conversational settings shape speakers' and listeners' categorizations in special ways. We focus on three aspects of conversation that have important implications for categorization: its multimodal nature, historical nature, and collaborative nature. To say that conversation is "multimodal" is to say that interlocutors can exchange information simultaneously on different information channels. Thus, when speakers categorize referents, they not only provide a verbal label, but also "give off" additional cues that can increase the efficiency with which category information is transmitted from one person to another. To say that conversation is "historical" is to say that the way a referent is categorized depends not only on the similarity of the stimulus to a set of target concepts but also on past acts of categorization. Finally, to say that conversation is "collaborative" is to highlight the fact that speakers and listeners work together to find categorizations that effectively identify a referent from a joint perspective. In what follows, we discuss research on these three aspects of conversation and elucidate their implications for theories of category learning and category use. Our discussion also considers the cognitive mechanisms underlying the various phenomena that we discuss (to the extent that they are known) in order to gain insight into how current models of categorization might be extended to the realm of conversation.

III. The Multimodal Nature of Conversation: Confidence Cues in Category Learning

One conversational situation to which the standard category learning paradigm appears to apply straightforwardly is that of an expert who teaches a set of distinctions to a novice. Learning in such a situation proceeds much like in a category learning experiment: the learner views a series of stimuli for which the expert provides a category label. For instance, consider a new employee at a fabric store who is taught the company's unique color categorization scheme. The trainer would point to a color sample and tell the learner, "We call this color *glur*." By exposing the learner to a variety of examples accompanied by the category label *glur*, and contrasting these examples with examples of other colors, the learner will eventually acquire the target set of categories.

After exposure to a sufficient number of labeling events, learners will not only be able to successfully classify stimuli but they will also have learned something about *category structure*, that is, about which items are more or less typical of a given category. Where does this knowledge about category structure come from? In the standard view of category learning, the only information provided along with the stimulus is the category label. Thus, knowledge about category structure is not communicated to learners via the expert but is generated by learners alone based on the distribution of examples they have encoded (e.g., based on overlapping features, Rosch & Mervis, 1975).

In conversation, however, experts will tend to provide evidence for the typicality of an example by the degree of confidence that they display in their categorization assertion (Barr, 2003). Because of the multimodality of conversation, speakers can express these confidence cues directly in their speech or through visual channels such as manual gesture or facial expressions. In this section, we focus on the confidence cues that are given by the relative fluency or disfluency of a speaker's linguistic performance. We discuss how these confidence cues are manifest in speech and then review evidence that listeners are sensitive to these cues. Finally, we discuss recent evidence that shows that learners take advantage of confidence cues in conversational category learning situations. This research challenges the standard assumption that categories are learned solely on the basis of pairings between stimuli and category labels.

A. DISFLUENCY AS AN INDEX OF SPEAKER CONFIDENCE

Categorization assertions are subject to the maxims of cooperative communication (Grice, 1975). In categorizing a stimulus for a learner, speakers strive to say things that are informative and true. A speaker who is uncertain about a categorization but withholds this uncertainty is acting uncooperatively. For example, imagine that the expert from the preceding example wished to refer to a fabric that was somewhat discolored due to aging. The fabric looks like it could belong to the color category *glur* or *blay* but is slightly more *glur*-ish. Although the expert might assume it more likely to be *glur*, it would be uncooperative for the speaker to assert "this one is *glur*" without qualification. Instead the expert would say something like, "I think this one is *glur*, but it could also be *blay*." The presence or absence of such verbal hedges (e.g., *I don't know, I guess, I think*) indicates the speaker's confidence in the categorization.

Verbal hedges are not the only cues to a speaker's confidence. Speakers will also give off signals that index their confidence through the fluency or disfluency of their linguistic performance. A speaker who asserts, "this is um ... *glur*?" is clearly far less confident than a speaker who asserts "this is *glur*!" The speaker's degree of fluency could potentially be a useful source of information for learners because it is associated with the speaker's confidence in the categorization. A speaker would be more likely to become disfluent when attempting to describe referents that are difficult to categorize, which could help the listener distinguish good and bad examples when learning the category.

A variety of studies has supported a link between general cognitive difficulty and disfluency. Speakers who interpret the meaning of a cartoon are more disfluent than speakers who simply recount its plot (Goldman-Eisler, 1968). Furthermore, speakers hesitate for longer when they describe stimuli that are rated as highly ambiguous (Siegman & Pope, 1966). The likelihood of disfluency is also positively correlated with the number of alternative lexical items from which a speaker must select at a given moment of speaking (Schachter, Christenfeld, Ravina, & Bilous, 1991; Schachter, Rauscher, Christenfeld, & Tyson Crone, 1994).

Furthermore, a study by Smith and Clark (1993) found that speakers are more likely to be disfluent when they lack confidence in their assertions. They had speakers answer factual questions varying in difficulty. They found that when speakers were uncertain about their answers, their lack of confidence was associated with a longer hesitation before answering, a greater likelihood of using "fillers" (e.g., *uh* or *um*, Maclay & Osgood, 1959) and a rising final intonation.

Given the presence of such confidence cues, an important question is whether learners use this information when they acquire categories. A study by Brennan and Williams (1995) showed that listeners indeed exploit fluency information to draw inferences about a speaker's level of confidence in an assertion. They recorded speakers' spontaneous answers to factual questions that varied in difficulty. Brennan and Williams (1995) then played the responses to a set of listeners, who rated how confident speakers' were in their knowledge of the answers. They found that listeners' judgments correlated with the length of time speakers hesitated before starting to speak as well as whether their speech included fillers. Specifically, longer pauses and the presence of fillers were associated with lower confidence ratings.

B. USE OF CONFIDENCE CUES IN CATEGORY LEARNING

Do learners make use of confidence cues when they learn categories? A developmental study by Sabbagh and Baldwin (2001) suggests that they do. Three- and four-year-old children witnessed an event in which an adult used a novel word to name a toy. The adult introduced the term in a way that indicated that they were either confident or uncertain about the proper categorization of the toy. The speaker's confidence was marked verbally as well as gesturally (e.g., "Look at the *modi*!" versus "I think it's a *modi*?" while shrugging the shoulders). Children were more likely to learn the name for the toy when the speaker expressed confidence than when the speaker expressed uncertainty.

Confidence cues can not only influence whether or not a category is learned but can also enable the learner to distinguish between good and bad examples of a category. Barr (2003) found that adult learners exploited confidence cues to learn the structure of a category, even when the cues were not explicit verbal hedges. In this study, participants attempted to learn a set of novel color categories by viewing color patches on a computer screen and listening to the spoken categorizations from an expert. Each category had a nonsense category label (e.g., *riallo, donlon*) that was paired with five different instances varying in shade, some of which would be easier to classify than others.

For each category, learners heard categorizations that varied in the level of the certainty expressed. In the most certain case, the label followed a short initial hesitation and was spoken with a descending pitch. In the least certain case, the label was preceded by a long initial pause that included the filler *uh* or *um*, and was spoken with rising pitch.

Each color category was represented by five color patches that varied in shade but that were drawn from the same part of the color spectrum (e.g., five "bluish" or five "greenish" patches). Figure 1 shows instances of the category *donlon*, a category consisting of greenish patches (represented here in shades of gray rather than green). Donlon was adjacent to another novel

Stimulus	Rank	Speech consistent condition	Speech inconsistent condition
○	1 (best example)	Donlon	hmm... Donlon?
◔	2 (good example)	Donlon	Donlon?
◐	3 (moderate example)	uhhh Donlon	uhhh Donlon
◕	4 (poor example)	Donlon?	Donlon
●	5 (worst example)	hmm... Donlon?	Donlon

Fig. 1. Sample item from Barr (2003) for the novel color category *donlon* with the stimulus-to-sound mappings for the Consistent and Inconsistent conditions. Characteristics of the speech tokens are represented schematically with the gray line in the background corresponding to the pitch contour and the distance from the left of the column corresponding to the length of the hesitation. Due to printing limitations, the stimuli are presented in black and white, although the actual color of the category *donlon* was a shade of green.

category in the set, *prado*, whose members were a slightly different shade of green. Barr operationalized the "goodness" of a color patch with respect to the category as its distance in color space from the boundary of another novel category used in the experiment. Thus, the stimulus ranked in Fig. 1 as the "best example" of donlon was farthest from the boundary with prado, while the stimulus ranked as the "worst example" was nearest to prado.

To find out whether listeners took advantage of confidence cues in learning the categories, two sets of materials were created for each category by altering the mappings between the speech and the color patches (see Fig. 1). In the *Consistent* condition, the speaker's confidence was consistent with the underlying category structure. The confident-sounding utterances were paired with the best examples of the category, and the unconfident-sounding utterances were paired with the worst examples. In the *Inconsistent* condition, the speaker's confidence was inconsistent with the category structure. The confident-sounding utterances were paired with the worst examples of the categories, and the unconfident-sounding utterances were paired with the best ones. If learners have a tendency to associate confident-sounding utterances with good examples and unconfident-sounding ones with bad ones, then learning should be better when they learn from the set containing consistent mappings.

This is precisely what Barr (2003) found. On average, learners acquired the categories 16% faster in the Consistent condition compared to the Inconsistent condition. Furthermore, typicality ratings for learners in the Consistent condition showed better internal differentiation of the members of a given category. The average difference in rating between the most and least typical category members of each category was significantly higher in the Consistent condition than in the Inconsistent condition. Hence, listeners take advantage of confidence cues when learning category structure, even when those cues are not explicitly verbalized in verbal hedges but take the form of hesitations, filled pauses, and variations in intonation.

C. SUMMARY AND IMPLICATIONS

The evidence reviewed in this section highlights the importance of confidence cues in category learning. Speakers reliably provide confidence cues to indicate when they are uncertain. Because conversation is multimodal, this confidence can be conveyed in a variety of ways: through gestures, facial expressions, verbal hedges, hesitations, fillers such as *uh* or *um*, or rising intonation. Confidence cues influence the likelihood that listeners will learn a category. Furthermore, because confidence cues covary with category structure, they enhance learning by differentiating good from bad examples. In sum, conversational settings offer a rich informational environment that promotes the transfer of knowledge from expert to learner far more efficiently than envisioned by standard approaches to category learning.

IV. The Historical Nature of Conversation: Establishing and Using Conversational Precedents

Standard models of categorization assume that categorization decisions are determined by ahistorical factors such as the similarity of a stimulus to a target category or the preference for classification at the basic level (Rosch, Mervis, Gray, Johnson, & Boyes-Braem, 1976). Accordingly, an object is classified as a *car* because it shares more features with the category *car* than it does with other categories at the basic level. However, these two factors are not sufficient to explain how referents are categorized in conversation because how language users categorize referents is also influenced by the history of the conversation.

Conversation unfolds over time with each new act building on those that preceded it (Lewis, 1979). Language users take this history into account when a speaker decides how to categorize a referent or when a listener searches for a referent based on a categorization provided by a speaker. Thus, the decision of how to categorize a referent will depend on how it and other entities have been previously categorized. Specifically, language users strive for consistency in how they categorize objects, and this consistency can overrule the influence of similarity or of preference for the basic level.

Language users track information pertaining to what entities have been classified before, how they were classified, and by whom. Following Barr and

Keysar (2002), we refer to the episodic traces that contain this information as *conversational precedents*. The use of conversational precedents in referential communication can reduce the uncertainty that arises due to variability in how a given object can be categorized (Barr & Keysar, 2002; Brennan & Clark, 1996). Upon first categorizing a referent as a *fedora*, a speaker establishes a precedent that influences how that referent will be categorized in the future. By consistently following the precedent (e.g., continuing to refer to it as the *fedora* instead of as a *hat*), the speaker can streamline coordination and avoid ambiguity.

Recently, psycholinguists have begun to examine how precedents are used in making conversational references. This research has identified two phenomena associated with the consistent use of precedents: *entrainment* and *preemption*. We review evidence for these phenomena in the following two sections. Then, we discuss evidence for the cognitive mechanisms underlying these phenomena, which can offer guidelines for how standard theories of categorization could be modified to accommodate these phenomena.

A. ENTRAINMENT

Entrainment is a phenomenon whereby conversationalists tend to categorize referents consistently with past usage. Entrainment is important for the study of categorization because it can override the default preference to classify a stimulus at a basic level of categorization.

A study of language production by Brennan and Clark (1996) examined entrainment in speakers' classification of everyday objects. Everyday objects can be categorized at different taxonomic levels using linguistic terms that vary in specificity. For instance, a shoe can be classified as *footwear*, as a *shoe*, or as a *loafer*. Typically, speakers exhibit a preference for the basic-level term, for example, *shoe* (Rosch et al., 1976). The basic-level term is conventionally considered the neutral or 'unmarked' term (Cruse, 1977). More specific terms are only justified when another object from the same basic category appears among the contextually given objects. For example, a shoe should only be called a *loafer* when it is necessary to distinguish it from a second shoe (e.g., a sneaker).

Brennan and Clark (1996) found that speakers' repeated use of specific terms led to entrainment, which overruled the preference for basic-level classifications. In the experiment, speakers described everyday objects for a listener. Early on, speakers described target objects in contexts that contained a second member of the same basic-level category, requiring them to use a specific term. For example, a shoe was called a *loafer* to distinguish it from another shoe in the display. Speakers used these specific terms multiple times, causing them to become entrained. In a later test trial, the objects appeared in a context in which the basic-level term would have been appropriate. For example, the shoe that they had previously described as a loafer now appeared as the only shoe in the display. Speakers nonetheless showed a tendency to continue using the specific term.

The phenomenon of entrainment has also been observed in language comprehension. Barr and Keysar (2002) found that listeners' expectations of speaker consistency overruled the default preference for basic-level terms. In one of their experiments, speakers established precedents to refer to certain objects using specific terms. Thus, a flower appeared in a display with another flower and was referred to as the *carnation,* while a car appeared in a display with another car and was referred to as the *sportscar*. In a later test phase, listeners saw a display containing only the same flower (carnation) and the same car (sportscar).

The critical question was: Would listeners expect the speaker to use the preferred basic-level categorizations (*car* and *flower*) or the subordinate-level entrained categorizations (*carnation* and *sportscar*)? What listeners actually heard in the test phase was the basic-level term *car*. Note that the word *car* overlaps with the initial syllable of the word *carnation*. If listeners expect the basic-level term, then they should consider only the car (sportscar) and not the flower (carnation). However, if they expect the subordinate-level precedents, then they should temporarily consider the carnation. Based on an analysis of listeners' eye movements, Barr and Keysar found that listeners expected the subordinate-level precedents. Thus, listeners' expectations are calibrated to what speakers actually do.

B. PREEMPTION

Preemption, the complement to entrainment, also has important implications for how referents are categorized in conversation. Just as entrainment can overrule the preference for basic-level classification, the phenomenon of preemption can overrule similarity in the categorization of a referent.

Preemption is a general principle of language use. According to preemption, the existence of a linguistic form for a given meaning preempts the creation of a new form for precisely the same meaning (Clark, 1991; Clark & Clark, 1979). In other words, language users strive to avoid synonymy. The phenomenon was originally discussed in the context of the creation of denominal verbs (Clark & Clark, 1979) in which an innovative verb is created based on a noun (e.g., *James spent the whole day blogging*, where the verb *to blog*, meaning to write text on an Internet log, is derived from the noun *blog*). Preemption explains why, for example, people would accept the phrase *to gurney a patient* to refer to the act of putting a patient on a gurney but would not accept *to hospital a patient* to refer to the act of putting a patient in a hospital. In the latter case, the existence of the verb *hospitalize* preempts the creation of a new verb with precisely the same meaning. Preemption has also been shown to operate in how children acquire language (Clark, 1990) in that children tend to avoid mapping a novel word to an object that already has a conventional name (Markman & Wachtel, 1988).

Preemption operates not only with respect to the more stable conventional practices in a community but also with respect to conversational precedents (Kronmüller & Barr, 2006). According to preemption, listeners should be disinclined to accept a new categorization for a referent that was already categorized in a different way. Thus, upon hearing a new categorization, listeners should tend to consider objects that have not yet been categorized, even if they are dissimilar to the mentioned category, and ignore objects that were already categorized in a different way, even if they are highly similar to the mentioned category.

Kronmüller and Barr (2006) sought evidence for preemption in a language comprehension experiment that used eyetracking to monitor listeners' search for referents. Listeners saw a series of test displays containing three unusual objects that lacked conventional names (see Fig. 2). Listeners heard a speaker categorize one of the three objects (the *target* object), and their task was to identify this object based on the categorization provided. In the "Old" categorization condition, the speaker categorized the target consistently with how he or she categorized it in the past. In the "New" categorization condition, the speaker provided a new categorization for the target, thereby breaking the

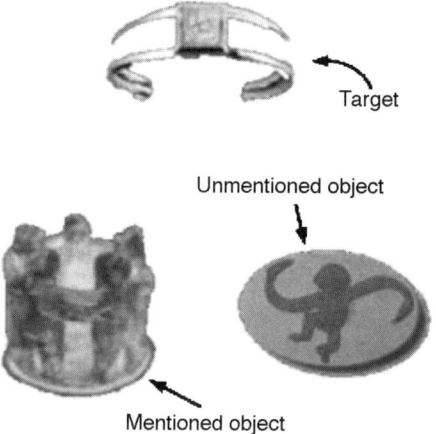

Fig. 2. Sample test display from Kronmüller and Barr (2006). Each test display contained a previously mentioned target object, another previously mentioned contextual object, and an unmentioned object.

established precedent. The new categorization was an equally good description of the target as the already-established categorization. If the established categorization preempts this new description then listeners should attempt to map the new description to an object in the display that had not yet been categorized, *the unmentioned object*.

Kronmüller and Barr (2006) examined fixations to the unmentioned object as listeners processed the referring expression. Note that in terms of similarity, the unmentioned object was always a much poorer match to the test description than the target object. If listeners' search for referents is guided only by similarity and not by preemption then they should be no more likely to look at the unmentioned object in the Old or New condition. In contrast, under the preemption hypothesis, fixations to the unmentioned object should be higher in the New than in the Old condition.

Figure 3 shows the proportion of trials containing a fixation to the unmentioned object over a series of 50 ms time windows, starting at the onset of the referring expression. Supporting the preemption hypothesis, listeners were far more likely to fixate the unmentioned object when they heard a new categorization than when they heard an old one. Fixations in

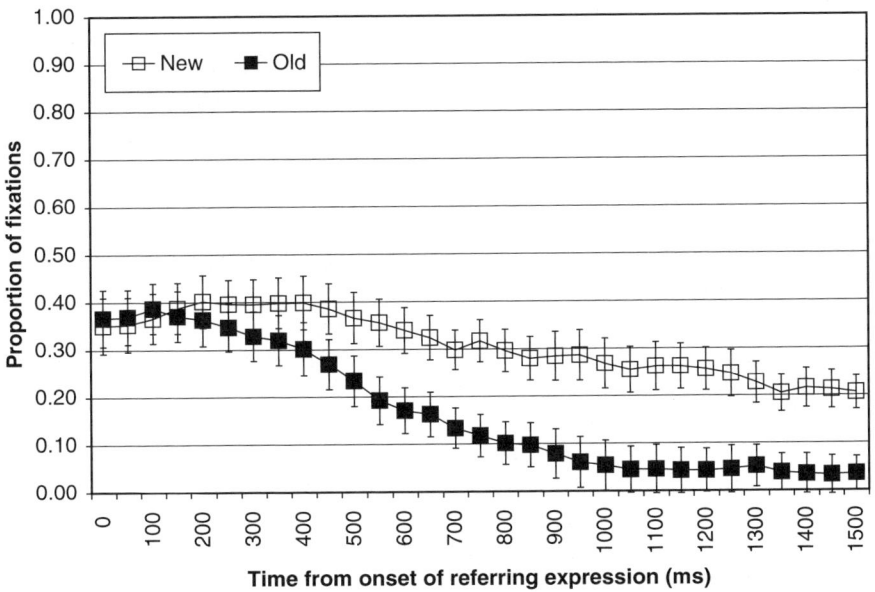

Fig. 3. Listeners' fixations on the unmentioned object in Kronmüller and Barr (2006), Old versus New expression conditions. Error bars represent the standard error of a difference between the two conditions. The data are averaged over 56 participants and 32 items.

the New and Old conditions began to diverge statistically at around 450 ms after the onset of the referring expression. This divergence indicates that when listeners heard a new categorization, they did not simply search for the object that was the best match to the mentioned category. Instead, they checked to see whether the categorization applied to the unmentioned object. Indeed, the preemption effect was so strong that it led listeners to select a nontarget object 13% of the time in the New condition. In the Old condition, they virtually never selected the wrong object (1%).

In sum, language users' categorization decisions are guided not only by similarity but also by conversational history in the form of precedents. Listeners expect consistency in how referents are categorized, and this assumption of consistency will even influence how listeners interpret novel categorizations. The fact that preemption effects have been found in language learning (Clark, 1990; Markman & Wachtel, 1988), in how novel expressions are coined (Clark & Clark, 1979), and now, in how listeners interpret references (Kronmüller & Barr, 2006) suggest that preemption is a principle with broad application in language use.

Current models of categorization, in which categorization decisions are based entirely on similarity and on preference for the basic level, have no provision to explain how precedents are used in categorizing referents. How might existing models be adapted to account for effects of entrainment and preemption? The answer to this question depends upon the nature of the mechanisms that underlie these effects. The explanation of these phenomena is the subject of an ongoing debate in psycholinguistics, which we turn to in the following section.

C. MECHANISMS UNDERLYING PRECEDENT USE IN CONVERSATION

A unified explanation for precedent effects in language use can be found in the *common ground framework* of Clark and colleagues (Clark, 1992, 1996). In an influential paper, Clark and Marshall (1981) argued that language users produce and interpret language against a shared body of knowledge, known as *common ground*. A piece of information is said to be part of the common ground between interlocutors when it is shared and known to be shared. The common ground between interlocutors includes world knowledge and language conventions that they believe to be shared based on evidence of their joint membership in a common community. It also includes information in the physical environment that they have joint access to, as well as shared knowledge about the history of the current interaction, including the precedents that have been established.

The common ground framework assumes the people make use of common ground when they make categorization decisions. For production, it implies that speakers should categorize referents in a way that reflects their common ground with the listener. Likewise, for comprehension it implies that when listeners interpret speakers' categorizations, they should restrict the information that they consider to their common ground with the speaker (Clark & Carlson, 1981). Entrainment and preemption effects are explained by invoking mutual agreements between interlocutors (Clark & Brennan, 1991; Clark & Wilkes-Gibbs, 1986). Entrainment takes place because once speakers and listeners have arrived at a mutually agreed upon way of categorizing a referent, they will continue to follow the precedent in order to reduce ambiguity and minimize collaborative effort (Clark & Wilkes-Gibbs, 1986). Preemption occurs because it would be uncooperative for speakers to depart from mutually agreed-upon precedents unless the departure is justified by, for instance, a change in context that makes the precedent ambiguous.

The common ground framework provides a single, comprehensive explanation for many aspects of language use. Despite its appeal, some have argued that routinely tracking common ground in real-time conversation may impose too much of a cognitive burden on interlocutors (Brown & Dell, 1987; Keysar, Barr, Balin, & Brauner, 2000; Pickering & Garrod, 2004). This view assumes that many of the adaptations that language users appear to make for their interlocutor are not the result of the use of common ground per se, but emerge out of the operation of much simpler cognitive processes and heuristics (for a review, see Barr & Keysar, 2006). We call this perspective on language use the *ordinary cognition approach*, as it assumes that many phenomena that seem to require an "interactional" explanation can be reduced to ordinary processes of cognition. This approach assumes that common ground plays a limited role in language processing. For instance, the perspective adjustment theory of Keysar and colleagues (Keysar, 2000) assumes that common ground is used largely to monitor production and comprehension processes, but otherwise exerts a limited constraint on language processing.

The ordinary cognition approach offers different explanations from the common ground framework for entrainment and preemption. The phenomenon of entrainment is explained by the simple cognitive principle that repeated use increases the availability of a categorization, and thus the probability that it will be accessed in the future. Preemption is explained as a default tendency to associate new categorizations with new referents.

The common ground framework and ordinary cognition approach have different implications for how theories of categorization can account for entrainment and preemption effects. It is possible to distinguish between these approaches by examining whether people use precedents in a way that depends on the identity of the person to whom they are talking. The main prediction of the common ground framework is that precedents should be used in a manner that is *partner specific*. In other words, the precedents that are established between two specific interlocutors should not be carried over beyond the original conversation, where there is no common ground to support their use. The ordinary cognition view predicts that the use of precedents is largely *partner independent*: speakers and listeners should use precedents in ways that tend to violate their common ground.

1. Partner Specificity Versus Partner Independence in Entrainment

According to partner specificity, speakers should not continue to use entrained precedents with a new listener who lacks knowledge of the precedents because this could impair the listener's comprehension. Likewise, listeners should not expect a new speaker to follow the precedents of a previous speaker when the new speaker is ignorant of the previous speaker's precedents. In contrast, partner independence predicts that interlocutors should continue using entrained precedents beyond the conversational context in which they were established.

Brennan and Clark (1996) reported evidence suggesting a partner-specific use of precedents in language production. They found that speakers who entrained on subordinate-level categorizations for everyday objects (e.g., calling a shoe a *loafer*) were more likely to revert to a basic-level description when they spoke to new partners who lacked access to the precedents than when they spoke to old partners. However, they also observed that reversion to basic-level terms emerged gradually and not immediately after a partner switch. Indeed, in the first trial after the partner switch, speakers who spoke to a new partner were just as likely to continue using the specific term as speakers who spoke to an old partner. Thus, it was possible that speakers used the established terms in a partner-independent manner and only adjusted back to the basic-level terms because they gradually discovered that the specific terms confused the new partner. It is not clear whether speakers would have reverted without feedback from the partner.

Malt and Sloman (2004) suggested that precedents are used in a partner-independent manner. According to Malt and Sloman (2004), speakers tend to reuse precedents because each successful use of a precedent makes it more cognitively available. In their study, a confederate speaker described common objects to a participant who played the role of matcher in a referential communication task. Each object was named in one of two possible ways (e.g., as a *trash can* or as a *wastebasket*). The matcher then performed the referential communication task again, assuming the role of director and interacting with a new participant, who took the role of matcher. This second matcher then went on to become director in a third iteration of the task, again with a new participant as matcher. Note that this third director would have had no direct interaction with the original confederate speaker, and therefore would have no direct knowledge of this speaker's precedents. The question was whether this third director would nonetheless prefer the terms established by the confederate. In support of the partner-independent use of precedents, they found that these third directors were more likely to use the confederate speaker's term than the alternate term.

Barr and Keysar (2002) examined the partner specificity of entrainment from the standpoint of language comprehension. In their experiments, listeners heard two different speakers refer to objects. The speakers were isolated from one another so that listeners would have no reason to believe that either speaker would know about the other's precedents. Barr and Keysar (2002) found that when a speaker described a referent in a manner consistent with an established precedent, comprehension was facilitated. However, they found no evidence to support the partner-specific use of precedents: the facilitation was identical whether the current speaker was the one who established the precedent or a different speaker who could not have known about the other speaker's precedent. This finding supported the partner-independent hypothesis of precedent use (see also Metzing & Brennan, 2003).

2. Partner Specificity Versus Partner Independence in Preemption

Although research on entrainment supports the partner-independent use of precedents, and therefore the ordinary cognition approach, research on preemption presents a more conflicting picture. In a study by Metzing and Brennan (2003), listeners interpreted speakers' descriptions of unfamiliar objects that lacked conventional names, such as a piece of metal that was described as *the shiny thing*. They found that listeners were slower to identify a target object when a new categorization was provided for an old object (e.g., the object called *the shiny thing* was now called *the metal coil*) than when a precedent was reused. Importantly, this preemption effect was stronger when the new categorization was provided by a speaker who had previously established a precedent for that object than when it was provided by a new speaker. The evidence for this was that when a precedent was broken, listeners were faster to look at the (old) target when the speaker breaking the precedent was new than when it was the speaker who originally established the precedent.

This speaker effect could be explained by the common ground framework, which assumes that preemption effects are partner specific. According to this explanation, preemption only takes place when an old speaker violates a precedent by using a new categorization for an old referent. It would not take place when a new speaker uses a new categorization for an old referent, given that none of the precedents of the former speaker would be in common ground with the current speaker. It is perfectly natural for a speaker who is unaware of a previous speaker's precedents to categorize an old referent in a new way. We call the hypothesis that preemption effects are limited to old partners the *partner-specific-preemption* hypothesis.

However, Metzing, and Brennan's speaker effect could also be explained within the ordinary cognition approach, under the *recovery-from-preemption* hypothesis (Kronmüller & Barr, 2006). According to this hypothesis, accepting a new categorization for an old referent requires the listener to "recover" from a preemption effect that takes place *any* time a new categorization is heard—independently of whether the speaker is new or old. To accept a new categorization for an old referent, a listener must recover from preemption by finding a reason for the breaking of the precedent, for why an old object is suddenly being categorized in a new way. When a precedent is broken by the speaker who established it, listeners would have difficulty finding a reason justifying the shift in categorization. When a precedent is broken by a new speaker, listeners would easily find a justification for the new categorization in noting that the old speaker's precedents are not in common ground with the new speaker. Listeners would therefore be faster to recover from preemption and accept the new categorization for the target when it is provided by a new speaker, which would explain the speaker effect observed by Metzing and Brennan (2003).

Note that the both partner-specific-preemption and recovery-from-preemption hypotheses predict that common ground is used in the case of broken precedents, where they differ is in terms of how and when it is used. According to the partner-specific-preemption hypothesis, listeners only consult precedents that are in their common ground with the current speaker. Thus, preemption will only take place in the case of an old speaker with whom precedents have been established. According to the recovery-from-preemption hypothesis, listeners experience preemption whenever they hear a new categorization because they consult whatever precedents are cognitively available, not just those in common ground. This preemption effect will lead them to consider any object that has not yet been categorized (i.e., the unmentioned object; see Section IV.B). On failing to map the categorization to a new referent, they will initiate a recovery process that can involve a search of common ground.

Kronmüller and Barr (2006) tested these predictions in an experiment in which listeners' eyes were monitored as they interpreted new categorization for old referents. The stimuli were nonsense figures such as those shown in Fig. 2. The new categorization was provided either by the speaker who established the precedents, or a new speaker who had not yet established any precedents.

The strategy was to assess the time course of speaker effects by examining fixations to the unmentioned object. As discussed in Section IV. B, preemption effects had an onset of about 450 ms after the beginning of the referring expression. The partner-specific-preemption hypothesis assumes that the preemption effect will be localized to the old speaker condition. Therefore, starting at 450 ms, fixations to the unmentioned object should be higher in the old speaker condition than in the new speaker condition. In contrast, recovery-from-preemption hypothesis assumes that fixations to the unmentioned object should be equally high during this period and only start to diverge once a later recovery process takes effect. Hence, it predicts that the speaker effect should occur much later than 450 ms.

The results are presented in Fig. 4 (top panel). Overall, the pattern of findings supports the recovery-from-preemption hypothesis: listeners experienced early preemption in both conditions but were able to use common ground to recover from it when the current speaker was new. As the figure shows, there was no reliable difference between these two conditions until very late in processing, around 950 ms at the earliest. Before this point, fixations to the unmentioned object were statistically indistinguishable, indicating that preemption took place in both cases. At around 950 ms, listeners in the new speaker condition began to look away from the unmentioned object. At this point, they seem to have realized that the old precedents were not in common ground with the current speaker, and therefore were no longer applicable. In contrast, fixations to the unmentioned object remained high in the old speaker condition. Listeners in the latter condition appear to have had a more difficult time recovering, as predicted by the recovery-from-preemption hypothesis.

Kronmüller and Barr (2006) sought further evidence regarding the nature of this recovery process. According to the ordinary cognition view, effects of common ground are mediated by a self-monitoring process, whose operation is optional and depends on the availability of sufficient cognitive resources (Keysar et al., 2000). To find evidence for monitoring, Kronmüller and Barr (2006) included a cognitive load condition, based on previous research suggesting that cognitive load would selectively interfere with the monitoring aspects of language processing (Horton & Keysar, 1996; Rossnagel, 2000). This interference would make it difficult for listeners to recover from the preemption effect. The results from the cognitive load condition are seen in the bottom of Fig. 4. Supporting the monitoring hypothesis, the recovery process was completely eliminated by cognitive load.

Taken together, the results of this experiment provide strong support for the idea that preemption effects are largely partner independent. Listeners do not consider only those precedents that are in common ground with the

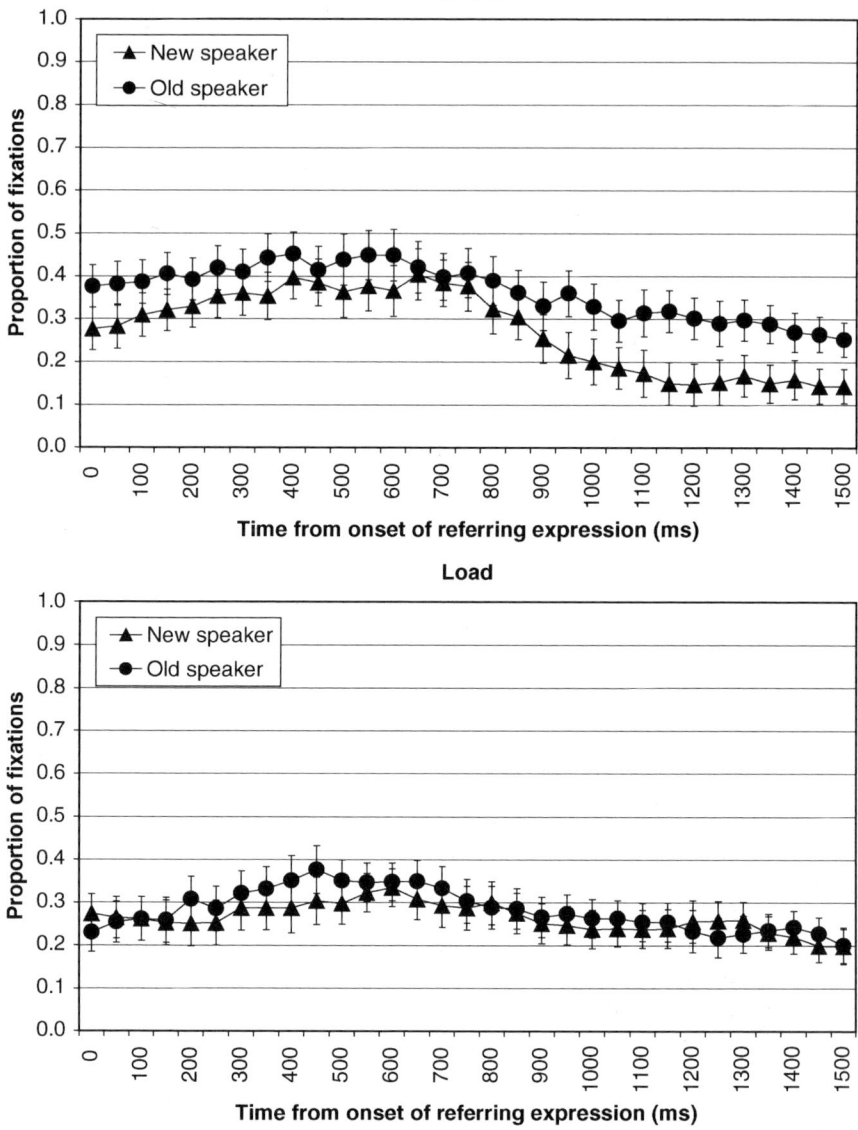

Fig. 4. Fixations on the unmentioned object in Kronmüller and Barr (2006). The top panel shows fixations for new versus old speakers in the No Load condition, while the bottom panel presents data for the Load condition. Error bars represent the standard error of a difference between the two conditions. The data are averaged over 56 participants and 32 items.

current speaker. Instead, they consider any available precedents, which results in preemption effects whenever a new categorization is heard. Listeners do, however, use common ground to recover from preemption effects when they fail to locate a new object that matches a new categorization. This use of common ground is supported by a late-onset, resource-dependent monitoring process.

D. SUMMARY AND IMPLICATIONS

To summarize, there is a historical dimension to interlocutors' categorization decisions that is not reflected in current models of category use. Specifically, interlocutors establish precedents regarding how a referent is to be linguistically categorized, and they tend to consistently follow these precedents when they speak and comprehend categorizations. This use of precedents is reflected in the complementary phenomena of entrainment and preemption. Entrainment is important because it suggests that the preference for a basic level of categorization can be overruled by the drive for consistency of expression. Preemption is important because it can override similarity in the search for referents.

The historical effects would seem to invite an explanation in terms of the accumulation of shared knowledge between interlocutors. Although people do appear to keep track of this information (Barr & Keysar, 2002), they do not appear to reliably use it in making categorization decisions. Instead, much of precedent use would seem to be explained by assuming that interlocutors use precedents because they are available, not because they are part of common ground. This is good news for categorization theories, which suggests historical effects can be explained without resort to common ground, a highly complex form of metaknowledge. Indeed, our discussion of mechanisms underlying these effects suggests that they can partially be reduced to ordinary processes of cognition. Still, the full story of how historical effects combine with effects of similarity or basic-level preferences is one that awaits further research.

V. The Collaborative Nature of Conversation: Socially Emergent Categories and Conceptual Alignment

Thus far, conversational category use and category learning have been discussed as though the responsibility for categorization decisions resides with one person: an expert teaches a category to a learner, or a speaker establishes a precedent that the listener uses to guide the search for a referent. Although this simplifies the analysis of how categories are used, in the end, this one-sided view is somewhat misleading because interlocutors influence one another through their actions, including the process by which they arrive at stable categorizations for a referent. In conversation, categorization is often a collaborative process.

A. Socially Emergent Categories

Clark and Wilkes-Gibbs (1986) made the crucial observation that referent categorization is typically accomplished collaboratively. Here is an example of one such case from their study (the interlocutors are attempting to identify a nonsense figure embedded in an array of other nonsense figures; Clark & Wilkes-Gibbs, 1986, p. 22):

(A) ... the guy reading with, holding his book to the left.
(B) Okay, kind of standing up?

Here, the first interlocutor (A) proposes an initial categorization for a referent, and the partner (B) elaborates upon the first speaker's description. On a subsequent turn, speaker A might choose to incorporate B's contribution along with A's own by, for example, referring to the same figure as *the guy standing up reading*, which would incorporate material contributed by both interlocutors.

The preceding example illustrates two important implications of collaboration for the categorization process. First, interlocutors do not simply select among preexisting categories when they categorize a referent but must often come up with new categorizations on the spot to meet their momentary needs. Second, these novel categories often emerge as a joint product of interlocutors' collaborative efforts. We refer to these collaborative categories that are created on the spot as *socially emergent categories*.

Collaborating on categorizations is often necessary because interlocutors' perspectives are likely to differ, and each interlocutor's knowledge about the other's perspective is limited. Different features of a referent, and therefore different ways of categorizing it, may be salient to different individuals. The categorization that would be most suitable from one person's perspective might not be adequate for that person's interlocutor. Hence, what interlocutors need to find is a categorization that will work from a *joint perspective*; in other words, a categorization that enables the referent to be identified from either interlocutor's perspective.

Evidence that interlocutors collaborate on references is ubiquitous in everyday conversation. For instance, it can be found in the way in which speakers introduce referents into discourse (Clark & Wilkes-Gibbs, 1986). Speakers tend to mark their initial categorization of a referent as tentative and subject to future revision by the use of verbal hedges of the sort reviewed in Section III (e.g., *It's sort of like an X, It's a kind of X*) as well as by rising question-like intonation (Brennan & Clark, 1996; Clark & Brennan, 1991). These are markers that the speaker's contribution is provisional—that the speaker is not fully committed to the categorization, leaving it open to revision. Such markers invite collaboration from the conversational partner.

Conversationalists are motivated to collaborate on how referents are to be categorized because it enables them to attain high levels of confidence that they mutually understand one another (Clark & Brennan, 1991). Furthermore, they are motivated to collaborate because it can reduce the personal effort that they must put into perspective taking. Finding a joint categorization through negotiation can be construed as a form of epistemic action (Kirsh & Maglio, 1994), an action whose intention is to gain information about the world and relieve the burden of having to compute that information oneself. Instead of attempting to guess what categorization a listener would find optimal for a given referent, speakers can simply offer up a categorization that is salient to them and assess its effectiveness through the interlocutor's feedback. In this way, collaboration becomes a proxy for the direct computation of mutual knowledge. In the preceding example, A saw in the abstract figure a likeness to a man who was reading, and offered this categorization to B. B was able to identify the figure based on A's categorization but sought confirmation by offering his or her own conceptualization of the referent. Through their contributions, the interlocutors revealed the kind of categorization that would effectively individuate the referent from their own perspectives. By combining this information, the interlocutors arrived at a joint categorization without having to compute the joint perspective directly.

Socially emergent categories are ubiquitous in conversation because language users are motivated to collaborate on references in order to maximize their accuracy as well as minimize their personal effort. Despite this ubiquity, these kinds of categories are nowhere to be found in the literature on category learning. Category research has traditionally focused on how people learn categories that already exist and not how people collaborate to form new categories. It characterizes the category learner as a socially isolated individual, whose categorization decisions are not subject to influence from any outside party. Such assumptions are incompatible with how categorization takes place in conversational settings.

B. Conceptual Alignment in Conversation and Beyond

Another phenomenon related to the collaborative nature of conversation is that interacting partners will tend to adopt increasingly similar ways of categorizing referents over the course of their conversation. Garrod and Anderson (1987) noted that interlocutors not only innovate new ways of describing referents but will also establish certain "interpretation rules," temporary conventions that govern how conventional terms map onto referents. They analyzed the linguistic behavior of pairs of participants (dyads) who worked together on a computerized task that involved moving a marker through a maze. They found that over time, both members of the dyad ended up using the same description schemes to refer to aspects of the maze. For example, some dyads appeared to describe locations in the maze according to an abstract matrix scheme in which rows and columns in the maze were designated by letters and numbers (e.g., *the marker is located in C4*). Others appeared to use a scheme in which the locations were designated as lying along a path (e.g., *it's three up and one over*). Importantly, the members of a dyad tended to adopt the same referring scheme and tended to use their schemes consistently over multiple games. It was rare that these schemes were negotiated explicitly (e.g., through one partner saying "let's describe locations by drawing a path through the network"). This suggested that they emerged through the stabilization of the rules of interpretation due to their repeated use by each member of the dyad.

The convergence in linguistic description is often explained by *conceptual alignment*, the idea that interlocutors come to conceptualize referents in similar ways (Garrod & Anderson, 1987; Garrod and Doherty, 1994; Markman & Makin, 1998; Pickering & Garrod, 2004). The term *alignment* is drawn from the theory of interactive alignment of Pickering and Garrod (2004). Under the conceptual alignment view, shared representations emerge as a by-product of the local coordination processes that take place in the dyad. These coordination processes can result not only in new socially emergent categories but can also alter language users' representations of conventional categories (Garrod & Anderson, 1987). Unlike the contractual view, according to which each conversation requires the forging of new agreements, conceptual alignment assumes that interlocutors will carry conceptual changes beyond the original conversation in which they were created. As a result, these categories can spread to other members of a language community, contributing to the establishment of community-wide conventions.

Evidence for conceptual alignment can be found in a study by Garrod and Doherty (1994), who examined the formation of referring conventions in a series of games played by dyads drawn from a closed community of players. They found that the community eventually converged upon a scheme for referring to locations in the maze, even though each participant experienced only a series of isolated partners, and was not aware that each partner they encountered was drawn from the same community of players. Garrod and Doherty (1994) suggested that the community-wide conventions were the result of a process of "dynamic concept formation." Over the course of many interactions, each individual would be exposed to a variety of categorizations from different individuals. The categorizations that best promoted understanding among different members of the community would tend to be reused, leading to stable conceptual representations. In contrast, less helpful conceptualizations would fall out of use. In essence, this view suggests that community-wide conventions can emerge as a by-product of the local processes of semantic coordination that take place in the dyad.

Other evidence that shared categories emerge through use can be found in agent-based simulations of the evolution of symbolic conventions (Barr, 2004; Hutchins & Hazlehurst, 1995; Steels, 1996). In agent-based simulations, a group of agents belonging to a population interact according to a set of rules programmed into the agents (Goldstone & Janssen, 2005). By manipulating parameters related to agent behavior and patterns of social interaction, the researcher can observe the conditions under which certain community-wide patterns emerge as a by-product of the interactions of the individual agents.

Using an agent-based model, Barr (2004) showed that semantic coordination processes at the dyadic level can lead to the emergence of shared representations at the community level, even when agents interacted with only a small subset of agents from the community. The agents played a simple communication game in which they could use any of four symbolic forms to refer to any of four meanings. At the beginning of each run, each agent's mappings between forms and meanings were randomized. In every epoch of the simulation, each agent played the game with another randomly assigned agent from the population. One agent in each pair was assigned to the role of "speaker," and attempted to convey one of the four meanings to its partner by selecting the form that was most strongly associated with that meaning according to that agent's own internal representation. The other agent was the "listener" and attempted to interpret the speaker's categorization by selecting the meaning most strongly associated with that form from its own internal representation. Agents adjusted their representations depending on whether their individual interactions were successful or unsuccessful. It was found that under a robust array of circumstances, stable conventions emerged at the population level as a by-product of these individual dyadic interactions. This convergence took place rapidly even for very large populations (up to 10,000 agents), on the order of only several hundred epochs. More importantly, convergence was likely even when agents' ability to learn about the behavior of other agents was limited by low memory capacity or by narrow sampling from a small neighborhood of agents.

Despite the growing number of researchers who have suggested that collaboration on references can lead to conceptual alignment, there has been little effort to find direct empirical evidence that language users' category representations change as a result of referential communication. An exception is a study by Markman and Makin (1998) that examined how engaging in a referential communication task with a partner affected performance on a subsequent nonlinguistic categorization task. Participants in their experiment worked together to build a model out of blocks. One of the participants, the director, was given access to the instructions for building the model, and the other, the matcher, was tasked with arranging the blocks according to the director's instructions. Each pair participated in a naming task before building the model, in the course of which they established agreements on how the various blocks would be named. After working together on building the model, each participant independently completed a task in which they were asked to sort the pieces used in the building into different categories. The sorting matrices of participants who built the model while communicating were compared to those who built the same model in isolation and did not communicate. The average agreement between the sorting matrices of dyads who build the same model was higher than that which was found between the matrices of a person who communicated and a randomly chosen person who had built the same model without communicating. This supports the idea that the communication process resulted in the members of a dyad categorizing referents in a similar way, over and above that which resulted from participating in a common building task.

Markman and Makin (1998) also found evidence supporting the hypothesis that referential communication promotes attention to both the commonalities among referents and differences related to the commonalities (or *alignable differences*; e.g., Markman & Gentner, 1993). Attending to commonalities is useful for finding ways of categorizing that can be generalized to many different objects. These base categorizations can then be used with modifiers to indicate differences from the common pattern. For example, participants in Markman and Makin (1998) came up with the base label *tile* to refer to certain kinds of pieces in the set. Different kinds of tiles were referred to as the *black tile* or the *two-pronged tile with the pole*. People were far more likely to use modifiers with base categorizations that were used for many different pieces than with base categorizations that were used for a small number of pieces. Based on these findings, Markman and Makin (1998) suggested that "categories are structured to facilitate the detection of commonalities and differences of similar items, because this information is useful for communicating about those items" (p. 341).

C. Summary and Implications

One of the tacit assumptions behind standard category research is that people learn and use preexisting categories in social isolation. The collaborative nature of conversation implies a very different picture. In conversation, language users work together to forge new categories on the fly in order to solve the coordination problems that they face. Because these socially emergent categories are constructed collaboratively, they can incorporate contributions from multiple interlocutors. Conversationalists are motivated to collaborate on categorizations because collaboration maximizes accuracy and reduced personal effort by circumventing the need to compute a joint perspective.

Collaboration also leads to convergence in how interlocutors represent concepts through the process of conceptual alignment. Evidence for conceptual alignment has been found at the level of the individual conversation as well as at the level of the language community. As Markman and Makin (1998) note, conceptual alignment provides a possible explanation for category coherence, and for how a community of language users arrive at the overlapping conceptual representations that are necessary for successful communication.

VI. Challenges and Prospects

The standard view in category research has rested on an idealization that abstracts away both from the goal of categorization and the settings in which categorization takes place. The study of conversational categorization—that is, of reference—highlights some inadequacies of current models and suggests important avenues for future development. Conversation is a setting that is multimodal, historical, and collaborative in nature. Its multimodal nature implies that interlocutors have access to an information-rich signal that enhances learning. Experts provide information not only about the category membership but also give off confidence cues that serve as an index of category structure. The historical nature of conversation means that interlocutors will base their categorization decisions not only on similarity or basic-level preferences but also on how referents have been categorized in the past. Finally, because conversation is collaborative, speakers and listeners will work together on how they categorize a referent. Through their efforts at coordination, they bring their conceptual representations into alignment. The local processes that bring about this coordination are important because they are also likely to underlie the generation of stable categories within a community of users.

Many of these aspects of conversational categorization are not readily explained by existing models. How serious are the challenges for extending categorization theories into the domain of conversation?

First, incorporating the confidence of an expert classifier into a category learning task seems largely unproblematic: the extent to which a particular instance will contribute to learning can be made proportional to the speaker's confidence signal. In most existing quantitative models, confidence can be operationalized as the strength with which a stimulus activates a category, relative to other possible categories. Yet a complete account of the use of confidence cues requires research that will fill some gaps in our current knowledge. What aspects of a speaker's behavior contribute to a listener's perception of uncertainty? Furthermore, speakers can be disfluent for a variety of reasons other than uncertainty about a categorization (e.g., they may know the classification but have trouble retrieving the label from memory). Can learners recognize the situations under which the fluency of a speaker's performance is no longer a valid index of category structure?

Current models would also require revision to capture the historical nature of conversational categorization. Fortunately, historical effects can be reduced to ordinary processes of cognition or simple heuristics. Despite appearances, they do not depend strongly on more complex mechanisms that incorporate common ground knowledge. Thus, entrainment can be viewed as a simple consequence of associative learning (Malt & Sloman, 2004), perhaps even repetition priming. Preemption might reflect a default heuristic to associate new categorizations with new information.

Finally, the aspect of conversational categorization that poses the most serious challenge for existing models is the collaborative nature of referring, and the accompanying notions of socially emergent categories and conceptual alignment. Unfortunately, the current understanding of this topic is not sufficiently developed to yield clear suggestions for implementation. Although the interactive process by which socially emergent categories are established has been well described (Clark & Brennan, 1991; Clark & Wilkes-Gibbs, 1986), and the resulting entrainment of descriptions has been documented (Clark & Wilkes-Gibbs, 1986; Garrod & Anderson, 1987), little is known about how such categories are represented and used or regarding their stability over time. The related notion of conceptual alignment also awaits further theoretical description. This would include investigation of alignment processes not only in the speaker–listener dyad but also how conceptual knowledge spreads to a community of language users (Garrod & Doherty, 1994). Such efforts are already underway in psycholinguistics (e.g., Barr, 2004; Pickering & Garrod, 2004) but could benefit from greater integration with category learning research. The promise of such an enterprise for theories of category use is that, by understanding the forces that shape conventional categories, we might be in a better position to understand why they are structured in the way that they are. The promise for language research is that by understanding how people attain similar category representations, we gain a deeper appreciation of how language can succeed in the face of ambiguity.

Of the many settings in which categorization takes place, conversation is clearly one of the most important. It is arguably the setting in which most categories are learned, as well as the setting in which a large portion of human categorization decisions are made. As a consequence, theories that ignore conversation will be of limited scope. Moreover, many conventional categories arise out of members' recurring need to share attention to particular entities and situations. Thus, conversation might be a primary engine that drives the development of conventional systems of categorization (Lewis, 1969). For these reasons, understanding how conversation works is essential for developing a comprehensive, ecologically valid understanding of how conventional categories are established and used.

ACKNOWLEDGMENT

We thank Mandana Seyfeddinipur for her valuable comments on a draft of this chapter.

REFERENCES

Ariel, M. (1988). Referring and accessibility. *Journal of Linguistics, 24*, 65–87.
Barr, D. J. (2003). Paralinguistic correlates of conceptual structure. *Psychonomic Bulletin & Review, 10*, 462–467.
Barr, D. J. (2004). Establishing conventional communication systems: Is common knowledge necessary? *Cognitive Science, 28*, 937–962.
Barr, D. J., & Keysar, B. (2002). Anchoring comprehension in linguistic precedents. *Journal of Memory and Language, 46*, 391–418.
Barr, D. J., & Keysar, B. (2006). Perspective taking and the coordination of meaning in language use. In M. J. Traxler and M. A. Gernsbacher (Eds.), *Handbook of psycholinguistics* (2nd ed.). San Diego: Academic Press.
Barsalou, L. W. (1991). Deriving categories to achieve goals. In G. H. Bower (Ed.), *The psychology of learning and motivation: Advances in research and theory* (pp. 1–64). San Diego, CA: Academic Press.
Brennan, S. E., & Clark, H. H. (1996). Conceptual pacts and lexical choice in conversation. *Journal of Experimental Psychology: Learning, Memory, & Cognition, 22*, 1482–1493.
Brennan, S. E., & Williams, M. (1995). The feeling of another's knowing: Prosody and filled pauses as cues to listeners about the metacognitive states of speakers. *Journal of Memory and Language, 34*, 383–398.
Brown, P. M., & Dell, G. S. (1987). Adapting production to comprehension: The explicit mention of instruments. *Cognitive Psychology, 19*(4), 441–472.
Brown, R. (1958). How shall a thing be called? *Psychological Review, 65*, 14–21.
Clark, E. V. (1990). On the pragmatics of contrast. *Journal of Child Language, 17*, 417–431.
Clark, E. V., & Clark, H. H. (1979). When nouns surface as verbs. *Language, 55*, 767–811.
Clark, H. H. (1991). Words, the world, and their possibilities. In G. R. Lockhead and J. R. Pomerantz (Eds.), *The perception of structure*. Washington, DC: American Psychological Association.
Clark, H. H. (1992). *Arenas of language use*. Chicago, IL: University of Chicago Press.

Clark, H. H. (1996). *Using language.* Cambridge, UK: Cambridge University Press.
Clark, H. H., & Brennan, S. E. (1991). Grounding in communication. In L. B. Resnick, J. M. Levine, and S. D. Teasley (Eds.), *Perspectives on socially shared cognition* (pp. 127–149). Washington, DC: American Psychological Association.
Clark, H. H., & Carlson, T. B. (1981). Context for comprehension. In J. Long and A. Baddeley (Eds.), *Attention and performance IX* (pp. 313–330). Hillsdale, NJ: Lawrence Erlbaum Associates.
Clark, H. H., & Marshall, C. R. (1981). Definite reference and mutual knowledge. In A. K. Joshe, B. L. Webber, and I. A. Sag (Eds.), *Elements of discourse understanding* (pp. 10–63). Cambridge: Cambridge University Press.
Clark, H. H., & Wilkes-Gibbs, D. (1986). Referring as a collaborative process. *Cognition, 22*(1), 1–39.
Cruse, D. A. (1977). The pragmatics of lexical specificity. *Journal of Linguistics, 13*, 153–164.
Garrod, S., & Anderson, A. (1987). Saying what you mean in dialogue: A study in conceptual and semantic coordination. *Cognition, 27*, 181–218.
Garrod, S., & Doherty, G. (1994). Conversation, coordination and convention: An empirical investigation of how groups establish linguistic conventions. *Cognition, 53*, 181–215.
Glucksberg, S., & Keysar, B. (1990). Understanding metaphorical comparisons: Beyond similarity. *Psychological Review, 97*, 3–18.
Goldman-Eisler, F. (1968). *Psycholinguistics: Experiments in spontaneous speech.* New York: Academic Press.
Goldstone, R. L., & Janssen, M. A. (2005). Computational models of collective behavior. *Trends in Cognitive Sciences, 9*, 424–430.
Grice, H. P. (1975). Logic and conversation. In P. Cole and J. Morgan (Eds.), *Syntax and semantics 3: Speech acts* (pp. 41–58). New York: Academic Press.
Gundel, J. K., Hedberg, N., & Zacharski, R. (1993). Cognitive status and the form of referring expressions in discourse. *Language, 69*, 274–307.
Horton, W. S., & Keysar, B. (1996). When do speakers take into account common ground? *Cognition, 59*(1), 91–117.
Hutchins, E., & Hazlehurst, B. (1995). How to invent a lexicon: The development of shared symbols in interaction. In N. Gilbert and R. Conte (Eds.), *Artificial societies: The computer simulation of social life* (pp. 157–189). London: UCL Press.
Keysar, B. (2000). The illusory transparency of intention: Does June understand what Mark means because he means it? *Discourse Processes, 29*, 161–172.
Keysar, B., Barr, D. J., Balin, J. A., & Brauner, J. S. (2000). Taking perspective in conversation: The role of mutual knowledge in comprehension. *Psychological Science, 11*(1), 32–38.
Kirsh, D., & Maglio, P. (1994). On distinguishing epistemic from pragmatic action. *Cognitive Science, 18*(4), 513–549.
Kronmüller, E., & Barr, D. J. (2006). Perspective-free pragmatics: Broken precedents and the recovery-from-preemption hypothesis. *Journal of Memory and Language,* in press.
Lewis, D. (1969). *Convention: A philosophical study.* Cambridge, MA: Harvard University Press.
Lewis, D. (1979). Scorekeeping in a language game. *Journal of Philosophical Logic, 8*, 339–359.
Maclay, H., & Osgood, C. E. (1959). Hesitation phenomena in spontaneous speech. *Word, 15*, 19–44.
Malt, B. C., & Sloman, S. A. (2004). Conversation and convention: Enduring influences on name choice for common objects. *Memory & Cognition, 32*, 1346–1354.
Markman, A. B., & Gentner, D. (1993). Splitting the differences: A structural alignment view of similarity. *Journal of Memory and Language, 32*, 517–535.

Markman, A. B., & Makin, V. S. (1998). Referential communication and category acquisition. *Journal of Experimental Psychology: General, 127*, 331–354.

Markman, A. B., & Ross, B. H. (2003). Category use and category learning. *Psychological Bulletin, 129*, 592–613.

Markman, E., & Wachtel, G. (1988). Children's use of mutual exclusivity to constrain the meanings of words. *Cognitive Psychology, 20*, 121–157.

Metzing, C., & Brennan, S. E. (2003). When conceptual pacts are broken: Partner-specific effects on the comprehension of referring expressions. *Journal of Memory & Language, 49*, 201–213.

Olson, D. R. (1970). Language and thought: Aspects of a cognitive theory of semantics. *Psychological Review, 77*, 257–273.

Pickering, M. J., & Garrod, S. (2004). Toward a mechanistic psychology of dialogue. *Behavioral and Brain Sciences, 27*, 1–22.

Rosch, E., & Mervis, C. B. (1975). Family resemblances: Studies in the internal structure of categories. *Cognitive Psychology, 7*, 573–605.

Rosch, E., Mervis, C. B., Gray, W., Johnson, D., & Boyes-Braem, P. (1976). Basic objects in natural categories. *Cognitive Psychology, 8*, 382–439.

Rossnagel, C. (2000). Cognitive load and perspective taking: Applying the automatic-controlled distinction to verbal communication. *European Journal of Social Psychology, 30*, 429–445.

Russell, B. (1905). On denoting. *Mind, 14*, 479–493.

Sabbagh, M. A., & Baldwin, D. A. (2001). Learning words from knowledgeable versus ignorant speakers: Links between theory of mind and semantic development. *Child Development, 72*, 1054–1070.

Schachter, S., Christenfeld, N., Ravina, B., & Bilous, F. (1991). Speech disfluency and the structure of knowledge. *Journal of Personality and Social Psychology, 60*, 362–367.

Schachter, S., Rauscher, F. H., Christenfeld, N., & Tyson Crone, K. (1994). The vocabularies of academia. *Psychological Science, 5*, 37–41.

Siegman, A. W., & Pope, B. (1966). Ambiguity and verbal fluency in the TAT. *Journal of Consulting Psychology, 30*, 239–245.

Smith, V. L., & Clark, H. H. (1993). On the course of answering questions. *Journal of Memory and Language, 32*, 25–38.

Steels, L. (1996). Self-organizing vocabularies. In C. G. Langton and T. Shimohara (Eds.), *Artificial life V: Proceedings of the fifth international workshop*. Cambridge, MA: MIT Press.

USING CLASSIFICATION TO UNDERSTAND THE MOTIVATION-LEARNING INTERFACE

W. Todd Maddox, Arthur B. Markman, and Grant C. Baldwin

I. Introduction

Most behavior is motivated. As we maneuver through the environment, we are constantly selecting behaviors from a large repertoire of possibilities. Cognition plays a large role in selecting a behavior, but the selected behavior is also strongly determined by our motivational state to approach positive outcomes or avoid negative outcomes. Cognitive research typically focuses on information processing and its effects on learning and behavior with little attention paid to the factors that drive or motivate one to act.

The influence of active goals on behavior has been the focus of recent social psychological research (e.g., Aarts, Gollwitzer, & Hassin, 2004; Ferguson & Bargh, 2004; Fishbach, Friedman, & Kruglanski, 2003; Higgins, 2000), but little work has examined the effects of motivation on learning (cf. Maddox, Baldwin, & Markman, in press; Markman, Baldwin, & Maddox, in press; Markman, Maddox, & Baldwin, in press). A complete understanding of the relationship between learning and behavior requires a focus on the interplay between motivation and cognition (Carver & Scheier, 1998; Higgins, 1997).

The broad aim of this chapter is to generate a renewed interest in bridging the artificial gap that has formed between research focused on motivation and learning. The two were intimately related in the 1950s and 1960s (Miller, 1957, 1959; Young, 1959), but since then they have diverged, partially because psychology became more divided and area driven. Work on learning became the domain of cognitive and animal psychologists, whereas motivation was studied by social and educational psychologists. Furthermore, research in cognitive psychology has often focused on the characteristics of particular tasks (such as classification or visual search), and so there has been little emphasis on integrating phenomena across domains.

There has been a parallel development in cognitive psychology and neuroscience. Cognitive psychology has begun to generate more integrative theories. At the same time, research in neuroscience makes clear that the brain does not distinguish between motivational areas and learning areas. In fact, some of the most important brain regions for learning, such as the prefrontal cortex, the anterior cingulate, and the caudate nucleus, are either directly or indirectly interconnected with brain regions known to be involved in motivation, affect, and personality such as the amygdala and the orbitofrontal cortex just to name two. In addition, detailed neurobiological theories are beginning to take hold that postulate-specific interdependencies between "cognitive" and "motivational/emotional/personality" brain regions (e.g., Ashby, Isen, & Turken, 1999; Bechara, Damasio, & Damasio, 2000; Gray, 1987; Pickering & Gray, 2001). Although the bulk of the theoretical development in this chapter will be behaviorally based, we will explore the neurobiological underpinnings in some detail in Section VIII.

The more specific aim of this chapter is to provide a framework for exploring motivational influences on learning. Specifically, we examine the influence of regulatory focus (Higgins, 2000) on perceptual classification learning. Perceptual classification learning provides an excellent domain for studying the motivation-learning interface because quick and accurate classification is central to the survival of all organisms and is performed thousands of times a day. In addition, a number of sophisticated mathematical models have been developed that provide the researcher with insight into the strategies that people adopt throughout learning.

In Section II, we briefly review regulatory focus theory (Higgins, 2000) and develop a framework for investigating the influence of motivation on behavior. The framework identifies a number of key personality, motivational, and environmental factors that interact to determine performance on learning tasks. Section III applies this framework to classification learning, and outlines two strong predictions that can be generated from the framework. Section IV reviews recently published studies from our laboratory and several ongoing studies that provide initial tests of these predictions. Section V extends the framework to the domain of decision criterion learning. We conclude with some general remarks.

II. A Framework for Examining the Motivation-Classification Learning Interface

The motivation literature makes a distinction between approach and avoidance goals (e.g., Carver & Scheier, 1998; Lewin, 1935; Markman & Brendl, 2000; Miller, 1959). Goals with positive states that one wishes to achieve are called *approach* goals, whereas goals with negative states that one wishes to avoid are called *avoidance* goals. Higgins (1987, 1997) proposed regulatory focus theory that extends this idea of approach and avoidance by suggesting that, orthogonal to approach and avoidance goals, there may be psychological states of readiness or sensitivity for potential gains/nongains or losses/nonlosses that tune the sensitivity of the motivational system. Specifically, a *promotion focus* activates an approach mode of processing that focuses the motivational system on the presence or absence of gains in the environment, whereas a *prevention focus* activates an avoidance mode of processing that focuses the motivational system on the presence or absence of losses in the environment.

Higgins and colleagues (Higgins, 1987, 1997; Higgins, Roney, Crowe, & Hymes, 1994) outline three aspects of regulatory focus. First, people differ in their *chronic focus* (also referred to as person focus). Chronic focus is an a priori predisposition toward a promotion or a prevention focus. Higgins (1987) suggested that a promotion focus is associated with a person's desire to achieve ideal states, which are defined as that person's hopes, desires, or aspirations. In contrast, a prevention focus is associated with a person's desire to achieve ought states, which are defined as that person's duties obligations, or responsibilities.[1] The strength of a person's predisposed focus toward an ideal or ought state can be measured in a number of ways. One that is popular is to have each person provide a list of attributes that describe how they ideally would like to be. For each attribute the person rates the extent to which they ideally would like to have that attribute and the extent to which they actually possess the attribute. A similar procedure is followed for attributes that describe how they ought to be. Large discrepancies between a person's ideal attributes and their beliefs about their actual attributes are associated with a promotion focus. Large discrepancies between a person's ought attributes and their beliefs about their actual attributes are associated with a chronic prevention focus (see e.g., Shah, Higgins, & Friedman, 1998 for details). The essential idea is that these discrepancies reflect the degree to

---

[1] Higgins (1997) suggests that a person's predisposition toward ideal end states and a chronic promotion focus versus ought end states and a chronic prevention focus is related to the environment in which they were raised. Children raised in a nurturant environment are more likely to have a chronic promotion focus whereas children raised in a more security minded environment are more likely to have a chronic prevention focus.

which people believe traits for ideal (i.e., approach) and ought (i.e., avoidance) states that are accessible for that individual are also part of their self-concept. To the extent that there are significant discrepancies, they likely reflect unfulfilled goals of the individual and consequently will help to determine chronic focus.

A second key aspect of regulatory focus is a person's *situational focus* (also referred to as incentive focus), which is induced by aspects of the current situation. If someone is pursuing a potential gain then they can be placed in a state of readiness for gain and nongain situations in general. Likewise, if someone is attempting to avoid a loss then they can be placed in a state of readiness for loss and nonloss situations in general.

Unlike chronic focus which is an attribute of a person, situational focus can be manipulated experimentally. Situational focus manipulations are relatively easy to instantiate. As one example, Crowe and Higgins (1997; see also Markman, Kim, & Brendl, 2005) told all participants that they would complete a recognition memory task followed by a second task. The promotion participants were told that if they did well on the recognition task, the second task would be one that they "liked," whereas prevention participants were told that if they did not do well on the recognition task the second task would be one that they "disliked" (liked and disliked tasks were determined separately for each participant based on pretesting). As a second example, Shah et al., (1998) had participants solve anagrams. The promotion participants were paid a base salary of $4 but were told that they could earn an extra $1 if they found 90% of the anagram solutions. Prevention participants were paid a base salary of $5 but were told that they would lose $1 if they missed more than 10% of the anagram solutions.

A third key aspect of regulatory focus is the idea of *regulatory fit* (Avnet & Higgins, 2003; Higgins, 2000; Higgins, Chen Idson, Freitas, Spiegel, & Molden, 2003; Lee & Aaker, 2004; Shah et al., 1998). This term has been used in a few different ways in the literature and so it is worth unpacking them a bit.

First, there is a potential fit between chronic and situational focus. That is, a person may have a chronic promotion focus (because of a large ideal-actual discrepancy) or a chronic prevention focus (because of a large ought-actual discrepancy). Individuals are likely to exhibit better performance in a cognitive task when there is a fit between their chronic focus and the situational focus induced by a task than when there is a mismatch between these foci. For example, in Study 1 from Shah et al. (1998), each participant completed two experimental sessions with a minimum of 3 weeks between sessions. In session 1, chronic focus (i.e., ideal and ought strength) was measured. In session 2, each participant was asked to complete ten anagrams under a situational promotion or prevention focus. The regulatory fit prediction was that people with a chronic promotion focus should perform better than people with a chronic prevention focus under a promotion situational focus, whereas people with a chronic prevention focus should perform better than people with a chronic promotion focus under a prevention situational focus. The results from Study 1 supported the predicted interaction.

A second type of regulatory fit focuses on the relationship between a person's current regulatory focus and the *reward structure of the task* (also referred to as goal attainment means; Crowe & Higgins, 1997; Higgins et al., 1994; Shah et al., 1998). Many tasks can be accomplished by multiple means. For example, in many learning experiments, people may receive points for some responses and lose points for others. One might try to maximize the number of points obtained by focusing on gaining points or alternatively by focusing on avoiding the loss of points. Situations in which one can gain points involve a gain/nongain reward structure. Situations in which one can lose points involve a loss/nonloss reward structure.

There is some reason to believe that people also perform better when there is a fit between the person's current regulatory fit and this reward structure. As one demonstration of this point, Shah et al. (1998) hypothesized a three-way interaction between chronic focus, situational focus, and the reward structure of the task. As outlined earlier, they predicted better anagram performance when chronic and situational foci matched than when they mismatched. They also predicted that the nature of the match—chronic promotion with situational promotion versus chronic prevention with situational prevention—would affect which means were used for goal attainment. Specifically, chronic promotion focus participants given a promotion situational focus should pursue gaining points more than losing points, and chronic prevention focus participants given a prevention situational focus should pursue avoiding losing points more than gaining points. Their Study 2 provided a test of this hypothesis. Session 1 measured chronic focus in the same way as in Study 1. In session 2, participants were asked to solve 6 "red" and 6 "green" anagrams and that the goal was to finish with at least 4 points. Participants were told that for each green anagram they would earn 1 point if they found all of the words. Participants were also told that for each red anagram they would lose 1 point if they did not find all of the words. The promotion situational focus participants were told that they would earn $4 but if they gained 4 or more points they would earn an extra $1. The prevention situational focus participants were told that they would earn $5 but if they failed to gain 4 or more points they would lose $1. As predicted, chronic promotion focus participants given a promotion situational focus pursued the green anagrams (the gains reward structure) more than the red (the losses reward structure), whereas chronic prevention focus participants given a prevention situational focus pursued the red anagrams more than the green.

For completeness, there is a third form of regulatory fit that involves value. In particular, people's judgment of the worth of objects is influenced by the fit between the processes by which they evaluate an object and their regulatory focus. As one example, Higgins et al. (2003) had people with a promotion or prevention focus evaluate items for what they would gain by obtaining the object or what they would lose by giving up the other object. Promotion-focused subjects valued objects more when they focused on what was to be gained by owning it than by what they would give up by not owning it. In contrast, prevention-focused subjects showed the reverse pattern, valuing objects more when they focused on what they would give up than on what they would gain.

The interaction between chronic focus, situational focus, and the reward structure of the task has been studied extensively in the literature (Higgins & Spiegal, 2004). Subsets of these motivational factors have been found to affect performance in a number of tasks including problem solving (anagrams; Shah et al., 1998), decision making (recognition memory; Crowe & Higgins, 1997), and consumer behavior (Lee & Aaker, 2004; Markman et al., 2005). This work has significantly advanced our understanding of the motivation-cognition interface. In the following section we apply this motivational framework to classification learning. To anticipate, we begin by examining the potential neurobiological underpinnings of regulatory focus theory and its interaction with classification learning. We also extend the notion of regulatory fit to explore the relationship between the processes engendered by a particular regulatory focus and the type of task being performed.

III. Applying the Regulatory Fit Framework to Classification

In this section we apply the regulatory fit framework outlined earlier to the task of perceptual classification learning. Because our interests lie primarily with drawing cause–effect inferences, we restrict our attention to manipulations of situational focus and the reward structure of the task. To be clear, we are *not* discounting the importance of chronic regulatory focus nor its interaction with the other forms of regulatory focus. On the contrary, an understanding of how chronic predispositions affect learning is critical to a complete understanding of the motivation-cognition interface. Even so, our work is experimental and thus a narrower focus is required.

Classification learning encompasses a huge literature (see Wisniewski, 2002 for a review) that includes semantic categories, natural categories, and artificial perceptual categories to name a few. Because our interest is in learning, we take the approach of constructing novel, artificial categories from collections of perceptual dimensions. This approach allows us to examine the processes involved in classification learning and to examine a wide range of category structures under controlled experimental conditions. This approach allows us to define rigorously the optimal classifier (a hypothetical device that maximizes long-run reward) and to compare human performance with that of the optimal classifier. In the following sections we review briefly the growing literature on the neurobiological underpinnings of perceptual classification learning and loosely tie these to the notion of regulatory fit.

A. NEUROBIOLOGICAL UNDERPINNINGS OF PERCEPTUAL CATEGORY LEARNING

Classification learning involves laying down a memory trace that improves the efficiency (i.e., accuracy and speed) of responding. It is now widely accepted that mammals have multiple memory systems (Poldrack & Packard, 2003; Schacter, 1987; Squire, 1992), and there is a growing consensus that multiple classification learning systems exist. Starting in the 1980s a mounting body of research suggested that participants have available multiple processing modes that can be used during classification. Well established in the literature is a distinction between classification based on a rule versus classification based on overall similarity (Allen & Brooks, 1991; Erickson & Kruschke, 1998; Folstein & Van Petten, 2004; Kemler-Nelson, 1984; Nosofsky, Palmeri, & McKinley, 1994; Rehegr & Brooks, 1993; Smith & Shapiro, 1989). Rule-based classification is accomplished when an individual forms an explicit verbal rule that distinguishes between members of different categories. Similarity-based classification involves classifying a new stimulus based on some function of the similarity between the new instance and a stored category representation.

Much evidence supports the claim that there are multiple classification learning systems and that they involve unique (though overlapping) neural systems. This empirical support comes from a wide range of research areas including animal learning (McDonald & White, 1993, 1994; Packard & McGaugh, 1992), neuropsychology (Filoteo, Maddox, & Davis, 2001a, 2001b; Maddox & Filoteo, 2001, in press; Myers et al., 2003), functional neuroimaging (Filoteo et al., 2005; Poldrack, Prabhakaran, Seger, & Gabrieli, 1999; Reber, Stark, & Squire, 1998; Seger & Cincotta, 2002, 2005; Smith, Patalano, & Jonides, 1998), and cognitive psychology (for reviews, see Keri, 2003; Maddox & Ashby, 2004).

One of the most successful multiple systems models of classification learning, and the only one that specifies the underlying neurobiology, is the COmpetition between Verbal and Implicit Systems model (COVIS; Ashby, Alfonso-Reese, Turken, & Waldron, 1998; Ashby & Waldron, 1999). COVIS postulates two systems that compete throughout learning—an explicit, hypothesis-testing system and an implicit, procedural-based learning system. COVIS assumes that, in humans, the two systems mediate the learning of different types of category structures.[2] Briefly, COVIS assumes that *rule-based category learning* is dominated by the explicit hypothesis-testing system that uses working memory and executive attention and is mediated by a circuit that includes the anterior cingulate, the prefrontal cortex, and the head of the caudate nucleus. Frequently, the rule that maximizes accuracy (i.e., the optimal rule) is easy to describe verbally. For example, Fig. 1A presents a scatter plot of stimuli from a rule-based condition with four categories. Each point in the plot denotes the length and orientation of a single line stimulus (see Fig. 1C for an example) with different symbols denoting different categories. In this example, the rule is to give a first response to short, shallow angle lines; a second response to short, steep angle lines; a third response to long, shallow angle lines; and a fourth response to long, steep angle lines. To solve this task, the explicit hypothesis-testing system learns the criterion between "short" and "long" and between "shallow" and "steep," and learns the mapping between short/long and shallow/steep lines and the four category labels.

In contrast, *information-integration category learning* is dominated by the implicit procedural-based learning system that depends on a reward signal to strengthen the appropriate (stimulus-category) associations in a relatively automatic fashion (Ashby & Ell, 2001; Ashby et al., 1998). This system is mediated largely within the tail of the caudate nucleus (with visual stimuli) and learning relies heavily on a dopamine-mediated reward signal.[3] Figure 1B presents a scatter plot of stimuli from an information-integration condition with four categories. Notice that the information-integration category structure can be derived from the rule-based category structure by

---

[2] It is important to note that we are not arguing that these are the only two classification learning systems. On the contrary, there is good evidence that at least two additional systems: an episodic-memory driven and a perceptual-priming system likely exist. The interested reader is directed to Ashby and Maddox (2005) or Keri (2003) for a review.

[3] In primates, all of extrastriate visual cortex projects directly to the tail of the caudate nucleus with about 10,000 visual cortical synapses converging onto each medium spiny cell in the caudate (Wilson, 1995). These medium spiny cells then project to prefrontal and premotor cortex (via the globus pallidus and thalamus; e.g., Alexander, DeLong, & Strick, 1986). The idea is that an unexpected reward causes substantia nigra neurons to release dopamine from their terminals in the caudate nucleus (Hollerman & Schultz, 1998; Schultz, 1992) and that the presence of this dopamine strengthens recently active synapses (Arbuthnott, Ingham, & Wickens, 2000).

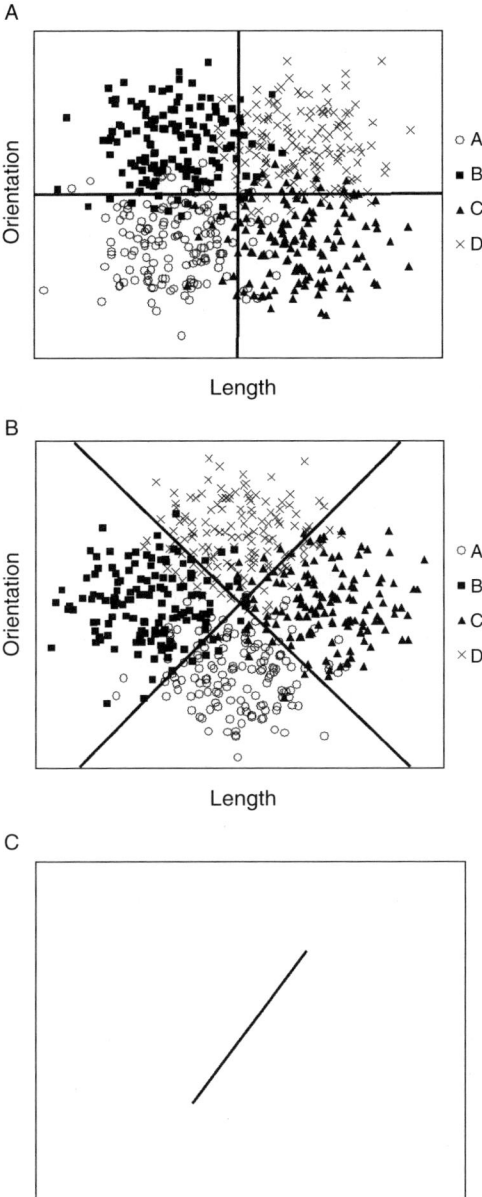

Fig. 1. (A) A four-category rule-based category structure with two dimensions: line length (in pixels) and orientation (in degrees). (B) A four-category information-integration category structure, created by rotating the rule-based structure 45° counterclockwise. (C) A representative stimulus.

rotating the location of each stimulus counterclockwise 45° in the length-orientation space. Unlike the decision rule in the rule-based condition, the resulting information-integration classification rule is nonverbalizable.

This represents only a cursory review of COVIS and the proposed underlying neurobiology. A more detailed discussion can be found in Ashby and Valentin (in press). For the present purposes, what is most important to note is that the hypothesis-testing system relies heavily on frontal brain regions, whereas the procedural-based learning system relies heavily on subcortical regions such as the tail of the caudate nucleus.

B. Neurobiological Underpinnings of Regulatory Focus

As reviewed earlier, regulatory fit leads participants to generate more alternatives in an anagram task (Crowe & Higgins, 1997; Shah et al., 1998). Solving anagrams requires the participant to select and test numerous alternatives. This process of selecting and testing alternatives can be defined generally as *cognitive flexibility*. The anterior cingulate, a frontal brain structure utilized by the hypothesis-testing system, is thought to be critically involved in the selection of alternatives and has been linked directly to cognitive flexibility (Posner & Petersen, 1990). In the following sections that develop and test our proposed motivation-learning framework, we will not elaborate on the possible neurobiological underpinnings but rather leave a more detailed discussion for the Summary and Future Directions section. For now suffice it to say that we assume that cognitive flexibility is at least partially mediated by the anterior cingulate.

C. Classification Learning Predictions

Our working hypothesis is that regulatory fit; specifically, a fit between situational focus and the reward structure of the task, leads to greater cognitive flexibility. Taken a step further, we suggest that cognitive flexibility can be loosely associated with frontal brain areas, in particular the anterior cingulate.

The complete set of hypotheses from this view are summarized in Table I. We can state our predictions in the following two parts.

Prediction 1: Regulatory fit manipulations should lead to better rule-based classification learning when cognitive flexibility is advantageous for solving the task, but should lead to worse rule-based classification learning when cognitive flexibility is not advantageous.

We define cognitive flexibility as an increase in one's ability or willingness to try different strategies across trials to achieve some stated goal, as opposed to sticking with a single strategy and making small incremental changes during learning. If the task is one for which a simple, highly salient

TABLE I
Regulatory Fit-Classification Learning Predictions

Task type	Reward structure	Promotion focus	Prevention focus
Rule-based: Flexibility	Gains	Better	Worse
Rule-based: Flexibility	Losses	Worse	Better
Rule-based: No flexibility	Gains	Worse	Better
Rule-based: No flexibility	Losses	Better	Worse
Information integration	Gains	Worse?	Better?
Information Integration	Losses	Better?	Worse?

Note: The "?" denote a more speculative prediction.

strategy will achieve the participant's goal or one in which the necessary rule is obvious from the start then the increase in willingness to try more complex rules associated with cognitive flexibility may not be acted upon. In contrast, if the task is one for which a complex, low-salience strategy is necessary to achieve the participant's goal or the rule is not obvious initially then increased cognitive flexibility should be advantageous.

Prediction 2: Regulatory fit manipulations should affect the hypothesis-testing classification system but not the procedural-based learning classification system. By extension, regulatory fit manipulations should affect rule-based classification learning more than information-integration category learning.

Prediction 2 follows because regulatory fit is assumed to lead to greater cognitive flexibility. Cognitive flexibility is associated with greater activity in the anterior cingulate which is a critical brain structure in the hypothesis-testing but not the procedural-based classification learning system. Because rule-based classification learning is dominated by the hypothesis-testing system, and information-integration classification learning is dominated by the procedural-based learning system, regulatory fit effects should be strongest for rule-based classification learning. Prediction 2 is more tenuous for reasons that will be discussed later.

The studies we have conducted over the past few years have addressed some of the predictions summarized in Table I. In the following sections we review this work. One series of studies examines the effects of regulatory fit on rule-based classification learning. In some cases cognitive flexibility is advantageous for solving the task whereas in others cognitive flexibility is *not* advantageous for solving the task. We then turn to a study that examines the effects of regulatory fit on information-integration category learning.

IV. Regulatory Fit Effects on Rule-Based Classification Learning

A. COGNITIVE FLEXIBILITY IS ADVANTAGEOUS

1. Maddox et al. (in press), Experiment 1 (Gains Reward Structure)

The first study we discuss explored a condition in which people learned rule-based categories. We designed the categories so that flexibility in the selection of a classification strategy would be advantageous. The task used a gains reward structure. This setting is summarized in the first row of Table I. From this table, we would expect that subjects given a situational promotion focus would perform better than would subjects given a situational prevention focus.

To create a setting in which cognitive flexibility was useful, the task was designed so that a simple, highly salient unidimensional rule yielded reasonable performance, but a more complex, less-salient conjunctive rule yielded higher performance that allowed the participant to exceed a performance criterion. Importantly, correct responses were rewarded with a gain in points on each trial, whereas errors led to no gain in points. Thus, there was a match between situational focus and the reward structure of the task for situational promotion focus participants, but there was a mismatch for situational prevention focus participants.

The stimulus on each trial was a line whose length, orientation, and horizontal position on the computer screen varied across trials. A scatter plot of the stimuli in three-dimensions along with the optimal decision criteria on length and orientation is displayed in Fig. 2A. The optimal decision rule was conjunctive and required the participant to set a criterion on length and orientation and to use the rule: respond A if the length is long and the orientation is steep otherwise respond B. A participant using the optimal length and orientation decision criteria could attain 100% accuracy, whereas the most accurate unidimensional rules on length, and orientation yielded 83% accuracy. The position dimension was irrelevant to solving the task (i.e., the optimal rule did not involve position) but was constructed in such a way that a unidimensional rule on position also yielded 83% correct. The position dimension was included because pilot studies conducted in our lab suggest that it is highly salient and thus we expected participants to focus initially on this dimension. To summarize, a participant could perform quite well while focusing on only one stimulus dimension such as position, but a conjunction of the length and orientation dimension information was required to achieve performance that exceeded the bonus criterion. Each participant completed several blocks of trials in the experiment.

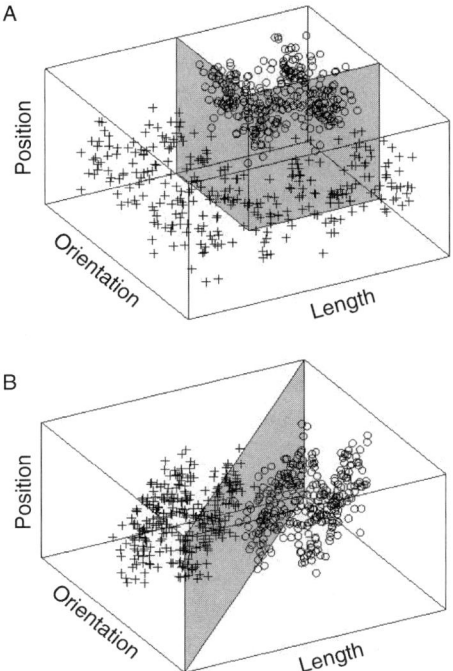

Fig. 2. (A) The two-category conjunctive rule-based category structure used in Maddox et al. (in press), Experiment 1. (B) A two-category information-integration category structure. In both panels, plus signs (+) denote category A, open circles (O) denote category B, and the gray planes represent the optimal decision bound. Copyright Psychonomic Society, Inc., 2006. Adapted with permission.

Participants in the situational promotion focus condition were told that they could earn an entry into a drawing for $50 if they exceeded a performance criterion during the final block of trials (equivalent to meeting or exceeding 90% accuracy). Participants in the situational prevention focus condition were given an entry into the drawing for $50 upon entry into the laboratory but were told that they had to exceed the same performance criterion in order to keep the entry. Notice that any participant using a unidimensional rule will not exceed the performance criterion. Instead, the participant must abandon the simple unidimensional rule (either on length, orientation, or position) in favor of the more complex conjunctive rule to exceed the performance criterion. Because discovery of the optimal conjunctive rule requires greater cognitive flexibility (i.e., a willingness to abandon the reasonably accurate, simple unidimensional rule in favor of the more complex conjunctive rule required to exceed the performance criterion), we predicted that participants given a situational promotion focus will discover the rule sooner, and thus will learn more quickly than participants given a situational prevention focus.

At the beginning of each block a "point meter" was set to zero. The criterion was shown as a line across the meter and was labeled "bonus." At the end of each block of trials the participants were given feedback on their performance in that block. If they exceeded the bonus criterion in the situational promotion condition, they were told "If that had been the last block of trials you would have earned an entry into the drawing for $50." If they exceeded the bonus criterion in the situational prevention condition, they were told "If that had been the last block of trials you would have kept you entry into the drawing for $50." If it was the final block, they were told whether they gained or kept their entry into the drawing.

Three sets of analyses were conducted on the accuracy data. First, we identified the first block of trials for which each participant met or exceeded the 90% performance criterion. This denotes the first block of trials for which the participant would have received feedback that, had that been the final block of trials, they would have earned an entry into the drawing (promotion focus) or they would have kept their entry into the drawing (prevention focus). As predicted, promotion focus participants exceed the performance criterion sooner than did prevention focus participants. Second, for each block of trials we compared the proportion of promotion and prevention focus participants who met or exceeded the 90% performance criterion. As predicted, more promotion focus participants (63.3%) exceeded the criterion during the final block than did prevention participants (36.7%). Finally, we computed the average accuracy in each block for the promotion and prevention participants. As expected, promotion participants were more accurate (91.3%) than prevention participants (86.5%) during the final block of trials. Taken together the accuracy-based analyses converge in suggesting that participants given a promotion focus (a) exceeded the performance criterion earlier in training, (b) were more likely in general to exceed the performance criterion necessary to earn an entry into the drawing, and (c) obtained higher overall accuracy rates.

The accuracy-based analyses support our claim that the regulatory fit between the situational promotion focus and the gains reward structure of the task led to greater cognitive flexibility. Implicit in this hypothesis is the assumption that cognitive flexibility led participants to abandon the highly salient unidimensional rule in favor of the more complex, less-salient conjunctive rule. To test this hypothesis rigorously we fit a number of decision-bound models separately to the block by block data from each participant. The details of the model-fitting procedure are outlined in Maddox et al. (in press).

We fit three models that assumed a unidimensional rule-based strategy: one that assumed a rule on length, another on orientation, and a third on position. We also fit a suboptimal conjunctive rule model that estimated the decision criterion values from the data, and the optimal conjunctive rule model that assumed the optimal decision criterion values.

Following the approach taken with the accuracy data, we conducted a number of separate analyses on the modeling results. First, as expected, the proportion of data sets best fit by the unidimensional position model was higher for prevention participants than promotion participants. This pattern suggests that prevention focus participants were less likely to abandon this simple rule in favor of the more complex conjunctive rule. Second, we identified the first block of trials for which a conjunctive rule model provided the best account of the data separately for each participant. Promotion participants' data were best fit by a conjunctive model earlier in learning than prevention participants. Finally, the proportion of participants whose data were best fit by a conjunctive rule model was higher for promotion participants than prevention participants.

Taken together these results suggest that a regulatory fit between a situational promotion focus and a gains reward structure leads to greater cognitive flexibility and thus better rule-based classification learning when the task is one that requires cognitive flexibility. Thus, this pattern supports the predictions in the first row of Table I.

2. Pilot Data (Losses Reward Structure)

Maddox et al. (in press), Experiment 1 provides support for our claim that a regulatory fit between the situational focus and the reward structure of the task leads to increased cognitive flexibility and better performance in a task for which a highly salient, simple rule is suboptimal, and a less salient, complex rule is optimal. Experiment 1 examined only a gains reward structure though.

In a recent pilot study conducted in our lab, we replicated Maddox et al. (in press), Experiment 1 but with a losses reward structure. As summarized in the second row of Table I, our motivation-learning framework predicts that—under these conditions—there will be a regulatory fit between situational prevention focus participants and the reward structure, and a regulatory mismatch between the situational promotion focus participants and the reward structure. Because the category structure is one that requires cognitive flexibility, and because situational prevention participants should be more cognitively flexible (under a losses reward structure), we predicted a pattern opposite of that observed in Maddox et al. (in press). Specifically, we predicted (a) faster, more accurate classification learning for situational prevention participants, and (b) an earlier shift away from the use of a unidimensional rule on position toward a conjunctive rule on length and orientation.

All aspects of the experiment were identical to those from Maddox et al. (in press), Experiment 1 except for the details of the point meter. In this study, participants started out with no points and lost either 1 point for a correct response or 3 points for an incorrect response. The 0 point on the meter was at the top of the screen, and the bonus line was below that. When the participant made a correct response the point meter went down 1 point and when they made an incorrect response the point meter went down 3 points. Participants earned or kept an entry into the drawing if they kept the point meter above the criterion line and lost or did not earn an entry if the point meter dropped below the criterion.

We followed the same data analytic procedure for these data as was used in Maddox et al. (in press), Experiment 1. Three aspects of the accuracy data were examined. First, as predicted, prevention focus participants exceed the performance criterion sooner than did promotion focus participants. Second, more prevention focus participants exceeded the criterion than did promotion participants. Finally, prevention participants were more accurate overall than prevention participants.

With respect to the model-based analyses, three analyses were conducted. First, the proportion of data sets best fit by the unidimensional position model was higher overall for promotion focus participants than for prevention focus participants, suggesting that promotion focus participants were less likely to abandon this simple rule in favor of the more complex conjunctive rule. Second, prevention participants' data were best fit by a conjunctive model earlier in learning than promotion participants. Finally, the proportion of prevention participants whose data were best fit by a conjunctive rule was larger than that for promotion participants.

3. Brief Summary

The results from Maddox et al. (in press), Experiment 1 and the pilot data above provide strong support for our regulatory fit/cognitive flexibility hypothesis. Participants completed a rule-based classification learning task for which a highly salient, simple unidimensional rule was suboptimal and a low-salience, complex conjunctive rule was optimal. Importantly, the bonus criterion could be met only if the participant abandoned the simple rule in favor of the more complex rule. Maddox et al. (in press) placed participants in a situation for which the reward structure of the task involved gains. Under these conditions, our regulatory fit hypothesis predicts better classification learning for situational promotion focus participants than for situational prevention focus participants. Promotion focus participants, learned faster, reached a higher asymptote, and were found to abandon the simple unidimensional rule in favor of the more complex conjunctive rule more quickly. In the pilot study, we placed participants in a situation for which the reward structure of the task involved losses. Under these conditions, our regulatory fit hypothesis predicts better classification learning for situational prevention focus participants than for situational promotion focus participants because the regulatory fit leads to greater cognitive flexibility. Prevention focus participants, learned faster, reached a higher asymptote, and were found to abandon the simple unidimensional rule in favor of the more complex conjunctive rule more quickly.

We turn now to a rule-based classification task for which cognitive flexibility should *not* be advantageous. These conditions are summarized in rows three and four of Table I. Because cognitive flexibility is not advantageous and because a regulatory fit between the situational focus and the reward structure of the task is hypothesized to lead to greater cognitive flexibility, we predict *worse* performance when there is a fit between the situational focus and the reward structure of the task than when there is a regulatory mismatch.

B. Cognitive Flexibility is not Advantageous

1. *Maddox et al. (in press), Experiment 2 (Gains Reward Structure)*

Experiment 2 of Maddox et al. (in press) examined the effects of regulatory fit on rule-based classification learning when cognitive flexibility was not advantageous for solving the task. We used the same gains reward structure used in Maddox et al. (in press), Experiment 1. As summarized in the third row of Table I, under these conditions, there should be a regulatory fit between the situational promotion focus and the gains reward structure that is predicted to lead to greater cognitive flexibility. Because cognitive flexibility is not advantageous, we predict better performance for the situational prevention focus participants than for the situational promotion focus participants.

We designed a classification task in which conservative changes in a person's criterion would lead to better performance in the task than would large changes that might be associated with high flexibility. As in Maddox et al. (in press), Experiment 1 we used a conjunctive rule-based classification learning task, but instead of a two-category problem where unidimensional rules existed that yielded good performance, we used a four-category problem where it was clear early in learning that a two-dimensional rule was required. The stimulus on each trial was a line whose length and orientation

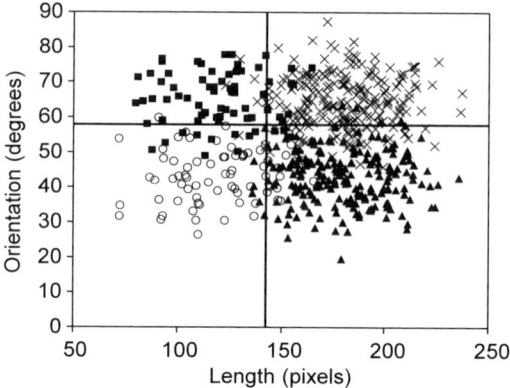

Fig. 3. Scatter plots of the stimuli along with the optimal decision bounds from the four-category conjunctive, rule-based category structure from Maddox et al. (in press), Experiment 2. Open circles denote stimuli from category A. Filled squares denote stimuli from category B. Filled triangles denote stimuli from category C. X's denote stimuli from category D. Copyright Psychonomic Society, Inc., 2006. Adapted with permission.

varied across trials. Figure 3 displays the category structures. The optimal rule can be described as follows: "Respond A if the length is short and the orientation is shallow; Respond B if the length is short and the orientation is steep; Respond C if the length is long and the orientation is shallow; Respond D if the length is long and the orientation is steep." Because the two-dimensional nature of the optimal rule is clear early in learning, the type of cognitive flexibility associated with qualitative shifts in the nature of the decision rule will not be useful. Instead, good performance will be achieved through slower, more incremental changes in the decision criterion values. These slower, more incremental changes should be associated with lower levels of cognitive flexibility and thus a prevention focus.

Two additional characteristics of the task were added to bias the task in favor of low cognitive flexibility. First, the category distributions overlapped requiring the participant to learn a "noisy" criterion between "short" and "long" lines and between "shallow" and "steep" orientations. Second, a base-rate manipulation was introduced. Specifically, categories C and D were presented three times as often as categories A and B. Base-rate manipulations affect the location of the optimal decision criterion and in this study shifted the location of the optimal length criterion away from the equal likelihood criterion (see Maddox, 2002 for details). When the base rates are unequal, the optimal classifier sacrifices accuracy on the low base-rate categories to increase accuracy on the more prevalent high base-rate categories effectively increasing overall accuracy and long-run reward. The fact that (a) the two-dimensional nature of the optimal rule is clear early, (b) the location of the optimal criteria are noisy due to category overlap, and (c) the base-rate difference shifts the criteria away from the equal likelihood criteria should provide an environment for which low cognitive flexibility is advantageous.

The regulatory fit manipulation is subtle and should not be expected to lead to differential patterns of performance under all conditions. For example, if one constructs a situation in which the "bonus" is easily attainable even with a suboptimal rule, there should be little effect of regulatory fit because both promotion and prevention focus participants should achieve the goal easily. In contrast, if we create a situation in which the bonus is rarely or never attainable, we should observe larger effects of the regulatory fit manipulation. To investigate this possibility, we examined the effects of regulatory fit on four-category conjunctive rule-based classification learning under two "goal states": one for which the bonus was easily attainable (the attainable goal condition) and one for which the bonus was unattainable (the unattainable goal condition). This resulted in a 2 situational focus × 2 goal state factorial design.

The situational focus manipulation was identical to that from Maddox et al. (in press), Experiment 1. Participants in the unattainable goal condition received 1 point for each correct response and no points for incorrect responses, whereas participants in the attainable goal condition received 2 points for each correct response and no points for incorrect responses. The bonus criterion was set to 75% of that obtained by the optimal classifier when 2 points could be earned for a correct response. Under these conditions, a participant achieving 100% accuracy in the unattainable goal condition would still not meet the performance criterion. The details of the point meter were identical to those from Maddox et al. (in press), Experiment 1.

Several analyses were conducted on the accuracy data. First, because the goal was attainable in the attainable goal conditions, we expected that situational promotion and prevention participants would meet or exceed the performance criterion early in learning and at the same rate. As expected, both groups achieved the goal early in learning. Second, as predicted, situational focus and attainability interacted in predicting performance. The interaction suggested that (a) situational focus had no effect on performance when the goal was attainable, (b) performance in the prevention-unattainable condition was high and equivalent to that observed in the two attainable goal conditions, and (c) performance in the promotion-unattainable goal condition was significantly worse than in each of the other three conditions. We predicted worse learning when there was a regulatory fit between the situational focus (promotion) and the reward structure of the task (gains) because this "fit" should lead to greater cognitive flexibility, which is disadvantageous for learning this category structure. We postulated also that this "fit" disadvantage should occur only when there goal is unattainable. Each of these predictions was supported by the accuracy data but it would be useful to determine whether the "fit" effect is truly due to greater cognitive flexibility.

We applied a series of decision-bound models to address this issue. The details of the modeling can be found in Maddox et al. (in press), but for now suffice it to say that we focus our modeling analyses on a model that assumes that the participant uses a conjunctive rule, but one for which the decision criterion values are estimated from the data. In addition to the two decision criterion parameters (one on length and one on orientation), the model includes a "noise" parameter. In short, the noise parameter provides an estimate of the trial-by-trial variability in the application of the decision criteria. The noise value should provide a direct test of our cognitive flexibility hypothesis, since greater cognitive flexibility, in the form of larger shifts in the decision criteria, should result in a larger value for the noise parameter. Thus, we predict larger noise estimates in the promotion-unattainable condition than in the other three conditions. In addition, we predict no difference in the noise estimates across these three remaining conditions. As expected, we found no difference in the noise estimates across the two attainable goal and the prevention-unattainable goal conditions, but that there was greater noise variability in the promotion-unattainable goal condition than in any other condition.

2. Pilot Data (Losses Reward Structure)

The next step is to replicate Maddox et al. (in press), Experiment 2 but with a losses reward structure. As shown in the fourth row of Table I, under these conditions our motivation-learning framework predicts that there will be a regulatory fit between the situational prevention focus and the reward structure of the task. Because we predict that a regulatory fit will lead to greater cognitive flexibility when the goal is unattainable, we predict worse category learning in the prevention-unattainable goal condition than in the other three conditions, a pattern opposite of what we observed in Maddox et al. (in press), Experiment 2. We are currently in the process of running this study.

C. RULE-BASED CLASSIFICATION LEARNING SUMMARY

Our working hypothesis is that a regulatory fit between the situational focus and the reward structure of the task leads to greater cognitive flexibility. Cognitive flexibility is a frontal-based cognitive process and thus changes in cognitive flexibility should affect learning in classification tasks that involve primarily frontal brain structures. These include rule-based classification learning tasks. In some cases, cognitive flexibility is advantageous for solving the task. Under these conditions, a regulatory fit between the situational focus and the reward structure of the task—that is, a situational promotion focus with a gains reward structure or a situational prevention focus with a losses reward structure—should lead to greater cognitive flexibility and thus better rule-based classification learning. Maddox et al. (in press), Experiment 1 and the pilot data presented above support this claim. In other cases, cognitive flexibility is *not* advantageous for solving the task. Under these conditions, a regulatory fit between the situational focus and the reward structure of the task—that is, a situational promotion focus with a gains reward structure or a situational prevention focus with a losses reward structure—should lead to poor rule-based classification learning because cognitive flexibility is not advantageous. Maddox et al. (in press), Experiment 2 supported this claim when the reward structure contains gains. We are currently running a study that tests this hypothesis when the reward structure contains losses. Thus, we have already found empirical support for the predictions in the first three rows of Table I and are currently running a study examining the predictions in the fourth row.

V. Regulatory Fit Effects on Information-Integration Classification Learning

As outlined earlier, we suggest a loose association between regulatory fit and frontal brain structures, such as the anterior cingulate, that support cognitive flexibility. A strong prediction then is that regulatory fit should have little, if any, effect on information-integration category learning since it is mediated primarily by subcortical structures such as the tail of the caudate nucleus. On the other hand, it is also possible that regulatory fit will have some effect on information-integration category learning through its effects on the hypothesis-testing system.

COVIS assumes that rule-based classification learning is dominated by the hypothesis-testing system, and that information-integration classification learning is dominated by the procedural-based learning system. Even so, COVIS also assumes that these two systems—hypothesis-testing and procedural-based learning—compete on each trial to determine the response of the system. In addition, COVIS assumes that there is a bias toward the output of the hypothesis-testing system early in learning. The idea is that the participant starts by testing out verbalizable rules and only if those fail (e.g., in an information-integration task) will the system begin to shift away from the hypothesis-testing system and toward the procedural-based learning system. Thus, it seems reasonable to suppose that any effects of regulatory fit on information-integration classification learning should be restricted to the early blocks of trials when the hypothesis-testing system is dominant. In addition, the effect could be advantageous or disadvantageous for learning. If increased cognitive flexibility leads the participant to focus more on hypothesis-testing strategies then cognitive flexibility should adversely affect information-integration classification learning. This weak prediction is summarized in the last two rows of Table I. This prediction, however, need not be borne out. It may be that participants who are high incognitive flexibility may be more willing to abandon hypothesis-testing strategies in favor of procedural-based learning strategies. At this point, we are taking an exploratory approach toward examining regulatory fit effects on information-integration learning. We assume only that regulatory fit effects should be restricted to the early blocks of trials when the hypothesis-testing system dominates and should disappear later in learning when the procedural-based learning system begins to dominate.

As an initial examination of the effects of regulatory fit on information-integration classification learning, and in an attempt to link this work as closely as possible with our previous work, we conducted a pilot study using the category structures in Fig. 2B. Notice that this is very similar to the category structure used in Maddox et al. (in press), Experiment 1, in the sense that we included a highly salient unidimensional rule on position that achieved reasonable accuracy, but an accuracy rate below that required to earn the raffle entry (situational promotion focus) or to keep the raffle entry (situational prevention focus). The best-fitting unidimensional rule on length and on orientation also yielded good performance, but performance below the bonus criterion. To exceed the performance criterion the participant had to focus exclusively on length and orientation and apply an information-integration strategy. In addition, we examine only the gains reward structure. The experimental procedure was identical to that from Maddox et al. (in press), Experiment 1.

To date, we have found little, if any, difference in the proportion of promotion and prevention participants reaching the criterion, although there is a small advantage for the prevention participants early in learning. In addition, the block-by-block accuracy rates are approximately equal. To more fully examine classification learning strategies, we fit a series of hypothesis-testing and information-integration models to the data. Interestingly, a large advantage emerged early in learning for the prevention participants with over 80% of the participant's data best fit by an information-integration model by the third block of trials. Although speculative, these data suggest that the increased cognitive flexibility for the situational promotion participants under this gains reward structure led them to apply hypothesis-testing strategies for longer than participants with a regulatory mismatch (i.e., the situational prevention participants). The fact that the strategy differences were not born out in the accuracy data are curious but not unfounded. It is often the case that qualitatively different strategies, such as hypothesis-testing and procedural-based learning, can yield equivalent performance. The fact that a performance difference emerges in the models but not in the accuracy data attests to the importance of including model-based analyses in these studies.

These pilot data are suggestive and provide initial support for the notion that a regulatory fit—that is, a situational promotion focus under a gains reward structure—leads to greater cognitive flexibility in information-integration tasks. Cognitive flexibility in this case leads the participant to abandon hypothesis-testing strategies later in the session than participants with a regulatory mismatch. Future work needs to address the situation in which there is a regulatory fit between a situational prevention focus and a losses reward structure. The tentative prediction (outlined in the final row of Table I) is that a regulatory fit between a situational prevention focus and a losses reward structure should lead to greater cognitive flexibility that leads the participant to abandon hypothesis-testing strategies later in the session than participants with a regulatory mismatch.

VI. Summary of Classification Learning Results

In the previous sections we reviewed work that examined the effects of regulatory fit on rule-based and information-integration classification learning. We tested the hypothesis that a regulatory fit between the situational focus and the reward structure of the task will lead to greater cognitive flexibility. When the task is one for which cognitive flexibility is advantageous, we see better rule-based classification learning for participants in the regulatory fit conditions. When the task is one for which cognitive flexibility is not advantageous, we see better rule-based classification learning for participants in the regulatory mismatch conditions. The results for information-integration classification learning are less clear. At the level of global block-by-block accuracy there appear to be no effects of regulatory fit between a situational promotion focus and a gains reward structure. On the other hand, the model-based analyses suggest that regulatory fit participants use hypothesis-testing strategies longer than regulatory mismatch participants. Clearly more work is needed.

VII. Regulatory Fit Effects on Decision Criterion Learning

In this section, we apply our motivation-learning framework to the task of decision criterion learning. We continue to examine the notion of regulatory fit between situational focus and the reward structure of the task, but we examine cases in which the reward structure of the task is biased toward one category over the other. This allows us to examine a different form of cognitive flexibility.

In all of the studies outlined earlier, the participant's task was to maximize reward (either by maximizing points earned or minimizing points lost). In every case this was equivalent to maximizing accuracy. In other words, the optimal decision rule simultaneously maximized accuracy and reward. This follows because the payoff matrices were unbiased in the sense that the payoff for being correct was identical across categories, and the payoff for being incorrect was identical across categories.

In the real world it is often the case that the payoff matrices are biased. For example, the reward is greater for correctly diagnosing a patient who exhibits chest pain as having a heart attack than it is to correctly diagnose indigestion. Similarly, the cost of incorrectly diagnosing indigestion in a patient who is having a heart attack could be fatal whereas incorrectly diagnosing a heart attack in a patient who is suffering only from indigestion is not life threatening. A critical aspect of learning under these biased payoff situations is that reward maximization requires the participant to sacrifice some measure of long-run accuracy. In other words, the decision rule that maximizes long-run accuracy is different from the decision rule that maximizes long-run reward. Across a number of studies reviewed by Maddox (2002), we have shown that participants often exhibit a bias toward accuracy maximization even though the strategy that maximizes accuracy leads to suboptimal reward maximization.

In one study, Markman, Baldwin, and Maddox (in press) examined the effects of regulatory fit on performance in a decision criterion learning task for which the payoff structure was biased toward one category and away from the other. In the gains condition, the participant gained more points for being correct than incorrect, and more points for being correct on category A then for being correct on category B. In the losses condition, the participant lost fewer points for being correct than incorrect, and lost fewer points for being correct on category A then for being correct on category B. The gains and losses conditions reflect the reward structure of the task. Situational focus was manipulated in a manner similar to that outlined earlier. Situational promotion participants were told that they could earn an entry into a drawing for $50 if they exceeded a performance criterion, and situational prevention participants were given the entry upon entering the lab but were told that they had to exceed a performance criterion to keep the entry.

The stimulus on each trial was a bar that varied across trials in height. Category overlap was large ($d' = 1.0$) making the task difficult. The category

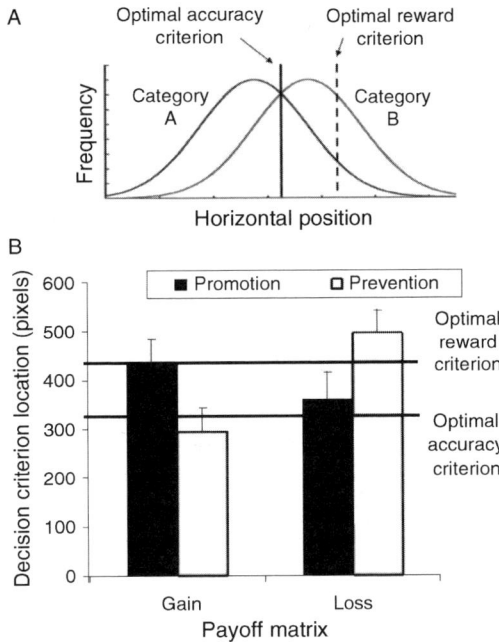

Fig. 4. (A) Category distributions and optimal reward and accuracy decision criteria from Markman et al. (in press). (B) Decision criterion estimates (averaged across participants). Copyright Blackwell Publishing, Inc., 2005. Adapted with permission.

structure is depicted in Fig. 4A. Situational focus was manipulated across participants whereas the reward structure of the task was run as a within-participant factor.

As stated earlier, when the payoff matrix is asymmetric the reward and accuracy-maximizing decision criteria are different, and in fact, a participant maximizing reward must sacrifice some measure of accuracy. Across a number of studies reviewed in Maddox (2002), we have found that participants have a bias toward accuracy maximization and only after extensive practice do they learn to shift away from this strategy toward a reward-maximizing strategy. We interpret this "shift" away from accuracy toward reward as a form of cognitive flexibility. We predict that a regulatory fit between the situational focus and the reward structure of the task will lead to greater cognitive flexibility and thus to more nearly optimal decision criterion learning. Specifically, participants given a situational promotion focus under a gains reward structure and participants given a situational prevention focus under a losses reward structure should show better learning of the reward-maximizing decision criterion.

The location of the best-fitting decision criterion relative to the accuracy and reward-maximizing decision criterion is displayed in Fig. 4B for each condition. Notice that the predicted interaction between situational focus and the reward structure of the task on decision criterion placement is supported by the data. Specifically, for the gain matrix, the best-fitting decision criterion is closer to the reward-maximizing criterion than to the accuracy-maximizing criterion for the situational promotion focus participants (a regulatory match) than for the situational prevention focus participants (a regulatory mismatch). Similarly, for the loss matrix, the best-fitting decision criterion is closer to the reward-maximizing criterion than to the accuracy-maximizing criterion for the situational prevention focus participants (a regulatory match) than for the situational promotion focus participants (a regulatory mismatch).

Although only a single study, these data suggest that the notion that regulatory fit leads to greater cognitive flexibility is fairly general and applies across traditional perceptual classification learning tasks (as outlined in detail in previous sections) and related tasks such as decision criterion learning. These data also suggest that the notion of cognitive flexibility can be instantiated in different ways depending upon the nature of the task. Regardless of the task, though, cognitive flexibility seems to open the participant up to examining alternative, and often less salient, strategies, such as applying a complex conjunctive rule when simple unidimensional rules, yield good (albeit suboptimal) performance (as in Maddox et al., in press) or abandoning a bias toward accuracy maximization in favor of reward maximization (as in Markman et al., in press).

VIII. Summary and Future Directions

This chapter offers a framework for examining the motivation-classification learning interface. We take as our initial model of classification learning, Ashby et al.'s (1998) COVIS model that postulates two-category learning systems: an explicit, hypothesis-testing system and an implicit, procedural-based learning system. COVIS assumes that rule-based category learning is dominated by the explicit, hypothesis-testing system that uses working memory and executive attention and is mediated by a circuit that includes the anterior cingulate, the prefrontal cortex, and the head of the caudate nucleus, and that information-integration category learning is dominated by the implicit, procedural-based learning system that is mediated largely within the tail of the caudate nucleus.

We take as our initial model of motivation, regulatory focus theory that postulates two forms of regulatory focus: a promotion focus that activates an approach mode of processing, and a prevention focus that activates an avoidance mode of processing. Following Higgins and colleagues (Crowe & Higgins, 1997; Higgins et al., 1994; Shah et al., 1998), we assume that a regulatory fit between two aspects of regulatory focus—situational focus and the *reward structure of the task*—is predictive of classification learning performance. Situational focus has to do with the global aspects of the person's classification learning environment and whether they are focused on performing well in the task in order to gain some reward (situational promotion focus) or in order to avoid losing some reward (situational prevention focus) on task completion. The reward structure of the task has to do with the local aspects of the person's trial-by-trial classification learning environment and whether they are focused on maximizing the number of points gained on each trial (gains reward structure) or are focused on minimizing the number of points lost on each trial (losses reward structure) in order to achieve the global task goal.

We extend the notion of regulatory fit to classification learning by hypothesizing that a regulatory fit between situational focus and the reward structure of the task increases cognitive flexibility. The hypothesis leads to two strong predictions. First, regulatory fit should lead to better rule-based classification learning when cognitive flexibility is advantageous for solving the task, but should lead to worse rule-based classification learning when cognitive flexibility is not advantageous. Second, regulatory fit manipulations should affect the hypothesis-testing classification system but not the procedural-based learning classification system. By extension, regulatory fit manipulations should affect rule-based classification learning more than information-integration category learning.

Two studies outlined in Maddox et al. (in press) and one pilot study summarized in this chapter provides initial support for the first prediction. When the reward structure involved gains, Maddox et al. (in press) found better rule-based classification learning for situational promotion participants than situational prevention participants when cognitive flexibility was advantageous, but found the opposite pattern when cognitive flexibility was disadvantageous. In a pilot study reviewed earlier where the reward structure involved losses and cognitive flexibility was advantageous, we found better category learning for the situational prevention participants (i.e., those with a regulatory fit) than for the situational promotion participants. The analogous study in which cognitive flexibility is disadvantageous is currently being investigated.

A pilot study provides initial support for the second prediction. In an information integration task where the reward structure involved gains, situational promotion participants showed greater cognitive flexibility than did situational prevention participants. Cognitive flexibility in this case led the regulatory fit participants to abandon hypothesis-testing strategies later in the session than participants with a regulatory mismatch. Future work needs to address the situation in which there is a regulatory fit between situational focus and a losses reward structure.

We also applied our regulatory fit hypothesis to a decision criterion learning task in which the reward structure involved gains or losses but also included a bias toward one category over the other (Markman et al., in press). Under these conditions, the participant whose goal is to maximize gains or minimize losses must sacrifice some measure of overall accuracy (Maddox, 2002). In this case, cognitive flexibility would be associated with a greater willingness to sacrifice accuracy, which appears to be an almost universal bias in these cases, in the interest of gain maximization or loss minimization. As predicted, participants in a regulatory fit condition—situational promotion focus with gains or situational prevention focus with losses—learned to apply a decision criterion that was closer to the optimal criterion and farther from the accuracy-maximizing decision criterion than participants with a regulatory mismatch.

A. Regulatory Fit, Cognitive Flexibility, and the Anterior Cingulate

In Section III. B, we suggested that the anterior cingulate, a frontal brain structure utilized by the hypothesis-testing system, is critically involved in the selection of alternatives. To be specific, our hypothesis is that regulatory fit leads to greater cognitive flexibility through increased anterior cingulate involvement. In this section we provide evidence in support of this claim.

Several lines of research support this claim. First, Ashby et al. (1999; see also Isen, 1993, 1999) proposed a neuropsychological theory of positive affect that assumes that positive affect increases dopamine release from the ventral tegmental area (VTA) into frontal brain areas, in particular the anterior cingulate. As one test of this hypothesis they cite work showing that a mild positive affect manipulation leads participants to generate more "associates" in the Remote Associates Task (RAT; Mednick, Mednick, & Mednick, 1964). Although regulatory fit and positive affect are not equivalent, many manipulations of positive affect involve a gain for subjects (such as an unexpected gift), and so they often involve a promotion focus. Second, in a recent pilot study, we (Baldwin, Markman, & Maddox, unpublished data) showed that a specific type of regulatory fit (i.e., a situational promotion focus versus a situational prevention focus along with instructions to maximize the number of associate generated) led the participant to generate more correct associates in the RAT, especially for the most difficult items. This result mirrors that for positive affect. Third, using event-related potential (ERP) Amodio, Shah, Sigelman, Brazy, and Harmon-Jones (2004) showed a relationship between chronic regulatory focus and activation in frontal brain areas.

We acknowledge that the proposed link between regulatory fit, cognitive flexibility, and frontal brain areas (in particular the anterior cingulate) is loose and speculative at this point. Even so, it provides a nice framework within which to examine the motivation-classification learning relation. Perhaps more importantly, it suggests a number of possible directions for future research and a number of potential connections with other cognitive functions as well as emotional, motivational, and personality traits. We briefly examine some of these issues later.

B. Future Directions

1. VTA Neurobiological Connectivity

What follows if regulatory fit increases dopamine release from the VTA? As outlined earlier, the VTA projects directly into the anterior cingulate, which is a fronto-cortical brain structure strongly implicated in flexible cognitive processing. The VTA projects directly to a number of other important brain structures as well. Most relevant to cognition, the VTA projects directly to the prefrontal cortex, which is known to be involved in working memory (for a review see Goldman-Rakic, 1987, 1995), and to the hippocampus (mostly CA1; Gloor, 1997), which is thought to be necessary for episodic memory consolidation (e.g., Gluck & Myers, 1997; McClelland, McNaughton, & O'Reilly, 1995). The VTA also projects to brain regions that have been implicated in emotions and personality. For example, the VTA projects directly to the amygdala. The amygdala is reciprocally connected to the hippocampus and to the orbitofrontal cortex (Gloor, 1997). The amygdala is thought to play a key role in the memory system for emotional events and stimuli (Cahill & McGaugh, 1998). As a final, related, note, it is worth mentioning also that the amount of dopamine available in the brain declines with normal aging (Gabrieli, 1995). This might partially explain the common finding that elderly people tend to be less cognitively flexible. An exciting avenue for future research would be to apply the notion of regulatory fit in normal aging with the ultimate goal of increasing (at least phasically) dopamine release to increase cognitive flexibility.

This brief review is not meant to be complete nor is it meant to motivate a set of specific predictions. Rather, we include it to emphasize the value of even a crude theory of the neurobiological underpinnings of the motivation-cognitive interface. If a regulatory fit leads to increased cognitive flexibility by increasing dopamine release from the VTA then this has implications not only for the processes associated with the anterior cingulate but also for processes associated with the prefrontal cortex, the hippocampus, the amygdala, and likely the many other brain regions indirectly connected to the VTA (e.g., orbitofrontal cortex, the head of the caudate nucleus, and so on). It is clear from this brief review that these brain regions include not only those involved directly in cognition but also those involved in emotion, motivation, and personality.

2. Applications to Related Cognitive Tasks

The notion that regulatory fit leads to increased cognitive flexibility should be examined in other cognitive tasks for which cognitive flexibility is advantageous or disadvantageous. Applications to tasks, such as solving anagrams and finding remote word associates, have already been conducted, but a number of more sophisticated tasks are available in the literature. For example, many studies examine tasks that involve repeated task switches (e.g., Mayr, Diedrichsen, Ivry, & Keele, in press). In tasks of this sort demands for flexible cognitive processing are high because of the need for shifts in attentional focus. In addition, the prefrontal cortex has been implicated in many of these tasks and based on the VTA-prefrontal cortex projection described earlier should be affected by regulatory fit manipulations. We are beginning to explore this domain.

A second task worth exploring is the so-called Bechara (or Iowa) gambling task (Bechara, Damasio, Damasio, & Anderson, 1994). On each trial in this task, the participant must select a card from one of four decks. The decks differ in the magnitude of gains and losses and in their long run expected reward. Like task switching, the Bechara task has been studied extensively in brain-damaged individuals including those with prefrontal cortex, amygdale, and orbitofrontal damage. Because the neural circuits involved in this task are being elucidated, this task may prove useful in extending our knowledge about the neurobiology of regulatory focus theory and ultimately lead to a deeper understanding of the motivation-learning interface.

3. Relation to Reinforcement Sensitivity Theory

Regulatory focus theory and the notion of regulatory fit have proved quite useful in our quest to examine the motivation-learning relation. Other "motivation-learning" theories have been developed. One that stands out is Reinforcement Sensitivity Theory (RST; Gray, 1982, 1987; Pickering & Gray, 2001). The details of the theory are beyond the scope of this chapter but, briefly, RST assumes that there are a small number of large-scale neural systems that control responding to motivationally significant reinforcers. RST proposes two systems: a behavioral approach/activation system (BAS) and a behavioral inhibition system (BIS). The BAS is supposed to mediate both approach and avoidance behaviors and is most relevant to regulatory focus theory. The BAS is activated by rewarding stimuli and the output of the system increases the probability of approach toward the desired goal. One novel aspect of the theory is that it makes direct links to personality research. Specifically, the theory proposes that the biological basis of fundamental personality traits is a function of individual differences in the sensitivity of the BAS system. In other words, people with high levels of BAS-related personality traits have a more responsive BAS than people low in BAS-related traits, and thus will experience stronger motivational and reinforcing effects. Although there is some controversy over which personality traits are BAS related, impulsivity, sensation-seeking, and extraversion have all been suggested (see Pickering & Gray, 2001 for a review).

Neurobiologically, it has been suggested that the BAS is located within brain regions innervated by dopamine-producing cells (Gray, 1987; Pickering & Gray, 1999). This latter connection makes RST especially relevant to our current focus as we also place a high premium on dopamine-mediated processes. To date, no attempt has been made to directly link regulatory focus theory and RST, and this chapter is not an appropriate avenue for such an attempt. Even so, there is clearly significant overlap between the two approaches and future work should attempt a more direct comparison.

4. Chronic Focus and Other Personality Characteristics

The studies reviewed in this chapter experimentally manipulated situational focus and the reward structure of the task. Chronic focus was not examined and cannot be experimentally manipulated. Rather chronic focus is a personality factor that the person brings with them into their environment. As suggested by the work reviewed in Section II, chronic focus is known to interact with situational focus and the reward structure of the task under some conditions. A complete understanding of the motivation-classification learning interface requires that personality factors, such as chronic focus, be included. It is very likely that the regulatory fit effects that we observed between situational focus and the reward structure of the task will be enhanced or diminished by a match or mismatch, respectively, with chronic focus. Future research should include measures of chronic focus and should expand the definition of regulatory fit proposed in this chapter (for relevant work, see Higgins, Shah, & Friedman, 1997; Idson, Liberman, & Higgins, 2000).

Extensions to other personality measures, such as depression, anxiety, and so on, should also be undertaken. Again the fact that the VTA projects directly or indirectly to so many brain regions that have been implicated in emotion and personality suggests that a more complete understanding of the motivation-learning interface will be obtained if this work is extended.

Expanding the scope of this work will increase our understanding of the interdependence of personality, motivation, and cognitive factors in predicting behavior (e.g., Idson et al., 2000).

5. Behavioral, Patient, and Brain Mapping Approaches to Studying the Motivation-Learning Interface

The motivation-learning framework developed in this chapter could have been described with little (if any) reference to the brain. From a social and/or cognitive psychological perspective this is adequate. In fact, because our data are collected from normally functioning individuals and are purely behavioral, some might argue that we should *not* make reference to the brain. We disagree. In our view, behavioral research of the sort presented in this chapter is informative to the cognitive neuroscience community, and more importantly can help bridge the artificial gaps between the study of interdependent processes (e.g., motivation and cognition) that preclude a full understanding of human behavior. Our approach is to extract from the vast neuroscience literature a set of conditions and constraints. We then outline an admittedly crude set of neurobiological underpinnings, but these lead to a surprisingly rich and testable set of neurobiologically inspired predictions. Without reference to the underlying neurobiology we would not be left with all the potential future directions outlined earlier.

Some might argue that one cannot make significant progress toward understanding the motivation-learning interface and the neurobiological underpinnings without examining patient with brain lesions or asking people to participate in an fMRI study. Again, we disagree. Significant scientific contributions can be made to cognitive neuroscience research using behavioral techniques like those presented in this chapter as well as by using patient with brain damage as participants or by using fMRI. Each has something unique to offer and the goal should be to identify points of convergence across approaches.

Indeed, there are a number of problems with the research program of localizing cognitive processes in the brain. As Uttal (2001) points out, there is a tendency to start the process of identifying brain regions by associating them with cognitive tasks that stand in for fundamental cognitive processes. However, the brain itself contains richly interconnected regions that are unlikely to respect the task divisions imposed by psychologists. Thus, developing integrative theories of the relationship between motivation and cognition based on behavioral evidence is a crucial step in the cognitive neuroscience program, even when none of the main dependent measures involve imaging or the use of data from brain-damaged patients.

IX. Closing Remarks

Our goal in writing this chapter was twofold. Our first goal was to offer a viable approach to studying the interface between research on motivation and classification learning. The hypothesis that a regulatory fit between situational focus and the reward structure of the task leads to greater cognitive flexibility provides a first step toward achieving this goal. Our second goal was broader in scope. We hope that the framework and empirical tests outlined in this chapter will lead to a renewed interest in bridging the artificial gap that has formed between research focused on motivation and research focused on learning. In the 1950s and 1960s learning and motivation research was intimately related and much progress was made (Miller, 1957, 1959; Young, 1959). Since that time, work on motivation and learning has diverged. Most research on motivation in humans has been done in social and educational psychology. In contrast, research on learning was generally pursued by cognitive and animal psychology. This separation is artificial and (in our view) detrimental to the advancement of a complete understanding of behavior. After all, the title of this book series is "The Psychology of Learning *AND* Motivation (emphasis added)". The work outlined in this chapter focuses on learning *and* motivation. We hope that other researchers will follow suit and more openly recognize in their work the intimate relationship between these two psychological factors.

ACKNOWLEDGMENTS

This research was supported in part by National Institute of Health Grant R01 MH59196 to WTM, and R21 DA15211 to ABM. We thank Greg Ashby, Richard Ivry, and Alan Pickering for useful discussions that influenced this work. We also thank Scott Lauritzen for help with data collection. Correspondence concerning this article should be addressed to W. Todd Maddox or Arthur Markman both at: University of Texas, 1 University Station A8000, Department of Psychology, Austin, Texas, 78712 (e-mail: maddox@psy.utexas.edu or markman @psy.utexas.edu).

REFERENCES

Aarts, H., Gollwitzer, P. M., & Hassin, R. R. (2004). Goal contagion: Perceiving is for pursuing. *Journal of Personality and Social Psychology, 87*, 23–37.
Alexander, G. E., DeLong, M. R., & Strick, P. L. (1986). Parallel organization of functionally segregated circuits linking basal ganglia and cortex. *Annual Review of Neuroscience, 9*, 357–381.
Allen, S. W., & Brooks, L. R. (1991). Specializing the operation of an explicit rule. *Journal of Experimental Psychology: General, 120*, 3–19.

Amodio, D. M., Shah, J. Y., Sigelman, J., Brazy, P. C., & Harmon-Jones, E. (2004). Implicit regulatory focus associated with asymmetrical frontal cortical activity. *Journal of Experimental Social Psychology, 40*, 225–232.

Arbuthnott, G. W., Ingham, C. A., & Wickens, J. R. (2000). Dopamine and synaptic plasticity in the neostriatum. *Journal of Anatomy, 196*, 587–596.

Ashby, F. G., Alfonso-Reese, L. A., Turken, A. U., & Waldron, E. M. (1998). A neuropsychological theory of multiple systems in category learning. *Psychological Review, 105*(3), 442–481.

Ashby, F. G., & Ell, S. W. (2001). The neurobiology of category learning. *Trends in Cognitive Sciences, 5*, 204–210.

Ashby, F. G., Isen, A. M., & Turken, A. U. (1999). A neuropsychological theory of positive affect and its influence on cognition. *Psychological Review, 106*(3), 529–550.

Ashby, F. G., & Maddox, W. T. (2005). Human category learning. *Annual Review of Psychology, 56*, 149–178.

Ashby, F. G., & Valentin, V. V. (2005). Multiple systems of perceptual category learning: Theory and cognitive tests. In H. Cohen and C. Lefebvre (Eds.), *Handbook of categorization in cognative science* (pp. 553–572). Elsevier, Ltd.

Ashby, F. G., & Waldron, E. M. (1999). On the nature of implicit categorization. *Psychonomic Bulletin & Review, 6*, 363–378.

Avnet, T., & Higgins, E. T. (2003). Locomotion, assessment, and regulatory fit: Value transfer from "how" to "what." *Journal of Experimental Social Psychology, 39*, 525–530.

Bechara, A., Damasio, A. R., Damasio, H., & Anderson, S. W. (1994). Insensitivity to future consequences following damage to human prefrontal cortex. *Cognition, 50*, 7–15.

Bechara, A., Damasio, H., & Damasio, A. R. (2000). Emotion, decision making, and the orbitofrontal cortex. *Cerebral Cortex, 10*(3), 295–307.

Cahill, L., & McGaugh, J. L. (1998). Mechanisms of emotional arousal and lasting declarative memory. *Trends in Neurosciences, 21*(7), 294–299.

Carver, C. S., & Scheier, M. F. (1998). *On the self-regulation of behavior*. New York: Cambridge University Press.

Crowe, E., & Higgins, E. T. (1997). Regulatory focus and strategic inclinations: Promotion and prevention in decision-making. *Organizational Behavior and Human Decision Processes, 69*(2), 117–132.

Erickson, M. A., & Kruschke, J. K. (1998). Rules and exemplars in category learning. *Journal of Experimental Psychology: General, 127*, 107–140.

Ferguson, M. J., & Bargh, J. A. (2004). Liking is for doing: The effects of goal pursuit on automatic evaluation. *Journal of Personality and Social Psychology, 87*, 557–572.

Filoteo, J. V., Maddox, W. T., & Davis, J. D. (2001a). A possible role of the striatum in linear and nonlinear categorization rule learning: Evidence from patients with Huntington's disease. *Behavioral Neuroscience, 115*, 786–798.

Filoteo, J. V., Maddox, W. T., & Davis, J. D. (2001b). Quantitative modeling of category learning in amnesic patients. *Journal of the International Neuropsychological Society, 7*, 1–19.

Filoteo, J. V., Maddox, W. T., Simmons, A. N., Ing, A. D., Cagigas, X. E., Matthews, S, et al. (2005). Cortical and subcortical brain regions involved in rule-based category learning. *NeuroReport, 16*(2), 111–115.

Fishbach, A., Friedman, R. S., & Kruglanski, A. W. (2003). Leading us not into temptation: Momentary allurements elicit overriding goal activation. *Journal of Personality and Social Psychology, 84*, 296–309.

Folstein, J. R., & Van Petten, C. V. (2004). Multidimensional rule, unidimensional rule, and similarity strategies in categorization: Event-related brain potential correlates. *Journal of Experimental Psychology: Learning, Memory, and Cognition, 30*, 1026–1044.

Gabrieli, J. (1995). Contribution of the basal ganglia to skill learning and working memory in humans. In J. C. Houk, J. L. Davis, and D. G. Beiser (Eds.), *Models of information processing in the basal ganglia* (pp. 277–294). Cambridge, MA: Bradford.

Gloor, P. (1997). *The temporal lobe and limbic system.* New York: Oxford University Press.

Gluck, M. A., & Myers, C. E. (1997). Psychobiological models of hippocampal function in learning and memory. *Annual Review of Neuroscience, 48*, 481–514.

Goldman-Rakic, P. S. (1987). Circuitry of the prefrontal cortex and the regulation of behavior by representational knowledge. In F. Plum and V. Mountcastle (Eds.), *Handbook of physiology* (pp. 373–417). Bethesda, MD: American Physiological Society.

Goldman-Rakic, P. S. (1995). Cellular basis of working memory. *Neuron, 14*, 477–485.

Gray, J. A. (1982). *The neuropsychology of anxiety: An enquiry into the functions of the septo-hippocampal system.* Oxford: Oxford University Press.

Gray, J. A. (1987). The neuropsychology of emotion and personality. In S. M. Stahl, S. D. Iverson, and E. G. Goodman (Eds.), *Cognitive neurochemistry* (pp. 171–190). Oxford: Oxford University Press.

Higgins, E. T. (1987). Self-discrepancy: A theory relating self and affect. *Psychological Review, 94*(3), 319–340.

Higgins, E. T. (1997). Beyond pleasure and pain. *American Psychologist, 52*(12), 1280–1300.

Higgins, E. T. (2000). Making a good decision: Value from fit. *American Psychologist, 55*, 1217–1230.

Higgins, E. T., Chen Idson, L., Freitas, A. L., Spiegel, S., & Molden, D. C. (2003). Transfer of value from fit. *Journal of Personality and Social Psychology, 84*(6), 1140–1153.

Higgins, E. T., Roney, C. J., Crowe, E., & Hymes, C. (1994). Ideal versus ought predilections for approach and avoidance distinct self-regulatory systems. *Journal of Personality & Social Psychology, 66*, 276–286.

Higgins, E. T., Shah, J., & Friedman, R. (1997). Emotional responses to goal attainment: Strength of regulatory focus as moderator. *Journal of Personality & Social Psychology, 72*, 515–525.

Higgins, E. T., & Spiegel, S. (2004). Promotion and prevention strategies for self-regulation: A motivated cognition perspective. In R. F. Baumeister and K. D. Vohs (Eds.), *Handbook of self-regulation: Research, theory and applications* (pp. 171–187). New York: Guilford Press.

Hollerman, J. R., & Schultz, W. (1998). Dopamine neurons report an error in the temporal prediction of reward during learning. *Nature Neuroscience, 1*, 304–309.

Idson, L. C., Liberman, N., & Higgins, E. T. (2000). Distinguishing gains from nonlosses and losses from nongains: A regulatory focus perspective on hedonic intensity. *Journal of Experimental Social Psychology, 36*, 252–274.

Isen, A. M. (1993). Positive affect and decision making. In M. Lewis and J. Haviland (Eds.), *Handbook of emotion* (pp. 261–277). New York: Guilford Press.

Isen, A. M. (1999). Positive affect. In T. Dalgleish and M. Power (Eds.), *The handbook of cognition and emotion* (pp. 521–539). New York: Wiley.

Kemler-Nelson, D. G. (1984). The effect of intention on what concepts are acquired. *Journal of Verbal Learning and Verbal Behavior, 10*, 734–759.

Keri, S. (2003). The cognitive neuroscience of category learning. *Brain Research Reviews, 85*, 85–109.

Lee, A.Y, & Aaker, J. L. (2004). Bringing the frame into focus: The influence of regulatory fit on processing fluency and persuasion. *Journal of Personality and Social Psychology, 86*(2), 205–218.

Lewin, K. (1935). *A dynamic theory of personality.* New York: McGraw-Hill.

Maddox, W. T. (2002). Toward a unified theory of decision criterion learning in perceptual categorization. *Journal of the Experimental Analysis of Behavior, 78*(3), 567–595.
Maddox, W. T., & Ashby, F. G. (2004). Dissociating explicit and procedural-learning based systems of perceptual category learning. *Behavioral Processes, 66*, 309–332.
Maddox, W. T., Baldwin, G. C., & Markman, A. B. (in press). Regulatory focus effects on cognitive flexibility in rule-based classification learning. *Memory and Cognition.*
Maddox, W. T., & Filoteo, J. V. (2001). Striatal contribution to category learning: Quantitative modeling of simple linear and complex non-linear rule learning in patients with Parkinson's disease. *Journal of the International Neuropsychological Society, 7*, 710–727.
Maddox, W. T., & Filoteo, J. V. (2005). The neuropsychology of perceptual category learning. In H. Cohen and C. Lefebvre (Eds.) *Handbook of categorization in cognitive science* (pp. 573–599) Elsevier, Ltd.
Markman, A. B., Baldwin, G. C., & Maddox, W. T. (2005). The interaction of payoff structure and regulatory focus in classification. *Psychological Science, 16*, 852–855.
Markman, A. B., & Brendl, C. M. (2000). The influence of goals on value and choice. In D. L. Medin (Ed.), *The psychology of learning and motivation* (Vol. 39, pp. 97–129). San Diego, CA: Academic Press.
Markman, A. B., Kim, K., & Brendl, C. M. (2005). The influence of goal activation on preference. Unpublished.
Markman, A. B., Maddox, W. T., & Baldwin, G. C. (2005). The implications of advances in research on motivation for cognitive models. *Journal of Experimental and Theoretical Artificial Intelligence, 17*, 371–384.
Mayr, U., Diedrichsen, J., Ivry, R., & Keele, S. W. (2006). Dissociating task-set selection from task-set inhibition in prefrontal cortex. *Cognitive Neuroscience, 18*, 14–21.
McClelland, J. L., McNaughton, B. L., & O'Reilly, R. C. (1995). Why there are complementary learning systems in the hippocampus and neocortex: Insights from the successes and failures of connectionist models of learning and memory. *Psychological Review, 102*(3), 419–457.
McDonald, R. J., & White, N. M. (1993). A triple dissociation of memory systems: Hippocampus, amygdala, and dorsal striatum. *Behavioral Neuroscience, 107*, 3–22.
McDonald, R. J., & White, N. M. (1994). Parallel information processing in the water maze: Evidence for independent memory systems involving dorsal striatum and hippocampus. *Behavioral Neural Biology, 61*, 260–270.
Mednick, M. T., Mednick, S. A., & Mednick, E. V. (1964). Incubation of creative performance and specific associative priming. *Journal of Abnormal and Social Psychology, 69*, 220–232.
Miller, N. E. (1957). Experiments on motivation. *Science, 126*, 1271–1278.
Miller, N. E. (1959). Liberalization of basic S-R concepts: Extensions to conflict behavior, motivation, and social learning. In S. Koch (Ed.), *Psychology: A study of a science. General and systematic formulations, learning, and special processes* (pp. 196–292). New York: McGraw Hill.
Myers, C. E., Shohamy, D., Gluck, M. A., Grossman, S., Onlaor, S., & Kapur, N. (2003). Dissociating medial temporal and basal ganglia memory systems with a latent learning task. *Neuropsychologia, 41*, 1919–1928.
Nosofsky, R. M., Palmeri, T. J., & McKinley, S. C. (1994). Rule-plus-exception model of classification learning. *Psychological Review, 101*, 53–79.
Packard, M. G., & McGaugh, J. L. (1992). Double dissociation of fornix and caudate nucleus lesions on acquisition of two water maze tasks: Further evidence for multiple memory systems. *Behavioral Neuroscience, 106*, 439–446.
Posner, M. I., & Petersen, S. E. (1990). The attention system of the human brain. *Annual Review of Neuroscience, 13*, 25–42.

Pickering, A. D., & Gray, J. A. (1999). The neuroscience of personality. In L. A. Pervin and O. P. John (Eds.), *Handbook of personality: Theory and research* (2nd ed., pp. 277–299). New York, NY: Guilford Press.

Pickering, A. D., & Gray, J. A. (2001). Dopamine, appetitive reinforcement and the neuropsychology of human learning: An individual differences approach. In A. Eliasz and A. Angleitner (Eds.), *Advances in individual differences research* (pp. 113–149). Lengerich, Germany: PABST Science Publishers.

Poldrack, R. A., & Packard, M. G. (2003). Competition among multiple memory systems: Converging evidence from animal and human brain studies. *Neuropsychologia, 41*(3), 245–251.

Poldrack, R. A., Prabhakaran, V., Seger, C. A., & Gabrieli, J. D. E. (1999). Striatal activation during acquisition of a cognitive skill. *Neuropsychology, 13*, 564–574.

Reber, P. J., Stark, C. E. L., & Squire, L. R. (1998). Cortical areas supporting category learning identified using functional magnetic resonance imaging. *Proceedings of the National Academy of Sciences of the United States of America, 95*, 747–750.

Rehegr, G., & Brooks, L. R. (1993). Perceptual manifestations of an analytic structure: The priority of holistic individuation. *Journal of Experimental Psychology: General, 122*, 92–114.

Schacter, D. L. (1987). Implicit memory: History and current status. *Journal of Experimental Psychology: Learning, Memory, and Cognition, 13*, 501–518.

Schultz, W. (1992). Activity of dopamine neurons in the behaving primate. *Seminars in the Neurosciences, 4*, 129–138.

Seger, C. A., & Cincotta, C. M. (2002). Striatal activity in concept learning. *Cognitive, Affective, and Behavioral Neuroscience, 2*, 149–161.

Seger, C. A., & Cincotta, C. M. (2005). The roles of the caudate nucleus in human classification learning. *Journal of Neuroscience, 25*, 2941–2951.

Shah, J., Higgins, E. T., & Friedman, R. S. (1998). Performance incentives and means: How regulatory focus influences goal attainment. *Journal of Personality and Social Psychology, 74*, 285–293.

Smith, E. E., Patalano, A., & Jonides, J. (1998). Alternative strategies of categorization. *Cognition, 65*, 167–196.

Smith, J. D., & Shapiro, J. H. (1989). The occurrence of holistic categorization. *Journal of Memory & Language, 28*, 386–399.

Squire, L. R. (1992). Memory and the hippocampus: A synthesis from finding with rats, monkeys and humans. *Psychological Review, 99*, 195–231.

Uttal, W. R. (2001). *The new phrenology*. Cambridge, MA: The MIT Press.

Wilson, C. J. (1995). The contribution of cortical neurons to the firing pattern of striatal spiny neurons. In J. C. Houk, J. L. Davis, and D. G. Beiser (Eds.), *Models of information processing in the basal ganglia* (pp. 29–50). Cambridge, MA: Bradford.

Wisniewski, E. J. (2002). Concepts and categorization. In H. Pashler and D. Medin (Eds.), *Steven's handbook of experimental psychology: Memory and cognitive processes* (3rd ed., Vol. 2, pp. 467–531). New York, NY: John Wiley & Sons.

Young, P. T. (1959). The role of affective processes in learning and motivation. *Psychological Review, 66*, 104–125.

INDEX

A

Absolute coordinate system, 167
Accuracy-maximizing criterion, for situational prevention/promotion focus participants, 238
Actions
    intentional *vs.* accidental, children's ability to distinguish, 56
    onset-, and endpoint-focused, 56
Active goals, influence on behavior, 213
Act-out tasks, 43
Acts of exclusion, 24
Adult learners, 187
Adult speakers, 36
Affective influences, 136–138
    category selection and stereotype activation, 138–141
    stereotype application and expression, 141–144
Affective resonance hypothesis, 138
Affective states, effect on category selection, 140
Affect, motivation, and inference, identification-based, 144–146
African American face primes, 132
African–American slavery, 25
Alignment, 204
Alternative currencies, 1–2
American national identity, 25
American National Standards Institute (ANSI), 77
Amygdala, 214, 241–242
Anagrams, 217–218, 222, 242
Anger, 143
Anxiety and fear, 142–143

"Appearance," 37, 43
    construction, 38–39
Approach goals, 215
Argument structure constructions, 52
Argument structure generalizations, advantages of
    category validity, 51–52
    construction, as predictors of sentence meaning
    corpus evidence of, 47–49
    experimental evidence for, 49–51
    languages, with more predictive verbs, 52
    predictive value of verbs in argument structure patterns, 46–47
    structural priming and its relation to constructions, 52–54
Argument structure patterns, predictive value of verbs in, 46–47
Assembly process, 71
Assertions, 183, 185
    speakers', lack of confidence in, 186
Assistive guitar, created following the product development process, 78
Associative learning, consequence of, 208
Assumption reversals, 115
Asymptote, 228
Attention, movement of, 161
Avoidance goals, 215

B

Babysitting, 5
"Back-to-basics" hypothesis, 140
Banca del Tempo (Bdt), 3
Bargh's automotive model, 136–137

Barter, 3
Behavior, 213
Behavioral approach/activation system (BAS), 242–243
Behavioral inhibition system (BIS), 242
Biases, stereotypic, 136
Bonne monnaie. See Good money
Bottom–up pathway, to social impressions, 123
Brain mapping, approaches to studying motivation-learning interface, 244
Brain sketching, 101–103
Brain storming, 100
Brennan's speaker effect, 198

C

"Cailloux," 5
Casenhiser and Goldberg experiment
 forced-choice comprehension task, sample test items used in, 39
 training stimuli used in, 38
Categorical identities, 126, 129
Categorization(s), 33
 assertion, 183, 185
 collaborating on, 202
 in concept generation, 79
 core of contemporary design methods, 68
 of customer population, 73
 decisions, 189, 194
  human, 209
  interlocutors', 201
 "decontextualized" approach to, 181
 of design problem, 106
 of functions and flows, 82–84
 importance of entrainment in, 190
 important process in problem solving, 113
 nonlinguistic, parallel facilitory effect in, 44–45
 of people and nonsocial objects, differences between, 124
 in product design and development, 68
 research, importance of setting in, 181–182
 social, schematic model of, 124–128
 tasks, 52
Categor(y)ies
 distributions and optimal reward and accuracy decision, 237
 dominance hypothesis, 126
 dominance, principle of, 135
 identification, basis for, 123

labels, 220
learning, 45, 161
 and category use, primary setting of, 182
 information-integration, 220
 rule-based, 220
 use of confidence cues in, 187–189
of patents, 89
representations, 79
 type of, 91
research, 203
 for searching and decomposing specifications, 79
selection
 effect of affective states on, 140
 influence of anxiety and happiness on, 139
structure, 185
validity, for constructions, 52
Caused motion, stimuli, 51
Chain migration, 19–20
Child language data exchange system (CHILDES) database, 47
Children
 act-out tasks, 43
 conservative learners, 43
 language acquisition in, 192
 learning of novel construction, 41
 process of learning language in, 33
Chronic focus, 215, 217
 and other personality characteristics, 243–244
Chronic integral affect, 137–138
Chronic regulatory focus, 218
Classification
 based on rule and overall similarity, 219
 definition of, 68
Classification learning, 214, 218–219
 multiple systems models of, 219
Classification learning system
 procedural-based, 223
 regulator fit-, 223
Clear motivation, 41
Club del Trueque, 3
Cognitive flexibility, 222–223
 gains reward structure, 224–227, 229–232
 losses reward structure, 227–228, 232
Cognitive flexibility, not advantageous
 gains reward structure, 229–232
 losses reward structure, 232
Cognitive psychology, 214, 219
Coherence, 127
Collaboration, for categorization, 202–203, 207

Index

Commodities, banned, 6
Commodity-based systems, 3
Common ground framework, 194–195, 198–199
Compadre, 18
Competition between verbal and implicit systems model (COVIS), 220, 233, 238
   review of, 222
Complex conjunctive rule, 227–228, 238
Component combination, 96
Compositionality, concept of, 161
Compositional structure, computational utility of, 166
Comprehension, 46
Concept generation, 68
   activity of, 75
   classifying schemes for, 92
   scaffolding of : category representations, 79
      function, function categories, and function diagrams, 80–89
      generalized engineering parameters, 89–91
      physical principle classification, 91
      physical principle diagrams, 92–96
      textual idea generators, 91–92
   tasks in, 74
Concept generation methods
   brainstorming and mind mapping, 100–101
   brain-writing methods, 101–103
   categories of, 96
   classification of, 99
   inputs to, 99
Concept selection, 75
Conceptual alignment, 204, 207–208
Confidence cues, 186
   use in category learning, 185, 187–189
   use of, 208
Configural information, 160, 166–167
Conjunctive rule, 227–228
Connectionism, 167
Connections, in trust network, 19
Conservative learning, 43
Constructional priming, 52
Construction(s)
   learning, a facilitory factor, 40–44
   learning, on the basis of input, 35–39
   motivation for learning, 52
   as predictors of sentence meaning, experimental evidence for, 49–51
   skewing of constructions toward particular verbs, 40
   structural priming and its relation to, 52–54

Consumer products, with functional labels, 80
Conversation
   categorization processes in
      reference, as kind of categorization, 182–183
      referent categorization, strategies for, 183–184
   category learning and category use, primary setting of, 182
   collaborative nature of, 201
      conceptual alignment in, and beyond, 203–206
      socially emergent categories, 202–203
      summary and implications, 206–207
   historical nature of: establishing and using conversational precedents, 189
      entrainment, 190–191
      mechanisms underlying precedent use in conversation, 194–201
      preemption, 191–194
      summary and implications, 201
   multimodal nature of, 185
      category learning, use of confidence cues in, 187–189
      disfluency as index of speaker confidence, 186–187
      implications, 189
   as site of category learning and category use, 181–209
Conversational categorization, 207–209
Conversationalists, 190, 203, 207
Conversational precedents, 190
Conversational settings, implications in categorization, 184
Corollary concepts, 115
COVIS. *See* competition between verbal and implicit systems model
Creativity and invention, 67
"Créditos," Argentine, 3
C-Sketch, concept generation method, 101, 104, 106
"Cue validity," 46–47
   of constructions, 51
   of verbs and constructions as predictors of sentence meaning, comparison of, 48
Customer(s)
   lead-, 74
   multimodal, 71
   needs, basis for engineering specification for product vision, 77

D

Decision-bound models, 232
Decision criterion learning, 238
Decision criterion, reward-maximizing, 237–238
Decision making, 218
Definite descriptions, use in categorizations, 184
Demographic categor(y)ies, 140
  negatively valenced, 139
Denominal verbs, 191
Dental anxiety, 143
Dependencies, adjacent and non-adjacent, 36
Design
  basic concept generation methods, 96–99
    brain sketching, c-sketch, 6-3-5, and gallery methods, 101–104
    design-by-analogy, 111–113
    engineering empirical results and categorization, 104–107
    insights for engineering from categorization literature, 113–115
    inventive problem solving, theory of, 107–111
    Osborn's brainstorming and mind mapping, 100–101
  discussion and "Golden Nuggets," 115–116
  Edison's approach to, 67
  motivation and overview
    Edisonian design, 65–68
    enhancing the art of design: classification and categorization, 68
  need-function-form definition of, 74
  product development and concept generation process, 68–73
    developing a concept, 74–76
    implementing a concept, 76–77
    product development and categorization, 77–79
    understanding the opportunity, 73–74
  scaffolding of concept generation: category representations, 79
    engineering parameters, generalized, 89–91
    function, function categories, and function diagrams, 80–89
    physical principle classification, 91
    physical principle diagrams, 92–96
    textual idea generators, 91–92
  strategies, 75

Design-by-analogy, 111–113
  examples of, 111
Design conflicts, 90
  generalized engineering parameters for description of, 90
  ironing, evolution of the product, 107, 110–111
Design problem
  "art enabling device for persons with disabilities," 85
  "dorm room washing device," 86
  "peanut sheller," 85
  peanut shelling
    mind map of, 102
    "6-3-5" modified method for, 104–105
Determiners, alternative, 36
Director, 196–197, 206
Disfluency as index of speaker confidence, 186–187
Ditransitive construction, 34, 49–50
Domain-general processes, 35
Donlon, 187–188
Dyad(s), 204
  matrices of, 206
  speaker–listener, 208
Dyadic interactions, 205

E

Earmarking, top–down, 12
"Ecomoney," Japanese, 3
Economic transactions, 7
Edisonian design, 65–68
Edisonian innovators, 65
"Edisonian invention," 66
Effort flow analysis, interfaces in, 93, 95
Egalitarian concepts, 132
Egalitarian culture, 131
Egalitarianism, 132
  motivational desire for, 133
Embodiment engineering, 76
Emigrants, categories of, 17
Emotion(s), 143, 242
  states of, 139
Empathy
  power of, 145
  role in social perception, 146
Endogamy, ethnic, 20
Endpoint-focused actions, 56

Index

Engineering conflicts, TIPS design principles to solve, 108–110
Engineering design, need-function-form definition of, 74
Engineering insights from categorization literature, 113, 115
English constructions, 37
English transitive construction, 39
 acquisition of, 36
Entrainment, 190–191, 195, 201, 208
 partner specificity *versus* partner independence in, 196–197
Envios, 14
Episodic integral affect, 137
"Epistemic motives," 129
Equality, 132
Error-related negativity (ERN), 136
Ethnic endogamy, 20
Euro, 10–13
Euroland, 10–11
European Commission, 11
European identity, 11
European Union, 12, 26
Everyday objects
 speakers' classification of, 190
 subordinate-level categorizations for, 196
Exclusion, 147
External motivation, 131
Eyetracking, 192

F

"Face inversion effect," 172
Face recognition, 171
Face-to-face interactions, 182
Facial expressions, 185
Facial recognition, 159, 172
 plausible theories of, 173
Facilitation, 36
Faenas, 16
Fairness, 132
Featural accounts, 158
Featural information, use of, 161
Feature-only representations, 168
Fedora, 190
"Feelings as information" model/approach, 141–142
Feuds, among kin groups, 22
Fixations, on unmentioned object, 200
Flash Eurobarometer Survey 2004, 11–12

Flow classes, basic flows, and synonyms, 83, 84
Forced-choice comprehension task, sample test items used in, 39
Forced-choice task, 44
Force flow analysis, 92
 basis for relative motion in, 95
 innovation from, 96
Force flow representation, relative motion permutations in, 95
Form and meaning
 pairing of, 43
 relations between, 35
Form–function pairing, priming of, 54
Form–meaning pairings
 novel, 37
 phrasal, 37
Four flow classifications, 95
Free silver proponents, 8
French nationalism and citizenship, 25
Functional and flow bases, nonobvious design analogy between pickup winder and electric vegetable peeler, 114
Functional descriptions, mapping of customer needs to, advantages of, 80–81
Functional model
 of popcorn popper, 88
 for subsystem of extraterrestrial probe, 87
Function and form, correspondences between, 34
Function classes, basic functions, and synonyms, 82–83
Function, function categories, and function diagrams, 80–89

G

Gains reward structure, 224–227, 229–232, 239
Gallery, concept generation method, 101, 106
Genealogy, 21
Generalization, 44, 54–55
 anchor point for, 57
Generic features, interpretations of, 177
Genovese trust networks, 22–23
Genuine money, 8
Geons, 158–159
 collection of, 167
Gestalt psychologists, 123
Gesture, manual, 185
Goals, approach and avoidance, 215
"Golden Nuggets," 115–116

Gold Standard Act, 8
"Good money," 4
"*Grain de sel*," French, 3
Greenbacks, 8
"Green dollars," Australian, 3
Guilt, 134, 137, 143

H

Happy moods, 141
"Hierarchical" letters, 162
HOURS, 3
Human categorization, 45
Hypocrisy, 143
Hypothesis-testing, 235, 238
  classification system, 239

I

Idea generation
  factors affecting, 104
  methods, 115
    empirical comparison of, 106
Idea generators
  categories of, 79
  textual, 91
Imagery, 161
Image variability, feature-based strategies to overcome, 169
Immigrant remittances, 2
Impressive universals, in expression of arguments, 54
Incentive focus. *See* Situational focus
Incidental affect, 137–138
Inclusion, 147
Individuation, 135–136
Information (in Shannon's sense), 164
Information-integration category learning, 223, 238–239
  effects of regulatory fit on, 223
Information-integration classification rule, 222
Integral affect, 137
Interlocutors
  accumulation of shared knowledge between, 201
  cognitive burden on, 195
Internal motivation, 131
International migration, United Nations report on, 14
International Standards Organization (ISO), 77

Invariance, 158
Invention, trial-and-error method for, 67
Ironing, evolution of the product, 107, 110–111
Ithaca HOURS, 3

J

Joint categorization, 202–203

K

Kin-based organizations, 22
Kinship networks, 20, 22
Kinsman, 18
Knowledge, shared body of, 194

L

Labeling, as categorization, 183
Label(s)
  in relationships, 18
  verbal category, 131
Language(s)
  comprehension, 192
  learning, 194
  lexicon of, 184
  with more predictive verbs, 52
  processing, 199
  strategies for categorizing referents from, 183
  "usage-based" model of, 43
  users, 184, 189, 191, 194–195, 203–205, 207
    community of, 208
Lead-customers, 74
Lead-lag usage, 73–74
Leapfrogging, 100
Learners, 187
Learning, 181, 185
  and behavior, relationship between, 213
  goal of, 182
  perceptual classification, 214
Learning linguistic patterns
  argument structure generalizations, advantages of, 45
  category validity, 51–52
  construction as predictor of sentence meaning, corpus evidence of, 47–49
  construction as predictor of sentence meaning, experimental evidence for, 49–51
  languages, with more predictive verbs, 52

predictive value of verbs in argument structure patterns, 46–47
structural priming and its relation to constructions, 52–54
constructions, 33–37, 40–44
form–function pairings, motivation of, 54–56
mapping novel phrasal patterns onto novel meanings, in children, 37–39
parallel facilitory effect in nonlinguistic categorization, 44
experimental demonstration of the parallel, 45
Learning system, procedural-based, 222
Legal tenders, 7–10
LETS. *See* Local exchange and trading systems
Lexical classification, 184
Lexical decision task (LDT), 139
Linguistic description, convergence in, 204
Linguistic expressions, mental representation of, 53
Linguistic generalization, 57
Linguists, 35
Linking rules, 35
Listener(s), 199, 205
expectations, 191
fixations on unmentioned object, 193
Local currency groups, 3
Local exchange and trading systems (LETS), 3
major variants of, 4
media, 5
networks, 5
regulation of membership, 5
Local monetary systems, insider–outsider categories, 2
Local money, 1
relations and categories, 3–7
Locative argument, 44
Long-distance migration
mediation of kinfolk in, 20
risks in, 19
stream, 18
Losses reward structure, 227–228, 232, 239
"Love token" gifts, 9
Luminance, 160
Lyon Croix-Rousse SEL, 5

M

"MacAMug" line drawings, 173
Manual gesture, 185

Mapping. *See also* Brain mapping; Mind mapping
of customer needs to functional descriptions, 80
novel phrasal patterns onto novel meanings, in children, 37–39
quick learning of, 43
between short/long and shallow/steep lines and four category labels, 220
between speech and color patches, altering, 188
Market analysis, need in product development, 73
Mark, German, 12
Markov random fields, 165, 177
Matcher, role in conversation, 196
Mechanical effort transmission, 93
Memory or judgment, mood-congruency pattern in, 138
Mental accounting systems, 2, 9–10
with earmarking practices, 13
Mental control, Wegner's model of, 134
Mental imagery, 161
"6-3-5" method, for concept generation, 101–105
Mexican migration to New York City, analysis of, 15
Migrant(s), 14
communities, transplantation and transformation of, 21
long-distance, 15
Migration
chain, 20
stream, long-distance, 18
Mind mapping, 100–101
of peanut shelling design problem, 102
"Misths," Italian, 3
Mistrust, 147
Modeling, need for design decision-making, 76
"Money illusions," behavioral impact of, 10
Money, standardization of, 8
Monitoring process, 134
Monometallists, 8
Mood-congruency, 139
pattern in memory or judgment, 138
Moods, 141
Motivation, 242
and cognition, interplay between, 213
and emotion, 144
external and internal, 131

Motivational influences
  social perception, self-regulation of, 132–136
  varieties of, 128–132
Motivation-learning interface, 213–214
  behavioral, patient, and brain mapping approaches to studying, 244
  classification learning, summary of results, 235
  decision criterion learning, regulatory fit effects on, 235–238
  framework for examining, 215–218
  information-integration classification learning, regulatory fit effects on, 233–235
  regulatory fit, cognitive flexibility, and anterior cingulate, 240–241
  regulatory fit framework to classification, 218
    classification learning predictions, 222–223
    perceptual category learning, neurobiological underpinnings of, 219–222
    regulatory focus, neurobiological underpinnings of, 222
    rule-based classification learning, regulatory fit effects on
      cognitive flexibility, advantageous, 224–228
      cognitive flexibility, not advantageous, 228–232
      summary, 232–233
    using classification to understand, 213–214
Motives, basic human, 129
Multiple classification learning systems, 219
Multiple memory systems, 219
"Multiple symbolizations," 9

N

NASA Martian rover with rock probe, 87
Nationalism and citizenship, 24–26
Neutral mood, 142
"New" categorization, 192, 195, 197–198
Nonchronics, 132
Nonlinguistic categorization, 56
  parallel facilitory effect in, 44–45
Nonsense category label, 187
Nonsocial stimuli, categorization of, 138

Novel construction, 39
  children's learning of, 41
Novel verbs, 37–39
  interpretations of, 50

O

"Object-raising" and "object-control" sentences, examples of, 54
Object recognition, 167
  process of, 163
Object representations, 158
Object, unmentioned
  fixations on, 200
  listeners' fixations on, 193
Occupational categor(y)ies, 140
  positively valenced, 139
"One-piece umbrella," application result of force flow diagrams, 98
Onset-focused actions, 56
Operating process, 134
Opprobrium, 130
Optimal decision rule, 224, 236
Optimal rule, two-dimensional nature of, 231
Optimization, methods of, 76
Osborn's brainstorming and mind mapping, 100–101
Overgeneralization, 169

P

Paisano, 18
Parallel facilitory effect in nonlinguistic categorization, 44
  experimental demonstration of the parallel, 45
Parallel monetary systems, 1
  social arrangements around, 7
Parentele, 22
Parsing square into arbitrary "features," 163
Partner specificity *vs.* partner independence
  in entrainment, 196–197
  in preemption, 197–201
Partner-specific-preemption hypothesis, 199
Patents, categories of, 89
Pattern, *ditransitive* formal, 34
Payne weapons, 137
"Peanut sheller," design problem, 85

Index

Peanut shelling design problem
   mind map of, 102
   "6-3-5" modified method for, 104–105
Pegged currencies, 3
Perceiver(s), 135, 138, 144
   dispositional and transient characteristics of, 127
Perceptual classification learning, 214, 219
Perceptual expertise, 171
Personality, 242
Pew Hispanic Center study, 14
Phrasal constructions, 46
Phrasal form–meaning correlations, 35
Physical classifying schemes, 91
Physical principles, diagrammatic representations of, 92–93, 95–96
Pickup winder, 113
   and electric vegetable peeler, nonobvious design analogy between, 114
Piggybacking, 100
Popcorn popper, hot-air, and corresponding functional diagram, 88
Precedents, 195–196
Preemption, 191–194, 201
   effects, 198–199
   partner specificity *vs.* partner independence in, 197–201
Prejudice(s), 131, 138
   reduction, self-regulation model of, 134
Prevention focus, 215, 226
   chronic, 216–218
   participants, 228
Prevention participants, 216
Primate visual system, selectivities within, 168
Priming, 53
   form–function, 54
Prix d'ami, 6
Procedural-based classification learning system, 223
Procedural-based learning, 222, 235, 238
Procreation, 18
Product architecting, 74
   categories of, 75
Product design, key observations in, 89
Product development
   and categorization, 77–79
   processes, 72
      General Motors EV-1 automobile, 69
      phases of, 71

Product development, and concept generation
   process, 69–73
   concept
      developing, 74–76
      implementing, 76–77
   opportunity, understanding about, 73–74
Productivity, 166
Products
   flexibility in, 69
   Nike ID shoes, 70, 71
   range, illustrating innovations in markets, 70
Progressive abstractions, 115
Promotion focus, 215, 226
   chronic, 216–217
Promotion participants, 216
Psycholinguistics, 194, 208
Psycholinguists, 35
Public weal, 25

R

Racial bias, 136
Racial prejudice, 127, 143
Racial stereotypes, 135
Rapid serial visual presentation (RSVP) tasks, 53
"Real" money, 1, 8
Reasoning system, 131
Rebound effect, 134
Recategorization, 135, 138
Recognition
   of complex objects, 157
   image-driven theories of, 160
   potential utility for, 168
   structural accounts of, 160
   view-based theories of, 162
"Recognition-By-Components" model, 159
Recognizing objects based on features, benefits of, 169
Recovery-from-preemption hypothesis, 198–199
Referent categorization, strategies for, 183–184
Referential communication, 182, 190, 206
Referents
   classification of, 184
   listeners' search for, 192
Referring
   collaborative nature of, 208
   expression, 193–194, 199

Regulatory fit, 216, 218, 222
  manipulations, 222–223, 231, 239
  prediction, 217
Regulatory fit-classification learning
    predictions, 223
Regulatory fit effects
  on decision criterion learning, 235–238
  on information-integration classification
      learning on, 233–235
  on rule-based classification learning
    cognitive flexibility, advantageous,
        224–228
    cognitive flexibility, not advantageous,
        228–232
    summary, 232–233
Regulatory focus, 215–217
  theory, 242
Regulatory match, 238
Regulatory mismatch, 238
Reinforcement sensitivity theory (RST),
    relation to, 242–243
Related cognitive tasks, applications to, 242
Relational encoding, 171
Relational information, 171, 177
Relational work, 3
  earmarking, techniques of, 9
  with legal tender, 9
  means of, 10
  in remittance systems, 17
Relations and categories, 1–2
  euro, 10–13
  legal tenders, 7–10
  local money, 3–7
  nationalism and citizenship, 24–26
  remittances, 13–17
  trust networks, 17–24
Relations, coarse or qualitative, 170
Remittances, 13–17
Remote Associates Task (RAT), 240
Rent money, separation from gift money, 9
Resultative constructions, 51
Retina, activation on, 164
Reversals, 115
Reward-maximizing decision criterion,
    237–238
Reward structure
  gains, 224–227, 229–232, 239
  losses, 227–228, 232, 239
  of task, 233, 239
Root motivation, 129

Rule-based category structure
  conjunctive, four-category
    optimal decision bounds from, 230
  conjunctive, two-category, 225
  four-category, 221
Rule-based classification learning, regulatory
    fit effects on
  cognitive flexibility, advantageous
    gains reward structure, 224–227
    losses reward structure, 227–228
  cognitive flexibility, not advantageous
    gains reward structure, 229–232
    losses reward structure, 232

S

Sadness, 141
  effects of, 142
Salient Participants in Prominent Slots (SPPS)
    Generalization, 55
SEL, 3
"Self information," 165
Self-regulatory strategies, 136
Sentence meaning
  comparison of cue validities of verbs and
      constructions as predictors of, 48
  construction as predictors of
    corpus evidence of, 47–49
    experimental evidence for, 49–51
    overall, 50–51
    predictor of, 51
Sentences, "object-raising" and
    "object-control," examples of, 54
Setting(s), 181
  involving category learning and category
      use, 182
Shared accounting systems, 26
Similarity and solidarity, 147
Simple transitive construction, 39
Sistema di Reciprocit Indiretta (SRI), 3
Situational focus, 216–217, 224,
    238–239
  manipulation, 231
Situational prevention focus, 225, 233
Situational promotion focus,
    224–225, 233
"Smiley face" emoticon, 173, 174
Smiley face images, 175–176
Social acceptance, desire for, 130
Social categories, 140

Social categorization, 137
 expanded model of, 133
 schematic model of, 124–128
Social identity theory, 130
Social impressions, 123
Social justice, 132
Socially emergent categories, 202–203, 207–208
"Social mnemonic," 183
Social perceivers, 139
Social perception
 category selection in, 139
 and judgment, 126
 self-regulation of, 132–136
Social target
 behavior of, 126–127
 mental representation of, 126
Social world, categorization of, 123
 affective influences, 137
  category selection and stereotype activation, 138–141
  stereotype application and expression, 141–144
  identification-based affect, motivation, and inference, 144–146
 motivational influences
  self-regulation of social perception, 132–137
 varieties of, 128–132
 social categorization, schematic model of, 124–128
Speaker(s), 185, 190, 196, 205
 consistency, 191
 effect, 198–199
Speaker–listener dyad, 208
Specification creation process, categories for, 79
Speech
 consistent and inconsistent conditions, donlon with the stimulusto-sound mappings for, 188
 with fillers, lower confidence ratings, 187
Staple remover, 96
 improvement in terms of component combination, 98
 schematic and force flow diagram of, 97
Statistical learning, 35
Stereotypes, 131–132, 138
 correction, 134
 and prejudice, 143
 suppression, 134–135

Stereotypic biases, 142
Stereotypic concepts, associated with the elderly, 145
Stereotyping, anger's effects on, 143
Stimuli and category labels, pairings between, 185
Stimuli for sorting experiment, 49
Stored images, 169
"Store energy," classifying schemes to generate concepts for, 93
Structural encoding, 162–163, 172
 classes of, 168
 utility of, 167
Structural information, 167
Structural representations, 165
 construal of, 174
Structure
 category-specific and category-generic, 168
 in mental representations, 157
Subject Verb Object Oblique$_{path/loc}$ formal pattern, 42
"Surprisal," 165
Symmetry detection, 161
Systémes d' change Local (SEL), 1

T

Tauschring, 3, 6
Textual idea generators, 91–92
 categories for probing questions, 94
Theory of inventive problem solving (TIPS), 89, 107, 110–111
 design principles to solve engineering conflicts, 108–110
 generalized parameters for, 90
ThinkCycle, 83
Time exchanges, 3–4
TIPS. *See* Theory of inventive problem solving
Tolerance, 132
Top–down pathway, to social impressions, 123
Training stimuli, 42
Transitive constructions, 50–51
Transitivity, 37
Transparency, perception of, 161
Trompe l'oeil, paintings of dollar bills, 8
Trust networks, 17–24
Typologists, 33

U

"Universal grammar," 35, 43
"Usage-based" model of language, 43
Us–them boundaries, 18, 25–26
Us–them categories, 24
Utterances, 43, 46
  confident-sounding, 188
  correlations between formal patterns and meanings of, 34
  VOO, 48

V

Valence, 142
Ventral tegmental area (VTA), 240
  neurobiological connectivity, 241–242
Verb(s)
  balanced frequency training condition, 41
  of communication, 48
  cue validity of, 47
  denominal, 191
  frequencies of, 41
  skewed frequency, 41
  skewing of constructions toward particular verbs, 40
  of sound emission, 48
Verbal hedges, 186–187, 189
Verb Object Locative (VOL) construction, 42
Verb Object$_1$ Object$_2$, 47
Verb Object Oblique$_{path/loc}$(VOO), 47
  utterances, 48
Viajeros, 14
Vision, reconsidering the role of structure in, 157–159
  defining structure
    structural representations, importance of features in, 164–166
    structure, as compositionality, 160–164
  structural, importance of being, 166–168
    category-generic structure, 173–177
    category-specific structure, 168–173
Visions, driving force in understanding market opportunities, 73
Visual abilities, "holy grail" of, 177
Visual and linguistic tasks for prelinguistic infants, characteristics of agents in, 56
Visual channels, 185
Visual cortex, 160
Visual object recognition, 158
Visual recognition, 164, 166
  structural models in, 159
VOO. *See* Verb Object Oblique$_{path/loc}$
Voting machine, invention of, 67
VTA. *See* Ventral tegmental area

W

Wagner's model of mental control, 134
Why method, 115
Woodward's study, 56
Words, lexical category of, 161
Workers' mutual aid, 18

CONTENTS OF RECENT VOLUMES

Volume 30

Perceptual Learning
 Felice Bedford
A Rational-Constructivist Account of Early Learning about Numbers and Objects
 Rochel Gelman
Remembering, Knowing, and Reconstructing the Past
 Henry L. Roediger III, Mark A. Wheeler, and Suparna Rajaram
The Long-Term Retention of Knowledge and Skills
 Alice F. Healy, Deborah M. Clawson, Danielle S. McNamara, William R. Marmie, Vivian I. Schneider, Timothy C. Rickard, Robert J. Crutcher, Cheri L. King, K. Anders Ericsson, and Lyle E. Bourne, Jr.
A Comprehension-Based Approach to Learning and Understanding
 Walter Kintsch, Bruce K. Britton, Charles R. Fletcher, Eileen Kintsch, Suzanne M. Mannes, and Mitchell J. Nathan
Separating Causal Laws from Causal Facts: Pressing the Limits of Statistical Relevance
 Patricia W. Cheng
Categories, Hierarchies, and Induction
 Elizabeth F. Shipley
Index

Volume 31

Associative Representations of Instrumental Contingencies
 Ruth M. Colwill
A Behavioral Analysis of Concepts: Its Application to Pigeons and Children
 Edward A. Wasserman and Suzette L. Astley
The Child's Representation of Human Groups
 Lawrence A. Hirschfeld
Diagnostic Reasoning and Medical Expertise
 Vimla L. Patel, José F. Arocha, and David R. Kaufman
Object Shape, Object Name, and Object Kind: Representation and Development
 Barbara Landau
The Ontogeny of Part Representation in Object Concepts
 Philippe G. Schyns and Gregory L. Murphy
Index

Volume 32

Cognitive Approaches to Judgment and Decision Making
 Reid Hastie and Nancy Pennington
And Let Us Not Forget Memory: The Role of Memory Processes and Techniques in the Study of Judgment and Choice
 Elke U. Weber, Wiliam M. Goldstein, and Sema Barlas
Content and Discontent: Indications and Implications of Domain Specificity in Preferential Decision Making
 William M. Goldstein and Elke U. Weber
An Information Processing Perspective on Choice
 John W. Payne, James R. Bettman, Eric J. Johnson, and Mary Frances Luce
Algebra and Process in the Modeling of Risky Choice
 Lola L. Lopes
Utility Invariance Despite Labile Preferences
 Barbara A. Mellers, Elke U. Weber, Lisa D. Ordóñez, and Alan D. J. Cooke

Compatibility in Cognition and Decision
　　Eldar Shafir
Processing Linguistic Probabilities: General Principles and Empirical Evidence
　　David V. Budescu and Thomas S. Wallsten
Compositional Anomalies in the Semantics of Evidence
　　John M. Miyamoto, Richard Gonzalez, and Shihfen Tu
Varieties of Confirmation Bias
　　Joshua Klayman
Index

Volume 33

Landmark-Based Spatial Memory in the Pigeon
　　Ken Cheng
The Acquisition and Structure of Emotional Response Categories
　　Paula M. Niedenthal and Jamin B. Halberstadt
Early Symbol Understanding and Use
　　Judy S. DeLoache
Mechanisms of Transition: Learning with a Helping Hand
　　Susan Goldin-Meadow and Martha Wagner Alibali
The Universal Word Identification Reflex
　　Charles A. Perfetti and Sulan Zhang
Prospective Memory: Progress and Processes
　　Mark A. McDaniel
Looking for Transfer and Interference
　　Nancy Pennington and Bob Rehder
Index

Volume 34

Associative and Normative Models of Causal Induction: Reacting to versus Understanding Cause
　　A. G. Baker, Robin A. Murphy, and Frédéric Vallée-Tourangeau
Knowledge-Based Causal Induction
　　Michael R. Waldmann
A Comparative Analysis of Negative Contingency Learning in Humans and Nonhumans
　　Douglas A. Williams
Animal Analogues of Causal Judgment
　　Ralph R. Miller and Helena Matute
Conditionalizing Causality
　　Barbara A. Spellman
Causation and Association
　　Edward A. Wasserman, Shu-Fang Kao, Linda J. Van Hamme, Masayoshi Katagiri, and Michael E. Young

Distinguishing Associative and Probabilistic Contrast Theories of Human Contingency Judgment
　　David R. Shanks, Francisco J. Lopez, Richard J. Darby, and Anthony Dickinson
A Causal-Power Theory of Focal Sets
　　Patricia W. Cheng, Jooyong Park, Aaron S. Yarlas, and Keith J. Holyoak
The Use of Intervening Variables in Causal Learning
　　Jerome R. Busemeyer, Mark A. McDaniel, and Eunhee Byun
Structural and Probabilistic Causality
　　Judea Pearl
Index

Volume 35

Distance and Location Processes in Memory for the Times of Past Events
　　William J. Friedman
Verbal and Spatial Working Memory in Humans
　　John Jonides, Patricia A. Reuter-Lorenz, Edward E. Smith, Edward Awh, Lisa L. Barnes, Maxwell Drain, Jennifer Glass, Erick J. Lauber, Andrea L. Patalano, and Eric H. Schumacher
Memory for Asymmetric Events
　　John T. Wixted and Deirdra H. Dougherty
The Maintenance of a Complex Knowledge Base After Seventeen Years
　　Marigold Linton
Category Learning As Problem Solving
　　Brian H. Ross
Building a Coherent Conception of HIV Transmission: A New Approach to Aids Educations
　　Terry Kit-fong Au and Laura F. Romo
Spatial Effects in the Partial Report Paradigm: A Challenge for Theories of Visual Spatial Attention
　　Gordon D. Logan and Claus Bundesen
Structural Biases in Concept Learning: Influences from Multiple Functions
　　Dorrit Billman
Index

Volume 36

Learning to Bridge Between Perception and Cognition
　　Robert L. Goldstone, Philippe G. Schyns, and Douglas L. Medin

The Affordances of Perceptual Inquiry: Pictures Are Learned From the World, and What That Fact Might Mean About Perception Quite Generally
    Julian Hochberg
Perceptual Learning of Alphanumeric-Like Characters
    Richard M. Shiffrin and Nancy Lightfoot
Expertise in Object and Face Recognition
    James Tanaka and Isabel Gauthier
Infant Speech Perception: Processing Characteristics, Representational Units, and the Learning of Words
    Peter D. Eimas
Constraints on the Learning of Spatial Terms: A Computational Investigation
    Terry Regier
Learning to Talk About the Properties of Objects: A Network Model of the Development of Dimensions
    Linda B. Smith, Michael Gasser, and Catherine M. Sandhofer
Self-Organization, Plasticity, and Low-Level Visual Phenomena in a Laterally Connected Map Model of the Primary Visual Cortex
    Risto Mikkulainen, James A. Bednar, Yoonsuck Choe, and Joseph Sirosh
Perceptual Learning From Cross-Modal Feedback
    Virginia R. de Sa and Dana H. Ballard
Learning As Extraction of Low-Dimensional Representations
    Shimon Edelman and Nathan Intrator
Index

Volume 37

Object-Based Reasoning
    Miriam Bassok
Encoding Spatial Representation Through Nonvisually Guided Locomotion: Tests of Human Path Integration
    Roberta L. Klatzky, Jack M. Loomis, and Reginald G. Golledge
Production, Evaluation, and Preservation of Experiences: Constructive Processing in Remembering and Performance Tasks
    Bruce W. A. Whittlesea
Goals, Representations, and Strategies in a Concept Attainment Task: The EPAM Model
    Fernand Gobet, Howard Richman, Jim Staszewski, and Herbert A. Simon
Attenuating Interference During Comprehension: The Role of Suppression
    Morton Ann Gernsbacher

Cognitive Processes in Counterfactual Thinking About What Might Have Been
    Ruth M. J. Byrne
Episodic Enhancement of Processing Fluency
    Michael E. J. Masson and Colin M. MacLeod
At a Loss From Words: Verbal Overshadowing of Perceptual Memories
    Jonathan W. Schooler, Stephen M. Fiore, and Maria A. Brandimonte
Index

Volume 38

Transfer-Inappropriate Processing: Negative Priming and Related Phenomena
    W. Trammell Neil and Katherine M. Mathis
Cue Competition in the Absence of Compound Training: Its Relation to Paradigms of Interference Between Outcomes
    Helena Matute and Oskar Pineño
Sooner or Later: The Psychology of Intertemporal Choice
    Gretchen B. Chapman
Strategy Adaptivity and Individual Differences
    Christian D. Schunn and Lynne M. Reder
Going Wild in the Laboratory: Learning About Species Typical Cues
    Michael Domjan
Emotional Memory: The Effects of Stress on "Cool" and "Hot" Memory Systems
    Janet Metcalfe and W. Jake Jacobs
Metacomprehension of Text: Influence of Absolute Confidence Level on Bias and Accuracy
    Ruth H. Maki
Linking Object Categorization and Naming: Early Expectations and the Shaping Role of Language
    Sandra R. Waxman
Index

Volume 39

Infant Memory: Cues, Contexts, Categories, and Lists
    Carolyn Rovee-Collier and Michelle Gulya
The Cognitive-Initiative Account of Depression-Related Impairments in Memory
    Paula T. Hertel
Relational Timing: A Theromorphic Perspective
    J. Gregor Fetterman
The Influence of Goals on Value and Choice
    Arthur B. Markham and C. Miguel Brendl
The Copying Machine Metaphor
    Edward J. Wisniewski
Knowledge Selection in Category Learning
    Evan Heit and Lewis Bott
Index

Volume 40

Different Organization of Concepts and Meaning Systems in the Two Cerebral Hemispheres
  Dahlia W. Zaidel
The Causal Status Effect in Categorization: An Overview
  Woo-kyoung Ahn and Nancy S. Kim
Remembering as a Social Process
  Mary Susan Weldon
Neurocognitive Foundations of Human Memory
  Ken A. Paller
Structural Influences on Implicit and Explicit Sequence Learning
  Tim Curran, Michael D. Smith, Joseph M. DiFranco, and Aaron T. Daggy
Recall Processes in Recognition Memory
  Caren M. Rotello
Reward Learning: Reinforcement, Incentives, and Expectations
  Kent C. Berridge
Spatial Diagrams: Key Instruments in the Toolbox for Thought
  Laura R. Novick
Reinforcement and Punishment in the Prisoner's Dilemma Game
  Howard Rachlin, Jay Brown, and Forest Baker
Index

Volume 41

Categorization and Reasoning in Relation to Culture and Expertise
  Douglas L. Medin, Norbert Ross, Scott Atran, Russell C. Burnett, and Sergey V. Blok
On the Computational basis of Learning and Cognition: Arguments from LSA
  Thomas K. Landauer
Multimedia Learning
  Richard E. Mayer
Memory Systems and Perceptual Categorization
  Thomas J. Palmeri and Marci A. Flanery
Conscious Intentions in the Control of Skilled Mental Activity
  Richard A. Carlson
Brain Imaging Autobiographical Memory
  Martin A. Conway, Christopher W. Pleydell-Pearce, Sharon Whitecross, and Helen Sharpe
The Continued Influence of Misinformation in Memory: What Makes Corrections Effective?
  Colleen M. Seifert
Making Sense and Nonsense of Experience: Attributions in Memory and Judgment
  Colleen M. Kelley and Matthew G. Rhodes
Real-World Estimation: Estimation Modes and Seeding Effects
  Norman R. Brown
Index

Volume 42

Memory and Learning in Figure–Ground Perception
  Mary A. Peterson and Emily Skow-Grant
Spatial and Visual Working Memory: A Mental Workspace
  Robert H. Logie
Scene Perception and Memory
  Marvin M. Chun
Spatial Representations and Spatial Updating
  Ranxiano Frances Wang
Selective Visual Attention and Visual Search: Behavioral and Neural Mechanisms
  Joy J. Geng and Marlene Behrmann
Categorizing and Perceiving Objects: Exploring a Continuum of Information Use
  Philippe G. Schyns
From Vision to Action and Action to Vision: A Convergent Route Approach to Vision, Action, and Attention
  Glyn W. Humphreys and M. Jane Riddoch
Eye Movements and Visual Cognitive Suppression
  David E. Irwin
What Makes Change Blindness Interesting?
  Daniel J. Simons and Daniel T. Levin
Index

Volume 43

Ecological Validity and the Study of Concepts
  Gregory L. Murphy
Social Embodiment
  Lawrence W. Barsalou, Paula M. Niedinthal, Aron K. Barbey, and Jennifer A. Ruppert
The Body's Contribution to Language
  Arthur M. Glenberg and Michael P. Kaschak
Using Spatial Language
  Laura A. Carlson
In Opposition to Inhibition
  Colin M. MacLeod, Michael D. Dodd, Erin D. Sheard, Daryl E. Wilson, and Uri Bibi
Evolution of Human Cognitive Architecture
  John Sweller
Cognitive Plasticity and Aging
  Arthur F. Kramer and Sherry L. Willis
Index

Volume 44

Goal-Based Accessibility of Entities within Situation Models
  Mike Rinck and Gordon H. Bower
The Immersed Experiencer: Toward an Embodied Theory of Language Comprehension
  Rolf A. Zwaan
Speech Errors and Language Production: Neuropsychological and Connectionist Perspectives
  Gary S. Dell and Jason M. Sullivan
Psycholinguistically Speaking: Some Matters of Meaning, Marking, and Morphing
  Kathryn Bock
Executive Attention, Working Memory Capacity, and a Two-Factor Theory of Cognitive Control
  Randall W. Engle and Michael J. Kane
Relational Perception and Cognition: Implications for Cognitive Architecture and the Perceptual-Cognitive Interface
  Collin Green and John E. Hummel
An Exemplar Model for Perceptual Categorization of Events
  Koen Lamberts
On the Perception of Consistency
  Yaakov Kareev
Causal Invariance in Reasoning and Learning
  Steven Sloman and David A. Lagnado
Index

Volume 45

Exemplar Models in the Study of Natural Language Concepts
  Gert Storms
Semantic Memory: Some Insights From Feature-Based Connectionist Attractor Networks
  Ken McRae
On the Continuity of Mind: Toward a Dynamical Account of Cognition
  Michael J. Spivey and Rick Dale
Action and Memory
  Peter Dixon and Scott Glover
Self-Generation and Memory
  Neil W. Mulligan and Jeffrey P. Lozito
Aging, Metacognition, and Cognitive Control
  Christopher Hertzog and John Dunlosky
The Psychopharmacology of Memory and Cognition: Promises, Pitfalls, and a Methodological Framework
  Elliot Hirshman
Index

Volume 46

The Role of the Basal Ganglia in Category Learning
  F. Gregory Ashby and John M. Ennis
Knowledge, Development, and Category Learning
  Brett K. Hayes
Concepts as Prototypes
  James A. Hampton
An Analysis of Prospective Memory
  Richard L. Marsh, Gabriel I. Cook, and Jason L. Hicks
Accessing Recent Events
  Brian McElree
SIMPLE: Further Applications of a Local Distinctiveness Model of Memory
  Ian Neath and Gordon D. A. Brown
What is Musical Prosody?
  Caroline Palmer and Sean Hutchins
Index